"Embark on a profound journey through Emmanuel Falque's inspiring work crossing the borders between philosophy and theology. Engaging the interplay of body, flesh, and spirit, and inquiring about themes of embodiment, suffering, and transformation. A deeply philosophical and existential exploration of meaning, resistance, and becoming."

—**Lieven Boeve**, full professor of fundamental theology, KU Leuven, Belgium

"This tribute to Emmanuel Falque most fittingly expresses the strength of a shared recognition—the recognition of a thinker whose all-consuming desire for truth has communicated a share of this desire to many. *To Die of Not Writing: Doing Philosophy of Religion with Emmanuel Falque* testifies to an essential thinker, not only by the breadth of interest he inspires, but also by the depth of insight attained—a rich contribution to the philosophy of religion."

—**Alexander Ferrant**, assistant professor of philosophy, Grand Séminaire de l'Archidiocèse de Montréal

To Die of Not Writing

VERITAS
Series Introduction

"The truth will set you free" (John 8:32)

In much contemporary discourse, Pilate's question has been taken to mark the absolute boundary of human thought. Beyond this boundary, it is often suggested, is an intellectual hinterland into which we must not venture. This terrain is an agnosticism of thought: because truth cannot be possessed, it must not be spoken. Thus, it is argued that the defenders of "truth" in our day are often traffickers in ideology, merchants of counterfeits, or anti-liberal. They are, because it is somewhat taken for granted that Nietzsche's word is final: truth is the domain of tyranny.

Is this indeed the case, or might another vision of truth offer itself? The ancient Greeks named the love of wisdom as *philia*, or friendship. The one who would become wise, they argued, would be a "friend of truth." For both philosophy and theology might be conceived as schools in the friendship of truth, as a kind of relation. For like friendship, truth is as much discovered as it is made. If truth is then so elusive, if its domain is *terra incognita*, perhaps this is because it arrives to us—unannounced—as gift, as a person, and not some thing.

The aim of the Veritas book series is to publish incisive and original current scholarly work that inhabits "the between" and "the beyond" of theology and philosophy. These volumes will all share a common aspiration to transcend the institutional divorce in which these two disciplines often find themselves, and to engage questions of pressing concern to both philosophers and theologians in such a way as to reinvigorate both disciplines with a kind of interdisciplinary desire, often so absent in contemporary academe. In a word, these volumes represent collective efforts in the befriending of truth, doing so beyond the simulacra of pretend tolerance, the violent, yet insipid reasoning of liberalism that asks with Pilate, "What is truth?"—expecting a consensus of non-commitment; one that encourages the commodification of the mind, now sedated by the civil service of career, ministered by the frightened patrons of position.

The series will therefore consist of two wings: (1) original monographs; and (2) essay collections on a range of topics in theology and philosophy. The latter will principally be the products of the annual conferences of the Centre of Theology and Philosophy (www.theologyphilosophycentre.co.uk).

Conor Cunningham and Joseph Terry, *series editors*

Available from Cascade Books

[Nathan Kerr	*Christ, History, and Apocalyptic: The Politics of Christian Mission*][1]
Anthony D. Baker	*Diagonal Advance: Perfection in Christian Theology*
D. C. Schindler	*The Perfection of Freedom: Schiller, Schelling, and Hegel between the Ancients and the Moderns*
Rustin Brian	*Covering Up Luther: How Barth's Christology Challenged the* Deus Absconditus *that Haunts Modernity*
Timothy Stanley	*Protestant Metaphysics After Karl Barth and Martin Heidegger*
Christopher Ben Simpson	*The Truth Is the Way: Kierkegaard's* Theologia Viatorum
Richard H. Bell	*Wagner's Parsifal: An Appreciation in the Light of His Theological Journey*
Antonio Lopez	*Gift and the Unity of Being*
Toyohiko Kagawa	*Cosmic Purpose*, translated and introduced by Thomas John Hastings
Nigel Zimmerman	*Facing the Other: John Paul II, Levinas, and the Body*
Conor Sweeney	*Sacramental Presence after Heidegger: Onto-theology, Sacraments, and the Mother's Smile*
John Behr et al. (eds.)	*The Role of Death in Life: A Multidisciplinary Examination of the Relation between Life and Death*
Eric Austin Lee et al. (eds.)	*The Resounding Soul: Reflection on the Metaphysics and Vivacity of the Human Person*
Orion Edgar	*Things Seen and Unseen: The Logic of Incarnation in Merleau-Ponty's Metaphysics of Flesh*
Duncan B. Reyburn	*Seeing Things as They Are: G. K. Chesterton and the Drama of Meaning*
Lyndon Shakespeare	*Being the Body of Christ in the Age of Management*
Michael V. Di Fuccia	*Owen Barfield: Philosophy, Poetry, and Theology*
John McNerney	*Wealth of Persons: Economics with a Human Face*
Norm Klassen	*The Fellowship of the Beatific Vision: Chaucer on Overcoming Tyranny and Becoming Ourselves*
Donald Wallenfang	*Human and Divine Being: A Study of the Theological Anthropology of Edith Stein*
Sotiris Mitralexis	*Ever-Moving Repose: A Contemporary Reading of Maximus the Confessor's Theory of Time*

---

1. Note: Nathan Kerr, *Christ, History, and Apocalyptic*, although volume 3 of the original SCM Veritas series, is available from Cascade as part of the Theopolitical Visions series.

Sotiris Mitralexis et al. (eds.)	*Maximus the Confessor as a European Philosopher*
Kevin Corrigan	*Love, Friendship, Beauty, and the Good: Plato, Aristotle, and the Later Tradition*
Andrew Brower Latz	*The Social Philosophy of Gillian Rose*
D. C. Schindler	*Love and the Postmodern Predicament: Rediscovering the Real in Beauty, Goodness, and Truth*
Stephen Kampowski	*Embracing Our Finitude: Exercises in a Christian Anthropology between Dependence and Gratitude*
William Desmond	*The Gift of Beauty and the Passion of Being: On the Threshold between the Aesthetic and the Religious*
Charles Péguy	*Notes on Bergson and Descartes*
David Alcalde	*Cosmology without God: The Problematic Theology Inherent in Modern Cosmology*
Benson P. Fraser	*Hide and Seek: The Sacred Art of Indirect Communication*
Philip John Paul Gonzales	*Exorcising Philosophical Modernity: Cyril O'Regan and Christian Discourse after Modernity*
Caitlin Smith Gilson	*Subordinated Ethics: Natural Law and Moral Miscellany in Aquinas and Dostoyevsky*
Michael Dominic Taylor	*The Foundations of Nature: Metaphysics of Gift for an Integral Ecological Ethic*
David W. Opderbeck	*The End of the Law? Law, Theology, and Neuroscience*
Caitlin Smith Gilson	*As It Is in Heaven: Some Christian Questions on the Nature of Paradise*
Andrew T. J. Kaethler	*The Eschatological Person: Alexander Schemann and Joseph Ratzinger in Dialogue*
Emmanuel Falque	*By Way of Obstacles: A Pathway through a Work*
Paul Tyson (ed.)	*Astonishment in Science: Engagements with William Desmond*
Darren Dyk	*Will & Love: Shakespeare and the Motion of the Soul*
Matthew Vest	*Ethics Lost in Modernity: Reflections on Wittgenstein and Bioethics*
Hanna Lucas	*Sensing the Sacred: Recovering a Mystagogical Vision of Knowledge and Salvation*
Philip John Paul Gonzales et al. (eds.)	*Finitude's Wounded Praise: Responses to Jean-Louis Crétien*
Martin Koci et al. (eds.)	*God and Phenomenology: Thinking with Jean-Yves Lacoste*
Steven E. Knepper (ed.)	*A Heart of Flesh: William Desmond and the Bible*

To Die of Not Writing

Doing Philosophy of Religion with Emmanuel Falque

Edited by
PABLO IRIZAR,
DONALD BOYCE,
and MARTIN KOCI

Foreword by
CYRIL O'REGAN

CASCADE *Books* · Eugene, Oregon

TO DIE OF NOT WRITING
Doing Philosophy of Religion with Emmanuel Falque

Veritas

Copyright © 2025 Wipf and Stock Publishers. All rights reserved. Except for brief quotations in critical publications or reviews, no part of this book may be reproduced in any manner without prior written permission from the publisher. Write: Permissions, Wipf and Stock Publishers, 199 W. 8th Ave., Suite 3, Eugene, OR 97401.

Cascade Books
An Imprint of Wipf and Stock Publishers
199 W. 8th Ave., Suite 3
Eugene, OR 97401

www.wipfandstock.com

PAPERBACK ISBN: 979-8-3852-0314-7
HARDCOVER ISBN: 979-8-3852-0315-4
EBOOK ISBN: 979-8-3852-0316-1

Cataloguing-in-Publication data:

Names: Irizar, Pablo, editor. | Boyce, Donald, editor. | Kočí, Martin, 1987–, editor. | O'Regan, Cyril, 1952–, foreword.

Title: To die of not writing : doing philosophy of religion with Emmanuel Falque / edited by Pablo Irizar, Donald Boyce, and Martin Koci ; foreword by Cyril O'Regan.

Description: Eugene, OR : Cascade Books, 2025 | Series: Veritas | Includes bibliographical references and index.

Identifiers: ISBN 979-8-3852-0314-7 (paperback) | ISBN 979-8-3852-0315-4 (hardcover) | ISBN 979-8-3852-0316-1 (ebook)

Subjects: LCSH: Falque, Emmanuel, 1963–. | Phenomenology.

Classification: BL51 .T6 2025 (paperback) | BL51 .T6 (ebook)

VERSION NUMBER 07/24/25

Contents

Foreword | xi
CYRIL O'REGAN

Contributors | xxiii
Acknowledgments | xxv
Preface | xxvii

Introduction: To Die of Not Writing | 1
PABLO IRIZAR, DONALD BOYCE, MARTIN KOCI

Writing and Dying
A Struggle unto Life | 17
SABINE FOS FALQUE

The Relief of Writing | 30
ANDREW SACKIN-POLL

Philosophy and Theology: Introspection and Personal Transformation | 48
MATTHEW W. KNOTTS

Flesh and Spirit

"You Are Not Your Own": Another Look at the Body,
Flesh, and the Falque-Henry Debate | 69
STEVEN DELAY

Falque's Physicalism and the Spiritualism of the Flesh:
Phenomenology and Metaphysics | 89
WILLIAM L. CONNELLY

Dwelling and Resistance

Embracing Our Animality Through Wind and Breath: Revisiting
Anaximenes's Err in Augustine's Confessions | 107
DONALD BOYCE

Augustine on the Metamorphosis of Restlessness | 128
PABLO IRIZAR

The Strength to Remain: On the Past and Future of Manence | 151
DAVID ALBERTSON

Sense and Non-Sense

"Become, Never Cease to Become What You Are": Chaos,
Struggle, and Creation in Nietzsche | 177
GAËL TROTTMANN-CALAME

Meister Eckhart and the Logic of Non-Duality | 188
SEAN J. MCGRATH

Emmanuel Falque, Reader of Sigmund Freud: From
the Id to the Extra-Phenomenal | 207
MATTHEW NINI

When Meaning Breaks: Thinking Sense and
Suffering with Emmanuel Falque | 225
SARAH HORTON

God and Finitude

God and Human Being: An Ellipse in Emmanuel Falque's Work | 243
CARLA CANULLO

SUBSTANTIA: Note on the Use of *substantia* by St. Augustine
and on Its Belonging to the History of Metaphysics | 254
JEAN-LUC MARION

Conclusion

Fraternity in Finitude: Emmanuel Falque and the
Future of Christian Philosophy | 269
DAVID ALBERTSON

Index | 279

Foreword

Cyril O'Regan

OF ALL THE IMPORTANT contemporary work in philosophy and theology it is perhaps the dynamic and multivalent ongoing work of Emmanuel Falque that is most primed to elicit gratitude. The reason for this is disarmingly simple: it is not that when given the opportunity, whether the register is philosophy or theology, that Falque affirms gratitude but rather that gratitude is built into the entire fabric of this work. It is in fact what essentially knits together its many-colored segments. Gratitude is affirmed in Falque's notion of the *loving struggle* (*le combat amoreux*) with a strong other in which the blessing of who I am is yielded rather than extorted. It is acknowledged in his insistence on the necessary hospitality of the discourses to each other, whether we are talking about classical, medieval, or postmodern philosophy, phenomenology, patristic or medieval theology, psychoanalysis, the languages of poetry and fiction. It is celebrated in his loving attention to the ecstatic speech of the Christian mystical tradition, aiming relentlessly at the sourcing silence and incommunicability that generates the hazard of word and image. It is also vouchsafed as the only possible response to the glorious fragility of finitude and the sensitivity and vulnerability of the human bodies that express it. And finally and shockingly, for Falque, whether one is a Christian or not, a once believer or an actual believer, in the Eucharist that is the fundamental expression of gratitude, the knot in which the amen of the broken and resurrected body of Christ blesses my life and death, links me to the living and dead by giving me a memorial speech, at once broken and eloquent, that marries all available discursive resources in the linking of heaven and earth, the divine and the human that refuses the temptation of apotheosis.

As already indicated, gratitude is enacted as well as affirmed. It is performed across a wide span of works that inhabit different intellectual territories, that require submission to different methodological rules, and that seem to emerge spontaneously rather than as items in a preordained program. One gets a good sense of the élan and sheer joy of Falque's thinking in his engagement with those thinkers that, in equal parts, he embraces and resists, for example, Augustine, Aquinas, and Bonaventure, Duns Scotus and Cusanus, but also Husserl, Heidegger, and especially Merleau-Ponty, Henry, and Marion. One can see gratitude's enactment also in the way in which he facilitates the conversation between the discourses of philosophy and theology have for each by setting aside the histories of their contrariety and estrangement and by facilitating what he believes to be their natural partiality for each other. And if one follows Ignatius Loyola closely enough in the imperative of discernment, one not only sees but embraces the versatility of this thinking, its different pathways, aspects, and above all its profession—even confession—of its multifariousness because of the wound or crack that spurs desire and around which constellate expression, gesture, and reflection as hyperboles of a nothing which is yet a something that demands and resists naming.

As affirmed and enacted in Falque's work, gratitude is also generative and provocative; it calls forth the urge to non-identically repeat. What is rendered in this volume is gratitude in different registers and idioms for the irreplaceable, incommunicable Emmanuel Falque who can only be who he is by being eucharistically shared, who is actualized in the tangle of each writer's loving struggle with him to understand what he means and what he evokes, to love the object of his love and love it in one's own way. Obviously, to be grateful to Falque is to attend to what he says, acknowledge and celebrate his manifold contributions to phenomenology, French thought, and historical studies. Yet, much more than this is involved; one has to come upon the *jouissance* that sources and circulates through his thinking, have a sense of the passion of thinking and the wound that makes it at once necessary and free. What is offered in this volume is a bead of thank yous that resolutely resist hagiography. For Falque, as for Heidegger, thinking is always emergent, always at the beginning, and thus, in genuine thinking, one necessarily sees thought against thought and, through that opposition, mind and heart against themselves. Thus, hagiography is non-thinking incapable of admiring and sponsoring thinking against as well as for. At the same time, the reader of the volume has to be grateful for the essays gathered in a volume that forswears any attempt to provide a comprehensive treatment of Falque's work.

Nonetheless, the essays, largely, but not exclusively, by students of Falque touch on central themes in Falque's work, themes such as desire, finitude and its bodily expression, the construction of phenomenology as first philosophy after the so-called *theological turn* in the French reception of phenomenology, the enacted reconciliation of philosophy and theology, and the Eucharist as the materialistic site of the identity-in-difference of immanence and transcendence, the material and the spiritual, the individual and the corporate, the living and the dead, as well as the dead and the living. Without attending specifically to any of the fine contributions that commend themselves, and at the risk of losing the flavor of their singularity, I would like to honor Falque by dint of the pedestrian labor of insinuating connectivity between all of the above elements rather than by rich and exhaustive description of each of the elements. I do so while recognizing that the elements chosen are not the only important topical features of Falque's work, even if they are representative. I also recognize that Falque's thought is entirely kinetic and always open to revision in emphasis and substance such that what is at one point central becomes peripheral at another point and vice versa. Above all, on the model of the integrity and judiciousness of the readers in this volume, a *loving struggle* with Falque from time to time involves the impertinence of interrogation, which, after Ricoeur, Falque might agree is the most respectful and meaningful act a reader can engage in when it comes to truth and the generation of community that shares it. I begin with a reflection on desire which is constitutively ironic: it is both a discrete topic and everywhere in Falque's work, just as it is nothing and something.

Desire

What motivates thinking? What is its interest and aim? These are questions that matter vitally for Emmanuel Falque. Classically, Plato defined philosophy (*philo-sophia*) as a form of *eros*, an aiming rather than accomplishment of the satisfaction in the order of knowledge correlative to the desire for consummation of sexual union that provides the basic metaphor and perhaps more than that for all of human beings' so-called higher aims. Falque affirms desire as primitive and does so no doubt with the entire history of its trajectory in French thought in mind with its constant oscillation and crossing of its philosophical pertinence as laid down by Kojève's reading of the *Phenomenology* as this is taken up by French thinkers from Bataille and Blanchot through Sartre and onward to Nancy and Derrida and also a certain reception of Freud both Lacanian and non-Lacanian as this finds expression in thinkers as different as Merleau-Ponty, Kristeva, Althusser, and in those thinkers such as Badiou and Žižek who articulate desire both in terms of Hegel and Freud, thereby indicating that desire is one and sexuality and thought simply its two most prominent modes. Of course, Falque does not fail to notice that *eros* in the *Symposium* is constituted by lack (*penia*) as fullness (*poros*) and its energy provided by the movement from the former to the latter as the realization of a fulfillment that is anticipated. While what counts as satisfaction depends on the different circumstances of thinking and sexual want, it is more than a little ironic that it is the classical Plato who essentially underwrites an entire French history of the reception of the construct of desire by speaking to the lack common to both, what Falque speaks variously to a *crack* (*fêlure*) and *disruption*.

Surely, however, a knowledgeable reader of Falque would have it that Falque's following in the wake of Merleau-Ponty, and his acceding to the claims of the body made not only in *The Phenomenology of Perception* but also the temporal posts of *The Structure of Behavior* and *The Visible and Invisible* would immunize him from the seduction of the transcendentalism of Platonism? Yet Plato or a certain Plato remains in play, as does the possible sibling or cousin of Platonism, that is, Christianity that Merleau-Ponty pushes to the margins. The Plato, who suggests more than he says, seems for Falque to be in equal parts generative and irreplaceable, whatever the distortions to be found in his major and minor texts. Whatever the errors he offers or misprisonings of the aim for truth, *pace* Heidegger, he is eminently redeemable. Certainly, he seems strong enough to break out in delicious interpretations of giving provided by a genius such as Plotinus who speaks to the paradox of the gift as giving what one does not have. This is a Plotinian insight elevated by Claude Bruaire with whose thought on the economy of the gift Falque is undoubtedly familiar. Of course, there can be no doubt that Falque is resolutely against the disjunctions between immanence and transcendence, the divine and the human, and the material and spiritual that routinely get sanctioned in the history of philosophy and also theology. Against these dualisms, which continue to be incorporated into thought when Platonism is explicitly rejected, Falque appeals to his crowd of witnesses, certainly Merleau-Ponty, the subtle materialism of Maine de Biran, but also theological figures such as the anti-Gnostic Irenaeus, the anti-Marcionite Tertullian, Franciscan thinkers such as Bonaventure and Duns Scotus.

I have pointed to Falque's awareness of the French history of desire in both its Hegelian and Freudian inflections and their crossing. This is not to claim, however, that his depth of engagement is equal. While he has dug deep regarding its Freudian inflection, as is evidenced in his book on Freud in which he accepts the dismantling of Freud's topography of *Id*, *ego*, and *superego* recommended by the likes of Ricoeur, he does not demonstrate the same knowledge of the Kojève-engendered French history of Hegel's view of desire and the economy of recognition. Nor is he under the obligation to do so and attempt the kind of synthesis provided by Derrida in *Glas*. Nonetheless, one can see the opportunity for Falque's deepening his analysis of desire by attending more to the aim of desire in a situation of agony which is that of mutual recognition that can be understood as a kind of blessing. In this context we might ask a blessing of what, a blessing of accomplishment, complementarity or the very desire that makes for approach but which keeps persons inalienably separated from each other? And what amount the fact that in the historical Hegel—in contrast to his French reception—the mode of knowledge correlative to desire, the mode of knowledge that is its coefficient is absolute knowledge rather than knowledge that is perspectival, incremental, recognitional, Hegel still looms, still needs to be engaged and defeated when he insists on the attainment of desire. Falque's position is highlighted and made more dramatic by means of the contrast that desire does not have an end and that its partial satisfactions come about when it comes into contact with the known unknown that is fundamentally incommunicable or inaccessible. Falque is his own best enemy here: he has given us so much here that he seems to compel us to look for more.

Finitude and the Body

The above discussion of desire naturally segues into uplifting a feature of Falque's thinking across his trilogy of trilogies, philosophical, theological, and methodological, concerning the irrefragable finitude and corporeality of the human subject. As already stated, Merleau-Ponty is a crucial influence in his specification of the embodied nature of the finite human subject, though Falque sees in Merleau-Ponty a carrying forward of Husserl's articulation of the *Lebenswelt* and the passive nature of the genesis of sense that imperils Husserl's speculations about transcendental constitution. At the same time, Merleau-Ponty's breakthrough is index to Heidegger's articulation of finitude in *Sein und Zeit* which, unfortunately, proceeds without an explicit discourse of the body notwithstanding the prominence of *being-in-the-world* in Heidegger's analytic of *Dasein*. If there is one thinker who might challenge Merleau-Ponty as a precursor, then, arguably, it would be Michel Henry—this despite the fact that throughout his work Falque is consistently engaged in a struggle with Henry that has in fact multiple registers. Acknowledging Henry's contribution to a reorientation of phenomenology that is of moment and formally similar to that of Merleau-Ponty in a number of works, but especially in *The Metamorphosis of Finitude*, Falque expresses worries about a number of facets of Henry's discussion of the *flesh*. More specifically he worries about the emphasis on the aboriginal unity of the self that does not tolerate non-identity, on immanence that forbids transcendence and ecstasy, and also about the relative ethereality of the flesh in contrast to heaviness of materiality of the body. While Falque understands the motivations about Henry's fundamental options, his decision against the materialist understanding of the body and his wish to preserve as inviolable a human subjectivity that is exceptional in the universe render his account implausible. For Falque, Henry is guilty of a reaction formation against any trace of a fundamentally embodied reality to the point perhaps of exhibiting a kind of closet Cartesianism.

On Falque's account, however, not all forms of materialist construals of the human subject are created equal. He distinguishes between the kind of subtle and non-reductive materialism of Maine de Biran and the standard representatives of the materialist reduction of the human subject of which there are multiple contenders, and with respect to which there is a distinguished French ancestry with d'Holbach being perhaps the most impressive and influential representative. Moreover, though Henry makes clear that Descartes is the poisoned root of modern philosophy in its idealist forms and a contaminant in phenomenology, Descartes still continues to exercise considerable influence in his thought: the rejection of the body in favour of the flesh arises from the fear that what he names *flesh* might be reduced to *res extensa*. With this in mind perhaps we have a clue with respect to the origin and maybe even the meaning of one of Falque's most famous constructs. I am speaking of his notion of the *extended body* (*corps épandu*) as a site of action and passion that cannot be reduced to its material constituents. Even though this notion develops positively out of his appropriation of Merleau-Ponty and negatively out of his probing of Henry's *chair épandu*, as witnessed especially in *The Metamorphosis of Finitude*, one can sense also the intended opposition to Descartes's *res extensa*. Indeed, it is difficult not to see it as a subversion of his lifeless notion of the body that was rejected by Maine de Biran and most eminently within the phenomenological movement Merleau-Ponty who flushes from phenomenology the Cartesianism lay deep in the folds of much of Husserl's later work. Perhaps it is also worth commenting on—if only in passing—that Falque acknowledges the precedent not only provided by Merleau-Ponty but also by Pope John Paul II. The expression of appreciation and gratitude, however, unlike what is the case with Falque's relation to Merleau-Ponty issue in progress either in conceiving the body and despite John Paul II immersion in phenomenology via Ingarden or reconceiving phenomenology.

Two points by way of moving to the second of the two registers regarding the body in Falque. First, a question: one wonders whether it is possible to define the body generically, whether the body, as the locus of incommunicability, is the locus of a unique selfing. Second, Falque is anxious to give credit where credit is due with regard to thinkers highlighting the body and resisting the more invidious strains of Platonism—especially anthropological dualism—within the Western intellectual tradition. Throughout the Western tradition any number of Christian thinkers expressed their support of the body, from Irenaeus to Scotus, Tertullian to Bonaventure. Of course, the makeup of the list of supporters is hardly accidental. The list suggests (a) that the influence of Platonism in the Western intellectual tradition is not absolutely hegemonic and (b) more specifically, that while anthropological dualism is prominent in the theological tradition, nonetheless, there is significant evidence of a counterforce. Perhaps the best way of understanding Falque on both of these points is to see him in opposition to Nietzsche's linking of Platonism and Christianity. For Falque, Christianity is no more exoteric Platonism than Platonism is incipient Christianity in its denial of the body, its evasion of its pathos, and its forswearing of the impossible possibility of resurrection.

Falque's invoking of theological figures as affirmative voices for the body is not in itself sufficient to conclude that he has not strayed into the borderlands where philosophy and theology meet, though it does mean that he has embarrassed somewhat the security of the distinction between the discourse that with goodwill (Kant, Husserl) and bad will (Enlightenment, Heidegger) has come to function in a modernity somewhat of an axiom. More about Falque's rendering of what Marion refers to as *demarche* in due course. The point I want to make here is different. It is not simply that Falque seems to grant recognition to theological voices, but more that he suggests that the Christian contribution to the proper understanding of the human subject is not simply a straightforward denial of Christianity's tendency to inscribe Platonic dualism, but in the devastating indirection of thinkers such as Augustine and Bonaventure and even more primitively Irenaeus that deconstructs Platonism by appeal to Christ in his incarnation, passion and death, and resurrection. If Augustine dramatizes this overcoming of Platonism in the *Confessions*, in book 4 of *Against Heresies* Irenaeus's Christ is presented not only as fully embodied, but his embodiment is a very condition of our salvation. Yet, for Falque it is, arguably, Bonaventure and more broadly the medieval Franciscan tradition that exhibits a special genius for revising the understanding of the human subject by the detour of the unveiling of Christ's body and its commitment to not shying away from its lifeless form. If Bonaventure's perspective on Christ fundamentally disturbs the regime of Platonism, even as he accepts to a considerable extent its fundamental insights and judgments, the trajectory of the Franciscan tradition and especially the iconography it spawned gave us not only a non-docetic Christ, but the means to think of ourselves differently, to turn nay into yea, the move perhaps beyond our hatred or at best our toleration of the human body to gratitude for its limitations.

Phenomenology

I have said quite a deal already in passing concerning Falque's embrace of phenomenology as *first philosophy* as well as about his complex relations to Husserl and Heidegger and to his immediate French precursors who can be classed as belonging to the *theological turn*. So rather than go over that ground again, here I want to highlight Falque's expansive reckoning with the phenomenological tradition that he carries out in *Hors phénomène* (2021), where *hors* importantly can be translated into English as *beyond* or *outside*. I will return to this distinction in translation shortly, but as a preliminary, it is important to point out that Falque's selected parameter for deeper investigation and fruitful conversation is with those species of phenomenology that emphasize the limits of intentionality. While this certainly leaves Levinas and Henry in play, the conversation that seems to be most important to Falque is that between himself and Marion, his former teacher. At the center of *Hors phénomène* is the loving struggle with Marion's notion of the *saturated phenomenon*, which is formally defined as the excess of intuition over intention. While Falque is fully aware of Marion's claim regarding the banality of the *saturated phenomenon*, given its generality, nonetheless, he entertains a kind of Derridian worry that the excessiveness of the phenomenon relative to intention is subtly and invidiously connected to *height* and thus connected to the kind of hyperousiological economy that dominates Neoplatonism and that seems to have been embraced by Marion in his early theologically saturated work. In addition, though Marion's take on revelation as the *ne plus ultra* of saturated phenomena is not questioned, the exclusive emphasis on the unconditionality of revelation that abrogates the conditions of its reception seems to risk totally devaluing the finite order, thereby falling into the trap set by Nietzsche that Christianity is the custodian of this dualism. Returning to the term *hors*, one might suggest that the lexical issue of translation is subordinate to the issue of understanding in the sense that the excess of intuition can be influenced by the vector from below to above or the vector of outside to inside. As suggested already, Falque worries about the insinuation of the former vector in Marion and seems to side with an earlier figure as Blanchot, who is not a canonic figure for him, when it comes to understanding what exceeds phenomenality: the vector of displacement cannot automatically be regarded as the ejection towards a height, but a displacement of the satisfied economy of from outside. Phenomenality is destroyed, as I am effectively turned inside-out. It might be said in passing that this chastening of the vertical vector in *Hors phénomène* is of a piece with Falque's resistance to Freud's topographical model of the self.

If the above specifies the fundamental difference between Falque and Marion on what is excessive in the phenomenon, it bears mentioning that Falque threads his formal discussion of what exceeds the phenomenon with the more old-fashioned existentialist analysis of limit experience found in the earlier generations of existentialist philosophy. There is definitely something Jaspers-like about Falque's analyses of what he calls *limited phenomena* such as serious illness, death of a child, and pandemic, among others, even if such analyses are also consistent with the kinds of analyses of moods prosecuted by Heidegger in *Being and Time*. Falque's analyses of a wide range of limited phenomena could be understood to separate him, on the one hand, from Levinas who focuses on the subversion of the intentionality of the subject by the other and, on the other hand, from Henry who thinks of intuition more a given state, which though intimated from time to time that from time in the philosophical tradition, is most fully disclosed in the New Testament (*I Am the Truth*) and the mystical tradition, especially in Meister Eckhart (*The Essence of Manifestation*).

Crossing of Philosophy and Theology

Falque not only supports a positive relation between philosophy and theology that has essentially been barred from the side of philosophy in the modern period—though he admits that the barring has also come from the side of theology—but also attempts to outline in a general way the borderlands in which they meet. Falque is not a genealogist. Thus, it is unfair to expect of him an account of the genesis of the dissociation and its sustaining protocols. For him, it is simply another phenomenon to be unveiled, one that has become acute in French phenomenology since Janicaud's objection to the *theological turn* and his argument that phenomenology can only be *first philosophy* if it has excised theological presuppositions. Falque realizes that Janicaud's pronouncements on the separation of the discourses are largely stipulative, even if—and here he is largely in agreement with Marion—there is some foundation for the view in Husserl (less) and Heidegger (more). Nonetheless, Falque acknowledges that the problem that Janicaud raises, that is, how to avoid the confounding of these discourses, is real. There may be borderlands shared by philosophy and theology, but how to describe it in general and how to describe it in such a way that the identity of each is preserved such that we are speaking of a melding of discourses but their genuine rapprochement and mutual fertilization. Here Stanislas Breton is exemplary for Falque, though one wonders whether Claude Bruaire might not also have suggested a way forward.

Falque does not present us with a set of protocols for the proper intimacy and distance between the two discourses that might be involved in what Falque—after Marion—calls their *crossing*. Indeed, there is more than enough evidence in his work as a whole and especially in *Crossing the Rubicon*, that he would not countenance such a project. Judgments regarding propriety or impropriety of crossing have to proceed inductively and more or less worked out on a case-to-case basis. Maybe Levinas's introduction of the concepts of *incarnation* and *revelation* into phenomenology makes him guilty of conflating the two discourses. Maybe not. Maybe in Marion's early work his articulation of the borderlands (*demarche*) risks confounding philosophy and theology in a marsh of indifference, thereby, perhaps, setting up an overcorrection in his accounts of saturated phenomenon and account of revelation that seems to drain the marsh by segregating philosophy from theology. Falque's basic intuition—for which there may not be an adequate conceptual provision—is that our reflective judgments necessarily have to balance the principled independence of the discourses with the possibility of codependence in concrete circumstances. In a sense, we are looking for metaphors of hyperboles of dynamic approach and distancing as both proxies and approximates to what a concept seems unable to provide.

In this context, Falque more than once hints at Chalcedon functioning as a kind of heuristic model. By means of the affirmation of Christ being one hypostasis while possessing two natures we are empowered how to see the relation between these two discourses that throughout history have each one in turn exercising prerogatives over the other. The Chalcedonian formula helps insofar as it specifies a mode of unity in which there is neither *confusion* nor absolute *separation* between philosophy and theology. In any case, Falque is persuaded that each of the discourses turns out to be a gift to the other, each giving the other something it does not have. Stated more crudely than Falque would put it, theology sometimes provides philosophy with what it needs to think, whereas philosophy can sometimes provide theology with the means of thinking. Looked at dynamically and kinetically, philosophy and theology are involved in a perpetual dance of approach and separation in the interest of illuminating the dynamic human subject in all of this concreteness and pathos, longing and reaching. And maybe with the introduction of the metaphor of dance, which is at the root of perichoresis, perhaps certain articulations of the Trinity may also help us think through and follow through on the relation between discourses and avoid segregation between philosophy and theology.

Eucharist

With Christ's entry as a means to think the relation between philosophy and theology rather than simply be an object of one (theology)—though Christ is a central object of reflection in all of Christian theology—we come to Falque's manifold reflections on the Eucharist throughout his work, but especially in *The Wedding Feast of the Lamb* (2016). The Eucharist is not only a fundamental filament in a complex web in a sense it is also the principle of unity of the web as such, insofar as it is in the Eucharist that the desire finds both its satisfaction even as it is given back to itself, that the finitude of the self is honored and the broken and mortal body comes to be loved beyond reason, and phenomenology is released from its asceticism into a fullness of response to reality that is multiple and pliant and which was always its birthright. The Eucharist is also the place where all of Falque's philosophical and theological thinkers with whom he is involved in *loving struggle* can repose together and provide mutual blessing, thereby joining with his spouse, four children where love and struggle go hand in hand, and also with numerous friends where by means of his words and physical gestures each is made to feel absolutely incommunicable and inaccessible and thus of absolute worth. As Christ's suffering and broken body tells us all that we need to know about our human bodiliness and the animality that cannot be excised on pain of making us angels or ghosts, the Eucharist reveals to us through our unity with Christ, the exemplar, our communion with each other based on our fundamental inseparability because of and not despite our equally fundamental differences. In communion our inalienable solitude is not seen to be pathological. Rather it is seen to be our glory rightfully awaiting recognition and receiving blessing.

As Falque sees it, in the Eucharist is constituted an inalienable *we* in which there lies the promise of loving recognition all the way down to our somatic base, and also, of course, our resilience as well as our pathos, our passion defined by the interval of the non-identity with ourselves that is our glory as well as our wrack of pain. There, too, lies the promise that even in the hopelessness of our suffering, the presumptive finality of death will not be denied and will be blessed in the resurrected body. Here *The Guide to Gethsemane* (2018) matches—if not surpasses—what one comes across on these topics in *The Wedding Feast of the Lamb*. Of course, the Eucharist is unimpeachably memorial, indeed, the site of attentive memory's maximum to the extent to which our memory of the passion, death, and resurrection of Christ is exploded by God's loving memory in Christ. We participate insofar as we are undone in the right way. And our hope for resurrection is grounded in this participation in which we our bodies will no longer be the carriers of inertia but the bearers of the ecstasy. There is something in Falque's account that makes us think of *epektasis* when it comes to imaging the eschatological state even if this is not necessarily his aim. At the same time, there are enough clues for us to think that this forever reaching or stretching is not unique to Eastern Christianity, though perhaps we see it most clearly in Gregory of Nyssa, Maximus the Confessor, and latterly Sergei Bulgakov. Given Przywara's discovery of its presence in Augustine and Balthasar's ratification, it would be difficult to imagine that he would deny it to the Western tradition. One after all can find it in Dante's *Paradiso* in which he exalts Augustine and Bonaventure as he does Aquinas.

While Falque's elevation of the Eucharist is momentous, it is not without precedent in French phenomenology. Of course, in this respect the early Marion stands out. Yet, more than the early Marion who takes issue with Hegel's casting and Lacoste who follows him taking issue with Heidegger's various substitutions, Falque conceives of the Eucharist as having as having a kind of semantic reach that is overarching even if it cannot explain itself or explain how it discloses the quivering web of vital meaning and the meaning of vitality. Moreover, yet for the same reason, it suggests that not only all of theology but also all of philosophy is doxological. If the Eucharist is the site of memorial form of thought, for the same reason it is the site of gratitude, at once global and inordinate. It is the gratitude of gratitude, its absolute altitude, that sounds and resounds the other notes of gratitude that his thought elevates and to which it lovingly attends.

Contributors

David Albertson
University of Southern California

Donald Boyce
Southern Methodist University

Carla Canullo
University of Macerata

William L. Connelly
Catholic University of Paris

Steven DeLay
Woolf University

Sabine Fos Falque
University of Tours

Sarah Horton
Catholic University of Paris/Australian Catholic University

Pablo Irizar
Newman Theological College

Matthew W. Knotts
Loyola Academy

Martin Koci
Catholic University of Linz

Jean-Luc Marion
University of Chicago

Sean J. McGrath
Memorial University/McGill University

Matthew Nini
University of Freiburg

Cyril O'Regan
University of Notre Dame

Andrew Sackin-Poll
University of Cambridge

Gaël Trottmann-Calame
Catholic University of Paris/LUMSA

Acknowledgments

Sarah Horton revised the French-to-English translation of Sabine Fos Falque's chapter. Pablo Irizar and Donald Boyce edited and prepared the French-to-English translations of the chapters by Canullo, Marion, and Trottmann-Calame. *Commonweal* graciously granted permission to reproduce David Albertson's concluding chapter, "Fraternity in Finitude: Emmanuel Falque and the Future of Christian Philosophy," originally published online on January 10, 2024. Alain Saudan provided biographical details related to Emmanuel Falque's early intellectual itinerary. William L. Connelly's contribution is a revised and extended version of the original text published with *Crossing: The INPR Journal*, on November 18, 2020. Sabine Fos Falque warmly and patiently encouraged and supported the project from its inception. This project was a work of collaboration; deep gratitude is owed to all involved, named and unnamed, including our families.

Preface

THIS PROJECT WAS BORN from a deep sense of gratitude. Everyone's story of encountering Emmanuel Falque is unique yet similar. On his sixtieth birthday the editors have arranged the present intellectual bouquet as an homage to the many contributions Emmanuel Falque has gifted and continues gifting to a generation of scholars in philosophy, theology, and beyond. Falque has nourished us all in unique ways. We reciprocally present this volume as a modest expression of sincere gratitude, which, as Augustine wisely reminds us, is the debt of love. Thank you, Emmanuel, from us all.

Introduction

To Die of Not Writing

Pablo Irizar, Donald Boyce, & Martin Koci

What does the existential ache captured by the assertion *to die of not writing* have to do with *doing philosophy of religion* with Emmanuel Falque? Everything. That's the heart of Falque's intellectual itinerary, as the cumulative impact of this volume's celebratory bouquet of contributions illustrates, and persuasively so.

The story begins with flesh and bones, the *sine qua non* of human existence. Emmanuel Falque was born on November 7, 1963, in Neuilly-sur-Seine, a French commune in the Île-de-France region. He studied philosophy at the University of Nanterre and obtained a graduate-level degree in theology at the Jesuit Faculty of Philosophy and Theology in Paris, the Centre Sèvres. Emmanuel Falque wrote a doctoral dissertation in philosophy on Bonaventure under the direction of Jean Luc-Marion at the University of Paris. In 2006, he completed a *habilitation à diriger des recherches* (HDR), a credential often required to direct doctoral research in some European countries. Emmanuel Falque began his teaching engagements at various *lycées* (high schools) of Touraine. Eventually, he joined the Faculty of Philosophy at the Catholic University of Paris (ICP), where he eventually served as dean and continues teaching and researching. In 2015, Falque cofounded the *International Network for Philosophy of Religion* (INPR). The

INPR has hosted numerous events around the world (France, Italy, Canada, US, Switzerland, UK) and continues to foster a geographical *spread body* for fruitful, authentic, collegial, amicable, and personal encounters for practitioners of philosophy of religion. Through the INPR, for nearly a decade now, most of the contributors have, in one way or another, lived out the experience of *doing philosophy of religion* with Emmanuel Falque. The experience is certainly, and firstly, one of encounters with Emmanuel Falque, in *flesh and bones*; an encounter with his disarmingly generous humanity, to which corresponds a complementary encounter with his monumental (and living) intellectual *oeuvre*. Emmanuel Falque's academic output is creative, insightful, and consistent, yet at times it is also quite challenging, as it spans various historical periods, writers, themes, and disciplines. Falque's thought moves in multiple directions, simultaneously traversing four fields. These are not phases or evolutions of his work but areas of interest that burst forth from him in hundreds of published articles, lectures, and books. Falque writes as though he were fighting a single *loving struggle* across four different fronts, each with a different battle that begins here, is paused there, and continues everywhere, but mostly as an endless and generative *storm in a skull*.

Falque's work can be categorized in different ways. For example, David Albertson and Mark Novak see a trilogy on method in *Crossing the Rubicon*, *The Loving Struggle*, and *By Way of Obstacles*.[1] However, the four categories Falque himself employs to delineate his work—categories or lines he is always crossing—are (1) *Patristic and Medieval Philosophy*, (2) *Philosophy of Religion*, (3) *Philosophy and Theology*, and (4) *Phenomenology*. To give the reader a general introduction, we will adopt Falque in his own words, if nothing else, to emphasize his constant work from all sides, consistently defying any neat categorization. Here we list some primary texts from each category in chronological order of their publication with the associated English translation and its respective publication date.

The key texts in *Patristic and Medieval Philosophy* are: *Saint Bonaventure et l'entre de Dieu en théologie* (2000), translated as *Saint Bonaventure and the Entrance of God into Theology* (2018) by Brian Lapsa and Sarah Horton; *Dieu, la chair, et l'autre: D'Irénée à Duns Scot* (2008), translated as *God, the Flesh, and the Other: From Irenaeus to Duns Scotus* (2014) by William Christian Hackett; and finally, *Le livre de l'expérience: D'Anselme de Cantorbéry à Bernard de Clairvaux* (2017), translated recently as *The Book of Experience: From Anselm of Canterbury to Bernard of Clairvaux* (2024) by George Hughes.

---

1. See Novak, Review of *By Way of Obstacle*; Alberton, "Fraternity in Finitude."

In *Philosophy of Religion*, Falque's earliest and perhaps most widely disseminated texts are all translated by George Hughes, who Falque credits[2] with having run the Pauline race of translating his triduum: *Le passeur de Gethsémani: Angoisse, souffrance et mort*; *Lecture existentielle et phénoménologique* (1999), translated as *The Guide to Gethsemane: Anxiety, Suffering, Death* (2018); *Métamorphose de la finitude: Essai philosophique sur la naissance et la resurrection* (2004), translated as *The Metamorphosis of Finitude: An Essay on Birth and Resurrection* (2012); *Les noces de l'Agneau: Essai philosophique sur le corps et l'eucharistie* (2011), translated as *The Wedding Feast of the Lamb: Eros, Body, and Eucharist* (2016). While *The Guide to Gethsemane* is Falque's earliest published text of all his work (1999), it is actually the most recently published English translation of the triduum (2018). Interestingly, Falque's earliest published work, *The Guide to Gethsemane*, is a text born out of pain, as the author's note lodged in the crack between the preface and the body of the work confesses.[3] Maybe pain does—as Sarah Horton suggests in her chapter—beg for "recognition and interpretation." Falque's most recent text in *Philosophy of Religion*, *La chair de Dieu* (2023), is currently available in French only. In English, the literal translation of the French is *The Flesh of God*.

In *Philosophy and Theology* sits Falque's challenge to both theologians and philosophers, *Passer le Rubicon: Philosophie et théologie; Essai sur les frontières* (2013), translated as *Crossing the Rubicon: The Borderlands of Philosophy and Theology* (2016) by Reuben Shank. We also include *François Philosophe* (2017), written with Laure Solignac, in this category, which has yet to be translated into English.[4]

The last and perhaps more prolific area of Falque's published work is *Phenomenology*. The key texts here are: *Le combat amoureux: Disputes phénoménologiques et théologiques* (2014), translated as *The Loving Struggle: Phenomenological and Theological Debates* (2018) by Bradley Onishi and Lucas McCracken; *Parcours d'embûches: S'expliquer* (2016) translated as *By Way of Obstacles: A Pathway Through a Work* (2022) by Sarah Horton; *Éthique du corps épandu* and *Une chair épandue sur le divan* (2018) written

2. Falque, *Guide to Gethsemane*, xvi.

3. "But what lay behind my reading of the Gospels here was something that was all the more crucial in that it happened so suddenly: the unbearable coincidence of the accidental death of one friend, and the suicide of another" (Falque, *Guide to Gethsemane*, between xxx and 1).

4. Although Falque does not include this coauthored text in his own bibliography, it stands out to the editors as another example of Falque's engagement with Philosophy and Theology while demonstrating just how engaged Falque remains with contemporary Catholic Theology as it is developed in papal sermons, encyclicals, and general theological debates.

with his wife, Sabine Fos Falque, which has not yet been translated into English; *«Ça» n'a rien à voir: Lire Freud en philosophe* (2018) translated as *Nothing to It: Reading Freud as a Philosopher* (2020) by Robert Vallier and William Connelly; and *Hors phénomène: Essai aux confins de la phénoménalité* (2021). Falque's preferred translation of the expression *Hors phénomène* is *Extra-Phenomenal*, even if a literal English translation for *hors* is not *extra*, but *out*. Perhaps, by *extra*, Falque has in mind the Latin proposition *ex* (out of), in which case *hors* appears to translate somehow into *extra*. This may capture Falque's insight that the *extra-phenomenal* is not just beyond phenomenality, but rather beyond ordinary phenomenality, yet somehow phenomenal.

In his bibliography, Falque places *Patristic and Medieval Philosophy* first. From early on, Falque has always thought through and with the intellectual giants of the Christian tradition. Falque's dissertation on Bonaventure with Jean-Luc Marion at the Sorbonne in 1998 was then published as the first text in this first historical trilogy. What does historical philosophy have to do with phenomenology? Surprisingly, Falque's coauthored book (with Laure Solignac) entitled *François Philosophe*, a proposal to think of Pope Francis as a philosopher, communicates Falque's turn to historical philosophy and interest in retrieving core insights from history to bridge thought and practice. According to Falque and Solignac, Pope Francis acts as a lover of wisdom or philosopher, as evidenced in his approach to discerning how to see a path of action forward in the tradition of Ignatius of Loyola. According to Falque and Solignac, for Pope Francis all action presupposes thought. More so, the authors argue, action is itself a mode of thinking. This is precisely the leitmotif of Falque's trilogy in historical philosophy. Bonaventure, the Cistercians, Anselm, and the early church fathers like Augustine and Tertullian all share the fundamental concern: thought and action go hand in hand because action is a mode of thinking. Falque's interpretation of figures in the history of philosophy teaches that authentic philosophical discourse is never without demands or responsibility.

The field of *Philosophy of Religion* (also known sometimes as *Natural Theology*) is perhaps what Falque is best known for internationally, based mainly on his *Philosophical Triduum* composed of three meditative reflections on Good Friday (*The Guide to Gethsemane*), Easter Sunday (*The Metamorphosis of Finitude*), and Holy Thursday (*The Wedding Feast of the Lamb*). In *The Guide to Gethsemane*, Falque explores how Jesus was gripped by fear of death with no resignation, certitude, or heroism. According to Falque, in the garden, Jesus authentically dies and shows us how to die—how to abandon our management of death, opting instead for a willingness to lose ourselves entirely and, therefore, also be lost in God's love. Falque warns against rushing through the garden with a neurotic self-certitude of heaven or immortality at the end of it. Sin, on this account, is not finitude itself but our refusal to accept our finitude. In *The Metamorphosis of Finitude* Falque asks, with Nicodemus, what it could mean to be *born again*. On Falque's account, the resurrection is not some distant historical or future thing, although it is also that, but is the transformation or transfiguration, which he prefers to translate as metamorphosis, of our being in time by placing within us a longing for the infinite. *The Wedding Feast of the Lamb* is an extended analysis of Christ's initiation of the Eucharist with the now liturgical words from the Christian Scripture: "this is my body" and "this is my blood." Christ, by assuming our animality in the Eucharist, saves us from bestiality, according to Falque's novel interpretation. Through Eucharistic activity, Christ descends to the Chaos, passions, and drives of our animality to embrace, transform, and *re*form them in God and as God.

The third category of work that bursts forth from Falque is writing on the overlap of *Theology and Philosophy*, which is, at times, *Philosophical Theology* but also sometimes (dare we say) *Theological Philosophy*. While one might understand Falque citing the latest papal encyclical, one can also catch him wading into obscure theological debates within church history to bring them to bear on the questions and problems he is exploring. It is often a relief to the reader that Falque has taken the time to recover others in church history who wrestled with the same questions and problems (e.g., what is the nature of Christ's body in the Eucharist? Can we chew it with our teeth? What is the nature of the soul? Are we the same after the resurrection?). In *Crossing the Rubicon*, Falque proposes a *counterblow* of theology on phenomenology, making the bold claim he repeats throughout the text that "the more one theologizes, the better one philosophizes."

Risking overstating the observation, we must nevertheless (and with confidence) claim that Emmanuel Falque is the first heir to the rich French phenomenological tradition, mainly in the vein of the so-called *theological turn*. So much of continental philosophy is about one's intellectual genealogy, and Falque has the benefit of being a clear heir and a *loving combatant* of Jean-Luc Marion (a student of Ferdinand Aliqué). In *The Loving Struggle*, Falque carefully traces the different veins of the French phenomenological tradition, arguing for a *loving struggle* between philosophy and theology to ensure the vitality of both rather than merely a *theological turn*. He continues the line of thinking on method in *By Way of Obstacles*, where he continues the work of *The Loving Struggle* arguing for thought in context, *catholic* thought (in the sense of universal, sweeping, inclusive), and for thought grounded squarely within the horizon of finitude—something that will allow us to embrace our humanity more fully. In *Éthique du corps épandu* (*Ethics of the Spread Body*), Falque expands on his very original idea discovered in his *Triduum* that there is a body, the *spread body*, that is neither purely objective (*res extensa* or *Körper*) nor purely interior (flesh or *Leib*). In *Nothing to It*, Falque reads Freud as a philosopher showing how the It or Freudian Id is not visible and never shows itself as a *phenomenon* despite being the underlying reality or source and force of all that does *show itself*. Finally, in *Hors phénomène*, a text currently being translated as *Extra-Phenomenal*, Falque expands on the way that what does not *appear* at all and is therefore strictly non-phenomenal, may be that which best characterizes us in our humanity. Here, Falque lets the *counterblow* or *backlash* of psychoanalysis—with its rich analysis and testament to trauma—ring out on phenomenology. Falque describes this not as a *turning point* as much as a *radicalization* or rooting of his work in deep soil, the fertile depth of trauma's extra phenomenality.[5]

In each text, it is clear that Falque thinks and writes at the borders or limits of each field. He is not satisfied with superficial solutions to philosophical and theological problems. He is not afraid to try to think that which often escapes thought—especially concerning the body. In each text, Falque thinks not from above but from below. By this, we mean he begins and ends with human experience, "the ordinary skeins of embodied life," as David Albertson puts it, "not yet saturated by divine glory."[6] Where some might be content (and quite legitimately) with thoughtless piety, Falque always attempts to think and speak his Catholic faith in a way that absorbs or learns from the criticism of thinkers such as Nietzsche, Heidegger, Freud, and Marx.

The contributions of this volume engage in varied ways and from distinct perspectives with a range of ideas in Falque's *oeuvre*, modeling in this way the rewarding practice of *doing philosophy of religion* with Emmanuel Falque.

Who else than *Sabine Fos Falque*, the wife of Emmanuel Falque, is better positioned to explore the intricate dance between conflict and affection in intimate relationships? In her contribution, "A Struggle unto Life," she illustrates the point by using real figures who experienced their loving struggles through writing and words.

Through the lens of famous literary couples—Catherine Pozzi and Paul Valéry, Franz Kafka and Milena Jesenská, Pierre Jean Jouve and Blanche Reverchon—Sabine Fos Falque examines the delicate balance between individuality and unity. She draws parallels between the struggle unto life and the biblical story of Jacob wrestling with the angel, suggesting that loving

---

5. See Falque and Costa, "Turning Point?"
6. Alberton, "Fraternity in Finitude," para. 4.

relationships often involve a transformative struggle. This interplay of love and conflict is presented as a source of anguish and inspiration, driving creative output while testing the boundaries of intimacy. It changes everything. And there is no better way to introduce the intellectual world of Emmanuel Falque than by these words written, certainly, *about life*, but much more importantly, *out of* love.

Andrew Sackin-Poll brings into discussion the power of literature and portrays the relationship between bodied life and writing. He takes an original angle on Falque's texts and puts them into dialogue with the philosopher Catherine Malabou as well as writers such as Georges Perec and Enrique Vila-Matas. The central argument, presented in a well thought-through poetic language, posits that writing is shaped by and simultaneously shapes the rolling depths of bodied life rather than unfolding in a detached, transcendental space. *The page* and *the bed* are presented as homologous spaces where the body spreads out, merging the writer's identity with the subject matter. Moreover, bodied life is influenced by contingency and accident, shaping the outward form of life and, consequently, the surface of the text. Masks and surfaces in literature are shown to relate to the plastic materiality of bodied life and its outward expression, each shaping the other. Sackin-Poll suggests that encountering the resistance and solitude within a text can open up new possibilities and transformations for the reader. Ultimately, the presence of the writer can be felt in the relief and contours of the text, marking a fragile, minimal contact between the solitudes of the writer and the reader. The rhythms, contours, and resistant aspects of a text are thus seen to offer a *relief* of the writer's bodied life, creating a tenuous link between the solitudes of the writer and reader, opening up the possibility for transformation and the discovery of new horizons.

Matthew W. Knotts follows the theme of transformation further and links Falque's work on the relationship between philosophy and theology with the Ignatian spiritual practice. He argues that Falque's focus cannot be reduced to academic purposes but underlines its importance for personal transformation within the individual. Knotts reaffirms Falque's argument that philosophy and theology examine the same reality from different perspectives, with human finitude as their common ground. He believes the encounter between the two disciplines leads to a transformative experience, especially in light of Christ's incarnation. At the same time, Falque's thought is deeply influenced by Ignatian spirituality, particularly the *Spiritual Exercises*, which emphasizes introspection, discernment, and the integration of intellectual reflection with lived experience. Ultimately, Falque's thought calls for a mutual engagement between philosophy and theology, leading to personal growth and a deeper understanding of the human condition.

Knotts appreciates the holistic dimension of knowledge acquisition and the possibility of integrating philosophy and theology within the individual presented by Falque and commends his work for further development in this direction. Naturally, this sounds very appealing to the ears of theologians; however, there is always the question of (secular) philosophers who will find the call challenging. In one way or another, Knotts has delineated an interesting path of research by explicitly linking Falque's intellectual activity with spiritual practice.

Steven DeLay's chapter contributes to Emmanuel Falque's ongoing loving struggle with Michel Henry regarding the relationship between the body and the flesh. DeLay begins by examining Falque's reading of the apostle Paul's view that the believer's body is a temple of the Holy Spirit, and asks what light phenomenology can shed on this idea. Then, the author reviews phenomenological approaches to the body, including the perspectives of Husserl, Merleau-Ponty, and Sartre, to contrast them with Henry's critique of historical phenomenology and his emphasis on the flesh (i.e., the subjective, lived body). The author proposes a rapprochement between Henry and Falque. Henry illuminates how our incarnate existence is grounded in Life, while Falque describes the transformation of the flesh by the Holy Spirit. The chapter concludes by suggesting that Falque's phenomenology of incorporation attests to the promise of eternal life in Christ, which makes phenomenological inquiry worthwhile. DeLay's work is provocative due to his intentional decision not to adhere to a distinction between philosophical and theological agendas. Many readers will find this contribution thought provoking.

In his exploration of the problem of the flesh, *William Connelly* proves to be an excellent student of Falque and follows his doctoral father in exploring the philosophical implications of our embodied existence. Connelly critiques phenomenology's limitations in grasping the depths of human experience beyond immediate consciousness, extensively examining Falque's concept of the *spread body* and his efforts to bridge the gap between phenomenology and the unconscious realms of human existence. The author also investigates the intricate relationship between spiritual and physical aspects of human nature, drawing on theological concepts to illuminate philosophical inquiries. He advocates for a more balanced approach that combines materialist theology with spiritualist philosophy, capable of addressing both corporeal and metaphysical dimensions of human experience. In a truly Falquean fashion, Connelly grapples with the challenge of articulating a comprehensive understanding of human nature that accounts for both its physical embodiment and spiritual potential, seeking to reconcile the apparent dichotomy between flesh and spirit in philosophical discourse.

Donald Boyce explores the concept of *breath* as a manifestation of God's presence within human animality. Boyce draws on Augustine and examines the role of wind and breath in *Confessions*, noting that while wind is often used metaphorically and negatively, breath holds a deeper significance. In Augustine's work, Boyce explores the connections between God and breath, highlighting how breathing in God through song and praise allows momentary access to the divine. The author also discusses the physiological repercussions of finitude and disordered love and how attention to breath can lead to a metamorphosis of finitude, enabling one to live fully in the present moment. The author engages with Falque's ideas throughout the text, particularly the concept of God inhabiting human animality and the importance of attending to the body's experiences. The text concludes by emphasizing the significance of breath as a constant reminder of human finitude and a means of participating in and experiencing God's presence in each moment of life.

Pablo Irizar broadens and deepens our understanding of emotions, particularly anxiety, by looking more closely at the early Christian treatment of the passions. Through an analysis of *restlessness* in the work of St. Augustine—something Irizar says is lost in a more secular treatment of anxiety—he shows how scholars often mistakenly reduce the early Christian concept of anxiety to stoic weariness about life. By closely examining music in the Augustinian corpus, Irizar argues that music, particularly in a liturgical context, offers a temporary remedy, foretaste, or *efficacious sign*, of the ultimate rest found in harmonious divine eternity. In his conclusion, Irizar suggests that while learning to abide *in* anxiety is important, we should not stop there. All five senses of restlessness—metaphysical, moral, psychological, existential, and normative—find their satisfaction, something more than mere psychological well-being, in God's redemptive eternity, where all things achieve *transformative* or *metamorphosing* harmony and unity. On this account, anxiety is not left behind but instead is *incorporated* by being *brought up*. While Irizar does not explicitly discuss Falque, his indebtedness is apparent through Irizar's emphasis on the passions and reliance on Falque's paradigm of the *metamorphosis of finitude*—a paradigm Irizar appropriates in his monograph *The Metamorphosis of Love*, which is an analysis of *body*, *word*, and *free will* in the work of Bernard of Clairvaux.

David Albertson explores the concept of *manence* in the work of Emmanuel Falque, based on the background of his predecessor Stanislas Breton. *Manence*, derived from the Greek μένειν and the Latin *manere*, denotes a mode of abiding or dwelling that is central to both philosophy and theology. Albertson traces the concept's emergence in ancient Greek and Christian Neoplatonism, highlighting the contrasting notions of the sudden event and the steadfast remaining. He then examines how Augustine of Hippo, departing from the Neoplatonic tradition, emphasizes God's intimate proximity to the self, rendering the divine presence an *anti-event* characterized by unwavering remaining. Finally, Albertson proposes Hadewijch of Brabant, a thirteenth-century Beguine mystic, as an unexpected medieval figure whose understanding of *manence* resembles Falque's most closely. Hadewijch's writings present a resolute commitment to remaining within the limits of human finitude, embracing the suffering and exile of embodied existence in solidarity with Christ's humanity. Her visionary experiences, often occurring during eucharistic communion, merge the erotic and sacramental aspects of remaining, offering a unique perspective on the strength found in abiding within the confines of immanence.

Gaël Trottmann-Calame explores Nietzsche's concept taken from Pindar of "becoming what you are" in a chapter that thinks with Falque's *Hors phénomène* using Falque's insights into the priority of becoming to explore what Nietzsche might mean by egoism. Nietzsche, as Trottmann-Calame observes, reinterprets becoming as a perpetual, chaotic process rather than a realization of a *form* or essence. For Nietzsche, and perhaps also for Falque, there is a metamorphosis of egoism because of the destabilization of the *I*—the stable *self* and foundation of most metaphysical philosophy. Trottmann-Calame suggests that true self-becoming—true egoism—is instead a mastering or *en*forming of the chaos, passions, and drives. This is not a mode of selfishness on Nietzsche's account, as Trottmann-Calame shows, but a necessary force for self-creation and growth—the way we create and recreate.

Sean J. McGrath's chapter explores the concept of non-duality (ND) as a perennial philosophy found in various Eastern and Western traditions, specifically focusing on the teachings of the Christian mystic Meister Eckhart. McGrath argues that ND is a rational position that can be advanced through argumentation. Thus, for McGrath, ND is not restricted to being an experience of transformed consciousness. The author presents three families of arguments for non-duality: epistemic, grammatical, and ontological. These arguments lead to three basic negative claims: ND cannot be conscious or an object of consciousness; ND cannot be spoken of categorically but only indirectly gestured to; and ND cannot be finite. Then, McGrath delves into Eckhart's teachings on ND, which led to his condemnation by the Avignon Pope John XXII in 1329. Eckhart's central claim was the identity of God and creatures in the ground, the abyss of potency from which both have emerged. This identification effectively collapses the distinction between creation and the divine. According to McGrath, the implication is not that creatures are divine or that the divine is a creature; following the apophatic tradition of theology, Eckhart wishes to emphasize the nothingness of human beings. McGrath insists on Eckhart's conviction that ND can be experienced ordinarily as the truth of everydayness. The text concludes by emphasizing Eckhart's distinctive doctrine of analogy and his radical apophasis, recognizing the limits of human language in speaking about God.

Emmanuel Falque is not known only for *crossing the borders* of theology and history of philosophy. Recently, he has engaged with psychoanalysis too. *Matthew Nini*'s chapter focuses on Falque's book on Sigmund Freud *Nothing to It* [«*Ça*» *n'a rien à voir* (2018)] and argues that Falque's engagement with the founder of psychoanalysis represents a crucial moment in the development of Falque's phenomenology. Through this engagement with Freudian psychoanalysis, particularly the concept of the Id (or Ça in French), Falque develops the notion of the extra-phenomenon, the experience that not only escapes the phenomenal realm but also destroys the very capacity for appreciating the phenomenal. Nini argues that Falque learns from Freud how to deal with the extra-phenomenal, and this apprenticeship involves learning how to tell jokes to approach the unsayable. This paradoxical methodology allows that which resists appearing to be included in the discourse on phenomena without being objectified. The insights gained from engaging with Freud's work are further developed in Falque's later work and the extra-phenomenal is transformed into the extra-phenomenon in *Hors phénomène*.

The contributors to this volume provide abundant proof to show the coherence and gradual development of Falque's thought, which finds its (current) pinnacle in *Hors phénomène*. Whether in theology or psychoanalysis, Falque integrates various sources into his phenomenology to go beyond phenomenology without betraying or leaving the phenomenological method behind. *Sarah Horton*'s chapter is exemplary in this respect. Her contribution, "When Meaning Breaks: Thinking Sense and Suffering with Emmanuel Falque," elaborates on the concept of the extra-phenomenal. Horton focuses on the breakdown of meaning and all of our interpretive categories in the face of traumatic experiences. The chapter opens with a useful philological clarification of possible translations of the French into English, and the author proposes to stick with the extra-phenomenal (an option for which we opted in the entire volume). The *extra-phenomenal* is neither the supra-phenomenal (exceeding thought) nor the infra-phenomenal (preparatory to phenomena), but rather it destroys the possibility of phenomenality itself. Horton clarifies that, for Falque, the extra-phenomenal is a fundamental aspect of the human condition, a *crack* that runs through all of us, making us susceptible to crises that shatter sense and subjectivity.

Something that at first sight appears as the impossibility of any possibility gives rise to an impossibility of impossibility, as the self is thrown back upon itself and transformed rather than utterly annihilated. For Horton, survival amid the breakdown of meaning is a crucial theme, for survival itself may be a resource from which one gains the strength to remain alive. Writing and creativity are presented as existential challenges that arise from the crisis of the extra-phenomenon, and Horton concludes by acknowledging Falque's work as the inspiring source for further thought and writing in the direction of existential survival when meaning breaks.

Carla Canullo's chapter, titled "God and Human Being: An Ellipse in Emmanuel Falque's Work," points out that Falque's thought can aptly be characterized by the biblical story of Jacob wrestling with the angel symbolizing the struggle—*a loving struggle*—between human beings and God. Falque's approach to philosophical thought is described as *bare-faced*; as he proceeds "with the face uncovered"—reminiscent of his *loving struggle* with his master Jean-Luc Marion. In contrast to much of French phenomenology after the so-called theological turn, Falque directly confronts the relationship between the divine and human; theology and philosophy; faithful to his maxim "the more one theologizes, the better one philosophizes." However, Canullo does not simply repeat the argument of *Crossing the Rubicon* and review the subsequent debate;[7] instead she makes a link between the early work of Falque (*Triduum philosophique*) and his most recent masterpiece, *Hors phénomène*. There, the concept of the passage comes to the fore and is presented as the hermeneutical key to the entirety of Falque's professional career: the passage which remodels not only the thought but also the person in the act of transformation.

Jean-Luc Marion's contribution, dedicated to his student Emmanuel Falque, examines Augustine's use of the term *substantia*. The context for Marion's contribution is Falque's argument that while Augustine is not a substance-metaphysician (and therefore escapes the critique of onto-theology), nevertheless Augustine remains a metaphysician who reconfigures and indeed inverses classical Aristotelian concepts in the *Categories* (or *Predicates*) such as substance and relation. For Falque, love as relation, based on Trinitarian considerations by Augustine, supplants substance in Christian thought. Against Falque, Marion argues that Augustine's use of the concept of substance (*substantia*) does not commit the Bishop of Hippo to metaphysics. Augustine, according to Marion, has a non-metaphysical understanding of substance. The author suggests that for Augustine, *substantia* does not adequately predicate God, as God lacks accidents and attributes. God is better described instead by the term *essentia*. Regarding

---

7. Koci and Alvis, *Transforming the Theological Turn*.

creatures, *substantia* is used negatively to highlight their mutability and lack of subsistence compared to God's immutability. The term is also employed in a pre-philosophical sense, denoting poverty or lack of stability. Thus, Marion concludes that Augustine's usage of *substantia* does not support the claim that his theology is situated within the framework of metaphysics (at least not in the classical sense of an Aristotelian *first philosophy*).

David Albertson's closing essay, which functions as an *envoi* to this volume, situates Falque as a central figure in emerging contemporary Christian debates about philosophy and theology. Together with Marion, Albertson notes, Falque takes on the Christian debates that began with *ressourcement* in the first half of the twentieth century and morphed into postmodern debates in the second half.

As we hope the present volume shows, Falque's intellectual itinerary is best characterized by a method of *transfiguration* through *traversing*, which is, at heart, nothing different from Falque's commitment to Catholicity. In Falque's quest for Catholicity, the drive to write and the longing for immortality can be found; to die of not writing is to say that one lives (on) by writing. In Falque's *oeuvre*, the aspiration to Catholicity, then, is not restricted to assenting to doctrine, asserting faith, and embracing a tradition, but it is the fullness of human *aperity* found in practice, in the liturgy of life and nature and in adopting an existential mode of self-transcendence through reason and philosophy, and with the aid of revelation and theology. At the very least (though ambitiously), we may conclude that the practice of *doing philosophy of religion* with Emmanuel Falque is about witnessing, experiencing, and becoming transfigured by the human longing for eternity within the liberating confines of finitude, always guided by the illuminating light of Christ.

Bibliography

Alberton, David. "Fraternity in Finitude." *Commonweal Magazine*, Jan. 10, 2024. https://www.commonwealmagazine.org/fraternity-finitude.
Falque, Emmanuel. *The Guide to Gethsemane: Anxiety, Suffering, Death*. Translated by George Hughes. New York: Fordham University Press, 2019.
Falque, Emmanuel, and João Paulo Costa. "A Turning Point? An Interview with Emmanuel Falque." Translated by Pablo Irizar and Donald Boyce. *Journal for Continental Philosophy of Religion* 5.2 (2023) 217–28.
Koci, Martin, and Jason W. Alvis, eds. *Transforming the Theological Turn: Phenomenology with Emmanuel Falque*. Lanham, MD: Rowman & Littlefield, 2020.
Novak, Mark. Review of *By Way of Obstacles: A Pathway Through Work*. *Reading Religion*, Mar. 24, 2023. https://readingreligion.org/9781666734140/by-way-of-obstacles.

Writing and Dying

A Struggle unto Life

Sabine Fos Falque

Ad E., in mea vita virum dilectum

Remember you.

Who are you?

You destroy me.

You're so good for me.

How could I have known that this city was made to the size of love?

How could I have known that you were made to the size of my body?

—Marguerite Duras, *Hiroshima Mon Amour*

Duras's raw words—scalpel-words—tell how much the struggle becomes entangled with love. How much this very entanglement feeds the desire to write. How much writing metabolizes the temptation of struggle. Even more so when we write, not together, but when we are two who are writing.

Catherine Pozzi and Paul Valéry, Franz Kafka and Milena Jesenská, Pierre Jean Jouve and Blanche Reverchon: lovers, of course, but more than that. The *between us* is not just a matter of bodies seeking and finding each other, but of a shared act of writing. Ultimately not common, but shared. Not intermingled but distinct. Each works in their own way, with their own rhythm, with the flesh of their words: the writing of one seemingly has nothing to do with the writing of the other. Nothing to do with it, nothing to it, and yet.

Certainly, in literature, love is often—even always—the object of investigation. But here, it's something else. Something intimate, almost secret, that cannot be explained and is revealed barely or almost by chance. Something sufficiently rare that upon discovering it, one is lost in a quiet wonder.

The *something* would be like drawing a shared force for writing out of the very experience of loving, basing the shared yet differentiated gesture of writing on what is felt and proven in loving. The experience of enjoying the verb combined with that of enjoying the flesh.

A link is made, immediately unmade, then tightened anew, from one body to another body, from one unconscious to another, but also from one writing to another. An intertwining is what weaves itself without even realizing it. From one to the other, but also from poetry to philosophy, from literature to psychoanalysis, from philosophy to listening to the unconscious. Each of them, crossing the Rubicon, or rather the Jabbok, to join the other on the other shore, is thereby changed, in his or her very being but also in his or her writings. Like Jacob, who, once his struggle with the angel is over, finds himself forever marked by it when he finally joins his family beyond the Jabbok River.[1]

Loving It

A quest as much as a fear, loving sustains the necessary illusion of being able to obtain everything from it, gives the jubilation of existing, even if in its wake there immediately creeps the panic of staying far away, of not being able to reach each other, or even more, of losing. Even if in its wake, like a basso continuo, there creeps also the struggle that naturally goes with it—even if we'd rather not.

While awaiting the arrival of Irmgard, his mistress, Simon, a character from Julien Gracq's *The Peninsula* (*La presqu'île*), crisscrosses a peninsula as one crisscrosses the bittersweet reserve of one's childhood. This is all that

---

1. In Genesis 32:23 and in the mural painted by Eugène Delacroix in 1861 at Saint Sulpice Church, Paris, France.

loving owes to childhood, isn't it? A slightly haggard drift. Alternating certainties and doubts. She'll come to him, he's certain, as he stands tall and as firm as a shore: she's embellished within him. The next moment brings him to the brink of a debacle: he won't know how to rush towards her if she comes. Yes, how will he know how to cope with his desire? And, after all, why should the world lend itself so easily to his desire? "I'm afraid . . . not afraid that she won't be there! Afraid to join."[2] Afraid, yes, of course. What if I didn't know? What to do? What is love based on? No one knows. There are so many risks involved in joining. Including the risk of the blurring of internal and external limits, the limits between what's mine and what's yours. Intermingling body and soul without, for all that, losing oneself amounts to the work of an artist. Should we then work at the art of loving?

Catherine Pozzi's words to her lover Paul Valéry: "I'm afraid of your arms, which immediately take the shape of my soul. So, you can enslave me and mysteriously create me as part of your flesh."[3] Terror of subjugation. As if being too close threatens Narcissus's integrity. Narcissus is a fragile but greedy flower born of a pure and exclusive alloy of self to self, with no possible Other. His demands would lead us to deposit the best part of ourselves in the beloved, haloed in the most intense shimmerings, with the best part of oneself waiting to be reflected. As if love were nothing more than that, this search for the same—even if it's in vain. What's more, collapse or execration could well result from this impossibility, and that would be the risk. A risk that most often threatens, in each one, the intimate act of writing.

The Loving Struggle, or Jacob's Struggle with the Angel

As we can see, there's nothing idyllic about these loves. A few cracks slip through into them, one's own and those of the in-between. To love, in Kafka's words, would be to consent, face to face with the other, to "strip naked before the ghosts,"[4] singular and common.

The impulse to love must certainly deal with the heaviness of being, as it were, each person's way of being in the world. Each *naked* person rooted in immanence and with "a fragile soul"—the human *tout court*, conceptualized by Emmanuel Falque beginning in his first book and continually—and for whom the whole world remains a mystery. A person who is an unexpected and profound world unto himself. Who, because of his terrible lucidity, finds himself without the slightest refuge, without asylum, exposed. Like,

---

2. Gracq, *Presqu'île*, 104, 167.
3. Pozzi, *Journal 1913–1934*, 180.
4. Kafka, *Lettres à Milena*, 267.

in Kafka's words, "a naked [human being] among clothed people."[5] Or a human being, in Faulkner's words, made up of "stench and grace" in continual struggle with the tension of desires. He's the one of whom we don't know whether he might suddenly become "abject or crazy."[6] Or, to follow Bernanos, he's the one whose soul can just as well be *criminal* as *holy*.[7] Yes, the infernal divisions of the *I*, the unpredictability of unconscious matters, the horizon of death and the incompressible thrust of anguish and doubt keep this *human tout court* in a state of threat. That's it, isn't it, a state akin to that of the tightrope walker between exaltation and fall—between Eros and Thanatos? That is to say, it's a struggle unto death.

The struggle consists of avoiding toppling over.

Jacob's struggle with the angel plays with the risk of toppling over. It was a bare-knuckle fight, pitting Jacob body-to-body against a stranger for no clear reason. Unconscious rivalries? Submission to an irresistible drive to hate? Compulsive repetitions of infantile struggles that are still going on? For a whole night, nothing and no one will separate them. They're relentless. Delacroix has brought all his power of conviction to bear, telling us both of the maniacal nature of the thing and the possibility, perhaps, of salvation. Yes, the human *tout court* could very well be saved, or at the very least exalted, even raised to divine heights—if only by the power of art here, writing elsewhere.

If we remain for a bit beneath Delacroix's painting, we discover that neither of the scene's protagonists is falling since, fighting with each other, they are in fact leaning on each other precisely to keep from falling. Against [*contre*] and very close [*tout contre*]. It's as if the struggle itself makes it possible to be together in an in-between space dense with surges of all kinds of drives—erotic and combative. At the end of the battle, there is no winner, but there is a transformation.

Could it be the same with man and woman as with Jacob's struggle with the angel? It is the angel of God in Genesis, of course; elsewhere, a metaphor for the struggle with what is unknown in the self; here, therefore, the struggle that constitutes the in-between. A couple: wrestlers? They pant together, naked torso against the naked torso, striving to win over the other, without screams or tears, but taken by the same destructive rage. Made up of "bloody entanglements, bitter fulfillments, defensiveness, nasty mouths,

---

5. Milena in Kafka, *Lettres à Milena*, 290.

6. That said, "Sometimes I aint so sho who's got ere a right to say when a man is crazy and when he aint" (Faulkner, *As I Lay Dying*, 233).

7. Falque, "Baiser de Satan"; Fos Falque, "Âme bric-à-brac."

devouring, blood sweat and retaliation"⁸—hatred in all its forms. Nothing but the all-too-familiar infernal component of desire, when it reveals all that desire contains of hatred.

Except that in the midst of unreason, amid combat, we hear the basso continuo of a kind of *loving power*. If only because, on this night, the forces seem equal. There can be no winner. And this is what allows us to hear this loving power, which would not be so much our nature as our quest. The power that makes us write is at the risk of a struggle of writing against writing.

Yes, through this combat it's as if they each seemed to be trying to know each other better through a *Who are you?* that, in the very hour of the struggle, doesn't wait for an answer. Seeking to know and be known takes time. It is by struggling until the very end of the night that they will discover it. Not before.

Delacroix's chosen colors and the impetus that is shared but that is to fight each other show the aspect of pleasure taken in the whole thing. Dark pleasures. The eroticism of the struggle in which the angel and the man, or man and woman, can stand upright only by bracing against each other. Neither the crushing war nor the fall. Even if the angel, dislodging the man's femoral nerve, thus obliges the man not only to lean on him but to keep his imprint in himself forever. Even if it means limping from it for life—at dawn Jacob leaves the combat limping—because, from the origin and for life, I cannot remain without the support of the other who makes me exist. Since indeed, from the dawn of life, man's flesh, burdened with a limp, bears the eternal imprint of his originary fragility—from the Latin *fragilis*, as if capable of being broken or fractured from within—and of the dependence it entails.

But let's take a closer look at the different forms of the struggle—body to body, but also writing against writing—thus entering into a kaleidoscopic reading, not only literary but clinical.

Catherine Pozzi and Paul Valery

To be joined with and to reach him, Catherine Pozzi gives her lover Paul Valery a few pages of her Diary to read shoulder-to-shoulder, to talk over and over again, because with "this fragile, perishable humanity that is mysteriously sweet to you, you must make an eternal home for yourself."⁹ He, too, has her read his lines. She reads them and marvels, and he loves to feel

---

8. See Jouve taking up for his own ends Jacob's combat with the angel in *Vagadu*, 799–801.

9. Pozzi, *Journal 1913–1934*, 157.

her marvelling at him: she will say of his verses that they are more than she ever hoped for from any living being. From the effect of this passion, he will retain the sensation of something immense, unlimited, immeasurable, like lightning falling on him from her lips.[10]

At that time, there is still no rivalry; the scent of his paper, his tobacco, and his body take on the same unique, possessed form. With him, she feels whole for eternity, naming him *ad infinitum*: "Lionardo mio—Friend—Name in the soul—O my only kingdom—Thought of my Thought—My everything in the world—The other face of my thought—Your presence, universe enough—This country of our thought—Found again, soul to soul—O eyes that I have sought unto their depths!"

The musicality of the words indicates the extent to which the act of loving was immediately linked to the act of writing: each wrote for him- or herself—diaries, notebooks, poems, essays—but also with a view to giving him- or herself to the other. On the lookout for assent, even praise, while never ceasing to connect love to thought. Sometimes he, Paul Valéry, even improvises and annotates in the margins of her own Diary, Catherine Pozzi, joining her here and there, looking for where they might be alike, confirming or contesting words and correcting the gap between points of view. She will also let him draw on the edges of her pages with pen, pencil, or watercolor, consequently letting him fill her being with his own—colors, shapes, images from within. "So many mornings, so many nights, in your notebooks, you've written to me. . . . Looking for me. And now I'm writing, looking for you, and it's dawn. Where is the point of thought that is health?" Later, but always too soon, the love will wither, the lover becoming, by dint of suffering, the soulless man or the madman. So, what happened? Perhaps, in her case, the arising of a shadow as dark as it is invisible, cast over the Ego and the world since a very early desolation, far back in time. In June 1916, André, her fiancé-brother-platonic friend, died. In June 1918, her father was murdered. The disappearance of the father and the beloved are merged over time into a single figure of loss. Since then, the present has allowed itself to be unraveled, right down to the roots of yesteryear, to the point where today she is prevented by it from playing, laughing, and crying—hence prevented from setting herself in motion to love. So much so that, every first day of the year, she writes in her Diary, as if in incantation, the same lines of loss and fidelity to the dead. Designation of pain, repetitive hammering even at the times when it's Paul Valery she loves. Identified with the lost—father and André—Catherine falls into a kind of internal constraint of fidelity, a psychic form of death occupying the living.

---

10. Valery cited in Pozzi, *Journal 1913–1934*, 721n45.

> My strength, André. . . . We will be intertwined because we must be, in a sun that is not yet and that we are helping to create through the infinite pain and the will of our love that does not know itself and yet finds. . . . My life, my spirit, I am the same thing as you for eternity. . . . My past life, my future spirit, I will be faithful to our meeting during eternity. . . . My life, my spirit, I am the same as you for eternity. . . . My past life, my future spirit, I will be faithful to our meeting for eternity. . . . Part of the present of my life, part of the spirit, I am still en route towards your eternity.[11]

A loss that becomes melancholized. A relentless commitment to digging the absent one's footprint. The death of the present desire is gone with the lost one. Is the victory won by unconscious matter, encrypted in "the realm of mnemonic traces of things"?[12]

Every other vibrant, fully fleshed love then becomes a source of reproach, complaint or, at the very least, dissatisfaction that nothing can soothe. Every disappointment, frustration, sensation of real or imagined prejudice against Paul Valéry—every ambivalent conflict linked, in addition, as much to her position as unacknowledged mistress as to her somatic fragility—will plunge her into destructive revolt or melancholy despondency. All the way to a fatal illness that will finally carry her away.

Milena Jesenská and Franz Kafka

Between her and him, a love, as always not devoid of narcissism, because in Milena Jesenská, Kafka will discover, for the first and only time in his life, someone who knows how to read his work, live it, translate it, and embrace it. As a translator—but not only a translator—she will indeed become Kafka's Czech voice. Her translations will serve as a means of expression for them, a kind of intermediary playground in which it was possible to play at approaching each other to get to know each other. He recognizes in her not only a gift of writing and style—"You are lightning: I never cease to be amazed at your speed: you make a ball of a handful of sentences, lightning strikes"[13]—but also a music of language inhabited by decision, passion, and, above all, "the intelligence of a seer." "Your translation is therefore faithful, and I feel as if I'm leading you by the hand, in my wake, through the underground passages of history, ugly, low, dark, almost endless corridors . . .

---

11. Pozzi, *Journal 1913–1934*, 163, 103, 273, 551, 656.
12. Freud, *Deuil et mélancolie*, 168.
13. Kafka, *Lettres à Milena*, 276.

to have, I hope, the wit to disappear when we emerge into the open."[14] A desire to come out into the open, of course, even if Kafka, terribly lucid, knows how to say to himself, "My life is hesitation in the face of birth"; and to Milena that he complains about "being born from the sunlight."[15] However, even if it's "impossible to live humanely in my family circle,"[16] and silence is the climate that suits him best, he will, several times, buckle down to the work of loving. Always with, between the lines, that originary fear of emotional contact with someone other than oneself. Kafka knows what leads him towards Milena, because he's sure of it: she's part of him; but the opposite is not true: he doesn't know the link that binds her to him, and in this respect, the link "belongs entirely to fear."[17] To horror, even. The kind that won't let go. He won't be able, besides, to hold the impact of her presence on him for long, even though it's not hostile. But the tension of not knowing what's being woven inside her, without him, out of range, and the uncertainty concerning the contents of her thought, plunge him into an incurable torment, the only way out of which would be to fall silent to remain true.

Falling silent and then hurrying—to escape the persecuting anguish—hurrying, therefore, to hide his face in Milena's lap, or to rivet his eyes to her eyes to take her face between his hands to run his fingers over her forehead, her ears and her temples and so on *ad infinitum* to make her his, to want to meet her to belong to her and to hear her laugh. Thus, mocking fear, letting it pass, they crisscross the hills behind Vienna and, following her, Kafka knows how to move briskly. Quite simply, he's doing well by her side. Thanks to this—but it doesn't last long enough—the fear no longer takes hold, even one-on-one. The vise loosens; Narcissus has thickened enough in his own flesh to stand up to fear, having gained consistency:

> A moment ago I took a good look at myself in the mirror and, even on close examination, I found myself to be a better face than I am to my own knowledge. It's a pure face, harmoniously modelled, almost beautiful in outline. . . . The look is by no means devastated, there's no trace of that, but it's not childlike either, it would, rather, be incredibly energetic, unless it was simply observant, since I was precisely in the process of observing myself and wanted to frighten myself.[18]

14. Kafka, *Lettres à Milena*, 30.
15. Kafka, *Journal*, 538; *Lettres à Milena*, 57.
16. Kafka, *Lettres à Milena*, 264.
17. Kafka, *Lettres à Milena*, 57.
18. Kafka, *Journal*, 238.

For at least a few moments, Kafka lets himself rest, enters into a tension-free capacity to experience himself as existing. At rest with his thoughts, in a quality of presence proper to one who lets himself be caught up in music, "without any disturbing observation of myself being able to intervene in this slow rush."[19] An impenetrable musical magic circle has formed, surrounding him like a second skin, the inner face of a psychic skin protecting him from the virulence of the persecutions secreted within his very being. In this way, thoughts about his thoughts grant themselves respite. The act of observation no longer takes itself as an object. Loving—in the sense of existing—becomes easier.

Except that the soul remains fragile, and the paradoxes of loving are unbearable for Franz—that alloy of the greatest peace and the greatest worry, of supreme freedom and at the same time supreme constraint. It's a tearing-apart that occupies him so much that he struggles to continue his work.

From then on, he will demand that their letters cease, a demand tantamount to a death sentence on their union. What's more, their letters were too *zigzagged*: once written, waiting feverishly to be read at last, finally being read, but too often out of sync and crossing each other's paths: all that randomness that drove him mad in the end.

> You no longer know what you've written, you no longer know what the other is answering, and, in any case, you're trembling. I understand your Czech very well, I hear your laughter too, but I roll around in your letters between the word and the laughter, so I only hear the word, and besides, my whole being is fear.[20]

Although each of them is caught up by the same facility for writing—and for writing with art, since they've seduced each other with it, brought together by the same infatuation for the word, the sentence, the story, and above all by the same ease with which they connect them to the affects that go with them—it won't be enough. By dint of being afraid and of not meeting each other body to body, words deprived of flesh have also become deprived of meaning and wither away. They hollow out and reveal the illusion that, by reading them, it would be easy to create presence. "Epistolary sorcery"? Vain "torture"?

The link is exhausted by being nothing but writing. Writing without a body and without a kiss dries up the soul. And this never ceases "to destroy me," he confesses.

That's why it's better to write a novel and resort to the sublimation processes it requires.

---

19. Kafka, *Journal*, 240.
20. Kafka, *Lettres à Milena*, 56.

Blanche Reverchon and Pierre Jean Jouve

Pierre Jean Jouve, interested in the beauty that can be made out of human pain and joy in order to make us love our dissonance, relies for this on Blanche Reverchon, his second wife, a Swiss psychoanalyst and translator of Freud. They will indeed work together on the translation of *Three Essays on the Theory of Sexuality* (1905). From Blanche, Jouve will accept the evidence of the unconscious matter that, at its very roots, makes one write. From her onwards, he will experiment with writing without a net, letting himself be drawn "into recounting straightaway the curiosities of a dream or a furtive life," even sketching out some interpretation—"Good gods, what a scandal!"[21]

Finding the power to write out of all that is unknown in oneself—scattered fragments—these are their common games.

Finally, at the very end of his poetic work, in "Trésor," Jouve bears witness to the easing that comes from love that has passed through the sieve of time and of the horizon of death—thus transformed as Jacob was after his night of struggle with the angel. A loving power turned towards her, Blanche, his real, living wife, not a mythical one like so many of his muses.

> I have a treasure that is you, and though constantly threatened by thieving Time: treasure. You are a treasure through the intervention you once dared to make to transform a hundred profound things in me and to lead me to myself. You are a treasure for your constant and faithful presence in all the whirlwinds, crises, and fleeting misfortunes. . . . You were a treasure for the bold and dangerous knowledge into which you plunged and nurtured me.[22]

Could it indeed be to Blanche that Jouve owes this writing of the death drive as of the life drive? Yes, through her he is initiated into the science of the Psyche, a *zone of images* in search of forms—it is from this material that he will henceforth draw for his writing. In this cauldron of boiling excitements, he works on *a poetics of the unconscious*. What he learns there is so considerable and so attractive, so revealing of things foretold, so heralding of a future, that he believes he is discovering a veritable *inner continent*. Dreams, daydreams, memories, imaginary constructs, bizarre acts, and incidental thoughts populate this continent, and Jouve, because he stays by Blanche's side, finds in it the impulses of an explorer.

21. Jouve, *En miroir*, 1076.
22. Jouve, "Trésor," 233.

So much so, in fact, that they construct from it a joint text published in 1933 in the *Nouvelle Revue Française*, seeking together to render visible and comprehensible the movement of an analysis based on the clinical material of a cure (that of Mademoiselle H . . .) that the psychoanalyst Blanche had entrusted to her lover. The Jouve couple—one a poet, the other a psychoanalyst—thus agreed to tell the story.[23]

He would later use this same material in an audacious, experimental way to turn it into something else: a novel. His main character, Catherine Crachat, is none other than an imaginative reworking of Mademoiselle H.'s treatment.[24] Jouve relies on the material provided by Blanche to create "the portrait of an analysis," by dint of hard work and creativity. Whereas the density of this unconscious matter should only have been accessible to those who had experienced it in analysis, Jouve, thanks to Blanche, accesses it on the same level. The result is a character of prodigious thickness, a curious *imago* formed in and by the in-between that makes up a couple.

Only a shared writing can permit such a challenge—a challenge akin to "capturing a very nasty conger eel from the depths of the sea."[25] Two people were not too many for throwing themselves into this operation. One in charge of bringing up from the depths the materials of the internal world; the other in charge of transforming their form so that they are bearable for consciousness—thus accessible to reading, in other words, to capture.

The last writings are still for Blanche and through her, in order to respond to her death—that death that always comes too soon. She who was his youth, his accomplice, his admirer, is no more, and her absence now gives free rein to anguish. "Treasure of strength and virtue, where is she?"[26] Fifty years of understanding each other, of building and reflecting, suddenly no longer form the basis—or not enough to continue enjoying life. But he will have to write a bit more—if only "to keep himself worthy of her." To the point of consenting to the dwindling of speech, as it were, to the point of "enduring what one is worthy of enduring: death without any phrase."[27]

Loving Intimacies

Could we conclude from such portraits of couples that there are good fights, in the sense of necessary ones? Doesn't the stumbling block of otherness

23. Jouve and Reverchon-Jouve, *Moments d'une psychanalyse*, 1555–91.
24. Jouve, *Hécate*; *Vagadu*; *Les aventures de Catherine Crachat*.
25. Jouve, *Vagadu*, 717.
26. Jouve, *Derniers écrits*, 1721–26, 1737.
27. Jouve, *Derniers écrits*, 1741.

give each of us the measure of our own strength? Strength to live, but also to write. There's nothing perverse or masochistic about it. A struggle, to be sure, but one that—if we are to believe Pierre Jean Jouve and Blanche Reverchon; Franz Kafka and Milena Jesenská; Catherine Pozzi and Paul Valery—could well have a transformative effect.

Provided that, beyond or through this body-to-body struggle, from the one to the other the expectation of being blessed can at least sometimes be said and heard—"I won't let you go until you've blessed me" (Gen 32:26)—in the sense of being, for as long as it takes, chosen as the beloved. Getting a word of blessing: hearing something good about yourself. Something like "I'm waiting for you to say something good about me, because without it I can't live or even write," or rather, to take up Jacob's struggle with the angel, "Without your blessing I couldn't consent to live while limping [*boitant*]."

The dislocated sciatic nerve has in fact obliged the man to lean on the other and vice versa: this dislocation [*déboitement*], admittedly uncomfortable, holds back the fall or even the drive to destroy.

> Not falling because I'm pressed against him, and not destroying because I'm not trying to annihilate him: such is the truth of wounded life, in the traumatic sense of the rupture—in this case, the sciatic nerve—by which I exist only by leaning on the other according to a resistance that allows me, if not to exist, at least to reveal myself through it. We are never two differentiated beings made to meet each other, but it is on the contrary by meeting that we differentiate ourselves.[28]

In this battle without a winner, at dawn, each one weighs on the other, allowing himself to be pushed around by him, in order to receive life from him, since we know with certainty that we owe each other everything. The Other, a divine creature or the man/woman to be loved, at last, accepts that he/she has not won, renouncing hatred for a moment, consenting to limping.

She, even more of a woman, weighs on him like a victor, yet with the opposite sensation of obeying him, in the sense of consenting to what he is. She finds in this a greater freedom of being, a kind of tranquility in being able to differentiate herself from him, while at the same time being blessed by him.

He, even more of a man, measures his power against hers, consents to it and takes pleasure in feeling like a man. Each offers the other a resistance—one force against another—thus giving existence and legitimacy to ambivalence as to differentiation. The enigma of this "I would have liked to destroy you, but I also love you. Who are you?"[29] is the heart of the in-between.

28. Falque, "Blessure originelle," 16.
29. Jouve, *Vagadu*, 801.

More than a struggle unto death, it is a struggle unto life. For, at the dawn of a whole night's struggle with the desired Other, everyone emerges blessed: saved from his or her own destructiveness. Something like: "You weigh with all your life on my life, but I consent to it because in this support our strengths are communicated and, even more, what is unknown in our strengths is revealed."

Including the strength to write.

Bibliography

Falque, Emmanuel. "Le baiser de Satan." Presented at Bernanos à l'œuvre, Institut Catholique Paris, Paris, France, Oct. 2023. https://www.youtube.com/watch?v=YGBnrW3nvBM.

———. "La blessure originelle ou le trauma de l'amour." *Imaginaire & Inconscient* 42 (2018) 11–19. Special issue, *Les traumas de l'amour*.

Faulkner, William. *As I Lay Dying*. New York: Random House, 2000.

Fos Falque, Sabine. "L'âme bric-à-brac: Un cabinet de curiosités." Presented at Bernanos à l'œuvre, Institut Catholique Paris, Paris, France, Oct. 2023. https://www.youtube.com/watch?v=jp4VIK7tfyw.

Freud, Sigmund. *Deuil et mélancolie*. Métapsychologie. Paris: Folio essais, 1968.

Gracq, Julien. *La presqu'île*. Paris: José Corti, 1970.

Jouve, Pierre Jean. *Les aventures de Catherine Crachat*. Œuvres II. Paris: Mercure de France, 1987.

———. *Derniers écrits*. Œuvres II. Paris: Mercure de France, 1987.

———. *Hécate*. Œuvres II. Paris: Mercure de France, 1987.

———. *En miroir journal sans date*. Œuvres II. Paris: Mercure de France, 1987.

———. "Trésor." *Proses*. Paris: Gallimard, 1995.

———. *Vagadu*. Œuvres II. Paris: Mercure de France, 1987.

Jouve, Pierre Jean, and Blanche Reverchon-Jouve. *Moments d'une psychanalyse*. Œuvres II. Paris: Mercure de France, 1987.

Kafka, Franz. *Journal*. Translated by Marthe Robert. Paris: Grasset, 1954.

———. *Lettres à Milena*. Paris: Imaginaire Gallimard, 1988.

Pozzi, Catherine. *Journal 1913–1934*. Paris: Phébus, 2005.

The Relief of Writing

Andrew Sackin-Poll

What distinguishes Emmanuel Falque from other religious thinkers and phenomenologists is a commitment to thinking *from below* and *a minima*. A basic axiom of his work is that thought takes shape and happens through the impassable finitude of immanent, embodied life on one side and encounter (or event) on the other. More recent work examines trauma, the resistance of presence, solitude, and the other's role in sense and possibility. As someone working in French literature, I have been interested in what Falque's more recent work might say about the *presence* of the author in the text in terms of the *resistance of presence* that he formulates in *Hors phénomène*. This is, then, partly a first attempt at outlining the relation between the writer, as a lived body, and the surface of the text, through writers like Georges Perec and Enrique Vila-Matas, and thinkers like Catherine Malabou and Emmanuel Falque, in an effort to think the *link* between solitudes that the latter outlines towards the end of that same work.

The Sheet, the Page, the Bed

In January 2019, I translated a paper by Emmanuel Falque called "The Resistance of Presence," for a talk he was due to present at the Divinity Faculty,

University of Cambridge.¹ One of the many pleasures of translation is inhabiting the thought of another. There are a number of memorable passages: the *plat à resistance*, the spread flesh of Freud's nudes, and the troubling and searing accounts of concentration camps.² Each has informed my own thought in different ways.³ But I want to focus on the image of Pascal's *ship of sense*, used towards the very end of the talk.⁴ As Falque describes, the image of this ship indicates, first, that "we are embarked," that is, already at sea, rolling upon the surface of the deep, and, second, that this shapes and is given shape through thought. I will add, in what follows, that this *ship of sense* can form a similar reciprocal relation through writing, telling, and narration. What resists sense does not lead to its collapse, only a mode of thought and writing that allows for this resistance to be made present. Whether through the expression of this in poetry and literary prose, as references to Rilke, Pessoa, and Proust in *Hors phénomène* suggest, or a loving vigil over others, as seen in *Éthique du corps-épandu*, Falque's thought maintains, not a mimetic relation of representation, but a form of *vigil* that permits the presence or patency of a resistance to shape sense.⁵

The image of the *ship of sense* implies a different model of storytelling, narration, and the relation that this holds with embodied life, one that places the rolling depths in touch with the surface of the text. This adds a dimension of bodied life to the textual surface. Writing, then, does not unfold in an absolute or transcendental space in a manner that might be regarded as detached from the material, sensuous data of life; rather, it is shaped by and shapes this data. The kind of relation that writing holds with bodied life that I wish to outline might be compared to Georges Perec's homologous formulation of the page and the bed that makes them interchangeable, even indistinguishable as a site for the body:

> The page is generally used in the sense of the greatest dimension. The same follows for the bed. The bed (or, if preferred, the

---

1. The talk took place on February 19, 2019, and was later published as "Resistance of Presence."

2. See Falque, *Hors phénomène*, 110, 113, 147–48.

3. Shortly after translating the talk, for example, I started thinking about the "ordinary body," which draws obliquely upon some of Falque's claims about resistance and the body. This was the subject of a short talk given at the Val d'Aulnay INPR Seminar in 2019, later published as Sackin-Poll, "Ordinary Contested."

4. See Falque, "Resistance of Presence," 141.

5. See Falque, *Éthique du corps-épandu*. For the literary references, see, for example, the numerous references to Fernando Pessoa, Marcel Proust, and Rainer Rilke in section 6 of *Hors phénomène*.

page) is a rectangular space, longer than wide, in which, or upon which, one usually lies down lengthways.⁶

How might one imagine a body spreading out across the page as though across a bed? The space of the page where one writes things down is homologous to the space of the bed where one lies down. This may be the narrator's bed in Proust's *Á la recherche du temps perdu*, where one reads: "for a long time I would go to bed early. Sometimes, the candle barely out, my eyes closed so quickly that I did not have time to tell myself: 'I'm falling asleep.' And half an hour later the thought that it was time to look for sleep would awaken me; I would make as if to put away the book which I imagined was still in my hands, and to blow out the light."⁷ Here, as the passage continues, the narrator, as a child, dreams through time and space, merging his own identity with the subject-matter of his bedtime reading, becoming a church, a quartet, the historical rivalry between European monarchs. Towards the end, in *Le temps retrouvé*, the narrator, now as an adult, hovers between waking and the downward pressure towards the grave. Even if the narrated child and narrating adult are no longer the same person, they occupy this same liminal state; the page and the bed, wakefulness and slumber.⁸ Staying with Perec, the same overlapping of homologous spaces appears in his *Un homme qui dort*, which contains passages describing a life alone, spread out in bed, where the hum and buzz of existence assumes an almost suffocating aspect.⁹ But it may also be the therapist's couch, where the patient spreads out across the couch, inscribing the symbolic and imaginary in the space of the therapist's room.¹⁰ Each offers a site for ruses, tricks, masks, and guises, overlaying a bodied life, less as its representation, more as its displacement and patency. They offer a site for the individual to set themselves down, as Perec makes clear in a punning draft note for *Espèces d'espaces*:

> After the page, *le pageot, le pieu*. I know no less a fortuitous pun; it is easily translated in English (sheet [*drap*]—leaf of paper [*feuille de papier*]) and comfortably gives rise to a series of metaphors, the most well-known of which furnish the reader

---

6. Perec, *Espèces d'espaces*, 564. Unless otherwise indicated, translations in this essay are entirely my own.

7. Proust, *Swann's Way*, 1.

8. For a discussion of living and dying in Proust, see Bowie, *Proust Among the Stars*, 267–318.

9. Perec, *Homme qui dort*, 224.

10. For a discussion of the relation between the therapist's couch and Perec's writing, see Magné, "Textus ex machina." I am thinking, here, too, of Emmanuel Falque's and Sabine Fos Falque's works in *Éthique du corps épandu*.

with an indispensable key to understanding "Time Lost": "for a long time, I went to bed (on paper [on sheets]) early."[11]

Here, I can rest, dream, remember. The metaphor of the bed-page is not, however, intended to unify the two into a novel rhetorical trope, but rather displace the *genesis* of writing from an absolute space to a *tiling* or *overlaying* around the resistance of a bodied life. It forms a moment of resistance within the text, like an opaque monad: "The bed is, therefore, the individual space *par excellence*, the elementary space of the body (the bed-monad [*le lit-monade*])."[12]

The superposing of the page and the bed provides a model of writing for the image of the ship rolling on the surface of the deep: the space of the page, the space of the bed, where I have often spread out, rested, and dreamt for a while, as Perec writes: "The bed: place for ill-formed menaces, space for contraries, space of the solitary body, encumbered by ephemeral harems, a foreclosed space of desire, an improbable place for taking root, a space for Œdipal dreams and nostalgia."[13] The theme of being *encumbered* by the rolling depths of *ephemeral* desires and impulses, spread out in this bed echo Falque's recent thought. Through the collapse of the bed-page via a paronomasia, writing is no longer an *absolute space* devoid of contact with the body or a representational space, granting sense and *saving* it, but extensive with the body lying in bed, brimming with dreams and desires. The page is like a new skin, wrapping around a resistant material, like bed clothes.

"I follow, riding the waves, pushed by the winds . . ."

The paronomasia between the sheet, bed, and page provides the metaphoric space to think the relation between the rolling depths of bodied life and the ship of sense. This touches on the relation between the author and text. Here, Falque's topic of *following* the body (from *je suis*, as *I am*, to *je suis*, as *I follow*), which can be imagined like riding the waves or being pushed by the winds, becomes relevant. When one is unwell, suffering, or cannot sleep,

> I can no longer say "I am my body" in the sense of identifying [myself] with this being [*l'être*] as one might repeat out of a desire to incarnate consciousness, but rather "Je *suis*"—that is, *suivre*, "to follow"—"I follow my body" in the paradoxical sense

---

11. Perec, *Espèces d'espaces*, 1053n2.
12. Perec, *Espèces d'espaces*, 564.
13. Perec, *Espèces d'espaces*, 565.

where the body is "ahead of me" or "precedes me"—from the verb *suivre* "to follow."[14]

I would add that moments of joy and laughter carry one along, too. There are times when I have laughed, even though it might not have been my intention (or even appropriate) to do so. Along the rolling contours and ridges of this space, the writer follows. This indicates a restlessness, a disquiet.

Even in an experience of *rooting* and *encumberment*, when lying in bed, there is movement: I follow. But the energy of this movement is no longer intentional. In *The Wedding Feast of the Lamb*, Falque describes how the *il y a*—that is, the resistant presence of the body—marks the absence of self, a point where the self is invaded by a mass of sensations, an event, an impersonal field of forces, that is neither given nor absurd, but the absence of meaning (*sens*).[15] This *invasion* is designated as a *limited phenomenon*—that is, a phenomenon that cannot formulate itself—and arises from this limit being exceeded by Chaos.[16] This touches upon a non- or a-signifying aspect of embodied life that concerns not only the human but the world more broadly. Life becomes, as Falque says, *bodied*, with the past participle form indicating how this precedes intentional life and *em*bodiment, that is, the granting of shape and form.[17] There is, then, something *creative* in the relation between this and the world; it marks what urges, flows, and pushes the body, as well as what drags it along. The health of the organism shapes thought, since "our well-being (or our ill-being) is rooted in life at the level of our most basic corporeality."[18] "I am tired," "I am excited," "I am content," "I am fuzzy," express physiological states, marking the health (or not) of the speaking and writing subject. "Chaos . . . goes deep down into our emotions as well as into our drives . . . [it] ensures that our embodiment, or our drives, reach into what we live without ever being able to signify what it is that we live."[19] This is the force that precedes signification, thought, and structure; it can only be *lived* in and through a bodied relation. Later, of course, the *limited phenomenon* will be complicated by addition of the *extra-phenomenon*. While the former concerns an informulable and excessive phenomenon that invades the self, urging and pushing it forward, the latter has already taken place, having torn this same self apart. This can only be *lived* via the

---

14. Falque, *Hors phénomène*, 132.
15. Falque, *Wedding Feast*, 21.
16. Falque, *Wedding Feast*, 22.
17. Falque, *Wedding Feast*, 25–26.
18. Falque, *Wedding Feast*, 26.
19. Falque, *Wedding Feast*, 26.

other, who opens an alternative world (see below), rather than urge and push oneself.

The question for Falque and for me: how might one compose a *world* in Chaos or reform one from trauma, vicariously via the other? Who is the agent of this? Underpinning this is an ethical *demand* to live (or *let live*) the animal or *non-human* that exceeds and shapes the limit of the otherwise human organization of the body and phenomenal experience. Contrary to the structures of intentional consciousness (Husserl), existential analysis (Heidegger), and even the ethical resolution of solitude through the Other (Levinas), Falque insists on the human being shaped by as much as shaping the rolling depths.[20] Towards the end of his discussion of Chaos, Falque quotes this passage from an interview with Gilles Deleuze:

> The problem is not that of being this or that within man, but rather of a becoming inhuman, of becoming the universal animal: not to see oneself as a beast, but to deconstruct the human organization of the body, to cross this or that zone of intensity of the body, each one discovering which zones are his or her own, and the groups, the populations, the species that inhabit them.[21]

The resolution and organization of the human, affectivity, and expression is subordinated to bodied life, which contains species, groups, populations, an entire community of souls. This makes the outward shape and form of a life contingent upon the rolling depths, the shifts in intensity, and the community within one, that I can sometimes only follow. The monstrous, the brutish, the animal, and angelic drive me along; *je suis*, I follow.

"Starting at the end . . ."

This puts bodied life in touch with contingency and accident. Rather than the form, whether intentional or existential, shape lived material, it is shaped by this same material, too. This introduces a very different sense of counter-intention to the *saturated* phenomena of the flesh (Henry), the Other (Levinas), and the Icon (Marion). The movement does not come from *outside* but within, where what might otherwise be called *excess* dims to a minimal resistant presence. Borrowing from Catherine Malabou, one might say that Falque's description of Chaos and the extra-phenomenal touches upon the *becoming-accident* of form, where the form and figure of a life is shaped by accident, rather than the other way. This idea of *becoming-accident* could be

---

20. See Falque, *Wedding Feast*, 24–30.
21. Deleuze, "Lettre," 23, cited in Falque, *Wedding Feast*, 27.

related to Janicaud's suspicion of the search for a *morphological ideal* in the material and texture of experience in predominantly Husserlian and post-Husserlian phenomenology.[22] Instead of seeking, first, the ideal structure of experience, phenomenological inquiry should attend to and let experience *come forth*, as the later works of Heidegger suggest, and thereby give shape to such inquiry. This is part of what distinguishes Falque's approach to phenomenology: the very limit of phenomenology becomes the starting point, rather than the terminus for a minimalist approach to immanent experience. It must be noted, however, that Falque's *minimalist* approach differs from Janicaud's own formulation.[23] While Janicaud's minimalist phenomenology may suspend the pretensions to systematicity or *first philosophy* in an effort to move beyond the Husserlian approach, it nevertheless remains bound to the question of *making seen* or *making visible*. By contrast, Falque's minimalist phenomenology or phenomenology *a minima* concerns itself with that which never comes to light, whether in terms of the *limited* phenomena or more radically in terms of the extra-phenomenology, which *resists* reduction, punching a hole (*trou*) in appearing and the very material for phenomenological inquiry. The ill-formed, *limited* phenomena and resistant extra-phenomena constitute the material for his phenomenological inquiry, raising anew questions about sense, materiality, and embodiment, as well as the relation these sustain with the real.

Within the context of literature, resolution or representation is not sought in writing; rather, the resistant aspect gives shape to writing, the surface of the page is molded to the rolling depths of bodied life; for example, Perec, who was an orphan of the Holocaust, uses various devices, tricks, and ruses as metonyms for loss and exile, like the missing letter *e* in the novel *La Disparition* (1969) and the weaving together of autobiography and a story of a fictional island in *W ou le souvenir d'enfance* (1975). This touches on the other, more destructive side to Chaos. As Malabou describes in the opening of her *Ontology of the Accident*, the Greek goddess of cunning, ruses, and wisdom, Metis, could assume numerous guises, from animals, like lions and birds, to elements, like fire and water.[24] The series of forms, shapes, and guises is not endless, however, but rather comprises a finite series. When the goddess reaches the end, the cycle begins again. There are other polymorphic gods, like Thetis and Proteus, each of whom is capable of slipping from one's grasp by changing form. In each instance of transvestitism, a set range of possible forms can be recorded. But this forms part of

---

22. Janicaud, *Phenomenology "Wide Open,"* 69.
23. See Janicaud, *Phenomenology "Wide Open,"* 64–81.
24. Malabou, *Ontology of the Accident*, 7.

the very nature of each deity. If their nature were to change substantially, then such transformations would no longer be ruses and tricks, but *betray an existential underground* that, through such transformation, renders the subject unrecognizable.[25] This is the other side to Falque's Chaos: when the possible runs out and the world collapses, there is an existential metamorphosis. Such moments are traumatic, sealing a life, at least initially, within the confines of its event. "The formation of a new individual is precisely this explosion of form that frees up a way out and allows the resurgence of an alterity that the pursuer cannot assimilate."[26] Beneath the guises and ruses, there stands, in one iteration of this extra-phenomenon, an inassimilable part: trauma. Returning to Perec, experience of exile and loss do not mark, for him, the terminal point of literature, but the starting point, the inassimilable and solitary part, around which might be constructed literary spaces, masks, sheets, and pages.

This describes, in a mythic and literary mode, the moment when bodied life sets sail, unmoored from prior, possible forms, leading to a *modal collapse* that deprives the subject of the possible. Alongside the habits, forms, and outwards signs of life born from intention, sense, and meaning that mark a gamut of possible forms, stands a "destructive" constituent born of accident. It is around such an *accident* that the superposed spaces are arranged. One starts at the end, so to speak. The surface, whether page or bed, that forms the *new skin* for the irresolvable depths of this life does not so much indicate or refer to a thing or object than roll along, transforming and metamorphosing in a reciprocal movement of shaping and shaped, without resolution, only vigil and witness.

This indicates a new, *inverse* form of irony. Instead of irony forming a negative moment through ruse or trickery, ironic distance offers a means for staging a presence under the sheet or page. The negative is replaced by the patency of a resistant event, like a trauma or loss, the positive *presence* of which gives shape and relief to the page, the sheet, the bed. This echoes a moment in Malabou's *La Plasticité au soir de l'écriture*, where she illustrates the relation between different forms and the *unity* of a life underneath through the analogue of transformation masks. The *transformation mask* does not disclose or represent the face underneath, as a painting might relate mimetically to a model; on the contrary, it only opens and closes upon other masks. The masks are not only a figuration of the face but also an articulation of a relation between the plastic, that is the material, bodied life, and the graphic, that is, the written. "Both modes of representation

---

25. Malabou, *Ontology of the Accident*, 9.
26. Malabou, *Ontology of the Accident*, 12.

symbolize the division between the actor and their role, the individual and their social persona."[27] But the outer appearance does not equate to a false appearance or *persona* that might otherwise betray the *true* inner self; rather, each shapes the other: the plastic materiality of bodied life and its outer sign. Each element is inextricably linked to the other. If the masks transform, then this results from the fact that plastic modes of expression always transform graphic (or written) modes of expression (and vice versa). "Thus, the mask reveals the *interchangeability* or the *relation of conversion between the plastic* and the *graphic, image* and *sign, body* and *inscription*."[28] The masks, forms, and surfaces metamorphose into one another, revealing surface under surface, along the waves that carry the ship of sense.

The tricks, ruses, and displacements spread out upon the page and the divan are not only tricks of language that betray a life; rather, they form part of this plastic movement and interchangeability described above. What the paronomasia between the page-sheet and the bed-sheet marks is thus the interchangeability between image and sign, body and inscription that Malabou's description of masks and plasticity indicate. This has consequence for thinking about the relation between the writer and the text. If the author is understood to follow, riding the waves, pushed by the winds, then they are more than a function of the text, but integral to the creative relation between bodied life and the surface of the text.

"A fated accident . . ."

The mask within the mask, surface upon surface, reiterates the *tiling* and *overlaying* of the bed and the page in the superposed spaces of literature indicated in the opening section of this essay. What the foregoing section indicates is how these surfaces relate to Falque's conception of Chaos and bodied life. This concerns, then, at once the relation between bodied life, the presence of the author (or at least the presence of bodied life), as well as the possible in literature. The relation between each element can be seen in an essay by the Spanish author, Enrique Vila-Matas, called "Mastroianni-sur-Mer." This essay was written as the author completed his novel *El viaje vertical*, published in 1999. The title, the vertical or rectilinear journey, contrasts with the archetypal epic return home, like Odysseus's voyage back to Penelope in Homer's *Odyssey*. While the latter, circular journey leads the hero homeward, the former, vertical journey traces a straight-line, with no destination, like a tangent of the circular one. The *hero* of this journey,

---

27. Malabou, *Plasticité au soir*, 15–16.
28. Malabou, *Plasticité au soir*, 16.

Frederico Mayol, is a septuagenarian, who finds himself having to begin again after the unexpected collapse of his marriage. As Vila-Matas writes, "The novel is the story of an initiation to culture, that is, a classic novel of apprenticeship, were the protagonist not at a stage in life when, generally speaking, nobody learns anything anymore."[29] This work could, then, arguably count as a peculiar *Bildungsroman*, with the apprenticeship taking place towards the end of a life, rather than at the beginning; it is a *coming-of-age* at a *certain age*, so to speak.

This marks another experience of the impossible: melancholy. Such an experience may not be precipitated by a specific event or trauma but result, perhaps, from a steady accumulation, a slow suffocation. However this may arise, melancholy is another iteration of *modal collapse*, when the world is reduced to a single, fixed horizon, with seemingly no way out. There are many aspects of this essay that could be discussed in relation to melancholy, irony, and the question of how a writer is present in a text. Whilst writing *El viaje vertical*, Vila-Matas recounts how he listened to Ennio Morricone's musical score for the film *Sostiene Pereira* in the background, writing that his music "describes magnificently the slow rhythm of the movement of an awakening consciousness."[30] This slow rhythmic awakening occurs at a dreadful moment when life seems exhausted, when the possible has run out, and, at the end of a life, the threat that it may have been wasted. To illustrate such petrifying moments, Vila-Matas draws on the example of the artist Rothko, who, he writes, at the end of his career, questions whether he has wasted his life: "During his last days, desolation gripped Rothko, as he obsessively asked himself whether the greater part of his work had not, in fact, become absolutely meaningless, being carried away by the temptations of a demonic art market."[31]

At the end of the road, the artist despairs. This echoes Falque's cry "the possible, the possible, otherwise I will suffocate!" in relation to the Robinsonade.[32] When one is stuffed into a corner and utterly at sea, it is the other that can, not so much *save us*, as open up an alternative world. This relies on an encounter that can take many forms: flowers by a bedside, whilst unwell, point toward the outside, a kiss, a little gesture opening a new world, a newspaper article or a song, indicating, by chance, an unexpected possibility. Each is, in a way, *epiphanic*, disclosing a solitude—I alone must follow, whether lying in bed, cracked open as a kiss topples over into love

---

29. Vila-Matas, "Mastroianni-sur-Mer," 99.
30. Vila-Matas, "Mastroianni-sur-Mer," 99–100.
31. Vila-Matas, "Mastroianni-sur-Mer," 108.
32. See Falque, *Hors phénomène*, 367–92.

or weighed down by melancholy—*and* another world—the other who is there with me, opening another world, propping me up. Through the other, a new form is granted and, in some instances, assumed. The example used by Vila-Matas is the existential metamorphosis of the character Pereira in Antonio Tabucchi's novel *Sostiene Pereira*.[33] Set during the collapse of the fascist regime in Portugal, Pereira's refusal of fascism, abuse, and authoritarianism not only amounts to a change in political view, but also his relation to life, ethically, aesthetically, and psychologically: "The whole life of Pereira changes. He realizes that it is never too late to change, [never too late] for this community of souls that inhabit us to enter one suddenly."[34] Entrance into this "confederation of souls" arrives after an existential conversion, a change in the *existential underground* of the protagonist. The self is *invaded* by something that exceeds and transforms it. What is interesting, here, concerns how the writer affects the reader, as Vila-Matas continues: "[Tabucchi] leads us to this distinct voice that always ends at the extreme point of incommunicability."[35] A metamorphosis takes place, one that runs all the way down, and discloses this *extreme point of incommunicability* that touches on solitude, modal collapse, and plasticity.

Before looking more closely at how the writer affects the reader, let us ask where is this *extreme point*? What makes up this *voice*? One thing is certain: it is indeterminate, superposing at once bodied life, solitude, and sign (upon the page). It is something like the *secret* of solitude, that is, bodied life, the pulse and rhythm of which marks the surface, like the transformation masks discussed above. Something of this secret may be indicated in the discussion that immediately follows this contrast between exhaustion and transformation, with the topics of music and encounter coming together neatly in another, amongst many, examples of *(re)birth* or reopening of the possible in Vila-Matas's essay:

> I was reading *La Jeune Parque*—a poem by Valéry that is considered to be one of the most difficult in the French language—and, in a footnote, I learnt that it is not, however, necessary to understand the entire poem, because the exquisite musical monotony (in the style of Debussy) articulates a trance state. Valéry considered the poem to be an accurate portrayal of an emotional awakening of a young woman, or rather a goddess; in any case, [it portrays] the awakening of a consciousness. "The theme of the work," Valéry says, "is the awakening

---

33. Tabucchi, *Sostiene Pereira*.
34. Vila-Matas, "Mastroianni-sur-Mer," 109.
35. Vila-Matas, "Mastroianni-sur-Mer," 109.

of self-consciousness." I remember reading something similar by Wallace Stevens, who writes: "poetry is the subject of the poem." And then I said to myself that the same could be said of some narratives and even lectures.[36]

References to the poetry of Valéry and, indeed, Stevens concern the nascency of thought. But the reference to Valéry is especially apt, drawing together rhythm, the materiality of thought, and encounter. The *monotonous music* refers to the rhyming scheme of the poem, the rhythmic beat of the poetic voice, indicating what precedes or evades comprehension, evoking an awakening from the aphasia of materiality to the luminosity of thought. This rhyming pattern, as a series of sounds, marking the beat of the poetic voice, poses the incommunicable depths and its untranslatable *meaning* to the movement of intentionality or other constitutive bases for sense.[37]

How might this relate to Falque's recent work? In his poetic evocation of this poem, Alain makes this clear when he writes that the poem is the inverse of thought: the innumerable caresses of the world, gestures made, steps half taken, and a host of inner movements, form the material basis for thought. Quoting at length, Alain writes,

> Tides of blood and lymphatic fluids, this flame enveloped, no less carried along to the movement of the wind than the flame of a torch; these powerful slumbers, short sleeps, these changes in gait, these relaxations, these outbursts, these envelopments around the self [*soi*], these tissues that float and unfold their fringes, like seaweed in saltwater, this entire little world, alarmed and reassured, this is what carries our thoughts.[38]

What carries thought is the pulse of the blood, the lymphatic fluid, the rhythm of one's gait, the folds within folds of the body, and the faint delirium of this little world or monad. This is the *pulse* of the body that marks part of the rhythm of Falque's Chaos—that is, the lived, bodied aspect of a life that *I* only follow. As Alain continues,

> Thus, when we close our eyes, and, at the point of sleeping, these stirrings of life are translated upon the dark ground [*fond*] by puffs, smoke, brilliant points, auroras, twilights; whence I sometimes think about faces, fields, forests, and cities.[39]

---

36. Vila-Matas, "Mastroianni-sur-Mer," 109.
37. See Rabaté, "Wet the Ropes!"
38. Alain, "Qu'est-ce que la *Jeune Parque*?," 31.
39. Alain, "Qu'est-ce que la *Jeune Parque*?," 31.

Here, once again, one finds oneself spread out across a bed or a page, drifting into sleep. As Jacques Derrida notes in his essay on the same poem, there is a need to write the voice, the chaos, the depths, and that this bodily aspect informs thought.[40] The rhythm, rhyme, and homophony of the poem, much like the puns in this essay (the sheet, page, and bed), signal this other aspect of thought. Likewise, Falque recognizes that one cannot sink into the depths, lost in the inchoate, but must always wager on sense.[41]

This poetic awakening across the surface and relief of the material pulse of the body neither advocates a corporeal solipsism, where the subject is enclosed in the flesh, like Henry's auto-affection, nor a purely textual space of writing, where the writer may be a function of the text. Here, I return to the *becoming-accident* of form, where the depths of bodied life shape the surface of the text, offering its relief and contours. The accidents of life shape a text; the serendipitous encounters that can transform a thought, open upon possibility, something that is true of this essay. In "The Prince and *la Jeune Parque*," for example, Valéry describes how, after twenty years, he returned to writing poetry, having grown weary of his scientific and philosophical inquiries.[42] But the habits of abstract thought were difficult to shake: "When I set myself once more to poetry . . . I was not slow to recognize many problems and enigmas of an abstract nature in the first flowers of my renewed season."[43] The *demand* to give speech to the *murmurings of an inner voice*, to transform *pure fragments* into a work, requires the *whole intellect*, making this tentative return difficult and tiring.[44] Frustrated, he walks about the city. After a while, he enters a café and, by chance, an article catches his eye about a singer. Reading the account of how the singer, Rachel, prepared for her roles and conveyed so well an affective as much as musical quality to her performances, Valéry, too, recognized the need for the voiced, which brings with it the bodily, to the surface of the page.

Even at the end of the road, there is a way out. This can be seen, again, in Vila-Matas's essay, which, at the end of a novel recounting a rectilinear journey in old age, retraces the steps of a writerly life in his own recovery of lost time:

> I look back on my life and the only thing that occurs to me to note is the perfidious nature of time, making us think that it never passes, yet, when we look back, it has passed too quickly,

40. Derrida, "Sources de Valéry."
41. See Falque, "Resistance of Presence," 141.
42. Valéry, "Prince and *la Jeune Parque*," 133–39.
43. Valéry, "Prince and *la Jeune Parque*," 134.
44. Valéry, "Prince and *la Jeune Parque*," 134.

though not sufficiently fast for me to be unaware that, being already one, there has been another, through all this time, always in me, let's calls him Mastroianni.[45]

Not dissimilar to Valéry's encounter and subsequent imbrication of the voiced and the written, the pulse of the body and poetic surface, Vila-Matas resumes something like an author's presence from the linking of superposed citations—the actor Mastroianni, the poets and writers Lorca, Pessoa, Stevens, Tabucchi, and Valéry, to name only a few—and the narrative running through the essay, drawing together the biography of the author and writing, as an immanent co-emergence between memory and text. This takes place, on one side, through film and fiction, with certain characters and scenes marking events in the writer's life, forming *a community of souls*, and, on the other, memory and biography, including scenes from the writer's life. The restlessness and disquiet of bodied life is felt through the oblique layering and superposing around a writer withdrawn, making the essay itself articulate a spiralling *Bildung*, as opposed to the circular journey of Odysseus and the line of Frederico Mayol. Pressed up against a deadline for a conference, and running out of road, the writer turns around themselves, revealing at once his own solitude and the others within him, as Vila-Matas writes, quoting a song by Pessoa: "an astonishing lucidity / in which one being, another is."[46]

The Relief of Writing

This poetic sojourn and chance, or maybe *fated*, encounter repeats itself in the work of Falque, who recounts similar *caresses* from the world in the genesis of his thought in anecdotes of *epiphanic* moments of thought, whether cracks in the pavement or standing on the beach, which punctuate an itinerary of thought that is continually moving, transforming, and metamorphosing in response to the rolling depths and encounters. Whether situating himself in the *impassable immanence* of human finitude (*Metamorphosis of Finitude*), the *chaos* of the deeps (*Wedding Feast*), or rolling in the *suffocating* mud crying out for the possible (*Hors phénomène*), Falque seeks to *humanize* and *incarnate* religious thought.[47] Implicit in this is the recognition that *incarnation* and *incorporation* is at once a demand and a

---

45. Vila-Matas, "Mastroianni-sur-Mer," 110.
46. Vila-Matas, "Mastroianni-sur-Mer," 109.
47. See Falque, *Metamorphosis of Finitude*, 15–20; *Wedding Feast*, 11–30; *Hors phénomène*, 367–92.

process, rather than something given once-and-for-all.[48] The metamorphosis of finitude becomes the rolling depths before, most recently, leading the *cogito* to stumble across its own solitude and the solitude of the other person (*autrui*) in a patient dialectical exhaustion of phenomenology, as it presses against the limit. This is a mode of thought that does not seek to resolve the inchoate depths into constitutional intentional nodes or essences, via eidetic analysis or save via the irruption of the Other; rather, the shape of bodied life forms the contours for thought, the relief of writing.

This may give the impression that this is a materialist, almost passive mode of thinking, subject to winds and waves of Pascal's sea. But this dialectical exhaustion, passing through various guises and masks, like Metis, leads to its inversion; the *untranslatable signifier*—the paronomasias—and the impersonal depths mark the starting point, rather than the limit of a thought. Trauma punches a whole (*trou*) in the possible masks of a life. This is not a constitutive event, in the usual sense, that is, once-and-for-all, but rather something known by encounter and repetition. A continual movement between the *downward pressure* and weight of bodied life—that is, the encumbered body in bed, the weight of exile and loss—and the lightness of the numerous surfaces that mirror, however obliquely, these depths mark a continual encounter with oneself via repetition, like a falling forward or upward along an undulating surface. This can take place in relation to oneself, as a discovery of solitude, or vicariously through others, as witness and vigil. Underpinning thought is the rhythmic pulse of bodied life, the awakening of *la jeune parque*. The demand is a pulse, which can be creative or destructive, as Malabou shows in her thought of plasticity. This is arguably the movement of *Hors phénomène*, leading not to the inchoate and suffocating depths of materiality, but to the *node of solitude* that forms the principle of an extra-phenomenal link to the impersonal aspect of solitude, which is neither *interchangeable* nor *communicable*. The depths form the *impersonal* that binds the *cogito* to the node of solitude that is encountered as an unknown: "The 'impersonal' aspect of solitude does not mean that I am interchangeable; wholly to the contrary: it only means that I discover myself [*moi-même*]."[49] Put another way, Falque encounters himself, as each does, less as an *a priori* foundational principle for the order of thought, like the transcendental *ego* (Husserl) or auto-affective flesh (Henry), more as a bodied life, with drives, impulses, dreams, desires, and memories, that is, a

---

48. For a brief discussion of incarnation as process and the relation between this and something like Falque's description of bodied life, see Keller, *Face of the Deep*, 218–21.

49. Falque, *Hors phénomène*, 422.

je that is dragged and pulled along as much as leading. This is articulated neatly in the refrain, *je suis*, I follow.

Yet this aspect, namely this impersonal and resistant dimension to oneself, which I would say has been implicit throughout, is *given* in relief, that is, the surface. The body and the sign do more than simply bring something into view. They form, as Malabou writes, "*le relief du langage.*"[50] Here, the layering of the mask, the bed, and the page return. Drawing upon and altering Falque's formulation of the *link*, the mask, bed, page, form a series of mutually supporting surfaces, including the reader, the other person. "The solitude of the other [*l'autre*] serves, in some sense, as 'a structure by return [*structure de renvoi*]' for my own solitude, not because I know it, but precisely the contrary, because I do not know it."[51] What resists along the relief of the page discloses a solitude that returns upon oneself, thus forming a link. The image Falque uses is drawn from mountaineering, capturing neatly the mutual risk involved as well as its fragility. "I am not 'without' the other [*l'autre*] in my solitude for so long as the other [*autrui*] 'keeps watch [*veille*]' over my own solitude—without, however, penetrating or violating it."[52] I wish to suggest, somewhat tentatively for now, that this *vigil* can take place in literary and poetic encounters, alongside face-to-face ones, where the resistant aspect is made patent. Each is held by the other, exposed to the community of souls that may enter one, as evoked by Tabucchi and Deleuze.

The presence of this resistance can be *detected* along the ridges, contours, and folds that form a relief, either within oneself, as one's *own* impersonal solitude, or the other person. To have that impersonal aspect of solitude made patent in relief, so to speak, opens up another world, another form or shape that is less than constituted, more than chaos, placing one in link with, in community with other ones-alone in solitude; indeed, it places one in touch with a whole constellation. Returning to Vila-Matas, who writes, *à propos* of Tabucchi, again,

> Dispersing his characters across universal horizons, concentrating them into a closed dimension, like small worlds in themselves, held in memory and distance. Consequently, the subtle thread of irony marks them and, very often, their painful tenderness; [they are] latent unities pulsing in their own and in the solitude of infinity.[53]

---

50. Malabou, *Plasticité au soir*, 104. I intend to develop further this notion of writing as relief.
51. Falque, *Hors phénomène*, 447.
52. Falque, *Hors phénomène*, 448.
53. Vila-Matas, "Mastroianni-sur-Mer," 117.

The expression of solitude is found through the enclosure of characters in "little worlds in themselves." Here, Perec's bed-monad [*lit-monade*]—that is, the body spread across a bed, written along a page, like a little world closed upon itself yet *extended* along a series of reliefs—forms part of a constellation of *links* amongst solitudes: Perec, of course, but also writers spread out in their beds, too, like Proust, and their readers. What is *incommunicable*, here, might be, in part, the *untranslatable signifiers* of sound and the poetic voice, forming the music and rhythm discussed earlier. This *latent unity* pulsing in the *solitude of the infinite* referring at once, I imagine, to the distance of these small worlds, these little *lit-monades*, and the chaotic plenum of this pulsating bodied life.

In contrast to Janicaud's minimalism, which charts the movement from invisibility to visibility, Falque's own minimalist approach charts the contours and reliefs of what never comes to light. This is attended, watched over by the other, in its opacity and resistance. Such a vigil forms parts its *form* or *shape*. With regard to literary texts, the page acts as a sheet, a thin pane, that *mirrors* this resistant aspect in a manner that is contiguous with yet irreducible to it. It shapes, gives form, without being *heuristic*—without searching for the *morphogical ideal* that both Janicaud and Falque criticize.[54]

The foregoing, I hope, gestures towards how Falque's *minimalist* approach to phenomenological inquiry, beginning *from below* within the ambit of bodied life, including its monstrous depths and impossible fissures, can be used to think the contours and relief of a life, cracks and all, in a way that reconfigures the relation between writing, the page, and the possible *vigil* held between a writer and reader. The puns—page, leaf, relief, *lit*, *relit*—signal the sonority of thought and the rhythmic beat of the depths. But this, as Falque says, is not to deny rationality, only set this in an encounter with the chaotic depths and the creative, pulsing rhythm of bodied life. More than this, however, the patency of these depths constitutes a *relief* of writing that marks the painful tenderness of its *positive* irony. Wrapped in the sheet, lying, spread out, across the page-bed; if you touch the sheet, run your fingers across its surface, there, along the contours can be felt the relief of writing. Underneath, if one taps gently, one might hear, in the hollow, the resonance of a solitude, like two, each in their cell, tapping against the wall, indicating that, one, the other, are not alone. Each might offer a counterbalance and support for the other in a fragile, minimal contact.

---

54. See Janicaud, *Phenomenology "Wide Open,"* 68–70.

Bibliography

Alain. "Qu'est-ce que la *Jeune Parque*?" In *Propos de littérature*, 31–32. Paris: Hartman, 1947.
Bowie, Malcolm. *Proust Among the Stars*. New York: Columbia University Press, 1998.
Deleuze, Gilles. "Lettre à un critique sévère." In *Pourparlers*, 11–23. Paris: Éditions de Minuit, 1990.
Derrida, Jacques. "Les Sources de Valéry: Qual, Quelle." *MLN* 87 (1972) 563–99.
Falque, Emmanuel. *Éthique du corps épandu*. Paris: Cerf, 2018.
———. *Hors phénomène*. Paris: Éditions Hermann, 2021.
———. *The Metamorphosis of Finitude: An Essay on Birth and Resurrection*. Translated by George Hughes. New York: Fordham University Press, 2012.
———. "The Resistance of Presence." Translated by Andrew Sackin-Poll. *Continental Philosophy Review* 56 (2023) 113–43.
———. *The Wedding Feast of the Lamb: Eros, the Body, and the Eucharist*. Translated by George Hughes. New York: Fordham University Press, 2016.
Janicaud, Dominique. *Phenomenology "Wide Open" After the French Debate*. Translated by Charles N. Cabral. New York: Fordham University Press, 2005.
Keller, Catherine. *Face of the Deep: A Theology of Becoming*. London: Routledge, 2003.
Magné, Bernard. "Textus ex machina (de la constraine considérée comme machine à écrire dans quelques textes de Georges Perec)." *L'Esprit Créateur* 26 (1986) 66–70.
Malabou, Catherine. *Ontology of the Accident: An Essay on Destructive Plasticity*. Translated by Carolyn Shread. Cambridge: Polity, 2012.
———. *La Plasticité au soir de l'écriture*. Paris: Éditions Léo Scheer, 2005.
Nancy, Jean-Luc. "The Young Carp." In *Expectation: Philosophy, Literature*, 203–29. Translated by Robert Bononno. New York: Fordham University Press, 2017.
Perec, Georges. *Espèces d'espaces*. Vol. 1 of *Œuvres complètes*. Edited by Chistelle Reggiani et al. Paris: Édition Gallimard, 2017.
Proust, Marcel. *Swann's Way*. Translated by C. K. Scott Moncrieff and Terrence Kilmartin. Revised by D. J. Enright. London: Vintage, 2005.
Rabaté, Jean-Michel. "'Wet the Ropes!': Poetics of Sense, from Paul Valéry to Jean-Luc Nancy." In Jean-Luc Nancy, *Expectation: Philosophy, Literature*, ix–xx. Translated by Robert Bononno. New York: Fordham University Press, 2017.
Sackin-Poll, Andrew. "The Ordinary Contested: Laruelle Contra Deleuze and Guattari." *Paragraph* 44.2 (2021) 238–56.
Tabucchi, Antonio. *Sostiene Pereira*. Torino: Loescher, 1995.
Valéry, Paul. "The Prince and *la Jeune Parque*." In *The Art of Poetry*, 133–39. Translated by Denise Folliot. Princeton: Princeton University Press, 1985.
Vila-Matas, Enrique. "Mastroianni-sur-Mer." In *Una vida absolutamente maravillosa*, 99–117. Barcelona: Penguin, 2012.

Philosophy and Theology

Introspection and Personal Transformation

Matthew W. Knotts

Introduction

*C*ROSSING THE RUBICON (2016) has provoked significant debate regarding Emmanuel Falque's novel understanding of the relationship between philosophy and theology.[1] According to King, Falque's understanding of the relationship between philosophy and theology applies at two distinct levels: that of the disciplines themselves on the one hand, and that of the individual thinker practicing either or both of these disciplines on the other.[2] Furthermore, King believes that the latter application offers greater opportunities for further development in future scholarship.

This contribution will focus on the latter distinction, namely, how Falque envisions the interaction between philosophy and theology as occurring especially within the individual, the final goal of which is personal transformation, which is also related to the concept of metamorphosis. Falque's analysis departs from the unique sociocultural context of France, shaped by its complex history of the relationship between church and state, and in turn

---

1. Originally published in French as *Passer le Rubicon* (2013).
2. See King, "On the Conversion of Philosophy."

the resulting politics of academic institutions.[3] It is well known that French society and academia are highly secular, which is a legacy of the French Revolution. However, Christianity is a prevalent area of study, even if for polemical purposes.[4] Falque also remarks on a curious aspect of the French education system. It—like other European countries—requires a robust philosophy curriculum for all students, while excluding theology, despite the fact of the integral relation of these disciplines in past centuries.[5] Furthermore, though Falque appreciates the necessity of allowing a philosophical and theological perspective to be heard in the secular academy, his attention is just as focused on the *ad intra* reconsideration of study and praxis within an ecclesial context.[6] However, as Koci notes,[7] the crucial issue for Falque is not the abstract relationship between disciplines,[8] nor even the political or social implications of this interaction, but the drama which unfolds as an internal struggle within oneself.

In this contribution, I discuss how Falque understands the integration of philosophy and theology within oneself. In other words, the same individual person is or can be both philosopher and theologian, while maintaining the legitimate distinction of these two disciplines. For example, Falque describes Thomas Aquinas in the following terms: "Aquinas is not a philosopher or a theologian but philosopher *and* theologian."[9] He continues that Aquinas "[maintains] *in the unity of the same being*, both philosophy and theology."[10] Whether and to what extent this is tenable is of course a question central to the critical engagement with Falque's thought.[11]

Furthermore, as Koci notes, Falque's project is partly autobiographical due to the fact that he studied both philosophy and theology and was formed in the Ignatian tradition of introspection and growth through spiritual exercises. In light of this observation, I also seek to demonstrate how the transformational aspect of Falque's philosophy admits of an inherently

3. Falque, "Philosophie et théologie."
4. Falque, "Philosophie et théologie," 201.
5. Falque, "Philosophie et théologie," 201–2.
6. Falque, *By Way of Obstacles*, 14.
7. Koci, "Phenomenology and Theology."
8. See Falque, "Philosophie et théologie"; *Crossing the Rubicon*.
9. Falque, *Crossing the Rubicon*, 148.
10. Falque, *Crossing the Rubicon*, 148.

11. See also Falque, *Crossing the Rubicon*, 150: "Only in uniting philosophy and theology can we see that we are consciously crossing the ford at the same time from philosopher to theologian and reciprocally from theologian to philosopher. The whole movement is held and maintained in the unity of the same being and according to a mutually fecund investigation."

Ignatian character, with particular reference to the *Spiritual Exercises* and Ignatian reflection.

Emmanuel Falque's Reconsideration of the Borders of Philosophy and Theology

Emmanuel Falque's ambitious and daring attempt to reimagine the relationship between philosophy and theology is expressed in his 2006 article "Philosophie et théologie: Nouvelles frontières," in which he calls for a new way of understanding the relationship between two disciplines often separated, if not opposed to one another.[12] Falque's revolutionary approach to the relationship between philosophy and theology in a postmodern context undoubtedly faces significant headwinds.[13]

To be sure, the secular situation of Western/North Atlantic nations exacerbates the difficulty of locating common ground between philosophy and theology. Falque acknowledges the complex history of France (socially, culturally, politically) and its implications for the practice of theology, especially in relation to philosophy.[14] Interestingly, Simon Goldhill has recently indicated the difficulties caused by the political situation of contemporary academia, in which theology is separated from—if not subjugated to—other disciplines.[15] The specialization of contemporary research also contributes to isolation within individual fields. Falque even regrets the fragmentation and separation of various subdisciplines within theology and philosophy, e.g., the divorce of systematic theology from the study of the Bible.[16]

Historically, philosophy and theology have been close siblings. According to Falque, "Ignatius of Loyola and Hadot have taught us that at least at their origins, and perhaps also ever since, theology and philosophy were and have always been 'spiritual exercises.'"[17] This genealogical affinity grounds the possibility of constructive and mutually supportive interaction between these two disciplines. Falque, following Étienne Gilson's perceptive note on Aquinas's method, envisions a mutually transformative relationship between

---

12. "Cet essai voudrait plutôt, et seulement, établir une sorte de programme—ou mieux, une *nouvelle manière* d'envisager *ouvertement* des champs faussement disjoints dans le cadre de l'institution laïque, comme aussi parfois ecclésiale" (Falque, "Philosophie et théologie," 203).

13. See Falque, "Philosophie et théologie," 203.

14. Falque, "Philosophie et théologie," 207.

15. Goldhill, *Christian Invention*.

16. Falque, *Crossing the Rubicon*, 24.

17. Falque, *Crossing the Rubicon*, 24.

philosophy and theology.[18] Crucial to Falque's position is surpassing the theological reduction of philosophy to a mere *instrumentum* or *ancilla*.[19]

Falque acknowledges the well-known theological turn in French philosophy, originating with Emmanuel Levinas's *Totality and Infinity* (1961). However, a concern may arise according to which philosophy, once the *mere servant* of theology, has reversed the previous relationship. Certainly, Falque rejects the appropriateness of interpreting philosophy as a mere servant, whether historically or conceptually. Moreover, he wishes—in a way appropriate to his emphasis on the importance of integration and transformation—to demonstrate how theology can and has critiqued philosophy, in particular phenomenology.[20] "The time has thus come," Falque writes, "to question phenomenology on the basis of theology and not always and again to develop theology phenomenologically."[21] One specific example of the way in which theology has challenged philosophy—or in Falque's terms, issued a *counterblow*—is through the critique of phenomenology according to which it has neglected the full significance of human corporeality.[22] "The questioning of phenomenology itself, and its very capacity to attend to non-sense or the organic body, arises from the counterblow of theology on phenomenology—not the opposite."[23] Remarkably, the theological critique of philosophy originates not simply in Christian thought but in its earliest sources, addressing one of the central questions of theology itself, Christology and the incarnation.[24]

Furthermore, Falque passionately argues for the common ground between philosophy and theology, namely, that they examine the same reality under different aspects.[25] Prior to *By Way of Obstacles*, Falque states, he had suggested that human finitude is the common point of departure for both philosophy and theology, a position he develops in *Crossing the Rubicon*.[26] King argues that "Falque does claim a conversion of philosophy by theology, but it is a conversion of the *meaning* of its central object: humanity."[27] Philosophy and theology inexorably and spontaneously lead to crossing paths

18. Falque, "Philosophie et théologie," 203.
19. Falque, "Philosophie et théologie," 203.
20. Falque, *Crossing the Rubicon*, 149.
21. Falque, *Crossing the Rubicon*, 150.
22. Falque, *Crossing the Rubicon*, 149.
23. Falque, *Crossing the Rubicon*, 148.
24. Falque, *Crossing the Rubicon*, 149–50.
25. See Falque, "Philosophie et théologie," 207.
26. Falque, *By Way of Obstacles*, 38–39.
27. King, "On the Conversion," 75.

with each other.[28] They differ not in terms of the object of inquiry but in their respective methods and points of departure.[29]

Falque points to the importance of René Descartes as a philosopher who in his third *Meditation* acknowledged the fundamental importance of the paradoxical presence of the infinite within the finite subject.[30] He juxtaposes Descartes's *proto-phenomenological* (my gloss) insight with the observation that theology begins from the assumption of humans' primordial orientation to God.[31] What philosophy understands as finitude theology glosses as creation and situates it in relation to God as *creator omnium*.[32] Nonetheless, philosophy's description of finitude does not suffer in any way for omitting *creation* from its analysis.[33] In fact, it would not be appropriate for philosophy to view finitude in terms of *creation*.[34] Rather, Falque advocates for philosophy and theology to develop complementary perspectives on the same human experience of finitude.[35]

In light of this inherent common ground, Falque calls for philosophy and theology to consider the same objects in their own respective ways. In advocating this, Falque acknowledges the possibility of difficulty and disagreement between these disciplines.[36] Ultimately, Falque calls for a rearticulation of the philosophically-expounded experience of finitude in the categories of theology.[37] "It is only by proceeding from and speaking to the mundane aspects of human experience that theology can affirm the meaningfulness of that experience and finally transform the meaning of human finitude."[38]

The precise sense of finitude for Falque is both informed by and distinct from contemporary philosophy. On the one hand, his thought is consistent with other Continental philosophers, for whom finitude is the essential starting point for the entire human condition.[39] Indeed, this concept is crucial for Falque: "Everything in reality depends on the philosophical interpretation

---

28. Koci, "Phenomenology and Theology Revisited," 907.
29. Koci, "Phenomenology and Theology Revisited," 907.
30. See Falque, "Philosophie et théologie," 205.
31. See Falque, "Philosophie et théologie," 205.
32. King, "On the Conversion," 77.
33. King, "On the Conversion," 77.
34. King, "On the Conversion," 82.
35. See Falque, "Philosophie et théologie," 208.
36. See Falque, "Philosophie et théologie," 210.
37. King, "On the Conversion," 75.
38. King, "On the Conversion," 78.
39. Falque, *By Way of Obstacles*, 34, 38–39.

of finitude itself."[40] Despite his unique philosophy, Falque acknowledges his debt to Heidegger in terms of construing finitude primarily in terms of how one interprets the implications of one's inevitable death. As he explains, "The question of finitude is less the question of Descartes, Kant, or Hegel than it is the interpretation that Martin Heidegger would give it, privileging the *world's closure* within the horizon of death over its opening onto some infinite that does not belong to it."[41] In my estimation, Falque's central focus for finitude is less about the metaphysical or epistemological aspects of the concept but its existential, phenomenological, and anthropological importance. To be sure, this does not thereby exclude or marginalize the epistemic, for Falque wishes to maintain that it is within finitude that one finds a common, shared humanity, thus grounding the possibility of a fruitful interaction between philosophy and theology.[42] Furthermore, finitude is at the heart of Falque's appropriation of the Christian mysteries for his philosophy. Through the incarnation, God unites himself with and dwells within human finitude,[43] whereby God in Christ embraces and lives finitude to its fullest extent.[44] The possibility of the transformation of finitude entails a heuristic rather than a didactic method[45]—more on which anon.

Personal Transformation

The precise way in which philosophy and theology are mutually transformative is in terms of the understanding of the human person.[46] However, Falque's proposal for transformation applies not only at the general level of the disciplines but also at the particular level of the individual.[47] Indeed, for him, the latter is primary. According to Falque, the relationship, even tension between philosophy and theology is first and foremost a matter of one's internal struggle which is prior to its realization in any kind of institutional

---

40. Falque, *By Way of Obstacles*, 36.
41. Falque, *By Way of Obstacles*, 36.
42. Falque, *By Way of Obstacles*, 34, 38–39.
43. Falque, *By Way of Obstacles*, 29–30.
44. Falque, *By Way of Obstacles*, 37.
45. King, "On the Conversion," 78.
46. King, "On the Conversion," 76.
47. King, "On the Conversion," 75.

structure.[48] The self—in the sense of the entire person—is the locus of the transformation of the relationship between philosophy and theology.[49]

As Martin Koci demonstrates, Falque thinks that both philosophers and theologians—in virtue of their shared object of inquiry—should venture into each other's territory.[50] Upon one's return, one's encounter with one's intellectual counterpart will result in personal transformation.[51] Whereas philosophy proceeds *heuristically* (that is, in my estimation, defeasibly), theology has often taken the *didactic* approach (the latter I gloss as *dogmatic*, but not in a pejorative sense).[52] Philosophers can develop new insights by creatively considering religious beliefs without thereby endorsing them or compromising the integrity of philosophy.[53] By venturing into one another's domain, philosophers and theologians gain a new perspective.[54]

One concern which one may raise with respect of Falque's thought is that such an interaction or encounter—indeed, transformation—jeopardizes the integrity of the disciplines. Of course, Falque argues vehemently against this interpretation.[55] In my estimation, his repeated use of the metaphor of travel is also illustrative. The philosopher who ventures abroad ever remains a philosopher, but sees things in a new way.[56] I believe that this can be likened unto the common experience of expatriates, which Falque himself wishes to evoke. One leaves one's home country, whether for study, employment, or even travel. Certainly, one's place and family of origin will always remain fundamental to one's identity. However, the encounter with that which is foreign irrevocably changes one. To give a trite example, one's palate may have to adjust to a new cuisine. But when one returns, this change is noticeable. For instance, the palate which once encountered familiar foods in one way will no longer encounter them in the same way. For philosophers, one encounters oneself in a new way, realizing differences,

---

48. "La *facultas* dit d'abord une capacité de la personne, et non la publicité d'une institution. Si donc il y a une 'unité' ou un 'conflit' des facultés (Kant), celui-ci se gérera d'abord en soi et pour soi-même au regard du mystère chrétien, plutôt que stratégiquement, et publiquement, dans le cadre des seules ambitions humaines" (Falque, "Philosophie et théologie," 205).

49. See Falque, "Philosophie et théologie," 209.

50. Koci, "Phenomenology and Theology Revisited," 905, 907.

51. Koci, "Phenomenology and Theology Revisited," 905.

52. See Falque, "Philosophie et théologie," 208.

53. King, "On the Conversion," 76.

54. King, "On the Conversion," 79; Falque, "Philosophie et théologie," 210.

55. See, e.g., Falque, *Crossing the Rubicon*, 147–52.

56. Falque, *Crossing the Rubicon*, 121.

borders, and changes *ex post facto*.[57] Thus one can speak of a certain loss, indeed a certain tragic loss of innocence, yet inevitably connected with the gain of one's greater insight, more nuanced perspective, and personal improvement and development.

Indeed, the mutually transformative encounter between philosophy and theology—indeed, between philosopher and theologian—is not only consistent with the general thesis of this contribution but also a major form of *transformation* in Falque's thought. The philosopher challenges the theologian to adopt a heuristic method and to ground theology in an orientation to the human condition, while the theologian challenges the philosopher to be open to that which lies beyond and summons it. As Falque explains,

> As the philosopher and the theologian cross the Rubicon, they will have no choice in passing each other but to let themselves be transformed—each one by the other. The first will teach the second about the human journey. The second will make the first see that he cannot refuse to open himself . . . to the transcendence of the One who comes to "metamorphose" everything, to the extent to which he has first assumed it in its entirety.[58]

Elsewhere, Falque calls upon theologians to embrace philosophy's heuristic methodology as a manner for inquiring into the experience and the implications of human finitude.[59] It seems that Falque also believes that the philosophical account of human finitude can challenge and deepen the theologian's understanding of the created nature of the human being.[60] "The challenge that Falque raises," writes King, "is for the practitioner, whether philosopher or theologian, to practice *both* philosophy and theology *in the same discourse*, directed at the same object."[61]

In *By Way of Obstacles*, Falque revisits themes he addressed in *The Metamorphosis of Finitude*.[62] The human condition—finitude—becomes the meeting point and the possibility of dynamic relationship between philosophy and theology.[63] One must recognize that finitude, far from being a deficiency or defined negatively against the infinite, is a starting point which is good in itself.[64] Falque stresses the importance of divine kenosis in

---

57. Falque, *Crossing the Rubicon*, 148–49.
58. Falque, *Crossing the Rubicon*, 151.
59. King, "On the Conversion," 76.
60. See King, "On the Conversion," 77.
61. King, "On the Conversion," 80 (italics mine).
62. Falque, *By Way of Obstacles*, 35–38.
63. Falque, *By Way of Obstacles*, 38–39.
64. Falque, *By Way of Obstacles*, 34–35.

the theological response to the question of finitude.⁶⁵ Christ's significance consists in his transformation of the human condition (in particular the reality of death) by uniting it with himself and then raising it to a new level through the resurrection. Thus, one can speak of a true metamorphosis or transformation. Furthermore, the action of the divine is primary. The human, called and addressed by God, is invited into transformative resurrection, without any prior expectation or promise of this. The transformation of finitude is the response to God's initiative in Christ.⁶⁶

The Significance of Christ for Falque's Philosophy

Christ's incarnation, and in virtue of this his subsequent transformation of humanity, grounds the possibility of the transformation of the philosopher through theology.⁶⁷ To expound upon this insight, I quote King at length:

> Starting with the human as such, theology can agree with philosophical accounts of the experiences of finitude, before seeing in what respect theology or revelation can transform the experience of finitude. For Falque, this is made possible fundamentally through the Incarnation—in God becoming human and therefore taking up the full weight of humanity in himself. This means that whatever is fully human is not foreign to God. Whatever philosophy says truly about humanity is borne in the person of Christ.⁶⁸

It is therefore possible to say that one first encounters God within one's fellow human being.⁶⁹ In virtue of the incarnation, one goes through the human to God, encounters God in and through humanity.⁷⁰ The Christian response to contemporary philosophy's fixation on self-creation is to stress that transformation is not primarily an act performed on one's own. The transformation of the human person comes through God in Christ.⁷¹ The-

---

65. Falque, *By Way of Obstacles*, 39.
66. Falque, *By Way of Obstacles*, 37, 39.
67. See Falque, "Philosophie et théologie," 210. For Falque, "L'homme-Dieu est donc légitimement, en régime chrétien, à la croisée des disciplines, philosophe en tant que 'Fils de l'homme' et théologien en tant que 'Fils de Dieu'" (Falque, "Philosophie et théologie," 206).
68. King, "On the Conversion," 77.
69. See Falque, "Philosophie et théologie," 206.
70. King, "On the Conversion," 77.
71. Falque, *By Way of Obstacles*, 38.

ology, enabled and supported by divine kenosis, leads philosophy beyond itself to new possibilities.[72]

Falque turns to the story of Jesus's appearance to two disciples on the road to Emmaus to elaborate his philosophical position. These disciples implicitly recognized the risen Christ prior to his miraculous disappearance at the breaking of the bread when they conversed with him on the way. As they later recounted, their hearts were ablaze as they walked and spoke with Jesus. According to Falque, through the disciples' encounter with the risen Christ, their discouragement and grief are brought into articulation in a theological idiom.[73]

Falque's constructive reimagining of the relationship between philosophy and theology resonates with the arguments of Goulven Madec, according to whom the medieval distinction between faith and reason differs from the patristic dispensation. Madec claims that the scholastic position does not reflect the understanding of early church fathers, such as Augustine, whose theory of knowledge is grounded in the twofold nature of Christ.[74] Falque's emphasis on the significance of Christology for both philosophy and theology is thus both historically faithful to the patristic tradition and also represents a promising opportunity for the reconfiguration of the relationship between the two disciplines.[75]

Falque himself suggests at least two reasons for the importance of engaging faithfully with the fathers of the church. First, and more generally, the weight of tradition requires the philosopher to be open to interaction with, if not transformation by, theology.[76] Second, and more specifically, several church fathers—not least of all due to their polemical responses to the Gnostics of their respective context(s)—stress the importance of Christ's robust physicality and corporeality, a crucial element of Falque's philosophy and its meeting point with theology.[77]

In describing his specific approach to the relationship between philosophy and theology, Falque invokes *spiritual exercises*, both in the sense of antique philosophy and the *Spiritual Exercises* of Ignatius of Loyola.[78] He

---

72. Falque, *By Way of Obstacles*, 39.

73. See Falque, "Philosophie et théologie," 206.

74. Madec, *Chez Augustin*, 13–15. "La rationalité, c'est *le Christ Verbe* qui la donne" (Madec, *Chez Augustin*, 14).

75. Knotts, "You Show Me Yours," 83–84.

76. Falque, *Crossing the Rubicon*, 148.

77. Falque, *Crossing the Rubicon*, 150.

78. Falque, *By Way of Obstacles*, 151–52, 187n21.

describes these as closely interrelated, and in what follows, I shall address the latter and illustrate the resonances of Ignatius in Falque's philosophy.

Falque's Philosophy: An Ignatian Perspective

The challenge Falque issues in *Crossing the Rubicon* is for philosophy to engage the whole person, "both intellectual reflection and lived experience."[79] These two distinct if complementary forms of inquiry are both integrated in the *Spiritual Exercises* of Ignatius of Loyola.[80] Falque clearly acknowledges the essentially Ignatian nature of his philosophy and methodology.[81] He maintains the importance of avoiding the division of thought and experience[82] which is essential to the Ignatian focus on the education of the whole person.[83] Crucial to both Falque's philosophy and Ignatian spirituality is the firm attachment to lived experience. As Falque writes, "The Spanish is always anchored in the *pathos* of our own humanity, which my work does not cease to also seek."[84]

The Spiritual Exercises

The *Spiritual Exercises* originate from a notebook that Ignatius began to keep during his retreat at Manresa, in which he recorded his experiences of meditating upon Scripture.[85] He gradually added to these thoughts throughout his life.[86] Ignatius retained this notebook when he began his studies in Paris (1528). They were eventually published as the *Spiritual Exercises* in 1548 and became the basis for a retreat.[87] Ignatius believed that his own experiences could help others to navigate their deepest yearnings, whereby they could find their path to God.[88] He advocated recording one's

---

79. Koci, "Phenomenology and Theology Revisited," 905.
80. Ignatian Spirituality, "What Are the Spiritual Exercises?"
81. Falque, *By Way of Obstacles*, 1, 7.
82. Falque, *By Way of Obstacles*, 1.
83. GSB, "Jesuit Education."
84. Falque, *By Way of Obstacles*, 8.
85. Hansen, "Spiritual Exercises."
86. Ignatian Spirituality, "What Are the Spiritual Exercises?"
87. Hansen, "Spiritual Exercises"; Ignatian Spirituality, "What Are the Spiritual Exercises?"
88. Hansen, "Spiritual Exercises."

thoughts daily and comparing them over the course of time.[89] Ignatius's method was influenced by his spiritual advisor, a Benedictine, who in turn was influenced by Thomas à Kempis's *Imitation of Christ* and Ludolph of Saxony's *Vita Christi*.[90]

The twofold purpose of the *Exercises* consists in overcoming one's selfishness and ordering one's life such that one can make truly free decisions, that is, free from any improper attachment to material things.[91] The *First Principle and Foundation* outlines how one must detach oneself from various worldly preferences and situate one's life in light of what will lead to one's true end, eternal life with God.[92] To achieve this goal, the *Spiritual Exercises* begins with scrutinizing oneself. Ignatius argues that if one follows Christ, one will flourish.[93]

The *Spiritual Exercises* is divided into four *weeks*. These are not considered actual seven-day periods, but rather phases of a journey with Christ to spiritual liberation and faithful commitment to God.[94] In Week 1, the retreatant reflects on how one has failed to respond to God's love. In Week 2, one reflects on Christ's life and ministry and resolves to amend one's life to follow and serve Christ. During the third week, one considers Christ's passion and death, and in so doing learns to see his sacrificial death and the Eucharist as ultimate expressions of his divine love. Finally, one meditates on Christ's resurrection and subsequent appearances prior to his ascension. The fruit of this portion of the retreat is a firm resolution to perform loving actions in service of Christ in the world.[95]

Three major forms of prayer structure the *Spiritual Exercises*, namely, meditation, contemplation, and discernment of spirits. The first of these is primarily intellectual, concerning the study of Scripture and Christ's life. Secondly, one moves to the affective level, praying rather than merely studying the Scriptures. Ignatius's imaginative methodology is informed by Ludolph of Saxony and Francis of Assisi. Finally, one moves to the discernment of spirits, whereby one focuses on how God is operative within one's inner life, including the emotions, the imagination, and one's deepest

---

89. Carroll, "Luther, Loyola," 170.
90. Hansen, "Spiritual Exercises."
91. Ignatian Spirituality, "What Are the Spiritual Exercises?"
92. Jesuit Resource, "First Principle."
93. Hansen, "Spiritual Exercises."
94. Ignatian Spirituality, "What Are the Spiritual Exercises?"
95. Ignatian Spirituality, "What Are the Spiritual Exercises?"

desires.[96] The last of these forms of prayer is especially pertinent to Falque's philosophy and method.

Transformation Through the Exercises

Personal transformation according to Falque always occurs in tandem with God.[97] In my estimation, one could say that for Falque, this is due to the fact that transformation is always an act that occurs as a result of God's activity, and is thus true transformation.[98] Ignatius shows how this is possible through his own exploration of the inner life. As Ignatius indicates in his *First Principle*, God is the natural end of the human being, created in his image. As Carroll writes, for Ignatius, the "human person [is] an autonomous substance that is naturally oriented towards the good."[99] Insofar as Falque wishes to establish the inseparable connection of theology and philosophical anthropology, his work is also fundamentally Ignatian: "In developing a vocabulary to describe the presence of God within us, [Ignatius] would inscribe God-talk on the fabric of human nature."[100]

The natural orientation to God affirmed by Ignatian theological anthropology, damaged by sin, admits of the possibility of restoration and redirection, namely, by ordering the movements of one's inner life and with the help of grace.[101] One must learn to see the world as creation, that is, in light of God as the ultimate reality and true goal of all things. Within the context of this perspective, one can order one's desires to the good. The *First Principle* can help one to realize this.[102] Ignatius's reflections provide insight into the often divided and conflicted self. In this respect, Ignatius speaks of the bad spirit in contrast to the voice of God. The former causes a state in the soul known as desolation, whereas the latter is the source of consolation.[103]

One's deepest desire is for God, and one can experience God within oneself.[104] Indeed, this is a fundamental and distinctive feature of Ignatian spirituality, namely the belief that God works in and through one's innermost desires. Hence attention to oneself leads one to hear God's call

---

96. Ignatian Spirituality, "What Are the Spiritual Exercises?"
97. Falque, *Crossing the Rubicon*, 24.
98. Falque, *By Way of Obstacles*, 37–38.
99. Carroll, "Luther, Loyola," 170.
100. Carroll, "Luther, Loyola," 174.
101. Carroll, "Luther, Loyola," 170, 172.
102. Carroll, "Luther, Loyola," 170.
103. Carroll, "Luther, Loyola," 173.
104. Carroll, "Luther, Loyola," 170.

and follow his will.[105] The Holy Spirit gently guides one within the soul.[106] Similar to Ignatius, Falque's thought rests upon the idea that God works in and through one's heart, including the imagination, emotions, and desires.[107] As Falque writes, "God himself, including in prayer or meditation, comes to transform and not to overcome images or the sensory, to inhabit and convert the senses rather than to abandon them."[108] For Ignatius, "our passivity is the means through which the activity of God takes place through our actions,"[109] yet this activity is always in cooperation with human freedom.[110] Human activity is called to participate in God's initial gift. Grace descends from God and returns to God through human nature, as Ignatius's *Suscipe* prayer expresses.[111]

The performance of the *Exercises* assumes the immanence of God and the capacity for discerning and learning from this presence. Falque boldly calls for philosophers to consider how one can perceive God in the contemporary world.[112] Elsewhere I have contended that it is in fact possible to do this, that is, to reconceive of the world as *creation*, to perceive the constituents of the world and the totality of being itself as so many *signa* and *uestigia* of God's presence. This kind of vision is not immediately available to the rational agent; rather, one must achieve it through a rigorous and continuous effort of study and purification reforming the entire person. Advancing in wisdom is a process that does not simply encompass the entire human being, but also assumes its inherent integrity. Personal transformation is necessary for advancing in certain forms of knowledge.[113]

Furthermore, I believe that the renascent appreciation of finitude in postmodern philosophy can provide resources for the articulation of theological positions, while also challenging them. Though traditional philosophical and theological sources clearly advocate the importance of inner conversion for the sake of attaining truth, such an approach can also be located in more recent philosophical sources, such as the work of Hans-Georg Gadamer.[114] For Falque too, what one perceives is partially premised on the

105. Carroll, "Luther, Loyola," 172.
106. Carroll, "Luther, Loyola," 170.
107. See Carroll, "Luther, Loyola," 174.
108. Falque, *By Way of Obstacles*, 8.
109. Carroll, "Luther, Loyola," 175.
110. Carroll, "Luther, Loyola," 174.
111. Carroll, "Luther, Loyola," 172.
112. Koci, "Phenomenology and Theology Revisited," 905.
113. Knotts, *On Creation*.
114. Knotts, *On Creation*. See King, "On the Conversion," 83.

internal state of the rational agent. For example, Falque suggests that the merely *utilitarian* perspective on an artwork will inevitably fail to divulge its aesthetic value.[115] From an Ignatian perspective, the modern critique of speaking of transcendence as present within the soul, especially in terms of God's action, is due to the gradual erosion of the conception of how one can conceptualize a non-competitive interaction of grace with human nature and similarly for how to articulate the activity of the transcendent within one's heart.[116]

Ignatian Reflection

Finally, I would like to suggest that Falque's summons to philosophers and theologians to examine a common problem from the other's perspective is congenial to the categories and the practice of Ignatian reflection. The purpose of reflection within an Ignatian perspective is to lead to and increase understanding.[117] Far from a merely subjective or emotional response to the content of one's study, reflection ultimately leads the learner to embrace the applicability and significance of the material for one's life.[118] It seems therefore that a transformative element is essential to Ignatian reflection, which in turn is fundamental for Ignatian pedagogy. Ignatian reflection involves, first, the analysis of information and, second, the discernment of the relationships among multifarious facts and the development of an enhanced perspective.[119] As one continuously returns to a particular point of consideration, one deepens one's insight into it. This is essential to Ignatian reflection. "Understanding," write Go and Atienza, "unlike simple knowing, entails seeing the meaning and value of what we are learning, relating them to other ideas, and spelling out their implications."[120]

Go and Atienza distinguish between three kinds of reflection: Conceptual, Metacognitive, and Personal.[121] They concisely explain these in the following manner: "While Conceptual Reflection aims at deepening the understanding of content and Metacognitive Reflection aims for a greater appreciation of learning and disciplinary thinking, Personal Reflection is

---

115. Falque, "Philosophie et théologie," 206.
116. Carroll, "Luther, Loyola," 175.
117. Go and Atienza, *Learning by Refraction*, 36.
118. Go and Atienza, *Learning by Refraction*, 86.
119. Go and Atienza, *Learning by Refraction*, 36.
120. Go and Atienza, *Learning by Refraction*, 38.
121. Go and Atienza, *Learning by Refraction*, 38–42.

focused on the implications of what has been learned in one's life."[122] Reflection ultimately builds to the final of these, which results in a change in the life of the learner.[123]

Go and Atienza also stress the importance of continuing reflection.[124] The consistent practice of reflection—especially under the guidance of an experienced teacher—will lead students to continuous insights about a particular subject, which can be formulated in terms applicable to the individual. Furthermore, the nature of reflection, though deliberately structured, allows for the possibility of novelty and surprise. The prudent pedagogue will anticipate some responses but remain open to unexpected insights as fruits of reflection.[125]

Genuine reflection occurs within a locus of instability and uncertainty.[126] Falque places an emphasis on how the nature of true experience and growth arises from placing oneself at risk. Indeed, it is possible that one's own inquiry does not result from one's initial, deliberate choice but rather from being drawn into reflection.[127] One becomes oneself and is transformed in virtue of an encounter with others.[128] For Falque, the *contre* of *ren-contre* is significant, due to the fact that authentic interactions with others assume an element of transformation.[129] The confrontation ("clash") with the other is an essential part of being human, yet this is not to be confused with violence.[130]

The emphasis on the importance of interpersonal interaction—as well as its involvement with confrontation—for one's identity has also been acknowledged in other areas of French philosophy. In his *La rencontre: Une Philosophie*, Charles Pépin explores the idea that one truly becomes oneself through one's encounters with others. Recent research from fields such as neurology and psychology has demonstrated that personal identity is constructed in and through a complex, interactive process. The realities of the recent pandemic have only reinforced the importance of social interaction for human development and flourishing. Returning to Falque, in his philosophy the other challenges one to change, and one must embrace this

122. Go and Atienza, *Learning by Refraction*, 42.
123. Go and Atienza, *Learning by Refraction*, 41.
124. Go and Atienza, *Learning by Refraction*, 89.
125. Go and Atienza, *Learning by Refraction*, 90–91.
126. See Go and Atienza, *Learning by Refraction*, 37.
127. Falque, *Crossing the Rubicon*, 24.
128. Falque, *By Way of Obstacles*, 14–15.
129. I am grateful to Pablo Irizar for this insight.
130. Falque, *By Way of Obstacles*, 9.

challenge before trying to change the other. According to Falque, "every philosophical gesture, like every thought, must first let itself be transformed by the other."[131] The encounter with the other requires first and foremost a sympathy of and companionship of thought.

The foregoing points, once situated within a theological context, allow for further development and articulation of what being human entails. One can put oneself at risk *qua* human and *qua* believer, with the latter building upon the former.[132] For Falque, life itself becomes a form of doing philosophy.[133] "One does not think independently of life. One thinks in one's life, one thinks life, and life itself, as I have said, is also an act of thought."[134] Falque incorporates Ignatian thought into his philosophy, insofar as he maintains the integral and reciprocal connection between philosophy and lived experience.[135] Falque locates here an overlap of philosophy and theology within the individual soul.[136] It is in the very act of living and the surprise and challenge of it that one is led to introspection.[137]

Closing Comments

This essay, though barely scratching the surface of Falque's thought, has revealed certain points of interest for contemporary research, which—in my opinion—can continue to lead to new developments in multiple fields. I especially appreciate Falque's emphasis on the holistic dimension of one's apprehension of and growth in knowledge, as well as the possibility of integrating both philosophy and theology within one and the same individual. Falque's attention to the importance of the internal disposition of the seeker of truth puts him at home both in a postmodern philosophical context, yet also in a tradition informed by Christian sources, as exemplified in Ignatius. Similar to Falque, I believe that inquiry into the nature of the self and one's finitude can be enriched by considering a number of complementary perspectives and integrating them into one complex and harmonious thought.

Furthermore, I am in fundamental agreement with Falque's decision to make the human person and the drama of finite lived experience the meeting point between philosophy and theology. This not to say, however,

---

131. Falque, *By Way of Obstacles*, 16.
132. Falque, *Crossing the Rubicon*, 24.
133. Falque, *By Way of Obstacles*, 8.
134. Falque, *By Way of Obstacles*, 16.
135. Falque, *By Way of Obstacles*, 16.
136. Falque, *Crossing the Rubicon*, 24.
137. Falque, *By Way of Obstacles*, 8.

that the finite is exhaustive of reality for Falque, nor is it to say that he embraces an uncritical naïveté about the infinite. Rather, he maintains that, while the starting point of finitude does not preclude proceeding to the infinite, it nonetheless remains a crucial task for philosophy to reconcile the ineluctable fact of human finitude with man's (in some circles) putative orientation to the infinite.[138] The common starting point of finite lived experience provides the common ground of inexhaustible depth, which the philosopher and the theologian can explore both individually and in mutually enriching dialogue.

I am also sympathetic to Falque's provocative, if promising, introduction of Christ into philosophical conversation, a move which is controversial for both secular and Christian thinkers alike. Nonetheless, I for one am convinced of the anachronistic nature of the division of philosophy and theology and the importance of the presentation of Christ as a source for deeper inquiry and insight into the human condition, regardless of how one categorizes it.

Emmanuel Falque has and continues to render a great service to scholarship through his monumental, decades-long work. It should fill the thoughtful reader with excitement and encouragement for the present and future of philosophy and theology.

Bibliography

Carroll, Anthony J. "Luther, Loyola and *La La Land*." *New Blackfriars* 99.1080 (2018) 163–76. https://doi.org/10.1111/nbfr.12340.

Falque, Emmanuel. *By Way of Obstacles: A Pathway Through a Work*. Translated by Sarah Horton. Eugene, OR: Cascade, 2022.

———. *Crossing the Rubicon: The Borderlands of Philosophy and Theology*. Translated by Reuben Shank. New York: Fordham University Press, 2016.

———. "Philosophie et théologie: Nouvelles frontières." *Études* 404.2 (2006) 201–10.

Gabelli School of Business (GSB). "Jesuit Education and Ignatian Pedagogy." Gabelli School of Business, September 2005. https://www.fordham.edu/gabelli-school-of-business/faculty/resources/jesuit-education-and-ignatian-pedagogy.

Go, Johnny C., and Rita J. Atienza. *Learning by Refraction: A Practitioner's Guide to 21st Century Ignatian Pedagogy*. Manila: Ateno de Manila University Press, 2019.

Goldhill, Simon. *The Christian Invention of Time: Temporality and the Literature of Late Antiquity*. Cambridge: Cambridge University Press, 2022.

Hansen, Ron. "Spiritual Exercises." *Santa Clara Magazine*, June 8, 2006. https://magazine.scu.edu/magazines/summer-2006/spiritual-exercises.

Ignatian Spirituality. "What Are the Spiritual Exercises?" Ignatian Spirituality, n.d. https://www.ignatianspirituality.com/ignatian-prayer/the-spiritual-exercises/what-are-the-spiritual-exercises.

138. Falque, *By Way of Obstacles*, 34–35.

Jesuit Resource. "First Principle and Foundation Resources." JesuitResource.org, n.d. https://www.xavier.edu/jesuitresource/resources-by-theme/first-principle-and-foundation-resources.

King, Christopher. "On the Conversion of Philosophy: The Problems and Promise of Emmanuel Falque's Theology of Philosophy." *Heythrop Journal* 42 (2021) 75–84.

Knotts, Matthew W. *On Creation, Science, Disenchantment, and the Contours of Being and Knowing*. London: Bloomsbury Academic, 2020.

———. "You Show Me Yours, I'll Show You Mine: Comparing Paradigms." *Philosophy and Theology* 29:1 (2017) 83–100. https://doi.org/10.5840/philtheol201611972.

Koci, Martin. "Phenomenology and Theology Revisited: Emmanuel Falque and his Critics." *Revista Portuguesa de Filosofia* 76:2–3 (2020) 903–26.

Madec, Goulven. *Chez Augustin*. Paris: Institut d'Études Augustiniennes, 1998.

Pépin, Charles. La recontre: Une philosophie. Québec: Allary, 2021.

Flesh and Spirit

"You Are Not Your Own"

Another Look at the Body, Flesh, and the Falque-Henry Debate

STEVEN DELAY

Introduction

IN THE PORTION OF his First Letter to the Corinthians, upbraiding them for tolerating the sexual immorality in their midst (the letter segues into a condemnation of fornication in general after having addressed the problem posed by a recent specific incident of sex between a woman and her step-son), the apostle Paul says of the believer's body, "What? know ye not that your body is the temple of the Holy Ghost which is in you, which ye have of God, and ye are not your own?" (1 Cor 6:19). For St. Paul, certainly, the believer's embodied finite existence, which is to be spiritual rather than carnal, must never neglect to remember that our incarnate existence is answerable to Christ. This experiential fact that salvation is worked out through and in the body is one he will iterate elsewhere, of course, perhaps most memorably, above all, in his letter to the Romans. What light can phenomenology shed on St. Paul's statement, by clarifying the nature of the fundamental relation between our corporeal life and God?

Admittedly, it may seem an unfitting choice to begin an examination, like the one to follow, of phenomenology's understanding of embodiment with a verse from a Pauline letter. Some no doubt would contend that the task of offering an analysis of the body should be a philosophical, as opposed to a theological, affair. Yet such a claim, which was considered compelling for much of the twentieth century during historical phenomenology's heyday, has become moot, given the present state of the discussion. With the progression of phenomenological philosophy's accounts of the body (or more exactly, as we shall see, the flesh [*der Leib* in German and *la chair* in French]) having by now long ago already crossed into unmistakably theological terrain (Dominique Janicaud, for one, noted so over thirty years ago when criticizing what he at the time termed the "theological turn" of French phenomenology), these words of Paul to Corinth, as it happens, are quite to the point. For just as phenomenology ever since Husserl has always sought to illuminate the body's role in our sensible perception of the world, so too it has now for some time aimed to exhibit our corporeal entwinement with God as well.[1]

That the problem of the body is an inherently theological one, in fact, is nowhere more apparent in recent memory than in Michel Henry's philosophy of the flesh, a phenomenology of incarnation (the term is to be heard both in the sense of our own embodied condition as selves as well as in the sense of the Word's having being made flesh) whose account of incarnate existence Emmanuel Falque's account of embodiment has challenged in various respects, and which has led to the latter's formulation of the notion of a *corps épandu* (spread body).[2] The debate between Falque and Henry over the relation of the body and the flesh, for which the theological matters of incarnation, redemption, and resurrection come to the fore, accordingly goes to the heart of the experience of oneself, of others, of the world, even of God.

Henry, who is known well for maintaining that there is no body without the flesh,[3] has been the subject of criticism on this score from Falque, who for his own part has just as adamantly insisted that, to the contrary, there is no flesh without a body.[4] In attempting to assess and to draw lessons from Falque's loving struggle with Henry, the questions quickly mount. To begin with, which of the two, body or flesh, has primacy over the other? In short, is it Henry who is correct to insist on the supremacy of the flesh? Or,

---

1. See DeLay, "Power at Work," for an analysis of how Emmanuel Falque, in particular, has contributed to this phenomenological work at the borderlands of philosophy and theology. For his own discussion of St. Paul and phenomenology's problem of the body, see Falque, *Metamorphosis of Finitude*, 53–61.

2. See Falque, *Wedding Feast*, 12–15.

3. Henry's lengthiest exposition and defense of the flesh's primacy is found in "Phenomenology of Flesh," part 2 of *Incarnation*, 93–167. Right after the publication of *Incarnation*, he offered a condensed presentation of the view in an interview with Isabelle Gaudé in the 2001 summer issue of *Le Journal des Grandes Écoles et Universités*. See Henry, *Auto-donation*, 165–69.

4. Falque, "Is There a Flesh," 139–66.

is it Falque who is right to insist on the body? Is there really any such priority, either way? What, indeed, do Henry and Falque mean by the flesh and the body? How does the phenomenon of embodiment concern the related phenomenon of revelation? To what extent, and how exactly, is Falque's phenomenology of religion to be assessed in terms of his account of the body? To what degree do Falque and Henry truly substantively disagree? And given the very reasonable assumption that Falque's thought on the body is key to his overall picture of existence if the criticisms that he has made of Henry's phenomenology of incarnation prove on close examination to be mistaken, does that diminish the significance of Falque's phenomenology of religion's contribution to phenomenology as a whole? Or, is there a fundamental insight lying behind his criticisms of Henry's philosophy of flesh that remains viable, and which accordingly invites a further and renewed line of questioning in keeping with the spirit of his work's central theological interests? These are all questions to which we will turn in due course. First, however, a preliminary word must be said about phenomenology's handling of the problem of the body, for the tradition's past analyses of the body, and their historical evolution, bear directly on the matters fundamentally at stake in Henry's and Falque's respective accounts of embodiment, as well as the differences separating them.

The Problem of the Body in Classical Phenomenology

Even the briefest summary underscores the body's importance for phenomenology. In one form or other, every significant phenomenologist of the twentieth century recognized the reality of there being a lived body (*der Leib*) that is irreducible to an object in the world, and so likewise irreducible to any scientific account of the body that one might find in physiology, biology, psychology, neuroscience, or cognitive science. This distinction between a lived body, or flesh, that experiences the world, and a mere material body physically extended in the world (*Körper*) is one that originates with Husserl, of course. As Falque will himself put the matter, "My flesh is that *through which I experience my own body phenomenologically*, and not the simple biological and molecular substratum that can be cured, or repaired, or modified."[5] As Husserl notes, the body, which is to say the lived body, the flesh, is what opens a perceived world. To be incarnate, in this sense, is to be in possession of a body—to have immediate and unfettered power over one's motor and perceptual capacities and the possibilities to which those capacities correspond. In the *Cartesian Meditations*, hence, Husserl terms

---

5. Falque, *Metamorphosis of Finitude*, 136.

this incarnate power, this power to perceive, move, and act, an "I can."[6] One's own flesh, as he says, "is not just a body but precisely an animate organism," to which belongs "*fields of sensation*," that is, perceptual horizons of sensorial experience whose governing ego, in the form of the *I can* just mentioned, "*rule[s] and govern[s] immediately.*"[7] As he observes, because the body perceives and touches kinesthetically, the sensations of perceptual experience and action flow in accord with an "I am doing."[8] This same point is one Merleau-Ponty will make repeatedly in *Phenomenology of Perception*: "My body is that by which there are objects," as well as that which in turn provides "a primordial field of presence," in short, "a perceptual domain over which my body has power."[9] Accordingly, Merleau-Ponty refers to there being a *body schema* (*schéma corporel*) which expresses the fact that "my body is in and toward the world,"[10] a fact in his view that makes such *moticity* worthy of the designation *original intentionality*.[11] While disagreeing with certain aspects of Husserl and Merleau-Ponty's view of embodiment, Sartre, for his own part, agrees with them over the main essentials. Thus, in *Being and Nothingness*, he more than once characterizes the body as "a point of view and a point of departure."[12] And for him, again like Husserl and Merleau-Ponty, the body is what makes possible intersubjectivity, for it is our bodily condition that explains how others encounter us, and we in turn them. The lived body is not merely that by which I experience the world, for in addition to this *body-for-me*, there is the *body-for-others*, namely, the experiential fact that, as an incarnate presence within the world, "I exist for myself as a body known by the Other."[13] The other, says Sartre, is "the *one who looks at me*,"[14] and if "the Other is always present to me inasmuch as I am always *for-others*,"[15] this is owing to our visibility, a fact itself in turn owing to our incarnate dwelling in the world. In a word, thus, as Sartre puts it, "my being-for-others ... is my *being-outside*."[16] The lived and sensing body, the flesh, opens the one common world in which we encounter everything

6. Husserl, *Cartesian Meditations*, 97.
7. Husserl, *Cartesian Meditations*, 97.
8. Husserl, *Cartesian Meditations*, 97.
9. Merleau-Ponty, *Phenomenology of Perception*, 94.
10. Merleau-Ponty, *Phenomenology of Perception*, 103.
11. Merleau-Ponty, *Phenomenology of Perception*, 139.
12. Sartre, *Being and Nothingness*, 355.
13. Sartre, *Being and Nothingness*, 375.
14. Sartre, *Being and Nothingness*, 281.
15. Sartre, *Being and Nothingness*, 304.
16. Sartre, *Being and Nothingness*, 309.

there that we do and in turn find ourselves encountered by others. As a brief sketch of historical phenomenology's conception of embodiment makes plain, the problem of the body is of supreme importance to understanding human existence. "The ambiguity of being in the world," Merleau-Ponty, for example, thus says, "is expressed by the ambiguity of our body, and this latter is understood through the ambiguity of time."[17] It is because the phenomenon of embodiment is key to our being-in-the-world that even Heidegger, who infamously has virtually nothing to say about the body in *Being and Time*, in effect also acknowledges its significance when he states in that work's §23 ("The Spatiality of Being-in-the-World"): "[Dasein's] 'bodily nature' hides a whole problematic of its own, though we shall not treat it here."[18]

Michel Henry's Philosophy of the Flesh and Radicalization of the Problem of the Body

This brings us to the matter of how Michel Henry's philosophy of the flesh addresses the problem of the body. In his final text *Words of Christ*, Henry says, "A human being is really twofold, visible and invisible at the same time."[19] What does that mean? And what explains it? As he notes immediately in the very next sentence, this duplicity of appearing corresponds to the body's own twofold mode of givenness. "The analysis of the body," he says,

> has established that the body is given to us in two different fashions: on the one hand, under the form of an external, visible body in the fashion of other bodies in the universe; on the other hand, each person lives inwardly in his or her own body under the form of the invisible flesh, suffering and desiring, and is at one with it.[20]

What Henry refers here to as the "external, visible body" is widely recognized by the philosophical tradition. And the latter, one might think, is a notion of embodiment already recognized by Husserl, Merleau-Ponty, and Sartre, as we have noted. It is the lived body (the "I can"), what Husserl terms *der Leib* and Sartre and Merleau-Ponty *la chair*, in short, the sensing body with which we move, act, and perceive, and which opens a field of perception, and allows us to encounter the world and all that shows itself

17. Merleau-Ponty, *Phenomenology of Perception*, 87.
18. Heidegger, *Being and Time*, 143.
19. Henry, *Words of Christ*, 49.
20. Henry, *Words of Christ*, 17.

within it. Moreover, it is this sensible body, which is itself visible, that is said to account for intersubjectivity, for it is by the body that one is seen by others, and by which one sees others. This incarnate existence is, to borrow again Sartre's turn of phrase, our *being-outside*.

Such, then, is historical phenomenology's body of *originary intentionality*, of transcendence, in other words, of what brings to sight what shows itself in what Henry himself, when criticizing historical phenomenology's understanding of the body, will term *the truth of the world*. This *truth of the world*—Henry also refers to it as *the word of the world*—designates a mode of phenomenality, of appearing. As he notes time and again throughout his texts, such phenomenality is that of ek-stasis, transcendence, exteriority, or visibility. The lived body, so understood, is what makes the perceived world available, and which is at the same time itself visible. Henry will reject this conception of the body that situates the embodiment in relation to the perceived world through transcendence in favor of an idiosyncratic notion of what he will term the flesh.

He in turn coins the expression *ontological monism* to name what he sees as a prejudice, according to which the philosophical tradition, including historical phenomenology, has focused solely on this one form of phenomenality—the world's truth or appearing. "In the philosophical tradition from which modernity arises," he states,

> the reply is demanded from the most ordinary experience: the things—stones, flowers, earth and sky, the products of the earth, tools and machines, humans themselves—all these realities show themselves to us in the world. Consequently, the widespread belief takes birth which defines what is called "common sense" and according to which the world is the environment of all possible manifestation. In other words: the universe of the visible is the only world which exists; it defines the ground of reality.[21]

This is the truth of the world, namely, that phenomena are what show themselves through an intentionality responsible for ejecting consciousness outside itself into exteriority. "Let us call this Word that finds its phenomenological possibility in the coming outside of an Outside the Word of the World,"[22] says Henry. At issue is phenomenality as such, reality's mode of appearing, not just any specific phenomenon or any particular object that appears. "The world," so Henry observes, "is not the set of things, of beings, but the horizon of light where things show themselves in their equality as

---

21. Henry, *Words of Christ*, 70.
22. Henry, "Speech and Religion," 220.

phenomena."[23] In other words, "A thing exists for us only if it shows itself to us as a phenomenon."[24] Or again: "The 'world's truth' is nothing other than this: a self-production of 'outsideness' as the horizon of visibility in and through which every thing can become visible and thus become a 'phenomenon' for us."[25]

In response to this longstanding tradition of ontological monism that has exclusively viewed manifestation as a matter of what lies outside, of what appears through intentionality, Henry contends that the world's horizon of visibility and exteriority cannot be the sole form of appearing. For one thing, were there no other kind of manifestation besides ek-static intentionality, there would be no experience at all. For, as Henry observed beginning with *The Essence of Manifestation*, transcendence can only disclose itself through a radical immanence that first experiences itself. As Henry explains, "If there existed no other truth than that of the world—there would be no reality at all anywhere but only, on all sides, death."[26] And the body itself is no exception to this phenomenological law of appearing. For what becomes of it in the hands of historical phenomenology, when reduced to the paradigm of visibility and exteriority?

According to Henry, consigned to the world's truth—to exteriority, ek-stasis, and thus the positive sciences that thematize it as a material object of knowledge—"It is now no more than an organism perceived from the outside, in terms of the world's truth, a bundle of objective processes."[27] Although historical phenomenology rightly rejects the naturalistic and scientistic theoretical framework that would have us understand the body as another material or physical object to be investigated in accord with the physical sciences, because it understands the body as what opens and sustains a world, and it understands embodiment in light of transcendence and intentionality, in terms of the world's truth, Henry argues it accordingly fails to recover the flesh's mode of purely immanent appearing. Husserl, Heidegger, Merleau-Ponty, and Sartre, along with the rest of the Western philosophical tradition,[28] consign the lived body to the horizon of the

23. Henry, *I Am the Truth*, 14.
24. Henry, *I Am the Truth*, 15.
25. Henry, *I Am the Truth*, 17.
26. Henry, *I Am the Truth*, 20.
27. Henry, *I Am the Truth*, 77.
28. According to Henry, there are a few figures who are notable exceptions to this reign of ontological monism, such as Meister Eckhart and Novalis. Maine de Biran is another one as well, and it is Biran, as we shall see in a moment, who inspires Henry's own philosophy of flesh. "Beginning with the Greeks and throughout the western tradition, with the exception of a few thinkers, a conception of appearing has come to

world's truth—exteriority, visibility, intentionality. In the last analysis, their conception of the body is beholden to ontological monism, to the notion that there is only one mode of manifestation, that of the world's visibility and exteriority.

Henry, in contrast, contends that even if the traditional phenomenological conception of the lived body resists a scientific reductionism that would treat the body as little more than an object subject to chemical and biological laws, by understanding the body as that which opens a world of perception, it nevertheless overlooks the flesh's auto-impressionality. The heart of auto-impressionality is its invisibility, that it is not shown in the light of the world. For this reason, Henry will often speak of its nocturnality. "The world is the reign of the visible, life that of the invisible."[29] Or again: "*The relation between the world and our life is here proposed under the form of a radical opposition between the visible and the invisible.*"[30] Hence, for Henry, the most fundamental and essential layer of revelation, namely, the one concerning the manner in which we are revealed to ourselves as the individual selves whom we are, occurs through the invisible pathos of transcendental self-affectivity. It is a form of radical immanent appearing he in later works calls the flesh. When, then, he writes, "It is in our invisible subjectivity where our actual reality is found,"[31] this assertion implies that it is in and through the flesh, through the pure immanence of transcendental self-affectivity, that we experience life.

As Falque observes, this is a drastic repudiation of historical phenomenology's understanding of the body as an organ of intentionality.[32] "How," as Henry asks, "is the intentionality that makes all things visible revealed—to itself?"[33] His own answer is that underneath all transcendence,

---

dominate, which is also that of common sense: the appearing of the world." See Henry, *Auto-donation*, 159.

29. Henry, *Words of Christ*, 15.

30. This essay's focus is Falque's objections, but it should be noted that others have expressed similar misgivings over Henry's philosophy of the flesh, and the phenomenology of life's ability to coordinate the radical abyss between the interiority of life's invisible self-affection, on the one hand, and the exteriority of the visible world's ek-static intentionality, on the other. See Marion, *Figures de phénoménologie*, 95–115. Jean-Louis Chrétien has pursued this same line of questioning as well, which he formulates by asking whether the two radically opposed forms of phenomenality Henry distinguishes, the "*parole du monde*" and the "*parole de la vie*," are "translatable." See Chrétien, *Reconnaissances philosophiques*, 169–90.

31. Henry, *Words of Christ*, 18.

32. For this reason, Henry will say that his philosophy of the flesh involves nothing short of a "reversal of phenomenology." See Henry, *Incarnation*, 93.

33. Henry, *Incarnation*, 47.

all intentionality, is a non-intentional, immediate, affective revelation. The perceived world and the intentionality responsible for opening this world's truth always already presupposes a more fundamental appearing, a form of revelation that explains how that very intentionality can be aware of itself. Didier Frank, for one, has clearly described the ek-static mode of appearing that Henry contends cannot account for itself. "The fundamental Husserlian claim about perception," says Frank, "is that things are given in the flesh, which is also to say that they are given to my flesh and through my flesh. Givenness in the flesh thus refers both to a mode of givenness and to the recipient of this givenness."[34] But how is what Frank terms here the *recipient* of such givenness in turn given to himself? How does what is given in perception reveal itself without oneself already having been revealed to oneself? According to Henry, as we have seen, Husserl, Heidegger, Sartre, and Merleau-Ponty have no answer to this fundamental question, because their phenomenologies of transcendence fail to thematize the radical immanence of life's transcendental affectivity, in short, the invisible auto-impressionality of the flesh. As Henry puts the point himself,

> For Husserl, the definition of pure phenomenality and of appearing is given by intentionality which is a movement by which consciousness ejects itself outside and it is precisely in this throwing itself outside itself that it is able to see what it can see. Consciousness is always consciousness of some thing, in the sense of a visible thing. . . . Yet Husserl, who was obsessed, of course, by the problem of life and which he rightly termed "transcendental," that is, non-biological, was unable to recognize its own mode of revelation.[35]

To what revelation exactly is Husserl, along with others, blind? Life's immanent self-affection. "Life," says Henry,

> is that which itself affects itself in the radical and decisive sense that this life that is affection, and that is affected, is not affected by anything other than itself, by no kind of externality and by nothing exterior to it. . . . Self-affection as life's essence implies its acosmic character, the fact that being affected by nothing other . . . it comes about in itself in the absolute sufficiency of its radical interiority.[36]

---

34. Frank, *Flesh and Body*, 39
35. Henry, *Auto-donation*, 160 (translation mine).
36. Henry, *I Am the Truth*, 105.

A string of characteristic formulations like the ones to follow describes the kind of self-revelation that Henry believes to be the condition of intentionality:

> To be a Self is indeed nothing other than this: to be given to oneself without this self-givenness being one's own doing.[37]

> The mode of revelation proper to life consists in the pure fact of experiencing oneself.[38]

> What matters is the way in which life gives itself this content that is itself. This self-giving that is a self-revelation is a transcendental affectivity, a pathos in which every self-experiencing is possible as *pathētik*, as affective in the very depths of its being.[39]

Hence, for Henry, recognition of transcendental life's mode of invisible revelation demands what he sometimes terms a *material phenomenology*, or a philosophy of the flesh. Moreover, a correct view of the body's self-givenness, he maintains, necessitates a complete reversal of historical phenomenology's problem of the body. "By opposing a more originary mode of manifestation (the immanent self-revelation of life in its invisible pathos) to the ek-static appearance of the world," he claims, "the phenomenology of life offers entirely new tasks for investigation."[40] And as mentioned, for Henry, chief among the phenomena to be investigated is embodiment, the *nocturnal* revelation of the flesh's invisible auto-impressionality. Indeed, for Henry, the pathos of life is the flesh: "In short, what is primary is the interior experience of my impressions, of my suffering, of my desire, of my anger, this pure affective impression which is the tissue of my flesh."[41]

Here, it might be observed that others besides Henry have used the term flesh. Sartre, for example, does not speak just of the body. He sometimes does speak as well of the flesh. What exactly is meant by it, then, if not what Henry wishes to designate by it? "The flesh," Sartre says, "is the pure

---

37. Henry, *Incarnation*, 182.
38. Henry, *I Am the Truth*, 199.
39. Henry, *I Am the Truth*, 106.
40. Henry, *Incarnation*, 89. Karl Hefty's excellent essay, which we will further mention shortly, scrutinizing the Henry-Falque debate provides a pithy summation of Henry's conception of flesh: "For Henry, the reality of flesh is invisible, irreducibly and in principle. In its original givenness, where it is given to itself as auto-impressional and the only place its givenness is original, it does not and cannot appear in the exteriority of world. Nor can flesh be extended to the world in the manner of Merleau-Ponty's touching-touched, sensing-sensed, feeling-felt chiasm" (Hefty, "Is There a Body," 62).
41. Henry, *Auto-donation*, 161 (translation mine).

contingency of presence."⁴² When one sees the other, the pure contingency of the other's existence, and in turn one's own, is manifest. The other rises up into visibility as a phenomenon without justification—a pure appearing whose presence in the world serves as a visible attestation of the fact that we find ourselves thrown into existence without ever having chosen so, without any given notion of what significance that very existence should possess but for the fundamental project to which we commit ourselves freely.⁴³ Although Henry and Sartre both use the term flesh, they ultimately disagree about what the term signifies. The difference can be highlighted with reference to the philosophy of Maine de Biran. For Henry, who in this respect follows Biran, the phenomenon of flesh designates an inner resistance, what Biran and Henry call a *sensation of effort*. Henry says,

> Because the action of any kind of power presupposes the action of the "I can," this original capacity of power must first be at work on its own basis, buttressed against itself as its own ground, wresting itself away from the radical passivity in which it is given in absolute life's self-givenness: *all feeling of action is in reality*, according to Maine de Biran's extraordinary intuition, *a feeling of effort*, and this effort is precisely not some modality of affectivity. Effort in its specific pathos marks how the "I can," with its original capacity to act shown back to its source, in the place of its generation in absolute life, and here given to itself in pathos, is in and by this pathos capable of deploying freely—itself, starting from itself, by its own strength, and as its own expense in some way—the power and strength which it has just been invested. This original pathos, which releases a strength and endows it with the strength to be exerted from itself and according to its own strength—to be more exact, when the test

---

42. Sartre, *Being and Nothingness*, 367. Merleau-Ponty uses the term also, though again in a sense that Henry will oppose: "The flesh is not matter, is not mind, is not substance. To designate it, we should need the old term 'element,' in the sense it was used to speak of water, air, earth, and fire, that is, in the sense of a general thing, midway between the spatio-temporal individual and the idea, a sort of incarnate principle that brings a style of being wherever there is a fragment of being. The flesh is in this sense an 'element' of Being" (Merleau-Ponty, *Visible and Invisible*, 139).

43. Camus is on to this phenomenon of pure contingency manifest in the body's sheer presence, which is to say, its "nudity," when he memorably describes the experience of seeing the man talking in the booth whose existence appears to be wholly gratuitous: "A man is talking on the telephone behind a glass partition; you cannot hear him but you see his incomprehensible dumb-show and you wonder why he is alive" (Camus, *Myth of Sisyphus*, 15).

of this force is exercised in these conditions in this way—*this* is the feeling of effort.[44]

The crucial thing to note regarding this characterization of embodiment is that the capacity to exercise one's bodily powers is itself said to be a power that does not derive from one's own power. What Husserl calls the *I can*, which is to say, the power of the ego, for Henry, is not the origin of its own power. Within the radical interiority of life is an Other—Life, or God. Henry is explicit about this: "As far as I am me, I affect myself. . . . But I have not brought myself into this condition of experiencing myself. I am myself, but I myself have no part in this 'being-myself': I experience myself without being the source of this experience."[45] The denial of Life, the forgetfulness that one is not the source of one's own power, constitutes what Henry terms the "transcendental illusion of the ego," the delusion of taking oneself to be an autonomous agent who is the origin of one's own life and its capacities. Along with many other similar passages, Henry offers the following description of this illusion:

> Experiencing each of its powers while it exercises it—and in the first place, the power it has of exercising them—the ego now assumes it is their source, their origin. It imagines that it possesses these powers, that they are its own in a radical way—produced by itself, and which it could produce each moment it is exercising them. As somehow the absolute source and origin of the powers that compose its being (the effective and acting being with which it identifies and by which it defines itself), the ego considers itself also the source and origin of this very being.[46]

Hence, in a word, "*Thus is born the transcendental illusion of the ego, whereby this ego takes itself as the ground of its Being.*"[47] Or again, said succinctly, "The first cause of people's forgetting their condition as Sons is the transcendental illusion of the ego."[48] "The more the ego exercises its power," as Henry further explains, "the more profound the experience it has, in the concreteness of its effort, of effecting this power, the more it attributes this power to itself, and the more it forgets the Life that gave it."[49] The transcendental illusion of the ego's self-sufficiency, which leads to experiencing one's bodily power as

---

44. Henry, *Incarnation*, 187.
45. Henry, *I Am the Truth*, 107.
46. Henry, *I Am the Truth*, 140.
47. Henry, *I Am the Truth*, 140.
48. Henry, *I Am the Truth*, 141.
49. Henry, *I Am the Truth*, 142.

though it were derived from oneself, oriented solely and exclusively to the world's horizon of visibility, elides the recognition of Life: "Forgetful of its 'me,' the ego is concerned with the world."[50]

Thus, according to Henry, a recognition of the flesh's interiority, and its origin within Life, necessitates a theological turn. To remain subject to the transcendental illusion of the ego is to live as what Henry himself will term a *prodigal son*, for it is to forget one's condition as a son of Life, as one who derives his very own life from Life, from God. For this reason, Henry will directly equate the life of the ego living apart from God as a form of idolatrous existence: "The majority lives like idolaters: They hardly care at all about the power that gives them life, and live in it only for themselves, and care, in all things and in others, only for themselves."[51] Or again: "*Phenomenologically*, someone who lives only for himself, who cares only about his own feelings and pleasures (as if he gave them to himself and as if the power that really gives them did not exist), who believes he leads an autonomous life and is not the beneficiary or debtor of any heritage or any promise—is that person not the prodigal Son?"[52] Here, quite plainly, any purported boundary between philosophy and theology is surmounted, for the presence of God is said to be attested in the experiential fact of our bodily capacity's origin in Life: "That God—or, if one prefers, Life—is more intimately within me than myself is not a mystical pronouncement, but a phenomenological one."[53] In turn, for Henry, what Christianity means by salvation consists in the *second birth* of which Nicodemus questions Christ. Salvation is a return to Life from the condition of spiritual death, a death wherein one lives as an autonomous ego estranged from the Life that sustains one as living.

> Christianity asserts the possibility that someone may surmount this radical Forgetting and rejoin the absolute Life of God—this Life that preceded the world and its time, eternal Life. Such a possibility signifies nothing other than salvation. To rejoin this absolute Life, which has neither beginning nor end, would be to unite with it, identify with it, live anew this Life that is not born and does not die—to live like it does, in the way it lives, and not to die. . . . To rejoin the absolute Life of God—would that not also be, though, for someone who has forgotten it, to find once again a condition that was once one's own, if it is true that in one's transcendental birth one came into oneself only in the very coming into itself of absolute Life?[54]

50. Henry, *I Am the Truth*, 142.
51. Henry, *Incarnation*, 152.
52. Henry, *I Am the Truth*, 162.
53. Henry, "Speech and Religion," 233.
54. Henry, *I Am the Truth*, 151.

Emmanuel Falque's Contribution to the Phenomenological Problem of the Body

Having recounted historical phenomenology's approach to the problem of the body and now in turn Michel Henry's critique of it, this brings us, at last, to the ultimate matter of Falque's phenomenology of incorporation, an account of the body which in many ways is formulated in direct opposition to Henry's philosophy of flesh. To what does Falque object?

Above all, Falque refuses Henry's prioritization of the flesh over the body. In this respect, Falque follows Sartre, who in *Being and Nothingness* rejects Biran's conception of embodiment. Of Biran, Sartre says,

> Either [the body] is a thing among other things, or else it is that by which things are revealed to me. But it cannot be both at the same time. Similarly I see my hand touching objects, but do not *know* it in its act of touching them. This is the fundamental reason why that famous "sensation of effort" of Maine de Biran does not really exist. For my hand reveals to me the resistance of objects, their hardness or softness, but not *itself*.[55]

Thus, whereas for Henry embodiment consists in the felt resistance of the flesh's own lightness or heaviness, owing to its own exertion and resulting fatigue, for Sartre, lightness and heaviness, and therefore fatigue as well, only occur through the weight of the organic, visible, and measurable body. And as Karl Hefty has noted, Falque agrees with the view articulated here by Sartre: "For Falque, heaviness or lightness can be felt only by a flesh that also weighs something, and thus also bears the properties of a worldly body."[56] Said otherwise, in a word, there is no flesh without a body. Falque says so himself: "there is 'no flesh without the body,' either in phenomenology or in theology."[57] Such is the phenomenological objection to Henry's phenomenology of flesh. But for Falque, of course, there is more importantly a theological basis for disagreement with Henry. The acosmic flesh of Henry's phenomenology of life is, in Falque's estimation, susceptible to the charge of angelism or Gnosticism. Moreover, as for the incarnation itself, Falque will relatedly contend that Henry's characterization of the Word becoming flesh neglects the central importance of the Word's having entered "into the historical process."[58] A phenomenology of the body, "unlike certain phenomenological interpretations of Christianity today," he says, must acknowledge

---

55. Sartre, *Being and Nothingness*, 328.
56. Hefty, "Is There a Body," 65.
57. Falque, *Metamorphosis of Finitude*, 137.
58. Falque, *Metamorphosis of Finitude*, 137.

the organicity and corporality of the lived body. Otherwise, so he says, "we are liable to forget its incorporation as the substance of the whole body (*Verkörperung*). And we then neglect 'animality' as a 'psychic' dimension of the Word incarnate."[59] What are we to make of Falque's objections?

In the course of carefully evaluating Falque's position, Hefty concludes that Falque's phenomenological and theological objections against Henry misfire, insofar as they misunderstand Henry's view.[60] If one follows Hefty's careful and persuasive assessment of the Falque-Henry debate, it might appear that the dispute is now settled: Falque is wrong. This is not the place to assess whether Falque has a way of responding directly to Hefty's rejoinders on behalf of Henry by reformulating modified versions of the original objections he has made. With an eye to concluding this brief overview of Falque's contribution to the problem of the body, I should like instead to suggest a way in which the heart of Falque's reservations over Henry's phenomenology of incarnation may in fact hit the mark, after all. To do so, it will be necessary to return to St. Paul, someone to whom Falque himself frequently recurs.

First, however, it must be noted that, contrary to the prevailing assumption, Henry himself never intended for his so-called *philosophy of Christianity* to substantively alter, much less supplant, the truth of Christianity. The phenomenology of life, as he understands it, ultimately is meant to clarify the truth of Christianity in a way wholly consistent with theological orthodoxy. At stake is an explication of Christianity, not a *demythologization* or *deconstruction* of it. Henry's own explanation of the relationship between the phenomenology of life and Christianity is in this regard illuminating:

> I wanted to write [*Incarnation*] and then I remembered Paul's texts on the mystical body. I then reread all the texts of the New Testament, and I understood that basically, without wanting in any way to reduce Christianity to a philosophy, it contained philosophical presuppositions, even philosophical theses, which are those of a phenomenology of life. I accordingly ventured a philosophical reading of Christianity based on phenomenology, but a reading which, instead of looking down on it, recognized in some way the truth, for in Christianity, and explicitly in the first verses from John's Gospel, it is said that God is Life.[61]

---

59. Falque, *Metamorphosis of Finitude*, 137. For his most thorough, and recent, presentation of the phenomenology of incorporation, see Falque, *Wedding Feast*, 100–132.

60. See Hefty, "Is There a Body," 62–71.

61. Henry, *Auto-donation*, 164 (translation mine).

This brings us to the most serious objection Henry's phenomenology of life invites, an objection that Falque in his own way is very much on to. In the last line of his essay for the *French Debate* volume, Henry invokes the famous exchange between Nicodemus and Christ concerning the second birth, by quoting the words in which Christ speaks of the Spirit: "The Spirit blows whither it will."[62] But this invocation of the Holy Spirit here by Henry in fact highlights what is perhaps the true aporia of his phenomenology of life. For Henry, self-experience is inherently inseparable from Christ, insofar as the very life we ourselves have is itself derived from Life. Following the prologue of John, Henry accordingly emphasizes that every living individual, simply in virtue of so living, is always already fundamentally related to Christ, who has brought each of us into the condition of living. Yet that same Gospel of John repeatedly emphasizes that the Holy Spirit will not be given until after Christ's glorification. Four key words of Christ on the matter come immediately to mind. First, in chapter seven of John's Gospel, we read the following:

> He that believeth on me, as the scripture hath said, out of his belly shall flow rivers of living water. (But this spake he of the Spirit, which they that believe on him should receive: for the Holy Ghost was not yet given; because that Jesus was not yet glorified.) (John 7:38–39)

And then in chapter fifteen: "But when the Comforter is come, whom I will send unto you from the Father, even the Spirit of truth, which proceedeth from the Father, he shall testify of me" (John 15:16). And finally, this time the words of chapter sixteen: "Nevertheless I tell you the truth; It is expedient for you that I go away: for if I go not away, the Comforter will not come unto you; but if I depart, I will send him unto you" (John 16:7). And finally, the culmination of this promise is recorded in chapter twenty, when the risen Christ returns to the apostles: "Then said Jesus to them again, Peace be unto you: as my Father hath sent me, even so send I you. And when he had said this, he breathed on them, and saith unto them, Receive ye the Holy Ghost" (John 20:20–21). As all of these words of Christ make clear, the Holy Spirit is given after Christ's ascension, a fact again attested in the account of Pentecost provided in the book of Acts:

> And when the day of Pentecost was fully come, they were all with one accord in one place. And suddenly there came a sound from heaven as of a rushing mighty wind, and it filled all the house where they were sitting. And there appeared unto them cloven tongues like as of fire, and it sat upon each of them. And

---

62. Henry, "Speech and Religion," 241.

> they were all filled with the Holy Ghost, and began to speak with other tongues, as the Spirit gave them utterance. (Acts 2:1–4)

Thus, in the Johannine texts on which Henry himself most heavily relies for his phenomenology of life, Christ states that the Holy Spirit will not have come until after he has been glorified. In Henry's phenomenology of life, however, there is no express role assigned to the Holy Spirit that reflects this, since everything about the human condition, which is explained almost exclusively in reference to the Son, proceeds as if there is no transformation in our self-experience brought about by the coming of the Holy Spirit. At least to my knowledge, Henry never explicitly addressed this apparent flaw in his philosophy of revelation and corresponding theological anthropology.

Falque, in contrast, has addressed this problem, much to his credit. It is this precise omission in Henry's phenomenology of incarnation just mentioned that Falque, above all, has done well to identify and rectify. According to Falque, salvation in Christ does not consist solely in a *return* to the radical immanence of Life's pathos, entailing an experience of embodiment whose experiential texture would in principle always already be available to everyone at any period of human history with or without the Holy Spirit. Instead, salvation involves a *metamorphosis of finitude*, which is to say, a change in how we inhabit and experience our bodies brought about through the power of the Holy Spirit. Missing from Henry's account of salvation was the power (*dunamis*) of the Holy Spirit. Falque explains this neglect of such power as stemming, at least in part, from phenomenology's general preoccupation with passivity, an approach typified in Henry's account of the pathos of life. As Falque says, "It has been the constant admission of weakness in Christianity that has only too rapidly led us to disregard the power of the Holy Spirit that is capable of bringing about our metamorphosis."[63] Henry's philosophy of the flesh, which does so well to underscore the immemorial presence of Christ revealed in the invisible pathos of our own flesh, nevertheless overlooks the further revelation of the Holy Spirit's deeper empowerment of that incarnate condition. Falque, however, quite explicitly recognizes that further donation. "As the transcendental condition of the body as well as of meaning," so he says, "the voice seeks a body for itself rather than coming from the body."[64] Or, put differently, "the force or the Holy Spirit—thus also the voice or the breath (*ruach/pneuma*) *desires* the body more than it takes its origin in a body and produces the *instituting signification* more than it has its provenance in the instituted meaning."[65]

63. Falque, *Wedding Feast of Lamb*, 9.
64. Falque, *Crossing the Rubicon*, 71.
65. Falque, *Crossing the Rubicon*, 71.

Falque is correct that if Christ's own resurrection changes everything, that considerably is in part because it has given us every reason to believe that we ourselves now have the hope of one day inheriting a glorified body as well. And if, as Falque insists, the resurrected body and the fleshly body are in some sense one and the same, this entails that the mortal body, the body of flesh and bone, the corruptible body of dust, must not be forgotten by phenomenology if the eternal horizon of our bodily finite condition is to be done justice. Such an approach is not at all to deny the spiritual body, but to explicate what the spiritualization of the body involves, by bringing into view life in the spirit.

Concluding Remarks

Following Falque, therefore, we may now conclude where we began, by turning back to St. Paul's First Letter to the Corinthians. Quite fittingly, he himself turns often to St. Paul.

> The essential feature of the Pauline system is that the flesh (*sarx*) always appears as a manner of being (admittedly negative or turned away from God) of the body (*soma*). And this *manner of being* does not condemn the body (*soma*), which for this reason also is identified with Christ, who is the Church.[66]

In the last analysis, it appears that a rapprochement, at least to some degree, emerges between Falque and Henry. Henry, in short, is correct to highlight the auto-impressionailty of the flesh, for this dimension of radical immanence is what explains the Johannine truth that each of us, simply in virtue of living, is a son of God always already. Falque, for his part, is correct to see that such a truth, as essential and fundamental and important as it is, does not alone suffice to account for the full revelation of God in Jesus Christ. For as Christ himself says in John's Gospel, it is the Holy Spirit who will come to transform those who believe. That transformation, that metamorphosis of finitude, takes place nowhere else but in and through the body. "True corporality," as Falque consequently says, "is not in our corporal and biological substance—important though that is in our *incorporation*—but in the way we live, accept, and receive this in our *incarnation*. The *experience of our bodies* is what makes our *flesh*."[67]

What we have here, then, is not a fundamental opposition between Henry and Falque, but rather a synergy, whereby each account highlights

---

66. Falque, *Metamorphosis of Finitude*, 55.
67. Falque, *Metamorphosis of Finitude*, 138.

something essential about both revelation and embodiment that the other did not provide on its own. Henry's philosophy of the flesh provides the basis on which it is possible to understand how our incarnate existence can in turn be transformed by the power of the Holy Spirit. Falque's phenomenology of incorporation describes that very transformation. The dispute between Henry and Falque over the problem of the body, thus, appears not to turn so much on whether there is a flesh without body, or a body without flesh, but on how it proves possible for the flesh to be empowered by the Spirit. Henry, more than anyone, has done well to illuminate how we are in principle capable of undergoing that transformation, insofar as life always already is grounded in Life. Such an account, however, remains incomplete without supplementation, which Falque's phenomenology of incorporation supplies through its focus on the role of the Holy Spirit. That God enables those who abide in Christ to use their bodies in a way aligned with the Spirit is, of course, a thoroughly Pauline motif, one Falque himself recognizes.

> The features that constitute and characterize Pauline anthropology, those on which the Christian dogma of the resurrection of the body is founded, are (a) the body (*soma*) as site of a relation with and openness to God, (b) the flesh (*sarx*) and the spirit (*pneuma*) as modalities of the body (*soma*), and (c) the distinction between the kinds of "flesh" (*sarx*) according to the quality of their glory rather than according to their substance. And it is from these features also, I believe, that we can arrive at a possible conceptualization in terms of the metamorphosis of finitude.[68]

How to conclude this evaluation of Falque and Henry's loving struggle? It seems only fitting to offer a final word that borrows from Falque's own formula regarding the desire to issue one's own words in response to the Word. *To die of not writing*: what then exactly does that mean? It means to need to keep writing, because there is always more to say, evermore to say, because the hope of the life to come, which is to say, eternal life in Christ, has made thinking this present one worthwhile now that death has been shown no longer to hold the last word over life. Transformed by the God revealed in Jesus Christ who subordinates all things, above all death, to himself, phenomenology in turn becomes an exercise in issuing words of life, because it is responsive to this promise of eternal life. Nowhere today is this translation from death to life, this transformation of our finitude, better attested in phenomenological philosophy than in Falque's thinking on the body.

---

68. Falque, *Metamorphosis of Finitude*, 55.

Bibliography

Camus, Albert. *The Myth of Sisyphus*. Translated by Justin O'Brien. New York: Vintage, 1955.

Chrétien, Jean-Louis. *Reconnaissances philosophiques*. Paris: Cerf, 2010.

DeLay, Steven. "The Power at Work Within Us." In *Transforming the Theological Turn: Phenomenology with Emmanuel Falque*, edited by Martin Koci and Jason W. Alvis, 187–201. Lanham: Rowman & Littlefield, 2020.

Falque, Emmanuel. *Crossing the Rubicon: The Borderlands of Philosophy and Theology*. Translated by Reuben Shank. New York: Fordham, 2016.

———. "Is There a Flesh Without Body? A Debate with Michel Henry." Translated by Scott Davidson. *Journal of French and Francophone Philosophy* 24.1 (2016) 139–66.

———. *The Metamorphosis of Finitude: An Essay on Birth and Resurrection*. Translated by George Hughes. New York: Fordham, 2012.

———. *The Wedding Feast of the Lamb: Eros, the Body, and the Eucharist*. Translated by George Hughes. New York: Fordham, 2016.

Frank, Didier. *Flesh and Body: On the Phenomenology of Husserl*. Translated by Joseph Rivera and Scott Davidson. London: Bloomsbury, 2014.

Hefty, Karl. "Is There a Body Without Flesh?" *Crossing: The INPR Journal* 1 (2020) 54–72.

Heidegger, Martin. *Being and Time*. Translated by John Macquarrie and Edward Robinson. San Francisco: Harper & Row, 1962.

Henry, Michel. *Auto-donation: Entretiens et conférences*. Paris: Beauchesne, 2004.

———. *I Am the Truth: Toward a Philosophy of Christianity*. Translated by Susan Emmanuel. Stanford: Stanford University Press, 2003.

———. *Incarnation: A Philosophy of Flesh*. Translated by Karl Hefty. Evanston, IL: Northwestern University Press, 2015.

———. "Pour une phénoménologie de la vie." *Le Journal de Grandes Écoles*, 2001, 46–47.

———. "Speech and Religion: The Word of God." In *Phenomenology and the "Theological Turn": The French Debate*, edited by Dominique Janicaud, 216–41. Translated by Bernard G. Prusak. New York: Fordham, 2000.

———. *Words of Christ*. Translated by Christina M. Gschwandtner. Grand Rapids: Eerdmans, 2012.

Husserl, Edmund. *Cartesian Meditations: An Introduction to Phenomenology*. Translated by Dorion Cairns. Dordrecht: Springer, 1999.

Janicaud, Dominique. "The Surprises of Immanence." In *Phenomenology and the "Theological Turn": The French Debate*, edited by Dominique Janicaud, 70–86. Translated by Bernard G. Prusak. New York: Fordham, 2000.

Marion, Jean-Luc. *Figures de phénoménologie: Husserl, Heidegger, Levinas, Henry, Derrida*. Paris: J. Vrin, 2015.

Merleau-Ponty, Maurice. *Phenomenology of Perception*. Translated by Donald A. Landes. London: Routledge, 2012.

———. *The Visible and the Invisible*. Edited by Claude Lefont. Translated by Alphonso Lingis. Evanston, IL: Northwestern University Press, 1968.

Sartre, Jean-Paul. *Being and Nothingness: An Essay on Phenomenological Ontology*. Translated by Hazel E. Barnes. London: Routledge, 1958.

Falque's Physicalism and the Spiritualism of the Flesh

Phenomenology and Metaphysics[1]

William L. Connelly

I looked, and tendons and flesh appeared on them and skin covered them, but there was no spirit in them.

—Ezekiel 37:8

FLESH EXISTS AS A tissue generated from successive passages of time through vast regions of space. In this sense flesh is historical. Rendering the flesh from the point of its successive generation, we come to terms with one of its principal qualities: folded tissue. The soft tissue of flesh bears the mark, or trace, of successive states and is indicated in heritable folds of tissue. Bred within this tissue is an intelligibility which is only indirectly apparent to consciousness. In essence, flesh is the durable and intelligible content of *productive activity*. The very composition of the material element bears a specific intelligibility inherent to itself. This composition is generated through the projection of specific activities through immense stretches of time and

---

1. Portions of this essay originally appeared as Connelly, "Intelligibility of the Flesh."

space. In this sense it is spread out—intelligible within the immediacy of direct contact, and also discernible through the congenital data bred into its very constitution. This intelligibility appears according to the Spinozan teaching: "The conatus with which each single thing endeavors to persist in its own being is nothing but the actual essence of the thing itself."[2]

The flesh—or the body in general—brings together two *heterogenous* realities into a coherent unity: the formal constitution of a material nature, palpable and teeming, and also a certain depth born within it, occupied by an intelligibility only latent to consciousness. These successive states—manifest in the flesh—are not fully lived out and do not necessarily manifest themselves in conscious life; they are inherited and carry within themselves latent content which may be expressed in life. They *express* themselves in terms of a *cycloïdal ontogeny*, through successive stages and a sequence of states, and are not explicitly apparent to consciousness in either an immediate or direct way. These data, present below the level of immediately lived perception, should not be excluded from a philosophical comprehension of the world. The very activity of successive production and sequential unfurling must necessarily be taken into consideration when coming to terms with the intelligibility of the flesh, just as Leibniz asserts for the world itself: "I call 'World' the whole succession and the whole agglomeration of all existent things. . . . For they all must necessarily be reckoned together as one world or, if you will, as one Universe."[3]

Between the immediately given phenomena and its successive depth, a link can be found, and a bond may be made, serving to bridge together an embattled void within the phenomenological tradition: ontology. While the conflict between phenomenology and ontology is perhaps the founding springboard of all philosophical inquiry, bringing this dynamism into clear relief yet remains one of its most lofty tasks. Whether it be under the guise of intentionality, in the *immediate givenness* of conscious life (Husserl), or in grasping phenomena scientifically where "everything about them" is treated "by exhibiting it directly and demonstrating it directly" (Heidegger), the phenomenological tradition has fixed itself upon immediate and direct apprehension of phenomena; and here, right from the start, the *school of phenomenology* appears to occlude the indirect, the inapparent, the riddled depths—the elusive *essence* of the things themselves.[4] But how can a philosophy devoted to the description of human experience systematically neglect—or bracket—these depths?

2. Spinoza, *Spinoza*, 283.
3. Leibniz, *Theodicy*, 131.
4. Husserl, *Crisis*, 233; Heidegger, *Being and Time*, 59.

Emmanuel Falque seeks to explore these depths, even going so far as to announce a "Descent into the Abyss," as he titles the first section of his *The Wedding Feast of the Lamb* (2016). Here he first introduces the notion of *the spread body*, and it is precisely within the context of a critique of phenomenology's limits that he brings this model into expression. He asserts that the phenomenological tradition has placed too much importance upon *signifying*, leading to illusory mirages which must be evacuated in order to truly render "the darkness in humankind, made up of passions and drives."[5] This leads him to conclude, "the borders of Chaos are inaccessible through a phenomenological approach." He reaches this conclusion by identifying two misleading tendencies of the phenomenological approach, firstly, in the "constant recourse to lived experience," and secondly, "the constant recourse to the ideal of passivity as against force." These critiques serve to lay out the parameters for a paradigmatic approach, where one cannot be satisfied to understand the body either in terms of its *lived* nature or in terms of its *extension* as an object in space: "The body spread out . . . is more than the simple extension of matter (the objectivity of the body) and more than pure selfhood of the flesh (subjectivity of the flesh)."[6] Here, with the paradigm of the spread-body, Falque points towards "the Chaos that only our human biological body encounters: the animal and instinctual."[7] He warns however, that "the point is not simply to deploy some kind of physiology of passions, like a contemporary neurology—one that privileges the somatic over the psychic; it is important simply to understand, and to seek, what is at the foundation of our embodiedness"; and this leads him to continue following "a line of thought based on *the strength of the body*."[8]

Falque continues to develop this notion of the spread body while further clarifying his critique of phenomenology, first focused upon the limit of phenomenality, especially in regards to *the night of phenomenology*, when "the possibility of meaningfulness is torn asunder" and not merely in terms of this *non-appearance* as simply "the privation of a phenomenon that could or should otherwise appear" but more fundamentally as the impossibility of appearing altogether (the *extra-phenomenal*)[9]—and secondly, he builds upon this theme in terms of questioning *the apriori of phenomenolization* in phenomenology and seeks to interrogate "this never interrogated apriori of

5. Falque, *Wedding Feast*, 15.
6. Falque, *Wedding Feast*, 15.
7. Falque, *Wedding Feast*, 15.
8. Falque, *Wedding Feast*, 25, 106.
9. Falque, "Extra-Phenomenal," 11. See also *Hors phénomène*.

manifestation and its possible signification."[10] These themes coalesce in his book *Nothing to It* (2020), where he seeks to amend these limits in terms of a *backlash* (or *counterblow*) of psychoanalysis in phenomenology, which he suggests will provide a means for orienting the psychic for its "descent into the abyss."[11] This is accomplished in a return towards the unconscious of Freud—in the *Id*, and the chaos of the passions and drives—whose thought provides, ironically, a certain framework for both delineating the psychic from the somatic, placing the *Id* and its drives at the border where the psychic is anchored to the somatic, but also by recognizing that even these divisions can't stand to hold as absolute. This in turns offers a means for recovering "the power of the 'force' that constitutes us."[12] It is here in the Freudian drive that Falque finds the nexus where "rooted in a body that is not only flesh" there may be found a certain collusion with *force* that here serves to clarify the constitutive powers of the will, and how one may place the psyche in relation to it.

Embarking upon this descent into the depths, Falque becomes heir and benefactor to the legacy of Maurice Merleau-Ponty, whose unfinished master-work was fixed precisely on this lacuna in the Husserlian phenomenological paradigm, and who left behind the very chart followed by Falque. For Falque, this journey leads toward "the obscure point of what is below or beneath signification intended by the Freudian 'unconscious' and recovered in the Merleau-Pontyan 'raw nature,'" and his conclusion is that philosophers must "come back to the organic body and not be satisfied with any attempted escape from it into the psychic."[13]

While Falque continues the course set out by Merleau-Ponty, Falque minimizes the ontological elements so central to the initial endeavor. One way to understand the course being charted out is to look at perhaps the first and most complete representation of this later work, his *The Visible and the Invisible* (1961), where Merleau-Ponty frames a general critique of the Husserlian *school of phenomenology*:

> It is necessary to take up again and develop the . . . latent intentionality which is the intentionality within being. That is not compatible with "phenomenology," that is, with an ontology that obliges whatever is not nothing to present itself to the consciousness. . . . It is necessary to take as primary, not the

---

10. Falque, *Nothing to It*, 104. See also Falque's forthcoming "counterpart" of this text, "Death of God."
11. Falque, *Nothing to It*, 100.
12. Falque, *Nothing to It*, 64.
13. Falque, *Nothing to It*, 64.

consciousness . . . with its distinct intentional threads, but the vortex . . . the spatializing-temporalizing vortex (which is flesh and not consciousness facing a noema).[14]

Falque's decision to approach this critique from the camp of the *masters of suspicion* (Nietzsche, Freud, Marx)[15] certainly has its value, though it also has a certain limitation. Falque finds in Merleau-Ponty a route to identify "a new mode of phenomenality, or rather another manner of describing our darkness."[16] While Falque certainly has justification in taking this task, and following the course set out by Merleau-Ponty in regards to a certain *depth psychology*, or a *phenomenology of the underground*, there is a certain tendency in his thinking which rejects the ontological impetus which had driven much of Merleau-Ponty's final endeavor. In radicalizing the Freudian aspect of Merleau-Ponty's thought (and injecting a strong Nietzschean element), he seems to overlook if not detract its ontological character. In one way Falque could be critiqued for a certain *romanticism of the flesh* where he subtracts its ontological character while leading towards a conception of flesh as statically opposed to the psychic, in this case stripping it of any inherent intelligibility while substantializing within the flesh a perpetual chaos and spontaneity without any subsisting order or structure. What remains is to more clearly describe how the intelligible nature of the flesh may be signified without idealization, and also to better describe the relation between the fundamental intelligibility of the flesh with human consciousness. It does not follow that just because the body is itself unconscious that it lacks an intelligibility; and further, the unconscious nature of the body would in no way negate any structural or organizing principle within it (even if operative at an unconscious level), which Falque's treatment of the body would seem to suggest.

These tendencies within Falque's treatment of the flesh—here characterized as a certain *romanticization*—are hedged against in his essay "In Flesh and Bones," where he introduces the concept of the *corps praxique*, in the turn towards the *real* or *effective* (*wirklich*) world, and the effort to "rediscover the objective" by means of praxis.[17] This is a necessary turn to make in order to escape the antagonism towards intelligibility which his thought tends to take. This is also a promising aspect to develop in light of

---

14. Merleau-Ponty, "Note from April, 1960," in *Visible and the Invisible*, 244. See also my own response to this question, "At the Confluence," 75.

15. Here Falque also takes a lead from Paul Ricoeur with his *école du soupçon*, as described in his *Freud and Philosophy*.

16. Falque, "Spiritualisme incarné," 228.

17. Falque, "In Flesh and Bones," 23–24.

his notion of *the ethics* of the spread body, particularly if it could be brought into conjunction with the research on "the facility of mystical theology" in his treatment of the *praxis experimentalis* involved in the *aesthetic operation* where "the mystical takes over from the theological, the theological from the philosophical, the philosophical from the mathematical."[18] Much progress could be made if this chain could be developed in light of the intelligibility of the flesh, where the material subsistence of the body (or bodies in general), can be viewed in terms of common structural patterns of organization rooted in mathematics, or intelligible forms, accessible and effective upon embodied life. The formal distinctions Falque makes between the psychic and the somatic are helpful, but only insofar as they show the fundamental integrity of composed beings; it seems worthwhile to try and link this chain, brought out in the context of *effective practice*, with his notion of the *spread body* particularly when expressed in the following terms:

> I am being held and maintained in life via "organic forces within me" that make me and render me alive, neither only via my matter or my *hylē* nor exclusively via my spirit or my *psychē* but via a "body" or a *soma* through which the whole of myself is expressed and hence also generated.[19]

I would contend that such a maneuver must also lead to a more fundamental *backlash* to the traditions of French spiritualism, one of whose primary concerns could be considered the very question of *force*.[20] Here, phenomenology finds itself overcome by such figures as Henri Bergson, Maurice Blondel, Felix Ravaisson, Maine de Biran, et. al., and here, perhaps finally, with the traditions of Neoplatonism. Falque recognizes the contribution of a number of these figures in some ways,[21] but his emphasis upon the school of suspicion (*l'école du soupçon*) seems to preclude their contributions. It must be said that the full thrust of Merleau-Ponty's later thought is more in the direction of Blondel's ontology and Henri Bergson's vitalism, than in the radicalization of Nietzsche's, or even Freud's, thought, to which Falque seems so fully committed in seeking out "*strategies to recover* chaos."[22] One missed opportunity in this drive towards the unconscious depths is in the clarification of the intelligible nature of the flesh, here brought out in the challenge this tradition of French spiritualism poses to philosophy, and

---

18. Falque, "All-Seeing," 765, 782, 784.
19. Falque, "Toward an Ethics," 101–2.
20. Janicaud, *Généalogie du Spiritualisme*, 6.
21. See Falque *Loving Struggle*, 49; Vieillard-Baron, *Supplément d'âme*.
22. Falque, "Extra-Phenomenal," 17.

which seems so necessary at this precise moment in time, the recovery of a certain *supplement for the soul*:

> The soul supplement is called by Bergson as a precise requirement for the modern industrial society. Technical progress has disproportionately increased the material capacities of modern man. . . . Consequently, if we do not want technical progress to serve only those men who are able to implement advanced scientific approaches and increase the difference between rich states and poor peoples, a counterweight is necessary: it is the "supplement of the soul" in the sense Bergson speaks of. In order to solve the problems of growth, there must be an ethical reference, a concern for justice, a spiritual impetus. Bergson wrote in 1932.[23]

Such models as the spread body can meaningfully contribute to this question, but this model needs to broaden its scope to be able to render a clear description of the *intelligibility of the flesh*, so as to clarify the dynamics and activities involved in the operations of the flesh, their relation to human cognition, and how they all relate to patterns of human behavior. One way to broaden this perspective is to reference another aspect of Falque's work in regard to the flesh, this time with his critique of *angelism*.

On the Relationship of the Spiritual and Physical in Man

Falque often employs the conceit of the docetic heresy that Christ's physical body was merely an illusion, and which denies the true flesh and blood incarnation of the Christ-Deity. This is used to illustrate a philosophical and spiritual point: there is no spirituality without the body, and that in fact it is a flat-out heresy to suggest as much. Theologically the point is obvious, however philosophically this point is taken up with more nuance and sophistication. Criticizing a philosophy of the lived body (Husserl) that fails to account for the extended body (Descartes), Falque issues just as stern a rebuke against any phenomenology that neglects the concerns of the flesh. But what does this mean? The point is clear enough when referring to the touching-touched, where the perception of the flesh being touched is simultaneously met with the act of another flesh extending a touch—a double movement of being touched, and of touching. Or in other words, an overlapping duality where neither "the 'sensing body' (phenomenal body), nor the 'sensed body' (objective body) constitutes the experience of the

---

23. Vieillard-Baron, "Introduction," in *Supplément d'âme*, 7–8.

body as such."[24] This *gap* (*écart*) is another phenomenological gorge eroded away with floods of ink, but is this landscape of any *non*-phenomenological interest? With Falque's notion of the *spread body*, we can begin to see the contours of a noteworthy landmark emerge. Here Falque conceives the flesh as both living *and* extended—both animate with life and breath, but also corporal and fleshly, even *meaty*. But, philosophically speaking, this intellectual geography has only been charted out, by Falque, in regard to *the depths* or again the *chaos of passions and drives* of *the body* of the *slab of meat* with *theology* doing all the work for making sense of the higher faculties of the *moral* and *metaphysical* dimensions of the human being—with the *transformation* of the body being accomplished by a *theology* from on high. Falque's discussion of spiritualism lacks the centering focus upon just this: *the moral* and the *metaphysical* aspects of the human being, or in other words: *the spiritual*.[25]

Falque goes to great lengths in hammering away the materiality of the body—warranting indeed a characteristic or even *distinctive physicalism*.[26] But does this distinct physicalism run its own heretical risks? With Falque's constant recourse to the *chaos of the passions and drive* (Nietzsche), of *the philosophy of the underground* or the *Id*, the *cauldron of seething desires* (Freud), are we not led astray to the extreme of another equally offensive *Ebionism*, which would—in philosophy—neglect the *spiritual*, the *moral*, even the *metaphysical* dimensions of the human being? Does not the critique of docetism on philosophical grounds justify a similar philosophical critique of the otherwise theological position of the *Ebionites*, who held that Jesus was a purely human figure, and that conformity to the law—or mere physical principles—was sufficient for salvation, i.e., circumcision, dietary laws, and Sabbath observance? Of course, we cannot claim this as a serious position, but Falque's line of argumentation is open to a counter-attack against the similarly veined heresy of the Ebionites. Doesn't Falque's physicalism tend towards a certain neglect of an equally weighted spiritualism?

This position can be deepened with Falque's continued advance against *angelism* or a certain theological or medieval tendency of *flight from the sensible* where the *angelic* is overemphasized at the expense of the *material*. Is there not an equally repugnant *flight from the spiritual*?[27] It is innovative and noteworthy for Falque to employ these theological currents to triumph phenomenology's *overcoming of metaphysics by the analytic of*

---

24. Falque, *God, the Flesh, and the Other*, 195.
25. See, for instance, Falque, *Spiritualisme et Phénoménologie*.
26. Davenport, "Falque's Fraternal Finitude," 49.
27. Falque, *God, the Flesh, and the Other*, 195.

the flesh but all the same it remains one-sided and lacking when seeking to find a *philosophical* analytic of the spirit, or a *philosophical* recovery of metaphysics. Now of course we can't criticize Falque for going in the opposite direction, as he clearly charted his course and laid out an intricate map of the opposing terrain, however, any serious development of the *concept* of the spread body would require just the same upon the other side of the gorge. Indeed, if this were to be the *doctrine* of Falque, it would require more substance to show the mutual dynamism and interface between the spiritual and physical in man, and not just a philosophical physicalism and a theologically materialist spiritualism; but rather, a theological materialism and philosophical spiritualism. In other words, it seems that Falque would benefit from treating theology from a non-confessional materialist position, and lead philosophy towards a rigorous spiritualism (confirmed by a sincere religious conviction) but with constant reference to the *forms* of religious life and how they relate to the *appearance* of religious consciousness. We of course already have this with his engagement of Nicolas of Cusa, thus proving the fertility of the point, but this would require a whole new conceptual phase, or orientation, away from the materialist traps of the *masters of suspicion* and towards the equally tendentious and modern philosophical tradition of those *masters of sympathy* such as Biran, Blondel, and even Bergson—here picking up upon the tradition of French spiritualism as handed down from Ravaisson (that he received from Biran via Cousin) to Lachelier, and from Lachelier to Blondel and Bergson.[28]

Greater attentiveness to this French philosophical tradition would help pave the way for a truly substantive and robust treatment of the spread body—where a *spatial* extension of the body is understood in concert with the *interior* extension of the *psyche*; and the living organism of the flesh is understood with reference to its inherent ontology—but here not a reductive spatial-temporalizing metaphysics (of the existential finitude), but rather one of virtuality and creativity (of the *cycloïdal ontogeny* infinite)—where the synergy of parts is emphasized over their separation. Here the concepts of *interior observation* and *psychological induction* become capital—making *reflexivity* the *method* for coordinating psychology and metaphysics; in turn redeeming metaphysics from its death absent psychology (psychologism) by recognizing that the true nature of pure thought "is an idea which is produced of itself and whose real nature we are unable to grasp except by *reproducing* it by a process of *a priori* construction or synthesis."[29] This makes

28. See how these themes are explored in my own work, Connelly, "Ritual and Thought." See also §7, "From Ideology to Spiritualism—Maine de Biran: The Primacy of Reflexive Analysis," in my doctoral thesis, "Unity of Thought."

29. Lachelier, "Psychology and Metaphysics," 88.

the metaphysical method of *reflexivity* the equal to the phenomenological method of the *reduction*. In this way, "the movement from analysis to synthesis is at the same time a movement from psychology to metaphysics."[30]

Franciscan Theophany and the Evolution of Philosophy of Religion

Regarding the proposed "rigorous spiritualism confirmed by a sincere religious conviction" I believe that attention to Falque's engagement with, and connection to, *the theophanic process*, provides genuine insight into the heart of Falque's work, both as it stands and where it might lead (perhaps most importantly as a doctrinal legacy of perennial value). First, we can all recognize that Falque's corpus has already influenced a generation of scholars, both philosophers and theologians, believers and unbelievers, helping them to make sense of a rapidly maturing and declining modernity, or postmodernity, that has led to where we are now, with multiple hazy and embattled horizons in the offing—a far cry from the naïve triumphalisms of the Enlightenment, making its *adult* reasoning seem like more that of an *infant*.[31] The return *to* religion, or the return *of* religion, is a phenomenon of

---

30. It seems here that the French phenomenological focus upon the description of experience takes precedence over the conditions of experience, thus neglecting the fully transcendental character of Husserl's phenomenological project. See, for instance, the insightful account of Mark Novak in his doctoral thesis, which incisively places Falque as primarily doing "descriptive phenomenology," whereas Henry analyzes "the conditions of appearing as such, and the nature of the human being in relation to this." While Novak is careful to identify how Falque does not "completely [focus] on what appears rather than how it appears," he is prudent and right to indicate how Falque is more interested in "discrete phenomena rather than their appearing as such" (Novak, "Saving Flesh," 258). Greater recovery of this transcendental aspect of phenomenology would help in building out the concept, or doctrine, of the spread body.

31. Curiously, Falque has neither been recognized nor honored with any distinction within the official philosophical establishment in France, as coronated by the Institut de France, which has not failed to continue delivering many prizes and awards on a regular basis. A marginal point to Falque himself, and almost embarrassing to bring up, as such distinctions are at best ceremonial, and at worst, careerist and institutional. Nevertheless, it is hard to fathom the absence of recognition for even one of its distinctions, given his genuine contribution to the culture of France, both internally, but also and especially abroad, with the abiding interest and relevance, if not excellence, of his work. To honor such work with ceremony is indeed an honor, and its glory is unassailable. Such an observation is grounded upon a larger critique of the prevailing philosophical environment (especially in France)—that Falque is certainly not immune to—which could be viewed in terms of a post-Deleuzian constitution of philosophy as the act of "creating concepts." The ambition for crafting a technically sound and socially tasteful "concept" for public display is certainly alluring and has its appeal,

our epoch, which is only slowly coming into clear relief—and whether it be in the rise of the religious revolutionaries in Iran, or the fall of atheist Soviet technocrats, or the emergence of new age spiritualities and the renewal of Roman Catholic orthodoxies, the question now becomes as focused as ever: How are we to manage our (humanity's) religious inheritance? What is the *significance* of religion in modern history, of religion in ancient history, of our presents and our futures? The question couldn't be more pressing. No longer a naïve question of belief or unbelief, of assent or rejection, the question of religion now has become one not only of *meaning*, and of *making sense*, and not only of just what exactly this *reality* labeled *religious* actually means, but also how it functions, how it is lived out, how its contents play out before our eyes in our minds and in our life, and how these experiences shape our lives, and the manner in which it survives, thrives, or declines. Here the topic of *place* is central, as where is one speaking from, from a position of culture, of heritage or family, of aesthetics, of metaphysics or of morals, of interloping intellectual interest, or of deep profound inner conviction, of personal insight or wisdom, or just simply from experience, the *place* of one's interest is often the deciding factor of its value—whether tacitly or not.

In the case of Falque, we know that his interest in religion comes from his own *theophany*—where he beheld the appearance of Christ to him—which transformed his life and set him on a course *with* God. This is a peculiar aspect of his person and his work which should now become a topic of interest, as he has shared his experience—first to a group of us at Port Royal in 2021, and secondly to a group of us in the foothills of Assisi in 2024.[32] I noted down on June 23, 2019, how "Emmanuel Falque shared a story with us today at the Abbey of Port Royale." He said that when he was young, he got in a fight with his brother who punched him in his face. He found a

---

and while the "creation of concepts" is indeed, and obviously, an essential element of philosophy, there is the risk of sterility, even *conceitedness*, in beginning and ending the philosophical endeavor—even qualifying it—upon the production of a concept. This amounts to a certain postmodern philosophical vacuousness, as the true and perennial task of philosophy emerges in *thoughtful ways of living and thinking* (Hadot), and manifests certainly in *essays* and in *speculation*, but above all else philosophy defines itself in terms of *doctrines*, and such doctrines are always and uniquely attached to the individual, but not as a concept, hypothesis, or idea, but rather an enduring *doctrine*. See for example Ollé-Laprune, *Philosophie*, 121–39. See also Blondel's account of his own "master's" philosophy, *Léon Ollé-Laprune*. As for the reach and appeal of his work, see Deketelaere, *Emmanuel Falque Reader*.

32. Since 2017, I have had the honor of working closely with Professor Falque, completing my PhD under his supervision and serving as secretary, alongside Domenico Cambria, for the International Network in Philosophy of Religion (INPR), which he founded and has led since 2015.

map and decided to go to the abbey of Port Royal to go speak to the monks. He rode his motorcycle there at night, in poor conditions, under the rain, and found that there were no longer any monks living there, but that there were some monks twenty kilometers away. He went there to find them, and then met with one out of the group who took him to a nice restaurant to talk about the situation. They decided for him to go to Assisi as a pilgrim. Upon going there, he rested his head in fatigue and then suddenly Christ appeared to him. From that moment everything changed for him. He then went around speaking to people about God. In the recent summer of 2024 in Assisi, he shared the same story to a group of around fifty of us and shared how it happened in the Basilica of St. Clair in front of San Damiano's Cross, which we all went to and visited together. The story continues and there are other colorful details, but the point here is to place this as an important element for understanding Falque, not only as a person, but also as a scholar.

In Falque's work we find a philosophical *tour de force* through the theological inheritance of the West, bosomed up upon the breast of the church's eldest daughter (France), where the pathos of a deep and abiding religious cultural inheritance exists as a rather clearly defined landscape—of as much cultural as religious value. This is to say that the Christianity of Falque is that of France, which is to say of an ancient and traditional variety so deep and so embedded that its embrace surpasses one's personal belief or acceptance, but not in a subterranean way (as largely in the United States), but in an immediate and pervasive way, shaping everything from the language and the institutions, to the streets and schools, even corner bakeries. In this way confessional, explicit and overt confessional theology is a ready given, and in Falque's work we find this same standard presence of religious reality as if *Eucharist* and *Holy Saturday* were natural givens like *sun* and *moon*, but such confessional theology is only intelligible to a shrinking minority of the global commons, and at the risk of *preaching to the choir* this French approach perhaps assumes too much while giving too little.

I think in this way Calvin Ullrich's point is made with great perspicacity, where he remarks that Falque's confessional commitment leads to a certain enigma where "the animality and organicity of the spread body" is undermined by a theological given which is never adequately explained or rendered intelligible outside of a confessional conceptual framework; here we are led to certain unanswered questions, specifically the *how* of any such spiritual transformation. This is perhaps, and probably, even obviously, not the work of Falque to do, but rather is up to those of us capable of seeding the fields pierced open by Falque's spade.[33]

---

33. Ullrich, "Spread Body," 10.

Nevertheless, this open and explicit inheritance represents a cultural legacy that speaks to much more than any local Christianity, but in fact resonates to the depth of Western culture, even humanity, and the facility to speak it out and frame human experience in terms of these religious forms presents a noteworthy and commendable achievement—particularly given the interest in Falque's work among non-Catholics, even non-believers. Nevertheless, there is a genuine danger of presuming a theological given which can automatically fill in and account for this or that philosophical or human existential. While it is not entirely true that Falque relies too much on theology, as he sometimes, even often, finds more in Heidegger or Merleau-Ponty than in the annals of Western theology, his work nevertheless assumes a theological background, and this background always stands as a normative spiritual given. This spiritual backdrop is also theologically given, enabling Falque to push a materialist philosophical *physicalism*, which is, again, enabled by a theologically materialist-spiritualism; with the *flesh* of Christ as the means of salvation (Tertullian), and here in his critique of docetism, there is the tacit recognition of the *synergy* between the divine and human natures of Christ, but he seems to instrumentalize a materialist theology that minimizes the spiritual aspects that it depends upon. In this way, it seems that a certain gnostic (Clement of Alexandria) or pneumatic (St. Paul) approach is appropriate to develop as an emendation to correct this imbalance.

Falque's philosophical physicalism is at once *non-confessional* but only as party to a religious assent of an inherent theological spirituality (personal theophany). His position does not account in any significant way for the inverse of the equation that he sets up and upon which his philosophy of the flesh is founded (*contra* docetism). A balanced and complete development of the philosophical paradigm would benefit from inverting his typical position: starting from a more truly material theology (not based upon a needed though hidden spirituality), and a spiritualist philosophy whose spirituality is affirmed, explicated, and understood, without recourse to any necessary theological confession. This does not suggest that the confession of one's own theology is to be cast away, hidden, or misplaced, but rather that, like the mustard seed, beginning small and inconspicuous, it can grow into a tree where birds can find shelter and rest.

Bibliography

Blondel, Maurice. *Léon Ollé-Laprune: L'achèvement et l'avenir de son oeuvre*. Paris: Bloud et Gay, 1923.
Connelly, William L. "At the Confluence of Phenomenology and Non-Phenomenology: Maurice Blondel and Emmanuel Falque." In *Transforming the Theological Turn:*

Phenomenology with Emmanuel Falque, edited by Martin Koci and Jason W. Alvis, 75–92. Lanham, MD: Rowman and Littlefield, 2020.

———. "The Intelligibility of the Flesh: A Response to Emmanuel Falque." *Crossing: The INPR Journal* 1 (2020) 155–62.

———. "Ritual and Thought: Spirituality and Method in Philosophy of Religion." *Religions* 1045.12 (2021) 1–36.

———. "The Unity of Thought: A Genealogy of Maurice Blondel's Spiritual Realism." PhD diss., Institut Catholique de Paris/Australian Catholic University, Melbourne, 2022.

Davenport, Anne. "Falque's Fraternal Finitude." *Research in Phenomenology* 49.2 (2019) 264–80.

Deketelaere, Nikolaas, ed. *The Emmanuel Falque Reader*. Key Writings in Phenomenology and Continental Philosophy of Religion. London: Bloomsbury Publishing, 2024.

Falque, Emmanuel. "The All-Seeing: Fraternity and Vision of God in Nicholas of Cusa." *Modern Theology* 35.4 (2019) 760–87.

———. "The Death of God and the Death of Man: Along the Guiding Thread of the Body." Translated by William L. Connelly. In *The Unthinkable Body*, edited by Rebeka A. Klein and Calvin D. Ullrich, 19–42. Tübingen: Mohr Siebeck, 2024.

———. "The Extra-Phenomenal." *Diakrisis Yearbook of Theology and Philosophy* 1.1 (2018) 9–28.

———. *God, the Flesh, and the Other: From Irenaeus to Duns Scotus*. Translated by William Christian Hackett. Evanston, IL: Northwestern University Press, 2015.

———. *Hors phénomène: Essai aux confins de la phénoménalité*. Paris: Hermann, 2021.

———. "In Flesh and Bones." *Crossing: The INPR Journal* 1 (2020) 5–27.

———. *The Loving Struggle: Phenomenological and Theological Debates*. Translated by Bradley B. Onishi and Lucas McCracken. Lanham, MD: Rowman & Littlefield, 2018.

———. *Nothing to It: Reading Freud as a Philosopher*. Translated by Robert Vallier and William L. Connelly. Leuven: Leuven University Press, 2020.

———. *Spiritualisme et Phénoménologie: Le "cas" Maine de Biran*. Chaire Etienne Gilson. Paris: Presses Universitaires de France, 2024.

———. "Le 'spiritualisme incarné' de Maurice Merleau-Ponty." In *Le supplément d'âme ou le renouveau du spiritualisme*, edited by Jean-Louis Vieillard-Baron, 221–47. De Visu. Paris: Hermann, 2016.

———. "Toward an Ethics of the Spread Body." In *Somatic Desire: Recovering Corporeality in Contemporary Thought*, edited by Sarah Horton et al., 91–116. New York: Lexington, 2019.

———. *The Wedding Feast of the Lamb: Eros, the Body, and the Eucharist*. Translated by George Hughes. New York: Fordham University Press, 2016.

Heidegger, Martin. *Being and Time*. Translated by John Macquarrie and Edward S. Robinson. Oxford: Blackwell, 1967.

Horton, Sarah, et al., eds. *Somatic Desire: Recovering Corporeality in Contemporary Thought*. Lanham, MD: Lexington, 2019.

Husserl, Edmund. *The Crisis of European Sciences and Transcendental Phenomenology: An Introduction to Phenomenological Philosophy*. Evanston, IL: Northwestern University Press, 1970.

Janicaud, Dominique. *Une généalogie du spiritualisme français.* La Haye: M. Nijhoff, 1969.

Koci, Martin, and Jason W. Alvis, eds. *Transforming the Theological Turn: Phenomenology with Emmanuel Falque.* Lanham, MD: Rowman & Littlefield, 2020.

Lachelier, Jules. "Psychology and Metaphysics (1885)." Translated by Edward G. Ballard. In *The Philosophy of Jules Lachelier*, edited by Edward G. Ballard, 57–96. Dordecht: Springer Science, 1960.

Leibniz, Gottfried Wilhelm. *Theodicy.* Translated by E. M. Huggard. Charleston, SC: Bibliobazaar, 2007.

Merleau-Ponty, Maurice. *The Visible and the Invisible; Followed by Working Notes.* Translated by Alphonso Lingis. Evanston, IL: Northwestern University Press, 1968.

Novak, Mark Fraser. "Saving Flesh, Redeeming Body: Phenomenologies of Incarnation and Resurrection in the Thought of Michel Henry and Emmanuel Falque." PhD diss., McMaster University, 2021.

Ollé-Laprune, Léon. *La philosophie et le temps présent.* Paris: Belin Frères, Libraires-Éditeurs, 1898.

Ricoeur, Paul. *Freud and Philosophy: An Essay on Interpretation.* Translated by Denis Savage. New Haven: Yale University Press, 1970.

Spinoza, Baruch. *Spinoza: Complete Works.* Translated by Samuel Shirley. Cambridge: Hackett, 2002.

Ullrich, Calvin D. "The Spread Body and the Affective Body: A Discussion with Emmanuel Falque." *Religions* 15.1 (2024) 30. https://doi.org/10.3390/rel15010030.

Vieillard-Baron, Jean-Louis. *Le supplément d'âme ou le renouveau du spiritualisme.* De Visu. Paris: Hermann, 2016.

Dwelling and Resistance

Embracing Our Animality Through Wind and Breath

Revisiting Anaximenes's Err in Augustine's Confessions

Donald Boyce

As our soul being air, holds us together, so breath (πνεῦμα) and air enclose the whole world.

—Anaximenes[1]

THERE IS A TENSION in the work of Emmanuel Falque. On the one hand there is that which speech cannot say,[2] but on the other hand there is a great call *to speak*. To speak in order to think,[3] but also, as the title of this text bears, *to die of not writing*. It is as if Falque, when it comes to the unspeakable Chaos, passions, and drives of our soul, says with the fourth-century North African St. Augustine to God, "I am earth and ashes

---

1. Fragment from *Aet. Plac.* 1.3 *Dox.* 278 (DK Fragment B2).
2. Falque, *Guide to Gethsemane*, 97–113.
3. Heidegger, "Seminar du Thor." This serves as one of the guiding principles at Falque's (he will have to forgive my use of the genitive) International Network of Philosophy of Religion (INPR) conferences.

but let me speak!"[4] Falque's method of going to the "limit of the phenomenon" gives "more weight to a 'philosophy of the organic,' one that does not forget or neglect our own proper animality."[5] While the method risks a kind of phenomenological heresy since it attends to the *extra-phenomena* (*hors phénomène*), it is a method I will follow in the analysis of *breath as an example of the way God inhabits our animality*.[6] Breath is how God sustains us even when we are *outside ourselves*—our thoughts so externalized that we can't even be with ourselves, let alone with God.[7] As Augustine says, God is actually "more inward than my innermost self (*Deus interior intimo meo*)."[8] The importance of breath is one Augustine attests to in *Confessions* and one that sits squarely in Falque's belief that God inhabits and transforms our animality. Yes, God is in our bodies as we are in his in the Eucharist (*The Wedding Feast of the Lamb*), but there is also a prevenient grace at work— one where God is always, already there as breath or air. Far from a *saturated phenomena*, breath is the quintessential example of a *limited phenomena* in Falque.

We must be careful however, for "by dint of speaking of the bodily unconscious, one can in fact silence through excess of consciousness that which lives in its own way.... We must be very careful not to subsume it into something else, in case we destroy through consciousness that body-to-body in which we are engaged."[9] While I will try to speak air or breath in order to think it, it is important to remember that "speech backs up the

---

4. Augustine, *Confessions* 1.6.7.

5. Falque, *Wedding Feast*, 1–4.

6. I use "extra-phenomena" here for the sake of consistency with the English translation of Falque's text, but I agree deeply with Sarah Horton's excellent footnote and argument for the use of "the-Outside-the-phenomena" in her chapter in this text.

7. See, for example, when Augustine asks how he could ask God to come into him, when if God were not already there Augustine would not "be" at all (*Confessions* 1.2.2) or the famous passage: "Late have I loved you, beauty so ancient and so new! Late have I loved you! And behold, you were within, but I was outside and looked for you there, and in my ugliness, I seized upon these beautiful things that you have made. *You were with me, but I was not with you*" (10.27.38).

8. *Deus interior intimo meo* (Augustine, *Confessions* 3.6.11) was the topic of the 2023 INPR conference in Los Angeles. I originally gave my energy or effort to thought on breath for a paper there. This paper was largely inspired by Karl Hefty's paper, "Soul or Life: Contours of a Forgotten Indecision," which he gave at the 2023 INPR conference in Montreal where the topic was "Forgetting the Soul." It is impossible to trace the legacy and richness of these conferences within the philosophical and theological world and I am deeply grateful for Falque to have lent his "force" to them over the last nine years.

9. Falque, *Wedding Feast*, 108.

flesh, but can never substitute for it."[10] The beauty of Emmanuel Falque is that one cannot swallow his work whole. More often than not, his work actually swallows the reader. One can find oneself chewing on Falque's sentences for months, if not years, before coming to grips with them. Maybe this difficulty is part of the appeal. Maybe it is simply because his texts find a way of speaking to something even more foundational and fundamental than our intellect—they don't speak, *but seep* into our bodies. No one is better at catching the reader with a stray phrase—laying the reader out on their back with the profundity and weight of their thought. And despite the heaviness of his thought, if you were in-person with Falque, he would put his arm around you with levity and a laugh, *well*, he would say smiling, as a warm invitation to conversation. An invitation *to speak in order to think*.

The idea of wind or breath—both πνεῦμα in Greek, which importantly can also mean spirit or soul—represents one of the most lived examples of *Deus interior intimo meo*. One that is true because God, whom we are late to, is always already *in* our bodies as the life of those bodies. It is one that fits squarely in the second creation account of Genesis where God breathes into Adam's nostrils the "breath of life" (Gen 2:7) as well as when God animates his church on Pentecost with his Spirit that comes like the "rush of a violent wind" (Acts 2:2). The concept is also already in Falque, though he chooses to focus his analysis on the body's experience of suffering and our integration into God in the *this is my body* of the Eucharist. In speaking of our animality that grounds us in and with God's creation, Falque looks first *to breath*. He says,

> Accius, a near-contemporary of Christ (first century before Christ), thus sees in the *animus* an essence of life (breath) in the same way that the Jewish tradition sees in Adam the figure of an "earthly one" (*adâmah*) in which the breath of life (*neshama*) is blown through the nostrils. "The Lord God formed man from the dust of the ground, and breathed into his nostrils the breath of life; and the man became a living being." (Gen 2:7). The "rite of breath" makes life, as Marcel Jousse tells us, and restores us to life. The theology of the breath (life) responds to

---

10. Falque, *Wedding Feast*, 63. "We speak, above all, by our bodies—indeed, more than by language—and that is what the eucharistic Last Supper in its celebration must not forget. A silence of the flesh is what is necessary, or at least expected, so that the surplus of speech does not cover what the body, by itself, has already known how to say better or say otherwise (§32). As the theologian Hans-Urs von Balthasar so rightly points out, 'The Eucharist, in particular, is the adaptation of our being to God by the descent of the Word *into our senses*, indeed, into our substance, which is something even *below the senses*. Not only does Spirit speak to spirit, but *Flesh speaks to flesh*'" (Falque, *Wedding Feast*, 129).

the anthropology of the dust (body)—instead of the substance of thought (soul) responding to the extension of a machine (body).[11]

It is my hope to pursue this *theology of life*, described here by Falque as a theology of breath. This breath is life-in-us prior to our *being there* (Heidegger) and even prior to our flesh (Henry, but also Marion, especially in *On Descartes' Passive Thought: The Myth of Cartesian Dualism*)—perhaps it is even God-in-us that we are always late to.

The search for beginning, origin, authority (ἀρχή) characterizes all philosophy. Augustine is a great conversation partner because he sits at the crossroads of Greek philosophy and Christianity. Since both a historical-philosophical and theological-biblical exploration of wind, breath, and air is beyond the scope of this chapter, I will focus on the exploration of God as *air* in Augustine's *Confessions*.[12] I do this because Augustine explicitly rejects this idea as it is described in Anaximenes, but also because, despite this, Augustine's auto, or hetero-biographical text—especially when we read breath as *speech*—bears witness to its truth.[13]

---

11. Falque, *Wedding Feast*, 75. "Or, as we have already seen (§5), if the breath [of God] is the same as the breath that gives life to all living creatures, and thus inscribes us biblically in the great sphere of animality, the dust or the clay is of a similar nature, or of the same texture: the clay with which 'the Lord God formed man from the dust of the ground' (Gen 2:7). The identity of the breath and of the clay does not take us beyond animality, as though Adam and Eve (Semitic tradition), or the rational human being (Greek tradition), had first been thought of independently from animals and their own animality. On the contrary, it brings us back to a common base, something we may see differently and from which we may eventually depart, but without ever denying this community of the psuchê. . . . The *anima*-lity in us is not an accident of our constitution that can be forgotten or that is simply overcome. We find this from the start in the Indo-European culture (*anima* and *animus*), as at the origin of Semitic culture (the clay and the breath)" (Falque, *Wedding Feast*, 77).

12. Alfred North Whitehead famously says that "the safest general characterization of the European philosophical tradition is that it consists of a series of footnotes on Plato" (*Process and Reality*, 39). I think it's just as accurate to say that the European philosophical tradition—especially the Catholic one to which Emmanuel Falque is party—consists of various debates around St. Augustine. If Augustine is a footnote on Plato, the entire gravity of Augustine's footnote shifts the conversation around his own concerns and questions. Instead of hiding this, I will say outright that this (i.e., thinking with and arguing over Augustine) is often an entire form of discourse in this field of philosophy.

13. "In short, it [*Confessions*] is not an *auto*- but a *hetero-biography*, my life told by me and especially to me from the point of view of an other, from close to the privileged other, God" (Marion, *In the Self's Place*, 45).

Recovering Anaximenes's Air as Breath, Soul, and Origin-of-Appearance

Given the above, one might think air/wind/breath is the perfect candidate for the saint who advocates incessantly for a return to the self—despite the pain and difficulty of such a turn. Augustine however, perhaps influenced by more materialistic (Aristotelian and Stoic) readings of the Presocratic philosophers, draws a firm line. He says clearly in *Confessions*, "*Anaximenes was wrong—wind is not God.*" Augustine is critical of Anaximenes three times in his corpus, once in *Confessions* (10.6.9), once in *City of God* (8.2), and once in a letter to Dioscorus (*Letter* 118). In *Confessions*, the prodigal son text-of-returns, we find the mention of Anaximenes in the middle of Augustine's intellectual ascent to God in book 10.

> I asked the sea and the depths and the creeping things with living souls, and they replied, "We are not your God; seek him above us." *I asked the blowing winds, and all the air with its inhabitants said, "Anaximenes was wrong; I am not God."* I asked the sky, the sun, the moon, the stars: "neither are we the God whom you are seeking," they said. And I said to all these things that surround the gateways of my flesh, "Tell me about my God—the God who you are not—tell me something about him." And they cried out with a loud voice, "He is the one who made us." My scrutiny of them posed the question; their beauty answered it.[14]

My hypothesis here is that at least part of the reason Augustine does not explore *wind* further as ἀρχή is because Augustine is reading Anaximenes through what has been called a "vague and inaccurate paraphrase" of Anaximenes by Cicero in *The Nature of the Gods* (1.26) and *On Academic Skepticism* (2.37.118).[15] However, in the oldest fragment of Anaximenes, the only one commonly accepted to be a direct quote,[16] Anaximenes connects ἀήρ with πνεῦμα. He says, "As our soul being air, holds us together, so do wind [or breath!] and air enclose the whole cosmos [οἷον ἡ ψυχὴ ἡ ἡμετέρα ἀὴρ οὖσα

---

14. Augustine, *Confessions* 10.6.9 (italics mine).

15. Kirk and Raven, *Presocratic Philosophers*, 147. While it is possible for there to be other sources for Augustine's knowledge of Anaximenes, we assume this to be the only one due to Augustine's reply to Dioscorus in *Letter* 118 in 411 which cites Cicero's texts concerning Anaximenes roughly ten years after *Confessions* is written. Augustine's interpretation of Anaximenes remains largely unchanged by 426 in the *City of God* where he says, "He left his pupil Anaximenes as his successor, who ascribed all the causes of things to the infinite air. Anaximenes did not deny the gods, nor did he keep silent about them. He did not believe, however, that they created the air but rather that they themselves originated from air" (8.2).

16. Kirk and Raven, *Presocratic Philosophers*, 149; Sallis, *Figure of Nature*, 22.

συγκρατεῖ ἡμᾶς, καὶ ὅλον τὸν κόσμον πνεῦμα καὶ ἀὴρ περιέχει]."[17] In Cicero's Latin paraphrases however, we only get *aera* rather than *spiritus, anima*, or *suspiria*.[18] There are other fragments of Anaximenes that Augustine could have had access to besides Cicero's (e.g., Hippolytus, who we know is cited heavily by Ambrose, in his *Refutation of Heresies* 1.7.4–6), but in each case, there is no mention of πνεῦμα (wind, breath, soul).[19] Anaximenes's ἀρχή is therefore only picked up by Augustine in its more literal form in book 10 of *Confessions* as *auras flabiles* or blowing winds.[20]

In this sense we might imagine Augustine saying with the biblical author in 1 Kgs 19:11 that God *did not* appear to Elijah *in the wind*. However, it seems likely that Augustine's denial of *God in the wind* might be more the result of his Platonic conversion—one that helps him overcome his constant tendency to *imagine* God.[21] In both the Septuagint and Jerome's Vulgate, the point (even more than the English) seems to be that God did not come in the great or loud spirit, or air, but in the thin or quiet air (i.e., the *whisper* as it is often translated in English). This theophanic moment in the Old Testament is one that reveals Christ. God does not come as a big-spirited loudmouth, but as the gentle, quiet spirit—*as the soft whisper of the breeze*. In the Septuagint this is God not of the great wind/spirit (πνεῦμα μέγα), but the voice, or sound, of a light breeze (φωνὴ αὔρας λεπτῆς).[22] The point shines equally

17. Fragment of Anaximenes from Aetius 1.3.4 (DK B2) in Diels, *Fragmente der Vorsoktraker*, 21. Some might argue the καὶ in "πνεῦμα καὶ ἀὴρ" is epexegetical (especially given the verb "περιέχει" is singular) and should therefore read "wind, that is, air." The epexegetical translation actually strengths the connection between πνεῦμα and ἀὴρ necessary for the argument below. I am indebted to Reid Comstock for observations such as this concerning the Greek.

18. For how Cicero's paraphrases draw largely from Aristotle's disciple Theophrastus see Runia, "Aristotle and Theophrastus."

19. It might go without saying that these "refutation of heresy" texts might not be the best place to find a charitable reading of the particular thinker being treated.

20. "Interrogavi *auras flabiles*, et inquit universus aer cum incolis suis, 'fallitur Anaximenes; non sum deus'" (Augustine, *Confessions* 10.6.9, italics mine).

21. See, e.g., "My heart cried out with fervor against all my phantasms, and I tried to drive away the whirling cloud of uncleanness from the gaze of my mind with a single blow; but no sooner had I dispersed it than it returned, in the twinkling of an eye, once again heaped together so that it pressed upon my sight and clouded it over, so that although I did not imagine you in the form of a human body, I was compelled to conceive of you as something bodily, extended in space—perhaps infused in the world or perhaps also diffused through infinite space beyond the world—but also incorruptible and inviolable and unchangeable, which I ranked higher than what was corruptible and violable and changeable" (*Confessions* 7.1.1). See also the argument below that Augustine does consider wind biblically, but primarily as "winds of false doctrine."

22. Cf. Aristotle's interesting note on φωνὴ in *De anima* 420b 5–6 that "voice is a certain sort of sound of some ensouled being ['Η δὲ φωνὴ ψόφος τίς ἐστιν ἐμψύχου]." I am again indebted to conversation with Reid Comstock for this connection.

through in the Vulgate: God did not come in the "great and strong wind/ spirit *(spiritus grandis et fortis),*" but in the "whistle of thin wind *(sibilus aurae tenuis).*"²³ In both cases, there is a juxtaposition between the *strong spirit* in which God *does not come,* and the gentle, whistling of breeze in which he does come. There is a good Biblical argument to be made then from the account in 1 Kgs that God, quite literally, whispers to us in the breeze.²⁴

There is also a philosophical argument for air. One that suggests we read the Presocratics with *phenomenological* ἀρχή in mind rather than material causality. John Sallis, in "Open Air: On Philosophy Before Philosophy," from his text *The Figure of Nature: On Greek Origins*, argues that later thinkers (especially Aristotle) who project or retroject "the signification of philosophy back upon the Milesians may also have had the effect of distorting and concealing the genuine concern and the decisive accomplishment of their thinking."²⁵ Even the very idea of *matter* (ὕλη) before Aristotle—let alone a *material principle*—according to Sallis, is anachronistic.

> The Milesians have no word for what will come to be called matter—not, however, because there is some lack in their language, some preconstituted meaning they cannot express, but rather because they do not think φύσις [nature] in this way at all; that is, they do not think it as involving a constituent for the expression of which the word ὕλη [matter] would be required.²⁶

Instead we should think ἀρχή—especially according to the Milesians—not as an element (στοιχεῖον or *elementum*), but as *"that from which things arise"*

---

23. We know Augustine was reading the Vulgate around the time of his writing *Confessions* due to his many, sometimes contentious, letters with Jerome (e.g., *Epistles* 28, 40).

24. For the sake of time and focus we will resist following this thread further into the essence-energies debate of the fourteenth century with Gregory of Palamas and Barlaam. We will simply say, as we do colloquially, that God's whisper, *is him* for what else do we know besides energies?

25. Sallis, *Figure of Nature*, 13. Later on Sallis points out that the idea that the Milesians even had a "view" (a concept steeped in the later Platonic concept of εἶδος—look, form, but also "view") could be seen as anachronistic. Sallis also points to Hegel's praise of Anaximenes as the synthesis of Thales (water) and Anaximander's (indefinite). In the *Lectures on the Philosophy of Religion* Hegel writes: "In place of the undetermined material of Anaximander, he [Anaximenes] again posits a definite natural element (the absolute in real form)—but instead of the water of Thales, that form is air. He found that a sensible being was necessary for the material; and air has, at the same time, the advantage of having greater formlessness. It is less corporeal than water; we do not see it, but feel it first in movement. Everything comes forth from out of it and dissolves again into it. He determines it as infinite as well" (cited by Sallis, *Figure of Nature*, 18).

26. Sallis, *Figure of Nature*, 16.

or "that by virtue of which they *come forth into the open*" as well as "that which has sovereignty over things, that which commands their coming forth, not merely at a point of origin but throughout their entire course."[27] In other words, air as ἀρχή or the principle of all things is about manifestation more than it is the hidden identity of things or the *stuff* of which they are composed. It is about how bodies appear or show themselves and are thus *constituted* by air, more than it is about air *changing into* other bodies.

The thrust of Augustine's argument against Anaximenes in *City of God* and his *Letter* 118 rests on the motion of air and therefore its being moved by some unmoved mover (God). But, at least according to Anaximenes, we only see air in its movement of something else (Fragment 7). As Sallis observes, "Air never shows itself as *itself* but rather is operative only in the manifestation of something differentiated from it."[28] And again,

> Air empowers the coming forth of things into manifestness. Its very invisibility, its transparency, its never showing itself as itself, is precisely what renders it capable of providing the site where things can come forth and be manifest. Air is what grants the transparent opening in which all other things can appear.[29]

To use a very simple example, we know it is not only temperature that affects the freezing point of a liquid, but also pressure or air. We also know that one's shape or form—their life force, but also their constitutive visual shape—depends highly on pressure.[30] Additionally, as Augustine points out, our speech depends on air to travel through[31]—it is the concrete way God

---

27. Sallis, *Figure of Nature*, 16 (italics mine). Sallis gives the example of the way ὕδωρ [water] is used by Plato in the *Timaeus* to describe fusible metal. On this reading Thales is not *just* talking about water as ἀρχή but also "the fusible"—something intrinsically prone to flow. Sallis admits his debt to Heidegger's account of φύσις.

28. Sallis, *Figure of Nature*, 23.

29. Sallis, *Figure of Nature*, 24. There might therefore be a connection between air when it is "equitable" and therefore "not manifest to sight" (Fragment A7) and Augustine's "heaven of heaven"—co-eternal with God and the place of becoming. See, e.g., Catherine Keller's account in *Face of the Deep*, 74–77. Furthermore, Keller suggests this "nothingsomething" is Monica/the church. While Keller believes this to be water (or liquid) as the amniotic fluid of birth, the reading also works with wind/spirit/breath—especially given the connection between the Holy Spirit, wind/breath, and the church.

30. This idea made headlines in June 2023 when a submarine carrying people on a tour of the Titanic wreckage imploded.

31. Augustine, *Confessions* 10.10.17. See also the explicit connection made between speech and the Incarnation in *On Christian Doctrine*: "In order that what we are thinking may reach the mind of the listener through the fleshly ears, that which we have in mind is expressed in words and is called speech. But our thought is not transformed into sounds; it remains entire in itself and assumes the form of words by means of

responds to Augustine's call to "let him speak" in book 1 despite the fact that he is dust and ashes. Could God be this *place of manifestation*—this *beyond being* that, while never showing itself, quietly and hiddenly holds things in being? If air is not God himself (Holy, *Idipsum*), is it not at least the closest way of speaking about—or better, *experiencing*—God *in prayer*? The highest divine name as one that overcomes us in the cool breeze or a deep breath: air. *Air is where we discover God in-nature-and-us—or better, discover ourselves in (praise of) God.* We do not even need to employ the language of deconstruction, but merely Augustine's own suggested hermeneutic,[32] in order to go back to *Confessions* and read Anaximenes's connection of air to breath (Fragment B2) back into the text.

Wind in *Confessions*

There are many places where Augustine mentions wind specifically rather than breath. In most cases Augustine's use of wind in *Confessions* is metaphorical and negative. For example, "Are not all these things smoke and wind [*ventus*]?"[33] and "Does not a soul that sighs after such fictions commit fornication against you, trusting in falsehoods and feeding the winds [*ventos*]? . . . For what does it mean to feed the winds [*ventos*] but to feed demons?"[34] So at the beginning of *Confessions*, far from God or anything like God, the wind is actually more like a demon. Augustine continues, "I was going astray in my pride carried by every wind [*omni vento*], yet in a most hidden way you were at the helm, steering me." Here the wind, as is the case in Eph 4:14,[35] is the wind *of false doctrine* that God steers us through. In a similar vein, in book 10, Augustine describes God as "a fragrance which

---

which it may reach the ears without suffering any deterioration in itself. In the same way the Word of God was made flesh without change that He might dwell among us" (1.13). I am indebted to Pablo Irizar for this and other help in my reading of Augustine.

32. See Augustine, *On Christian Doctrine* 1 (esp. 1.36.40) for how interpretation should build up the twin loves of God and Neighbor. This is also in line with Augustine's hermeneutic for reading Genesis in *Confessions* 12.1.1, 12.26.36—32.42; cf. Riel, "Hermeneutical Event," 258: "The criterion of truth is not the capturing of a true reference intended by the text or its author, but the intention of the one who interprets the text. It is a matter of 'walking in the truth,' a truth that is present in us and which we recognize in the Bible as a *signum*. If and when we approach the signs with the right questions, then the truth will happen."

33. Augustine, *Confessions* 1.17.27.

34. Augustine, *Confessions* 4.2.3.

35. "So that we may no longer be children, tossed to and fro by the waves and carried about by every wind of doctrine, by human cunning, by craftiness in deceitful schemes" (Eph 4:14 ESV).

no wind [*flatus*] disperses."³⁶ In most cases, wind appears only as *the winds of doctrine* or *the opinion of man*.³⁷ In general, wind/air without breath in *Confessions*, at least for our purposes, is largely unfruitful. We will therefore need to reinscribe breath back into Augustine's *Confessions* in order to rethink Anaximenes's err of air. It is a descent to Anaximenes because we move back down the divided line into an image (i.e., air) of truth, but also because we go, with Falque, to that which is below speaking—below even sense.³⁸ But as Augustine tells us so clearly, down is often actually the way up: "*Come down, then, that you may ascend*, and ascend to God. For you have fallen by rising up against God."³⁹

Augustine's Other Conversion: God-in-the-Flesh

While much ink has been spilt over Augustine's intellectual or Platonic conversion in distinction from his *Catholic* conversion in *Confessions*,⁴⁰ there is a conversion that goes largely unnoticed in the scholarly literature. This is perhaps because it is a conversion-in-the-flesh; a pre- or *infra-linguistic* conversion that goes ahead of Augustine.⁴¹ This is a conversion that turns Augustine around even when he is unable to turn himself around. It is as if the descent of the Word into the flesh—into our own bodies—takes place as the movement from the front of our brain down into the speechless lower brain—down our spine and into our bodies where we often hold things we cannot know or speak. This is the death of the Word before resurrection. A kind of psychoanalytic *resurrection* through the Word that is also and

36. Augustine, *Confessions* 10.6.8.

37. Interestingly enough, Falque picks up this type of idiomatic usage in *The Metamorphosis of Finitude*. Falque refers to the different attempts to think of eternity as "*flatus vocis*"—literally "breath of voice" or "empty word," that the translator, George Hughes's note reads more idiomatically as "mere wind" (*Metamorphosis of Finitude*, 23, 129). There are other times Augustine uses wind but they are literal and almost exclusively in regard to Augustine's journey to Rome, e.g., *Confessions* 5.8.15: "I pretended that I had a friend whom I did not want to leave until the wind [*vento*] changed and he could set sail" and "The wind blew [*flavit ventus*] and filled our sails, and the shore receded from our sight."

38. Falque, *Wedding Feast*, 129. See also Augustine's own version of this Platonic ascent/descent in *On True Religion* 55–56.

39. Augustine, *Confessions* 4.12.19 (italics mine).

40. See for example, Dobell, *Augustine's Intellectual Conversion*, or an earlier formulation of the argument in O'Connell, "On Augustine's 'First Conversion.'"

41. I am drawing largely from the work of Emmanuel Falque here in *Nothing to It*, but also in the conclusion of *Guide to Gethsemane*: "The In-fans [without-speech] or the Silent Flesh." For more on our belatedness to self, see Marion, *In the Self's Place*.

primarily a *recollection*. This is an often-silent psychoanalytic reading of the way the Word—Christ, but also form or the speech through which God creates and we imitate—enters into Chaos or the unconscious, so that we might begin to steer our Chaos by naming it.[42]

For Augustine, this conversion in his flesh has to do *with breath*. This is a bit of a *hidden conversion*, passed over for more obvious ones in book 9. It is when Augustine describes how even if he wanted to go back to his job as a rhetorician, *his lungs were too weak*. As Augustine tells us in *Confessions*:

> As it happened, that summer my lungs had begun to give way under the strain of too much work teaching. I found it difficult to breathe, and the pains in my chest betrayed the weakened state of my lungs. . . . At first this concerned me because my symptoms *were practically forcing me to set down the burden of my teaching position*, or, if I could be cured and recover, at least to take some time off. But once the wholehearted will to be still and see that you are the Lord had arisen in me and become firmly fixed—as you know, my God—I actually began to rejoice in having this honest excuse to mitigate the offense I would cause to people who for the sake of their children wanted me never to be free.[43]

As Evagrios points out in his texts *On Prayer*, when the demons have lost the initial battle they return as angels.[44] In this case, as the voice of parents who want Augustine to continue teaching for the benefit of their children. God-in-the-Flesh—below word or reason in his body—cooperating with Augustine's desire and intention helps him complete his turn.

Additionally, in book 7 Augustine claims his pride not only makes it difficult to rest, *but also to breathe*.[45] When the lower things become higher things, we are overcome with anxiety which has a striking physiological element if we allow ourselves to attend to it. In both cases, Augustine's *body knows before he does—it says* no *before he does*. On this reading, Augustine's

---

42. The reading is often implicit in Falque. For example, his *Triduum Philosophique*, but also in *God, the Flesh, and the Other*. I have had the pleasure of conversing with Emmanuel Falque's wife, Sabine, who is a distinguished psychoanalyst and I can only imagine the weight and impact her thinking has had on the development of Falque's—or better, *the* Falques' thought.

43. Augustine, *Confessions* 9.2.4 (italics mine).

44. Evagrios the Solitary, *On Prayer* §95 in *Philokalia*, 1:66.

45. "But because in my pride I rose up against you and charged against the Lord with my head held high and all my defenses at the ready, even those lower things were set above me and oppressed me, and I could not rest, could not breathe (*nusquam erat laxamentum et respiramentum*)" (Augustine, *Confessions* 7.7.11).

wholehearted will to *be still and know God* actually *follows and flows out of his physiological inability to do otherwise*. For Augustine there is never a separation between spiritual pain on the one hand and physical pain on the other—similar to Plotinus, pain is seen as the body grabbing or interrupting the soul/mind's attention.[46] Modern medicine is beginning to rediscover there are other causes besides the material. There is a plethora of recent research for example, into the idea that autoimmune diseases might have spiritual or psychological realities as their cause.[47]

Breath in the Beginnings: Genesis

In *Confessions* 7.1.2 Augustine expressly denies the idea that God fills all things by *breathing though* them. He says, "Such was my opinion, for I could not conceive of anything else. But it was false."[48] At this time Augustine is still wrestling with the idea that one can picture God and therefore God has different parts where he could be more in one thing than another. He tries yet again, this time with his famous sponge image in 7.5.7 where Augustine imagines creation to be a sponge filled by God who like a sea, infinite on all sides, fills it. "Every party of the sponge would of course be filled with the immeasurable sea," he says.[49] More satisfied with this image, he moves to the more metaphysical consideration: "But this good God created good things, and see how he encompasses and fills them. Where then did evil come from?"[50] While Augustine is much more satisfied with his water/sponge image, the concept of soil air (i.e., that there is a certain sense in which soil "breathes" in order to aid the respiration of plants and animals) helps solve for his concern that God (as air) might be unevenly distributed.[51] Air, at least on this account, is much like the water in Augustine's sponge image.[52] In fact, it might even be better because we can answer the

46. See, for example, Augustine, *On Music* 11.5.9.
47. See a summary of these findings throughout Mate, *Myth of Normal*, 11–17.
48. Augustine, *Confessions* 7.1.2.
49. Augustine, *Confessions* 7.5.7.
50. Augustine, *Confessions* 7.5.7.
51. Blum et al., *Essentials of Soil Science*, 53–54.
52. Plato treats something similar to this in *Parmenides* 131. In regard to participation of the one (form) in its many instantiations (individuals) Parmenides says, "So, being one and the same, it will be at the same time, as a whole, in things that are many and separate; and thus it would be separate from itself." Socrates replies, "No it wouldn't. *Not if it's like one and the same day.* That is in many places at the same time and is none the less not separate from itself. If it's like that, each of the forms might be, at the same time, one and the same in all" (italics mine). Of course, Parmenides moves the image

metaphysical question more easily in terms of air: the air is there, but we struggle to breathe it. This not breathing, a dying, is not evil itself, but a catalyst for evil—something evil can easily become *grafted onto*, to use the language of *The Metamorphosis of Finitude*. Rather than accepting God's gift (breath/air) the trick of Satan is that he gets us to think there is something more. Something else we waste or ignore air trying to get.

It is surprising that Augustine has more issues with air imagery than water since air, as we've seen—or not seen—is a much more apt image for the way God fills all things, allowing them to appear at all biologically (Hebrew soul), but also in terms of their known shape, form, or look (Greek soul). There may be anti-Manichean reasons for this. There is some hint of this in *Confessions* 3.10.18, where Augustine says,

> But if one of their saints ate a fig that had been plucked by someone else's misdeed and not his own, he would transform it within his stomach and breathe out (*anhelaret*) angels; indeed, in his prayers he would sigh out (*gemendo*) particles of God and belch (*ructando*) them forth.[53]

While Augustine wants to avoid picturing God—something he learned from the Platonists—he may also want to avoid coming too close to what he might see as a Manichean (mis)understanding of God. That is despite the fact that Anaximenes's view can be seen as faithful to the Hebrew tradition where upon death the dust returns to the earth and the spirit/breath returns to God.[54]

So how does Augustine treat breath in the beginnings? That is, in Genesis, but also at Pentecost? Interestingly, it is not in books 12 or 13 in his analysis of Genesis where Augustine refers to Gen 2:7 (where God breathes the *breath of life* into Adam's nostrils), but in another beginning: where Augustine discusses his desire to be freed from the "honey-trap of concupiscence" even while he sleeps and from the addiction to the pleasure that results from the passing from lack to fullness in eating in book 10.[55] Augustine, while admiring Paul says,

---

back to a material thing sail and leads the interlocutors astray. I would also point out that the idea that there is no air in space can be reconciled to Fragment A7 where on Anaximenes's account space air is actually just where air is "equitable" (i.e., where it does not appear at all).

53. Augustine, *Confessions* 3.10.18. There may have also been a healthy bit of skepticism regarding how the Paraclete appears since Mani claimed this title for himself. See Augustine, *Confessions* 5.5.8 and *Against the Fundamental Epistle* 6.7.

54. In Mani's "Hymn to the Father of Greatness" he says, "Let your brightness shine upon us, sweet source *and breath of life*!" Cf. Eccl 12:7 where upon death the dust returns to the earth and "the spirit/breath returns to God who gave it."

55. Augustine, *Confessions* 10.30.42.

> He had no strength in himself, for he was that same dust—*dust into which you breathed your inspiration,* so that he said these words that have kindled my love for him: "I can do all things," he says, "through him who gives me strength." Give me strength, so that I may be able to do all things.[56]

Here at least, Augustine seems to artfully avoid the idea that the breath breathed into Adam's nostrils is God. He reaffirms this after *Confessions* in *The Literal Meaning of Genesis.*[57] But there is still hope for breath in Augustine—maybe not as Holy Spirit, but as Word. This is because the *inspiration* God breathes into Paul is his words, words which are also always already God's. This is actually the only connection, albeit tacit, to the wind of Pentecost in the text. God's breath is ultimately and primarily about speech (and understanding speech)—God's speech in both cases.[58] In book 13, for example, Augustine says, "But he speaks no longer in his own voice; he speaks in your voice. For you sent your Spirit from the highest heaven through him who ascended on high and opened the floodgates of your gifts, so that the flowing stream might gladden your city."[59] Augustine's focus on speech rather than wind at Pentecost—a focus on unity of Word despite multiplicity—will remain Augustine's focus at least into 416 (e.g., *Sermons* 267–71).

"I Breathe You in a Little": God, Breath, Song, and Sighing

The last recovery of wind as breath in *Confessions* is in the explicit connection between God, breath, and speech. Augustine often connects his experience of, or inability to experience, God in terms of his breath. While it could be argued that this is only an image or metaphor for the way Augustine is feeling, we should take Augustine at his word: thinking about his description as an actual description of how his body interacts with and responds to God, here, air or breath. The first section will explore the physiological

---

56. Augustine, *Confessions* 10.31.45 (italics mine).

57. "Now, at any rate, I will affirm nothing as certain about the soul, which God breathed into the man by blowing into his face, except that it comes from God in such a way as not to be the substance of God and yet to be incorporeal; that is, not a body, but a spirit, not begotten of the substance of God nor proceeding from the substance of God, but made by God" (Augustine, *Literal Meaning of Genesis* 7.28.43).

58. "What we know through the Spirit of God no one knows but the Spirit of God. To those who speak in the Spirit of Good, it is rightly said, 'it is not you who speak'; and likewise to those who know in the Spirit of God, it is rightly said, 'It is not you who know'" (Augustine, *Confessions* 13.31.46).

59. Augustine, *Confessions* 13.13.14.

repercussions of finitude which disordered love is grafted onto, the second section will look at two places where Augustine connects "breathing God in" to songs of praise, and the final part will serve as a very cursory look at the way sighing functions in *Confessions*.

One of the ways Augustine describes sin in book 1 is the kind of life where breath goes forth, but does not return. "But that [loving the Latin language because of the literature], too, came from sin, from the vanity of the life by which I was flesh and a breath going forth and not returning."[60] Here, breathing out is connected to a kind of vanity—a vanity that tries to shape the external world rather than accepting the gift of breath. Augustine's ambition, and perhaps ambition in general, puts us firmly in a kind of exhale mode. Common expressions such as "he is sucking up all the air in the room" and "he's working so hard he's going to give himself a heart attack" are not just ways of speaking, but have a literal, physiological foundation that Augustine's careful description attests to. As Augustine says, "Still, more than anything else, it was bodily things that held me captive, as though they were pressing down on me *and suffocating me; I was gasping for breath* under the weight of the masses that were the objects of my thought, and I could not breathe the clean and pure air of your truth."[61] Interestingly, it is not a problem with the air (i.e., with God or God's breath who he gives indiscriminately to all), but with Augustine's ability to draw that breath, what he calls the "clean and pure air" of God's truth. God is there in the "thin whistle of wind" that is also in me, sustaining me—*Deus interior intimo meo*.

In books 9 and 13 there are explicit connections to *breathing God in* in song. To put it in the language of book 1, when our breath returns to God in song and praise, we can finally breathe God in—at least a little. In book 9 the context is Ambrose's use of hymns to make a unity out of the multiplicity and therefore create a kind of united front against Arianism. Augustine describes his weeping during these hymns: "And it was for this reason that I wept so much when your hymns were sung; for so long I had been sighing [*suspirans*] for you, and now at last I had begun to breathe [*respirans*] you in—so far as air [*aura*] was free to move in a house of grass."[62] This is likely the closest we get to Anaximenes's formulation: "As our soul being air, holds us together, so breath (πνεῦμα) and air enclose the whole world" (B2). This is although Augustine expresses some skepticism regarding our ability to

60. Augustine, *Confessions* 1.13.20. See also 6.10.17: "There were three mouths gaping open in their need, breathing out their poverty each upon the other, and looking to give them their food in due season."

61. *Sub quibus anhelans in auram tuae veritatis liquidam et simplicem respirare non poteram* (Augustine, *Confessions* 5.11.21).

62. Augustine, *Confessions* 9.7.16.

breathe God through his blending of 2 Cor 5:1 and Isa 40:6, "so far as air was free to move in a house of grass [i.e., earthly life or flesh]." Augustine makes the same qualification in the second passage: "breathing God" is possible, but at best fleeting. We can raise ourselves up in attention to the phenomenon of wind—our attention moving mimetically to the breath-in-us—but it's momentary and impossible to sustain. As Augustine says in book 13,

> I too say, "Where are you, my God?" and behold, you are here. For a little while I draw breath in you as I pour out my soul over me with a noise of exultation and thanksgiving, of the sound of one celebrating a festival. And still my soul is sorrowful, for it falls again and becomes a great deep, or rather, realizes that it is still a great deep.[63]

While we can reach God momentarily, we are always falling back into the deep. The chaos that the Spirit hovers over in the beginning, out of which God/We *speak* creation, is also in us.

The first time Augustine *breathes in God*, these breaths are connected to weeping. This is the kind of weeping that often characterizes the mystical experience. The anxious person cannot breathe, while the mystic breathes heavily because of the overwhelming pleasure of deep, real breaths. This is also the exhale of abandonment that Falque describes of Christ on the cross: "Speech is gradually buried in the flesh on the day of the Passion; it is his flesh that speaks out in his cry ('Then Jesus gave a loud cry and breathed his last' [Mark 15:37]), rather than his speech, which keeps silent in his *logos*."[64] There is a kind of pleasure associated with this later kind of exhalation. Since exhalation is the autonomic part of the breath cycle, it is a kind of *risk of finitude* encoded into our bodies—a risk of finitude where we exhale without actually knowing if we will draw breath again. The collective inhale during the resurrection of humanity will be an echo of Christ's first breath in the tomb. There has been a rise in the popularity of breathwork and high-intensity exercise classes.[65] These practices can be seen as an attempt to physiologically imitate this mystical experience of abandonment and since the experience is bodily it can be pleasing even without an explicit spiritual content in one's mind. It is as if the mystical arrives through the back door of the body.[66] In both cases (books 9 and 13) we inhale God and

63. Augustine, *Confessions* 13.14.15.

64. Falque, *Wedding Feast*, 202.

65. See, e.g., Barry's Bootcamp, Orange Theory, and other group exercise companies focused on high intensity. See also someone like Andrew Huberman who emphasizes breath for "human optimization" in *The Huberman Podcast*. I am indebted to Martin Koci for this and other popular examples.

66. I am thankful to Thomas Carlson whose comment on this during the 2024 Los

exhale praise. For Augustine it is not just about taking a bigger inhale, longer breaths, or some kind of breathwork, but is the concrete way in which our breath—already God's—returns to and for God (here, concretely air/wind).

Finally, there is the experience of *sighing* in *Confessions* that is also connected to the phenomena of breath. Sighing, like pain, on this account is a kind of oriented speechlessness. As Falque observes,

> Voice is always addressed or directed (cry, groan, moan), even when the possibilities of speech are exhausted (reason and articulate discourse). One becomes without speech, or "illogical"'(*a-logos*), before becoming without voice or voiceless (*a-phonê*). The voice, or *phonê*, is that which remains hidden under the *logos* because it has not, or has no longer, that strength to express itself otherwise—when it is hidden in a flesh in which it has become exhausted: "Then Jesus gave a loud cry and breathed his last" (Mark 15:37).[67]

Sighing, which demands a more in-depth treatment than I can offer here, is something that occurs throughout *Confessions* as the hallmark sign of restlessness.[68] It is a kind of belatedness to breath, that through emphasis of breath, tries to recapture all of the breaths missed or unattended to. Interestingly, we are always sighing, even after conversion. As Augustine says of the church, "O House full of light and splendid in form, I have loved your beauty and the place where the glory of my Lord abides, my Lord who fashioned you and holds you in his grasp! On this pilgrimage of mine may I sigh with longing for you. And I ask the one who made me to hold me also in his grasp in you, for he made me also."[69] Maybe there is a way in which this sighing—an oriented plea for God to come—is a way of attending to his already being there *even if we are late*. Maybe there is a metamorphosis of finitude at work in breath.

Angeles meeting of the INPR made it apparent that this small observation could fill, and might better deserve, a lifetime of work and exploration.

67. Falque, *Wedding Feast*, 88.

68. For example, Augustine, *Confessions* 6.5.8: "I thought upon these things, and you were with me; I sighed, and you heard me." See also 6.14.24; "I sigh for you day and night!" (7.10.16); "And I did not stand still in enjoying my God; no, I was seized by your beauty; but no sooner was I drawn to you than I was torn away by my own weigh, and I feel into the depths with a sigh" (7.17.23). "I went about my usual affairs with increasing anxiety, and every day I sighed for you" (8.6.13). See also *Confessions* 10.34.53; 11.29.23; 12.15.21; 13.13.14.

69. Augustine, *Confessions* 12.15.21.

Conclusion: Breath as a Metamorphosis of Finitude

The *metamorphosis of finitude* Falque speaks of might happen most naturally in attention to breath—this attention is a rebirth in each moment and the gratitude it engenders erupts across time and space. When we slow down enough to observe the wind gently blowing the trees, for example, there is a mimetic force that causes us to slow down and observe *our own* breathing, still however God's. In hearing the earth breathe [exhale] we are able to observe a truth, *the ultimate truth*, humming right beneath the surface of our projects and attention. We are reminded through this magnification of attention *that God's breath out there is always already one with his breath in me*. This *breath of life* quietly maintains our *shape* or *form* (εἶδος) even and especially while we are outside ourselves. The cool breeze that touches our skin reminds us that the world moves, but just as importantly that we move and breathe in union with it. There are no subject/object dualisms and simply put: *it breathes*. Some might call this a mystical panentheism, others, emphasizing a distinction between God's essence and energies, an overflowing theophany. In either case, *it is God*. God who we are in constant participation with whether we attend to it or not.

Finitude is, from the start, inscribed in how our bodies work. Without the continuous activity of breathing, we will die. Breathing is not something that happens only *after* the fall—as if there were no need for breath in our prelapsarian state. Instead, breath is a beautiful part and constant reminder of our finitude. In learning to breathe, to attend to breath, we learn to love and live into our limits. While breathing occurs in all of us at the vegetative level of our soul—i.e., it is something that occurs passively without any kind of attention or intentionality on our part—it is also something that we can do actively. *Voluntary* control of breath therefore straddles the different kinds of body treated in phenomenology and Falque in a unique way. Attention to breath, similar to the metamorphosis of finitude championed by Falque, is a manner or mode of living in the body.[70]

Wind. Air. Breath. Life. Anaximenes was right that this is ἀρχή. While Augustine explicitly misses this—especially given the fragments we have that Augustine likely did not—Augustine's *Confessions*, his very speech, *his very body*, testifies to it. More than an ability to observe life in nature, we also have the ability to observe, *to feel*, the breath of all living things in

---

70. "But what revives of me, as I have said above (§14), and as I shall discuss further (§29), is not my biological or organic body but the *manner* that I have of living through this same body. In short, the body that is most truly my own, but that is the property of God more than myself (§14), is what God resurrects at the heart of my inner self" (Falque, *Metamorphosis of Finitude*, 59).

nature. Watch the wind, feel the wind. Breathe. To use some of the riches of *The Guide to Gethsemane* and try to speak breath in terms of death: there is a spiritual death that is the death lost (in anxiety) or wasted (false or empty speech) breath. This kind of death is not bad in-and-of-itself. In *Confessions* we see the very beginning of the way this lost spiritual breath and lost biological breath (literal death) are interwoven. They follow each other or are grafted onto each other. *The body quite literally* wastes breath through fleeing its finitude and limitations. We rush towards death in not breathing or breathing too much. Attention to breath helps us receive the gift of metamorphosized finitude. Despite the clarity that comes for thinking in terms of death, the impetus for this chapter was actually life. Sitting outside holding my youngest daughter—bathing in the gentle breeze in what could only be called God, or at least *divine energies*. Feeling myself breathe. Feeling her breathe. Seeing the world breathe. In the wind, I breathe, we breathe, it breathes—this is a *metamorphosis of finitude*. As Falque says of joy, "The 'moment of eternity' is not the *making eternal of a moment* but the *joy of the eternal in the moment of all moments in time*."[71] It is one thing to, like Martha in the death of Lazarus, believe in the resurrection (John 11:21). It is another thing to experience it today in each breath.

> "Lord," Martha said to Jesus, "if you had been here, my brother would not have died. But I know that even now God will give you whatever you ask."
> Jesus said to her, "Your brother will rise again."
> Martha answered, "I know he will rise again in the resurrection at the last day."
> Jesus said to her, "I am the resurrection and the life. The one who believes in me will live, even though they die; and whoever lives by believing in me will never die. Do *you* believe this?"

Bibliography

Aristotle. *The Complete Works*. Edited by Jonathan Barnes. Princeton: Princeton University Press, 1984.

Augustine. *Against the Fundamental Epistle of Manicheaus*. Translated by Richard Stothert. Vol. 4 of *Nicene and Post-Nicene Fathers*, Series 1. Edited by Philip Schaff. Buffalo, NY: Christian Literature, 1887.

———. *Sermons (230-272B) on the Liturgical Seasons*. Translated by Edmund Hill. Vol. 3.7 of *The Works of Saint Augustine: A Translation for the Twenty-First Century*. New Rochelle, NY: New City, 1993.

---

71. Falque, *Metamorphosis of Finitude*, 116.

———. *The City of God*. Translated by William Babcock. Vols. 6–7 of *The Works of Saint Augustine: A Translation for the Twenty-First Century*. Hyde Park, NY: New City, 2012.

———. *Confessions* [English]. Translated by Thomas Williams. Cambridge: Hackett, 2019.

———. *Confessions* [Latin]. Edited by Carolyn Hammond. Loeb Classical Library. 2 vols. Cambridge: Harvard University Press, 2014.

———. *The Literal Meaning of Genesis*. In *On Genesis*. Translated by Edmund Hill. Vol. 13 of *The Works of Saint Augustine: A Translation for the Twenty-First Century*. Hyde Park, NY: New City, 1996.

———. *On Music*. In *The Immortality of the Soul; On Music; The Advantage of Believing; On Faith in Things Unseen*, 169–384. Translated by Robert Catesby Taliaferro. Fathers of the Church 4. Washington, DC: Catholic University of American Press, 1947.

———. *On True Religion*. In *Augustine: Earlier Writings*, edited and translated by John H. S. Burleigh. Philadelphia: Westminster, 1953.

———. *Teaching Christianity (On Christian Doctrine)*. Translated by Edmund Hill. Vol. 11 of *The Works of Saint Augustine: A Translation for the Twenty-First Century*. Hyde Park, NY: New City, 1996.

Blum, Winifried, et al. *Essentials of Soil Science*. Stuttgart: Schweizerbart, 2017.

Diels, Hans. *Die Fragmente der Vorsokratiker*. 2.1. Berlin: Weidmann, 1906.

Dobell, Brian. *Augustine's Intellectual Conversion: The Journey from Platonism to Christianity*. Cambridge: Cambridge University Press, 2009.

Evagrios the Solitary. *On Prayer*. Translated by G. E .H. Palmer et al. In vol. 1 of *Philokalia: The Complete Text Compiled by St. Nikodimos of the Holy Mountain and St. Makarios of Corinth*. New York: Farrar, Straus and Giroux, 1979.

Falque, Emmanuel. *By Way of Obstacles: A Pathway Through a Work*. Translated by Sarah Horton. Eugene, OR: Cascade, 2022.

———. *God the Flesh and the Other: From Irenaeus to Duns Scotus*. Translated by William Hackett. Evanston, IL: Northwestern University Press, 2015.

———. *The Guide to Gethsemane: Anxiety, Suffering, Death*. Translated by George Hughes. New York: Fordham University Press, 2019.

———. *The Metamorphosis of Finitude: An Essay on Birth and Resurrection*. Translated by George Hughes. New York: Fordham University Press, 2012.

———. *Nothing to It: Reading Freud as a Philosopher*. Translated by Robert Vallier and William L. Connelly. Leuven: Leuven University Press, 2020.

———. *The Wedding Feast of the Lamb: Eros, the Body, and the Eucharist*. Translated by Georges Hughes. New York: Fordham University Press, 2016.

Hefty, Karl. "Soul or Life: Contours of a Forgotten Indecision." Paper presented at the International Network for the Philosophy of Religion (INPR), Montreal, April 26, 2023.

Heidegger, Martin. "Seminar du Thor 1968." In *Four Seminars*, 10–35. Translated by Andrew Mitchell and François Raffoul. Indiana: Indiana University Press, 2012.

Hippolytus. *Refutation of Heresies*. Vol. 5 of Ante-Nicene Fathers. Edited by Arthur Cleveland Coxe. Revised and edited by Kevin Knight. https://www.newadvent.org/fathers/0501.htm.

Husserl, Edmund. *Cartesian Meditations: An Introduction to Phenomenology*. Translated by Dorion Cairns. The Hague: Matinus Nijhoff, 1960.

Keller, Catherine. *Face of the Deep: A Theology of Becoming*. London: Routledge, 2003.
Kirk, G. S., et al. *The Presocratic Philosophers: A Critical History with a Selection of Texts*. Cambridge: Cambridge University Press, 1983.
Mani. "Hymn to the Father of Greatness." Gnostic Society Library. https://gnosis.org/library/hymnfa.htm.
Marion, Jean-Luc. *In the Self's Place: The Approach of Saint Augustine*. Translated by Jeffrey L. Kosky. Stanford: Stanford University Press, 2012.
———. *On Descartes' Passive Thought: The Myth of Cartesian Dualism*. Translated by Christina Gschwandtner. Chicago: University of Chicago Press, 2018.
Mate, Gabor. *The Myth of Normal: Trauma, Illness, and Healing in a Toxic Culture*. New York: Penguin, 2022.
O'Connell, Robert J. "On Augustine's 'First Conversion' Factus Erectior." *Augustinian Studies* 17 (1986) 15–29.
Plato. *Parmenides*. Translated by Mary Louise Gill and Paul Ryan. In *Plato: Complete Works*, edited by John Cooper and D. S. Hutchinson. Cambridge: Hackett, 1997.
———. *Symposium*. Translated by Alexander Nehamas and Paul Woodruff. In *Plato: Complete Works*, edited by John Cooper and D. S. Hutchinson. Cambridge: Hackett, 1997.
Riel, Gerd van. "The Hermeneutical Event of Truth in Augustine." In *Felici Curiositate: Studies in Latin Literature and Textual Criticism from Antiquity to the Twentieth Century*, edited by Guy Guildentops et al., 249–74, Belgium: Brepols, 2017.
Runia, David. "Aristotle and Theophrastus Conjoined in the Writings of Cicero." In *Cicero's Knowledge of the Peripatos*, edited by William Fortenbaugh and Peter Steinmetz, 23–38. New York: Routledge, 1989.
Sallis, John. *The Figure of Nature: On Greek Origins*. Indiana: Indiana University Press, 2016.
Theoleptos of Philadelphia. In vol. 3 of *Philokalia: The Complete Text Compiled by St. Nikodimos of the Holy Mountain and St. Makarios of Corinth*. Translated by G. E. H. Palmer et al. New York: Farrar, Straus and Giroux, 1984.
Whitehead, Alfred North. *Process and Reality*. New York: Free Press, 2010.

Augustine on the Metamorphosis of Restlessness

Pablo Irizar

Retrieving the Passions

WITH THE INTRODUCTION OF the secular notion of *emotion* to replace or rehabilitate the ancient concept of *passion* (against rationalistic tendencies), the rich moral, religious, and metaphysical register of the experience of anxiety—disquiet, or restlessness to use Augustine's language—regrettably and often became exclusively restricted to the category of psychology in Western modernity.[1] So, in reaction to the resulting impoverishment of the complex existential experience of anxiety, in *Anxiety: A Philosophical History*, Bettina Bergo commendably attempts to retrieve and expand the experiential horizon and conceptual register of anxiety by considering "anxiety as a mode of sensibility and as an emotion."[2] However, in her historical synopsis of the word's origin and development in philosophical discourse, Bergo inexplicably reduces the early Christian concept of anxiety to the Stoic "stifling *taedium vitae*."[3] By disregarding the textured analysis of anxiety in early Christian discourse, she misses the

---

1. Dixon, *From Passions to Emotions*, 1–25, esp. 1, 3, 4.

2. Bergo, *Anxiety*, 4.

3. Bergo, *Anxiety*, 4. Bergo overlooks early Greek philosophical approaches to anxiety. For complement, see Horwitz, *Anxiety*, 19–35.

opportunity to explore how early Christian approaches to anxiety provide valuable resources to understand fear,[4] the cause of anxiety, and to deal with its consequences, namely "the possibility of rejecting paralysis and quieting our panic"[5] by means of *abiding with* anxiety first.[6] Building on Bergo's aim to retrieve philosophical understandings of the *emotions*, which early Christians call *passions*, and in response to her reductive characterization of early Christian views on anxiety, the present chapter considers the passion of restlessness or disquiet in Augustine's *Confessions* as a late antique equivalent of anxiety, with added corresponding moral, religious, and metaphysical implications observable especially in Augustine's rich reflections on music and its suitability for liturgical practice. It is argued that in *Confessions*, fitting (*conveniens*) or harmonious music is a temporal remedy for human restlessness or *disquiet*, which is the defining character of the human condition, and, albeit incomplete, music's remedy is an eschatological foretaste of the soul's harmony, otherwise fragmented by the metaphysics of time and the moral weight of sin. Therefore, music's remedy is also an immanent reminder of redemptive rest, fully possibly in God's eternity alone. Against the backdrop of early Christian reflections on the use of liturgical music and Augustine's contributions, this contribution analyzes two passages of *Confessions*, namely 9.14–15 and 10.49–50.[7] The conclusion notes that Augustine proposes a metamorphosis of restlessness within a metaphysics of redemption which prescribes abiding not in anxiety but seeking and expecting the final and inevitable harmony of rest of which anxiety is but a temporal trace.

Music and the Passions

By turning to Augustine's explicit and often speculative reflection on the *passions*, commentators often neglect the practical insight found in his discussion of music, which, following the early Christian context, centers on

---

4. "The Greeks defined anxiety broadly as 'the expectation of evil' [*The Nichomachean Ethics*].... Nevertheless, they focused on fear that arose in dangerous situations, in particular, combat. Aristotle (384–22 BCE) provided the most extensive discussion, emphasizing how normal fear and anxiety stem from threatening situations: 'Let fear, then, be a kind of pain or disturbance resulting from the imagination of impending danger, either destructive or painful.... For that is what danger is—the proximity of the frightening [*The Art of Rhetoric*]'" (Horwitz, *Anxiety*, 20).

5. Bergo, *Anxiety*, 35.

6. Bergo, *Anxiety*, 35.

7. All subsequent references to O'Donnell's commentary on these passages come from O'Donnell, *Augustine Confessions*, 105–12, 218–20.

the moral dimension of the passions provoked by music's delight.[8] Early Christian references to music are based on the authority of canonical scriptural sources. In the New Testament, these are about Christian worship and rituals, including weddings (Matt 11:17), funerals (Matt 9:23), and prayer (1 Cor 14:15; Acts 16:25; Jas 5:13). The performance of music, according to other scriptural sources, should be restricted to singing (Eph 5:19; Col 3:16), accompanied by instrumentation in the framework of the apocalypse (Matt 24:3), and lasting even in heavenly worship after the resurrection (Rev 5:8).[9] Interestingly, the apocryphal New Testament includes scarce hymns (*Acts of Thomas* 108 and *Acts of John* 94–97), which are not "rich in musical allusion."[10] The New Testament also includes putative canticles like the Magnificat (Luke 1:46–55), the Benedictus (Luke 1:67–79), and the Nunc Dimittis (Luke 2:29–35). Christological hymns are also noticeable in the Pauline epistolary tradition (Phil 2:6–11; Col 1:15–20; Heb 1:3). McKinnon alerts, however, that "while singing is mentioned frequently [in the Bible], it is complicated to determine just what is being sung and in what liturgical circumstances."[11]

Among early Christian writers, interpretations of scriptural passages referring to music fall under two general interpretative lines: "figurative or concrete."[12] Figurative references occur in preaching, exegesis, and exhortation, whereas concrete references are primarily liturgical. In the course of time, chants based mainly on the Psalms became common in early Christian worship, private devotions, the monastic tradition, cathedral offices, and the Eucharists.[13] McKinnon notes that by the year 480, "Gennadius gives us what might be the earliest extant reference to the concept that psalms relate thematically to readings."[14] On this basis, the question may be raised as to the suitability of speaking about a patristic musicological tradition. In response, while noting the scarcity of textual evidence, Pizzany does not hesitate to answer in the affirmative. Treatises on music in Greek include,

---

8. "Augustine's teachings on the passions and affections are to be found in *The City of God*, especially books IX and XIV, as well as in connection with the narrative of his own struggle with the passions in his *Confessions*, and in several other texts such as *The Free Choice of the Will*, *The Trinity* and the *Expositions on the Book of Psalms*" (Dixon, *From Passions to Emotions*, 27).

9. Ferguson, "Music," 788. For a complete list, see McKinnon, *Music*, 12.

10. McKinnon, *Music*, 24.

11. McKinnon, *Music*, 12.

12. Smith, *Music*, 169.

13. Smith, *Music*, 189–221.

14. McKinnon, *Music*, 170.

for instance, Nicomachus, Gaudentius, and Ptolemy.[15] A trend illustrating a Latin "musicological tradition" is evident, Pizzany argues, in the work of Augustine, Cassiodorus, Boèthius, and Isidore of Seville. However, he observes that during this period, "music is mostly treated as a mathematical discipline and detached, as such, from its artistic aspect" and "divorced from contemporary practice."[16] Moreover, Pizzany regrets that the patristic tradition gives no information on "the technique and execution of its theoretical presuppositions."[17] This may be, drawing from Ferguson, because "theoretical treatises dealing with the abstract characteristics of music had little or nothing to do with ecclesiastical music."[18] Ferguson also notes that even "the word *musica* rarely was used concerning Christian song, indicating the recognition that classical music was something different."[19] From this vantage point, he concludes, it is not possible to speak of a "Christian musicological tradition."[20] The apparent absence of interest in the practice and reflection on music may be due to early Christian prudential concerns and moral caution. In this regard, Marrou states that the patristic tradition exhibits "more prohibitions, warnings, and cautions than encouragements."[21]

Notwithstanding the relative scarcity of musicological treatises, reflections on music in patristic literature, which center around the liturgical practice of Eucharist or agape meals (Tertullian, *Apologeticum* 39.18), progressively shaped foundational theological questions on the use of voice and instrumentation, which were in turn informed by the underlying question of music's relation to the regulation of the passions of the soul.[22] While early writers attest to the predominance of responsorial singing, some writers like John Cassian (*Institutes* 2.5, 12) later insist on the solo rendering of chants.[23] Cassian was concerned with having music mirror the unity of the body of Christ (1 Cor 12:27): unison of voice in solo chants is an image of the unity of the body of Christ and his church. Basil of Caesarea (*Epistula* 207) identifies three acceptable forms of "congregational signing": responsorial,

15. Pizzany, "Music," 2:850.
16. Pizzany, "Music," 2:850.
17. Pizzany, "Music," 2:850.
18. Ferguson, "Music," 789.
19. Ferguson, "Music," 789.
20. Ferguson, "Music," 789.
21. "Plus d'interdictions, d'avertissements, de mises en garde que d'encouragements" (Marrou, "Théologie de la musique," 501).
22. Ferguson, "Music," 788. Patristic sources in this essay are cited from Ferguson, Music"; Pizzany, "Music."
23. Ferguson, "Music," 788.

antiphonal, and unison singing.[24] Antiphons were introduced into the Roman liturgy, first by Ambrose in Milan, as reported by Augustine, and eventually also more extensively by Pope Celestine,[25] with an emphasis upon expressing congregational unity—and also the unity of the body of Christ—by singing with "one voice." The call to sing with "one voice" was a standard reference found early on, for instance, in the writings of Ignatius of Antioch (*To the Ephesians* 4.2)[26] and referred often to the unison of (predominantly) vocal music.[27] Over the centuries, questions arose on the appropriateness of introducing female voices in congregational chant. In the opposing camp were figures like Cyril of Jerusalem (*Procatechesis* 14) and Isidore of Pelusium (*Epistula* 1.90). Isidore of Pelusium notes the female "silence in the synagogue" based on "the immoral connotations of female singers, and the use of choruses of women."[28] Evidence to the contrary is found in Eusebius of Caesarea (*Historia ecclesiastica* 7.30.10), who notes that Paul of Samosata, Bishop of Antioch, supported the female chorus, and who finds support for choirs of virgins by Ephrem the Syrian. Authors like Clement (2 Clem 9:10), Basil (*Homiliae in Psalmos* 29.3), Augustine—who cites an ancient Church tradition on singing "always with the mouth of the heart (Ps 33:3)"[29]—and John Chrysostom (*Homilia* 19) emphasized the importance not only of the voice but also of the heart. The figurative interpretation of singing meant that "the opposition to women's choruses was extended to all participation in the liturgy."[30] The use of instruments for worship was also disputed among early Christians because of their prevalence in "pagan sacrifices and in the Jewish temple."[31] Some justified the instrumental usage in Jewish worship (John Chrysostom, *Expositio in Psalmos* 149.2) but did not condone the Christian use, explaining that God allowed instrumentation "to prevent the Jews [from] being led by attraction to it into idolatry."[32] A complimentary view by John Chrysostom (*Expositio in Psalmos* 150) interpreted instruments not literally but as metaphors for the human body, which was

---

24. Ferguson, "Music," 788.

25. "In the mid-fifth century Arnobius quotes Pope Celestine's reference to the singing of an Ambrosian hymn" (McKinnon, *Music*, 169).

26. Smith, *Music*, 176.

27. Ferguson, "Music," 788.

28. Ferguson, "Music," 789.

29. Augustine, *Enarrationes in Psalmos* 106.1; McKinnon, *Music*, 159.

30. Ferguson, "Music," 789.

31. MacMullen, *Christianizing the Roman Empire*, 74–75.

32. Ferguson, "Music," 789.

considered the only instrument worthy of divine praise.[33] Unapproving attitudes towards using instruments in Christian worship were mainly shaped by "antagonism to idolatry and immortality associated with banquets, the theatre, and other entertainment."[34] Besides questions on the kind of voices used and appropriateness of musical instruments in early Christian liturgies, patristic writers often noted how music affects the passions, with the consensus that music, "by combining pleasure with profit is a means of giving beauty to the moral character."[35] Ferguson summarizes this attitude well: the moral import of Christian music was "intended to glorify God, to edify the faithful by lifting thoughts above and reaffirming the faith, to improve conduct and to proclaim the truth."[36] In early Christianity, then, positive attitudes towards music recognized the power of music in elevating the passions, worshiping God, and cultivating moral character.

Rejecting the Passions?

According to a standard (and not entirely inaccurate reading of history), by the fourth century, within the monastic tradition starting with St. Anthony, and later among writers like Evagrius Pontus in the East and John Cassian in the West, Stoic influences shaped Christian reflections on the passions. Writers like Evagrius considered the passions as obstacles to spiritual progress and therefore prescribed the quieting or even the eradication of the passions, for the sake of *apatheia* and *ataraxia*, the tranquility of spirit achieved by becoming without passions, the goal of asceticism.[37] Some have wrongly attributed to Augustine a similar attitude. For instance, in Sorabji's account of what Nagy and Boquet have later called the "Christianization of emotions,"[38] the "Stoic theory of how to avoid agitation was converted by early Christians into a theory of how to avoid temptation."[39] The implications are, first, that the passions are temptations and therefore to be rejected—a view against which Wetzel has argued[40]—and, second, that the Christian moral life depends on reaching a form of Stoic apathy, the opposite of the disturbances of a passion (*pathos*)—an impossible situation according to

33. Ferguson, "Music," 789.
34. Ferguson, "Music," 789.
35. Ferguson, "Music," 789.
36. Ferguson, "Music," 790.
37. Boquet and Nagy, *Medieval Sensibilities*, 34–40.
38. Boquet and Nagy, *Medieval Sensibilities*, 9.
39. Sorabji, *Emotions and Peace of Mind*, 8.
40. Wetzel, "Augustine," 349–63, esp. 354–55.

Dixon.[41] On the contrary, Boquet and Nagy maintain that, according to Augustine, upon experiencing a passion, the wise Christian should "not seek to moderate it, still less get rid of it. Rather, he would analyze it."[42] Indeed, Augustine (and a number of early Christian writers) are not merely baptized Stoics, for, as Boquet and Nagy note, "In the process of including all [passions] within the will, [he] also seemed to restore them to rationality."[43] Likewise, observing early Christianity's sympathy and even affinity towards Stoicism, its principles and proponents in late antiquity (like Cicero, Gellius, Seneca, and Apuleius),[44] Byers notes Augustine develops Stoic psychological principles by adopting "core principles, with some disagreement about applications and creative elaboration of new implications and applications. The disagreements are owing to differences in ontology and in diverging notions of 'complete' human happiness."[45] Augustine also goes beyond the Stoics by drawing from Platonism, as noted by Knuuttila: Augustine "did not share the Stoic view that the [passions] are opposed to right reason. He preferred to think, like the Platonists, that there is an emotional level in the human soul."[46] Sorabji's account is further complicated in considering Augustine's reflections on the practice of music to prompt the passion of joy in liturgical jubilation.

Reminiscent of the early Christian landscape, Augustine adopts a division, yet also aims for an integration, of musical theory and liturgical practice because, as Hübner notes, the Greek word for music (μουσική) includes theory and practice.[47] It is possible to reconstruct some of Augustine's views based on scattered references in his *Letters* and *Expositions on the Psalms*. On the side of liturgical practice, Augustine addresses, compliments, and enriches the early Christian panorama on questions around church music, especially the singing of psalmody in the liturgy. He confirms the

---

41. "Augustine rejected apatheia as an appropriate goal for someone living according to God's word" (Dixon, *From Passions to Emotions*, 59).

42. "What motivated the fear he experienced? Why did he feel moved by desire? What was the object of his disgust? Emotion called for enquiry and introspection. It was thus recognized as a cognitive aptitude: through emotion, man would understand the world, evaluate his human and material environment, and above all determine the place he wished to take in it" (Boquet and Nagy, *Medieval Sensibilities*, 25).

43. Boquet and Nagy, *Medieval Sensibilities*, 25.

44. Byers, *Perception*, 61.

45. Byers, *Perception*, 56.

46. Knuuttila, *Emotions*, 156–57.

47. "Das griechische Wort μουσική bezeichnet über den modernen Begriff hinaus sowohl Musikpraxis als auch Musiktheorie" (Hübner, "Musica," 123).

composition and chanting of hymns by Ambrose.[48] Augustine also believes that a Psalm is distinct from a chant.[49] Augustine defines the chanting of hymns as "praises of God with song; hymns are songs containing the praise of God. If there be praise, and it is not of God, it is not a hymn; if there be praise and praise of God, and it is not sung, it is not a hymn. If it is to be a hymn, therefore, it must have three things: praise, and that of God, and song."[50] Sound can be produced by various instruments—the Greek word *organum* refers to all musical instruments—and the human voice is divided into voice, breath, and striking.[51] Voice is preferred, and musical instruments are to be avoided, while the knowledge of music and musical instruments supports the interpretation of Scripture.[52] The reserve toward instruments is related to festival-like abuses, as in the case of the "evil custom" of eating and drinking to celebrate the feast of St. Leontius.[53] Augustine thus insists on the difference between Greek instruments, like the cithara, and the Psalter.[54] Psalmody, expressed by the sound of the voice, is the proper form of a Christian song. Augustine states that Psalms are divine readings, together with the gospel and the apostle, during the Eucharist.[55] He defends the singing of Psalms at various parts of the Eucharist.[56] On one occasion, Augustine refers to a reader chanting the wrong Psalm, and generously decides in preaching to "follow the will of God in the error of the reader, rather than our own will in our previous intention."[57] There is also a possible reference to the singing of Psalms by the congregation: "we sang to the Lord."[58] This suggests the practice of liturgical antiphonal psalmody in Augustine's time, where the congregation responds to a soloist.[59] Psalms are recited in response to readers and usually follow with an explanation, where allegorical exegesis is standard.[60] Augustine, furthermore, gives evidence of

---

48. Augustine, *Retractationes* 1.20, cited in McKinnon, *Music*, 166.
49. Augustine, *Enarrationes in Psalmos* 47.1, cited in McKinnon, *Music*, 157.
50. Augustine, *Enarrationes in Psalmos* 72.1, cited in McKinnon, *Music*, 158.
51. Augustine, *Enarrationes in Psalmos* 150.7, cited in McKinnon, *Music*, 160.
52. Augustine, *De doctrina christiana* 11.28, cited in McKinnon, *Music*, 165. Also, Augustine, *De doctrina christiana* 16.26, cited in McKinnon, *Music*, 164.
53. Augustine, *Epistula* 29.10–11, cited in McKinnon, *Music*, 163.
54. Augustine, *Enarrationes in Psalmos* 56.16, cited in McKinnon, *Music*, 157.
55. Augustine, *Sermo* 165, cited in McKinnon, *Music*, 161.
56. Augustine, *Retractationes* 11.37, cited in McKinnon, *Music*, 166.
57. Augustine, *Enarrationes in Psalmos* 138, cited in McKinnon, *Music*, 160.
58. Augustine, *Sermo* 14, cited in McKinnon, *Music*, 161.
59. McKinnon, *Music*, 164.
60. Augustine, *Enarrationes in Psalmos* 40, cited in McKinnon, *Music*, 157.

responsorial psalmody in the liturgy: "The psalm which we have just now heard sung and responded to in singing, is short and highly beneficial."[61] Psalms were sung in response to a chanter,[62] and the response to the Psalms is, at times, the alleluia.[63] Alleluia is sung with sacraments during certain times of the year—paschal season for fifty days, after Lent, signifying the resurrection of Jesus and "blessed eternity"[64]—according to an old church tradition, but always with the mouth of the heart (Ps 33:3).[65] Again, "the Church maintains the usage of ancient tradition" in singing Alleluia during paschal season, in various liturgical services, including the Eucharist, with the verbs "to say" and "to sing" used interchangeably.[66] Much debate surrounds the use of *iubilatio* and its relation to the Alleluia of the Mass.[67] Liturgical music ultimately elicits and results in the expression of jubilation or joy. According to Augustine, jubilation is without words: "One who jubilates does not speak words, but it is rather a sort of sound of joy without words since it is the voice of a soul poured out in joy and expressing, as best it can, the feeling, though not grasping the sense . . . the elevation of an exultant spirit, and this is called jubilation."[68] The practice of liturgical music thus centres on the celebration of the passion of rejoicing, which is according to Paul "a fruit of the Spirit" (Gal 5:22) and which, importantly, as Roberts notes, "sometimes includes suffering."[69]

Augustine's music reflections arise from and are rooted in practical theological questions. He wrote a treatise, *On Music*, intended as the hinge between the *Trivium* and *Quadrivium* of a larger, albeit incomplete, pedagogical project started in 388 on the *artes liberales*.[70] The collection of *On Music*—in Augustine's view, a "trivial and childish"[71] project—consists of six books, the last of which was completed years after the first set. The first five books are concerned, in Augustine's words, "only such as pertain to that part called rhythm,"[72] which is what the Greeks understood by observing

---

61. Augustine, *Enarrationes in Psalmos* 119.1, cited in McKinnon, *Music*, 159.
62. Augustine, *Sermones* 352.11.1, cited in McKinnon, *Music*, 162.
63. Augustine, *Sermo* 29A, cited in McKinnon, *Music*, 161.
64. Augustine, *Enarrationes in Psalmos* 1, cited in McKinnon, *Music*, 156.
65. Augustine, *Enarrationes in Psalmos* 106.1, cited in McKinnon, *Music*, 159.
66. Augustine, *Sermones*, 252.9, cited in McKinnon, *Music*, 162.
67. Augustine, *Enarrationes in Psalmos* 32.11, cited in McKinnon, *Music*, 156.
68. Augustine, *Enarrationes in Psalmos* 99.4, cited in McKinnon, *Music*, 158.
69. Roberts, "Emotions" 1.1.
70. Hübner, "Musica," 125.
71. Augustine, *De musica* 6.1.
72. Taliaferro, "On Music," 153. See Augustine, *De musica* 6.1.

"dimensions which music has in common with grammar—such as sound itself—and aspects which are proper only to music."[73] The last book closely follows *On Music* by Aristides Quintilianus. It can be inserted in the Platonic tradition of *Timaeus*, with emphasis also on the Pythagorean "hierarchy of numbers as constitutive of the soul,"[74] even if, as Taliaferro rightly notes, "no strictly Pythagorean treatise on rhythm exists."[75] Marrou concludes that in Augustine's *On Music*, the pleasure of music must be overcome for higher immaterial realities, such that the music's purpose, and indeed the purpose of all art, is to crush itself.[76] In this reading, there is no music for its own sake; instead, music serves a moral purpose, which is, according to Marrou, to evoke pleasure through desire only to terminate it by overcoming it. Thus, he contends that, for Augustine, music has the practical purpose of purifying the listener from passions rooted in sensible, as opposed to intelligible, reality. However, *On Music* is irreducible to a rejection of the passions. Thus, Taliaferro is of the view that in *On Music* Augustine explores the relationship between the experience of time and the possibility of redemption: "For," writes Taliaferro, "if time is an irreversible succession of before and after, then there is no Redemption possible; what has been, has been."[77] As Augustine concludes in *Confessions*, redemption is possible only if "time is a kind of distention"[78] of the soul, a distention containing the past and the future. For Taliaferro, the temporality of passion and pleasure inevitably opens the possibility of music's redemptive function. Moreover, beyond *On Music*, Augustine elsewhere insists on the importance of liturgical music for regulating the passions and ultimately for the flourishing of human life. Thus, McKinnon states that Augustine, "the most renowned of all church fathers, East and West, makes an appropriately significant contribution to [early Christian music], matched only by Ambrose, John Chrysostom and perhaps Basil."[79]

Does Augustine reject the passions, then? The answer must be decisively *no*. On the contrary, in the opening lines of *Confessions*, Augustine turns the passions, construed within the classical tradition as "disturbances of the soul," into the defining characteristic of the human condition—"our

---

73. Deusen, "De Musica," 575.
74. Taliaferro, "On Music," 154.
75. Taliaferro, "On Music," 154.
76. Marrou, "Théologie de la musique," 501.
77. Taliaferro, "On Music," 163.
78. Augustine, *Confessiones* 11.30.
79. McKinnon, *Music*, 153.

hearts are restless, until they rest in [God]"[80]—and, consequently, the aspiration of joy and peace, the opposite of disquiet and restlessness, in the Holy Spirit, becomes the aim of liturgical music. Augustine's "Christianization of emotions," to the limited extent that the expression applies, consists not in transforming passions into temptations but in pursuing the *right* order of the passions, primarily through therapy for restlessness with liturgical music. This is evident in *Confessions*, namely at *Conf.* 9.14–15 and *Conf.* 10.49–50, where Augustine explores to what extent therapy of the passions is possible and for what purpose.

The Consolation of Music

Throughout *Confessions*, Augustine expresses restlessness (or disquiet) through the experience of passions, for which a divine encounter, initiated by the joy of grace or the sorrow of sin, provides a therapy of consolation. On two rare occasions in *Confessions* where Augustine discusses music and passions in tandem, liturgical music is presented as a fleeting antidote to existential restlessness. Set during a liturgy sometime after Augustine's baptism by Ambrose on Easter of 386, in the first passage (*Conf.* 9.14–15), liturgical music elicits the passions. It orients them towards the spiritual profit of the listener, which is an experience of consolation in the form of rest, albeit imperfect.[81] Addressing God, Augustine writes,

> How much I wept at your hymns and canticles, deeply moved by the voices of your sweetly singing church. Those voices flowed into my ears, and the truth was poured out in my heart, whence a feeling of piety surged up and my tears ran down. And these things were good for me. Not long since had the church of Milan begun this mode of consolation and exhortation, with the brethren singing zealously together with voice and heart. It was just a year, or not much more, since Justina, mother of the boy-emperor Valentinian, persecuted your servant Ambrose on behalf of her heresy, into which she had been seduced by the Arians. There my mother, your handmaid, bearing a principal part of the anxiety and sleeplessness, lived in prayer; while we, still cool to the heat of your spirit, were stirred nevertheless by the stunned and shaken city. At that time the custom began that hymns and psalms be sung after the manner of the eastern

---

80. Augustine, *Confessiones* 1.1.

81. O'Donnell notes that this is among the earliest mentions of Arians in the Augustinian corpus. On the Arian persecution of Ambrose, see Augustine, *Epistula* 44.7; Ambrose, *Epistulae* 20, 21. See also O'Donnell, *Augustine Confessions*, 105–12.

regions lest the people be worn out with the tedium of sorrow. The practice has been retained from that time until today and imitated by many, indeed, by almost all your congregations throughout the rest of the world.[82]

In this passage, the practice of faith expressed in the beauty of liturgical music surges the passions of sorrow and the affect of piety.[83] Music, in turn, produces consolation and exultation against "the tedium of sorrow" and the "anxiety" of sleeplessness. The stillness of Stoic apathy is not the aim but rather the spiritual benefit afforded by the inspiring—literally, the giving of *spirit*, which Boyce analyzes as *air*—movements (*excitare*) of the passions. The incarnational transformation of spirit in voice—an image of Christ's incarnate union of *logos* and *flesh* in Augustine's *On Christian Doctrine*—results in an authentic consolation of spiritual rest in harmony's unity, which is unlike Stoic absolute motionlessness akin not to music but to silence. Rest from restlessness is not apathy but authentic *dwelling* of *flesh* and *spirit* in Christ's incarnation (John 1:1) through an otherwise impossible *redemptive metamorphosis* of time and eternity. Thus, Augustine anticipates a paradigm of consolation not in metaphysical obliteration but in the right (re)ordering of reality, the passions included and especially the passions, only to result in harmony and rest in God. In this passage, however, harmony consists only of human integrity. Augustine also observes that the voices of the "sweetly singing church" with "hymns and canticles" revealed zeal in the unity of "voice and heart." With "hymns and canticles," Augustine alludes to Paul at Col 3:16, thus situating the usage of church music within Scripture and introducing, as O'Donnell notes, a discussion on "the right use of church music" in the context of an "invention" story. The "invention" is based on the narrative of Augustine's birth into Christianity through baptism. O'Donnell insists on "the harmony and unity of the visible church in which Augustine has been (in the narrative sequence) baptized."[84] The expression of church unison externally expresses the spiritual integrity of Augustine's newly and now fully embraced faith. Music, and the passions it conjures, are not only of voice or body; they are of a wholesome human experience. Augustine uses the image of the heart to indicate the spiritual core of human beings and the locus of God's encounter and transformation of human beings in conversion.[85] The heart is the core of what it means to be human and the locus for experiencing humanity. Elsewhere in *Confessions*,

---

82. Augustine, *Confessiones* 9.14–15; McKinnon, *Music*, 154.
83. Augustine, *Confessiones* 9.14–15: "affectus pietatis."
84. O'Donnell, *Augustine Confessions*, 110.
85. Augustine, *Confessiones* 1.1; 13.1.

Augustine calls the heart the state and place "where I am whomever I am."[86] Music's consolation gives a glimpse of the integrity of human experience, where the believer finds rest through the ipseity of identity in the liturgy. This ipseity is otherwise dissipated in memory by the experience of physical and temporal distance from the past. Therefore, music's consolation of passions is constitutive of human *being* by means of transient rest.

Fittingness as Measure of Delight

Rest is music's consolation. However, with the consolation of music, Augustine is aware of the immanent danger of becoming entrapped by delight's temporal glimpses of rest. True and complete rest is possible only in God, after death, even if liturgical music can afford some glimpses thereof. In the following passage (*Conf.* 10.49–50), Augustine wrestles with determining the measure of delight and proposes the harmony of fittingness (*conveniens*) as the internal and external measure for recognizing the rectitude of delight. Fittingness orders delight's motion from restlessness towards rest while also accounting for the impossibility of reaching perfect rest while in time.

Written in the context of an extended reflection on seeking God in memory and in anticipation of a discussion on time, creation, and redemption, Augustine quibbles about the delight of church music and, on this occasion, shows that therapy of the passions is not an end, but a means to an end. In the lengthy passage, he writes,

> The delight of the ear drew me and held me more firmly, but you unbound and liberated me. Now I confess that I repose just a little in those sounds to which your words give life, when they are sung by a sweet and skilled voice; not such that I cling to them, but that I can rise out of them when I wish. But it is with the words by which they have life that they gain entry into me, and seek in my heart a place of some honor, even if I scarcely provide them a fitting one. Sometimes I seem to myself to grant them more respect than is fitting, when I sense that our souls are more piously and earnestly moved to the ardor of devotion by these sacred words when they are thus sung than when not thus sung, and that all the affections of our soul, by their own diversity, have their proper measures (*modos*) in voice and song, which are stimulated by I know not what secret correspondence. But the gratification of my flesh—to which I ought not to surrender my mind to be enervated—frequently leads me astray, as

---

86. Augustine, *Confessiones* 10.4.

the senses do not accompany reason in such a way as patiently to follow; but having gained admission only because of it, seek even to run ahead and lead it. I sin thus in these things unknowingly, but afterwards I know. Sometimes, however, in avoiding this deception too vigorously, I err by excessive severity, and sometimes so much so that I wish every melody of the sweet songs to which the Davidic Psalter is usually set, to be banished from my ears and from the church itself. And safer to me seems what I remember was often told me concerning Athanasius, bishop of Alexandria, who required the reader of the psalm to perform it with so little inflection of voice that it was closer to speaking than to singing. However, when I recall the tears which I shed at the song of the Church in the first days of my recovered faith, and even now as I am moved not by the song but by the things which are sung, when sung with fluent voice and music that is most [fitting] (*conuenientissima modulatione*), I acknowledge again the great benefit of this practice. Thus I vacillate between the peril of pleasure and the value of the experience, and I am led more—while advocating no irrevocable position—to endorse the custom of singing in church so that by the pleasure of hearing the weaker soul might be elevated to an attitude of devotion. Yet when it happens to me that the song moves me more than the thing which is sung, I confess that I have sinned blamefully and then prefer not to hear the singer. Look at my condition! Weep with me and weep for me, you who so control your inner feelings that only good comes forth. And you who do not behave thus, these things move you not. You however, O Lord my God, give ear, look and see, have pity and heal me, in whose sight I have become an enigma unto myself; and this itself is my weakness.[87]

Augustine's initial hesitation towards music concerns pagan resemblances, the quality of chants, and the moral dimension of the passions. He writes of his realization and caution over the power of sweet sounds of music to move the soul, which also awakens the passions: "When I sense that our souls are more piously and earnestly moved to the ardor of devotion." As O'Donnell notes, elsewhere Augustine expresses concern and is cautious about how the movement of the soul should not lead to movement of the body in the form of liturgical dance because of pagan connotations "as had happened at Cyprian's shrine in Carthage on his feast not many years before."[88] The pagan elements aside, while again acknowledging the power of hymns to

---

87. Augustine, *Confessiones* 10.49–50; McKinnon, *Music*, 154–55.
88. Augustine, *Sermo* 311.5. See O'Donnell, *Augustine Confessions*, 105–12.

instill piety and stir divine love, Augustine complains about the quality of church music, for instance, in *Epistula*:

> On the question [of music], so useful for moving a pious mind and for igniting the affects of divine love, various customs exist and most members of the church in Africa are more lazy, so the Donatist criticize us, because we soberly sing the divine hymn of the prophets in the church, while they themselves are intoxicated to the song of human psalms with the genius of the composers, as if they were being kindled to the trumpets of exhortation.[89]

When done well, Augustine admires the power of music and song to raise the human spirit towards God and is ashamed of the sober singing of prophetic hymns due to laziness. Poor church music is of no spiritual profit and fails to convey the true meaning of the prophetic song, which is to intoxicate the human spirit with God. While Augustine exhorts against the body's movement and values good church music, he maintained scruples about the moral questions surrounding the soul's movements. Thus, as McKinnon notes, consistent with the early Christian landscape, for Augustine, "the motivation of moralism is at least as strong as that of antipathy toward idolatry."[90] O'Donnell further notes that this leads to Augustine's hesitant attitude toward liturgical music. Augustine stresses the importance of church music,[91] but "the suspicion lingered long."[92] Augustine first describes the moral concerns behind his suspicion of church music which he conveys through his ambivalent attitude towards church music. Augustine first acknowledges the value of music.

> Sometimes I seem to myself to grant them more respect than is fitting, when I sense that our souls are more piously and earnestly moved to the ardor of devotion by these sacred words when they are thus sung than when not thus sung, and that all the affections of our soul, by their own diversity, have their proper measures (*modos*) in voice and song, which are stimulated by I know not what secret correspondence.[93]

On the other extreme, Augustine sometimes acknowledges the fear of deception.

89. Augustine, *Epistula* 55.34.

90. Augustine, *Confessiones* 10.49–50; McKinnon, *Music*, 3.

91. Augustine, *Enarrationes in Psalmos* 18.1.

92. O'Donnell, *Augustine Confessions*, 105–12. O'Donnell cites Augustine, *Contra Iulianum* 4.66.

93. Augustine, *Confessiones* 10.49–50; McKinnon, *Music*, 154–55.

> Sometimes, however, in avoiding this deception too vigorously, I err by excessive severity, and sometimes so much so that I wish every melody of the sweet songs to which the Davidic Psalter is usually set, to be banished from my ears and from the church itself.[94]

Augustine then states the ambivalence:

> Thus I vacillate between the peril of pleasure and the value of the experience, and I am led more—while advocating no irrevocable position- to endorse the custom of singing in church so that by the pleasure of hearing the weaker soul might be elevated to an attitude of devotion.[95]

The question for him is, what to do with church music to avoid the excess of delight while obtaining spiritual profit? The response has an external component and an internal component. Internally, the listener uses music to enjoy God. The enjoyment is licit when it is not for music's sake but for reaching God through music. When describing music, he writes that he delights "not such that I cling to them, but that I can rise out of them when I wish."[96] Augustine develops at length in the first books of *On Christian Doctrine*, which he wrote at around the same time as *Confessions*, the distinction between use (*uti*) and enjoyment (*frui*).[97] In a succinct passage, he explains: "For to enjoy a thing is to rest (*inhaerere*) with love in it for its own sake. To use, on the other hand, is to employ whatever comes to one's disposal, to obtain the object of love, if it is a right object of love."[98] However, he then qualifies that only the Triune God is the *true* aim of human enjoyment because in God alone is fully satisfactory rest possible, and all things, including people, are to be used to enjoy God.[99] Proper music uses delight, internally and externally, to lead toward the enjoyment of God—failure to do so results in the idolatry of self, as Marion calls it.[100] Externally, musical modulation provides a framework to order the internal use of delight. Modulation thus regulates delight, hence the need for specific

---

94. Augustine, *Confessiones* 10.49–50; McKinnon, *Music*, 154–55.

95. Augustine, *Confessiones* 10.49–50; McKinnon, *Music*, 154–55.

96. Augustine, *Confessiones* 10.49–50; McKinnon, *Music*, 154–55.

97. On the analogy *honestum* (*to kalon*)/*utile*//*frui*/*uti* or beautiful/useful//enjoy/use, see Fontanier, *Beauté selon saint Augustin*, 197–204.

98. "Frui est enim amore inhaerere alicui rei propter seipsam. Uti autem, quod in usum venerit ad id quod amas obtinendum referre, si tamen amandum est" (Augustine, *De doctrina christiana* 1.4, translation mine).

99. Augustine, *De doctrina christiana* 1.5.

100. Marion, *In the Self's Place*, 84.

liturgical music. This Augustine learns from Athanasius, "who required the reader of the psalm to perform it with so little inflection of the voice that it was closer to speaking than to singing."[101] The little inflection ensures a delight, but a delight that does not become the enjoyment of music. The measure of rightly ordered internal use of music and the external modulation for proper enjoyment is what Augustine calls fittingness. Fittingness is an approach to God and reality as truth through beauty rather than the gnoseological correspondence of reality and or Platonic identity. Fittingness is a wholesome characterization of the harmony of reality, where the place of human beings is rightly ordered vis-à-vis God and neighbor.[102] Moreover, metaphysical order precedes and prescribes the moral order: modulation makes fitting music, just like the order of the passions offers human beings glimpses of rest.

A Metaphysics of Redemption

Achieving a fitting albeit incomplete measure of delight is possible only because of the metaphysical state of reality, which is, for Augustine, disordered yet longing for order, of which the restless passions are but an instantiation. Towards the end of *Confessions*, Augustine writes, "Out of order, things are restless; restored to order, they are at rest."[103] While longing for metaphysical order, humans remain restless. Restlessness occurs, in the first place, because of the disordering of a preordained metaphysical configuration of reality. From this perspective, the drama of human redemption is about reordering disorder and chaos. The fittingness of music operates within the metaphysics of redemption. In the fittingness of music, delight orders human fragmentation towards eternal rest. Fittingness for Augustine, however, is broader. That which is fitting orders things rightly by using all things for the enjoyment of God alone. This produces an order of reality grounded in the moral capacity of human beings to become God-like or images of God through Christ, according to Gen 1:26. However, the ordering of reality, of things and signs, and of things through signs, by human beings, is possible only because God has preordained an otherwise fragmented reality. Temporality, in other words, may be reordered towards the eternal only because the eternal has reordered temporality. According to Augustine, reality is fitting for the eternal because the eternal engenders the temporal, and thus reality longs for rest. However, for this, temporality must enter eternity, for

101. Augustine, *Confessiones* 10.49–50; McKinnon, *Music*, 154–55.
102. Fontanier, *Beauté selon saint Augustin*, 35–40.
103. Augustine, *Confessiones* 13.9.

there is metaphysical disorder and all resulting forms of restlessness as long as time exists. Augustine explains this transfiguration of finitude through the fittingness of the incarnation, which is a *metamorphosis of love*. Fittingness is harmony and, like the harmony of music, there is also, by analogy, Augustine explains, harmony or co-adaptation between the eternity of the logos and the finiteness of humanity.[104] The harmony between restlessness and rest is the metaphysical prerequisite for the moral reordering of desire through fitting music. In *On the Trinity*, Augustine explains,

> For I mean by this co-adaptation (*coaptationem*)—as occurs to me just now—what the Greeks call [harmony]. But this is not the place to demonstrate the power of the consonance of single to double that is found in us especially and is naturally so implanted within us—and by whom except by him who created us?—that not even the unskilled can fail to notice it whether singing themselves or listening to others. Through it, indeed, high and low notes are so in concord that whoever departs from it offends grievously not just the discipline, in which most are inexpert, but our very sense of hearing. But a long discourse is required to demonstrate this, while one who knows how, can make it clear to the ears themselves on a well-regulated monochord.[105]

The metaphysical framework of co-adaptation, considered as harmony, renders a redemptive interpretation of music's power to "hold" and "liberate" human beings in the liturgy (*Conf.* 10.49–50). Augustine views music as therapy for the restlessness of the passions. Music's delight in the church first *seizes* and *holds* Augustine and offers, in this way, a glimpse of rest. The rest is real, so music is therapeutic to the fragmentary condition of metaphysical restlessness. However, though real, the rest of music's delight is temporal and momentary. Augustine's passion is *held* in suspense by the rapture of music only to disintegrate into the flux of fragmentation of time and, therefore, to restlessness, either turning into concupiscence of the passion's disquiet (moral restlessness) or resulting in an awareness[106] of the soul's dilation (metaphysical restlessness). Music, therefore, cannot "cure" the human condition but only relieve, momentarily, the pain of its consequent disintegration; music is not an end, but how deliberation is

---

104. McKinnon restricts the interpretation of this congruency to sinfulness and rightenousness.

105. Augustine, *De Trinitate* 4.4; McKinnon, *Music*, 167.

106. For the trinitarian modes of self-presence in Augustine's *De Trinitate*, see Wetzel, *Augustine*, 72–75, esp. 73: "Self-presence still has for [Augustine] a threefold aspect: the mind simultaneously recalls itself (past), sees itself (present), and wills itself to be continued (future)."

achieved: "You unbound and liberated me."[107] Augustine refers to Jesus, the second person of the Trinity, mediator of God and humanity, time and eternity, whose divine work is salvation. Through the initial grip of music's delight, in other words, Jesus first reaches out, then unbinds Augustine, and finally liberates him—a process corresponding to the threefold moments of a metamorphosis of restlessness through music, which is grace, conversion, and salvation. The power of music's metamorphosizing power then, for Augustine, lies in that, through its proper use, restlessness, moral and metaphysical, is the portal for redemption now, through the work of God's grace. Augustine writes, "I confess that I repose just a little in those sounds to which your words give life." Echoing the preexistent Word at John 1:1, the implication of this is, as O'Donnell observes, that the Word is before sounds and that the Word vivifies the sounds that express it. Finally, the eternal Word gives through the sounds that communicate it a place of repose, rest, and a glimpse of redemption. This rest, in turn, is transformative and reveals the enigma of the human condition, which God alone illuminates, for restlessness seeks redemption, just as it is being redeemed: "Look at my condition!" The place of restlessness is no longer metaphysical or moral, but understanding interiority through a life recounted from the vantage point of God's eternity, in the light of which human experience is an insufficient aporia: "I had become a great question to myself, and I asked my soul why it was sad and why it was so disquieted within me, and I had no answer to give myself."[108] Restlessness is incomprehensible without redemption. For this reason, Paul Rigby connects resurrection and restlessness in his Ricoeurian reading of *Confessions* as narrative.[109] The image of rest is the Trinitarian relational unity in the difference of musical harmony, which the singing of the psalter represents, reminiscent of the harmony of the tripartite soul in Plato's *Republic* (which is the essence of justice or order). The voice, flute, and string are united "as mind, spirit, body; but by similitude, not by properties."[110] Harmony is achieved through co-adaptability of the similitude of love: "My weight is my love: by it, I am carried, wherever I am carried"[111] for "God is love" (1 John 4:16). In the image of God, which resides in the intellect, the ordering part of the human soul, human beings are

---

107. As cited by O'Donnell. See Augustine, *Confessiones* 1.16; 6.26; 7.27; 11.1.

108. Augustine, *Confessiones* 4.9.

109. Rigby, *Theology of Augustine's Confessions*, 213–37.

110. As cited by Hübner, "Musica," 12. See Augustine, *Enarrationes in Psalmos* 150.8 (translation mine).

111. Augustine, *Confessiones* 13.10.

capable of God's unity (*capax dei*)[112] and, therefore, of rest after the perfect harmony in the image of the Trinity.[113]

Abiding with Anxiety?

Bergo concludes her study by suggesting that it is possible to overcome paralysis and deal with the panic of anxiety by first learning to *abide with it*.[114] For Augustine, abiding with restlessness is a start but not enough: the metamorphosis of restlessness is incomplete without rest. This is because at least five senses of anxiety, considered as restlessness, are identifiable based on our discussion of *Confessions*. First, the metaphysical sense, which conditions the human experience of life in terms of a sequence of events.[115] Second, the moral sense, based on the human ordering of desire through the use and enjoyment of things, is the only aspect of reality. Third, the psychological sense includes the human forms of self-presence, ipseity, and fittingness. Fourth, the existential sense defines human life as restlessness seeking rest in God, whose eternity alone quenches the human longing for wholesome peace of rest. Finally, there is the normative sense, according to which all creation must return to its initial rest in God, which is possible only through the work of redemption. Accordingly, the Aristotelian interpretation of anxiety as fear's "anticipation of evil" is too narrow, indeed it is insufficient, to fit Augustine's Christian concept of restlessness. Therefore, any antidote for "anticipation of evil" alone is insufficient to *cure* the disquieting ache of human life.[116] Likewise, the therapy for restlessness is irreducible to a mere

112. Augustine, *De Trinitate* 14.15.

113. Dixon, *From Passions to Emotions*, 31–35, esp. 31: "Augustine read the doctrine of the *imago Dei* in the light of the second part of this verse [of Gen 1:26] and hence argued that the *imago* was situated in that part of the soul that marked man out as superior to the animals, namely the intellectual part of the soul."

114. Bergo, *Anxiety*, 34.

115. Contrast with Dixon, *From Passions to Emotions*, 56: "Passions were, in Christian psychologies, signs of our fallen state. They were symptoms of the sickness of the soul and of the disordered nature of man."

116. "St. Augustine (354–430), the most influential theological writer in this era, emphasized that relief from anxiety stemmed from faith in the teachings of Jesus Christ, a result he himself had experienced: 'I neither wished nor needed to read further. At once, with the last words of this sentence, it was as if a light of relief from all anxiety flooded into my heart. All the shadows of doubt were dispelled.' Augustine's notion that 'our heart is restless, until it repose in Thee' epitomized the idea that faith in God was the best therapy for anxiety. However, religion was not only the remedy for, but also the cause of, anxiety. Belief in God and an eternal afterlife could relieve anxiety but at the same time lead to tremendous uncertainty. Preoccupations with whether one

cognitive ascent to an abstract belief in God for psychological well-being.[117] Within this rich moral, religious, and metaphysical framework of the passion of disquiet, *abiding with anxiety*, as Bergo prescribes, is inevitable in the metaphysical sense, imperative in the moral sense, foundational in the existential sense, instructive in the psychological sense, but unnecessary, and indeed antithetical, in the normative sense. While *abiding with anxiety* is a multifaceted state of restlessness, it is not an end but, as his reflections on music show, merely a step towards attaining momentary glimpses of temporal liberation from restlessness, which are glimpses of the promise of eternal rest in God. Restlessness or disquiet thus holds the promise of eternal rest. To the question, early in *Confessions*, "Who will grant me rest in you?"[118] Augustine supplicates at the end,

> O Lord God, grant us peace—for you have bestowed all things on us—the peace of rest, the peace of the Sabbath, the peace on which no night ever falls. For when all these very good things have run their course, this whole supremely beautiful order will pass away. Truly both morning and evening were made in them.[119]

Rest from restlessness is in God's redemptive eternity alone[120]—the only compelling basis for a hypothesis of a *metamorphosis of restlessness*—where all things are one simple in the triune God, and therefore, ever at rest, ever creative, because God *sees* all things and they come to be: "we see things you have made because they are, but they are because you see them."[121] A metamorphosis of restlessness within the paradigm of Augustine's *metaphysics of redemption* is founded upon recognizing that to be one is to be perceived by the timelessness of God's eternity, where all things inevitably are pulled

---

was a member of the elect chosen to enter the kingdom of heaven and guilt over the consequences of sinning were potent sources of anxiety. Fear of perpetual damnation in the afterlife was a particular source of terror that persisted through the Reformation in the sixteenth century" (Horwitz, *Anxiety*, 37).

117. "Of course the sovereign cure for worry is religious faith. . . . The turbulent billows of the fretful surface leave the deep parts of the ocean undisturbed, and to him who has a hold on vaster and more permanent realities the hourly vicissitudes of his personal destiny seem relatively insignificant things. The really religious person is accordingly unshakable and full of equanimity, and calmly ready for any duty that the day may bring" (James, *Talk to Teachers*, 224). Brief reference in Horwitz, *Anxiety*, 168.

118. Augustine, *Confessiones* 1.5.

119. Augustine, *Confessiones* 13.50.

120. Similarly, Dixon, *From Passions to Emotions*, 59: "An eternity of rest, not of motion."

121. Augustine, *Confessiones* 13.53.

by the weight of love towards the accomplishment of their restorative or redemptive restless rest.

Bibliography

Augustine. *Confessions*. Translated by Thomas Williams. Indianapolis: Hackett, 2019.
———. *Confessiones* [Latin]. PL 32.
———. *Contra Iulianum*. PL 45.
———. *De doctrina christiana*. PL 34.
———. *Enarrationes in psalmos*. PL 36–37.
———. *Epistulae*. PL 33.
———. *De musica*. PL 32.
———. *De ordine*. PL 32.
———. *Retractationes*. PL 32.
———. *Sermones*. PL 38.
———. *De Trinitate*. PL 42.
Bergo, Betina. *Anxiety: A Philosophical History*, Oxford: Oxford University Press, 2020.
Boquet, Damien, and Piroska Nagy. *Medieval Sensibilities: A History of Emotions in the Middle Ages*. Translated by Robert Shaw. Medford, MA: Polity, 2018.
Byers, C. Sarah. *Perception, Sensibility and Moral Motivation in Augustine: A Stoic-Platonic Synthesis*. Cambridge: Cambridge University Press, 2012.
Deusen, Nancy van. "De Musica." In *Augustine Through the Ages*, edited by Alan Fitzgerald et al., 575. Grand Rapids: Eerdmans, 1999.
Dixon, Thomas. *From Passions to Emotions: The Creation of a Secular Psychological Category*. Cambridge: Cambridge University Press, 2003.
Ferguson, Everett. "Music." In *Encyclopedia of Early Christianity*, edited by Everett Ferguson et al., 787–90. London: Garland, 2016.
Fontanier, Jean-Michel. *La beauté selon saint Augustin*. Rennes: Presses universitaires de Rennes, 2008.
Horwitz, Allan. *Anxiety: A Short History*. Baltimore: John Hopkins University Press, 2012.
Hübner, Wolfgang. "Musica." In *Augustinus-Lexikon*, edited by Robert Dodaro et al., 4.1/2:123–30. Basel: Schwabe, 2012.
James, William. *Talk to Teachers on Psychology: And to Students of Some of Life's Ideals*. New York: Holt, 1899.
Knuuttila, Simo. *Emotions in Ancient and Medieval Philosophy*. Oxford: Oxford University Press, 2004.
MacMullen, Ramsay. *Christianizing the Roman Empire*. New Haven: Yale University Press, 1984.
Marion, Jean-Luc. *In the Self's Place: The Approach of Saint Augustine*. Translated by Jeffrey L. Kosky. Stanford: Stanford University Press, 2012.
Marrou, Henri-Irénée. "Une théologie de la musique chez Grégoire de Nysse?" In *Christiana Tempora: Mélanges d'histoire, d'archéologie, d'épigraphie et de patristique*, edited by Jacques Fontaine and Charles Kannengiesser, 365–72. Paris: N.p., 1972.
McKinnon, James. *Music in Early Christian Literature*. Cambridge: Cambridge University Press, 1989.
Migne, J.-P., ed. *Patrologia Latina* [PL]. 217 vols. Paris: N.p., 1844–1864.

O'Donnell, James. *Augustine Confessions*. Vol. 3. Oxford: Oxford University Press, 1992.

Pizzany, U. "Music." In *Encyclopedia of Ancient Christianity*, edited by Angelo Di Berardino et al., 2:850–51. Downers Grove, IL: InterVarsity, 2014.

Quasten, Johannes. *Music and Worship in Pagan and Christian Antiquity*. Translated by Boniface Ramsey. Washington, DC: National Association of Pastoral Musicians, 1983.

Rigby, Paul. *The Theology of Augustine's Confessions*. Cambridge: Cambridge University Press, 2015.

Roberts, Robert. "The Emotions in the Christian Tradition." *Stanford Encyclopedia of Philosophy*, Mar. 10, 2021. https://plato.stanford.edu/archives/spr2021/entries/emotion-Christian-tradition.

Smith, John A. *Music in Ancient Judaism and Early Christianity*. London: Routledge, 2007.

Sorabji, Richard. *Emotions and Peace of Mind: From Stoic Agitation to Christian Temptation*. Oxford: Oxford University Press, 2002.

Taliaferro, Robert C. "Introduction to On Music." In *The Immortality of the Soul; On Music; The Advantage of Believing; On Faith in Things Unseen*, 153–68. Fathers of the Church 4. Washington, DC: Catholic University of America Press, 2010.

Wetzel, James. *Augustine: A Guide for the Perplexed*. London: Continuum, 2010.

———. "Augustine." In *The Oxford Handbook of Religion and Emotions*, edited by John Corrigan, 349–63. Oxford: Oxford University Press, 2009.

The Strength to Remain

On the Past and Future of Manence

DAVID ALBERTSON

He knows the blessedness of infinity, he has felt the pain of renouncing everything... and yet the finite tastes every bit as good to him as to someone who never knew anything higher, for his remaining in finitude has no trace of a dispirited, anxious training... as if it were the most certain thing of all.

—KIERKEGAARD, *FEAR AND TREMBLING*

IN A PASSING REMARK in the middle of *The Wedding Feast of the Lamb*, Emmanuel Falque makes an assertion one might easily overlook. He states that "the ultimate goal of my triptych of books" is "looking at what it is to 'abide.'"[1] That is, according to Falque himself, the Johannine figure of abiding, remaining, or dwelling (Greek, μένειν; Latin, *manere*)—in its fullest philosophical significance—is the fulcrum of the *Philosophical Triduum*. Falque names this concept *manence*, following the lead of Stanislas Breton (1912–2005), the French Passionist priest, philosopher, and theologian who

---

1. Falque, *Wedding Feast*, 50.

also taught at the Catholic University of Paris.² In what follows I explore manence beyond its occasional appearances across Falque's writings. Falque is right, in my judgment, that the concept subtends his lifelong efforts to intertwine phenomenology with Catholic theology and to compel both fully to embrace finitude. As he observes, manence even underlies the difference between him and Jean-Luc Marion on the saturated phenomenon and on the event.³ How well do we understand manence and its history, and why might it represent the heart of Falque's theological and philosophical project?

The primary sense of μένειν in the Gospel of John is eucharistic: those who eat the flesh and drink the blood of Jesus will *abide* (μένει) in him and he in them (John 6:56). The dominical mandate to *remain* plays a central role in the Farewell Discourse:

> Remain [μείνατε] in me, as I remain in you. Just as a branch cannot bear fruit on its own unless it remains [μένῃ] on the vine, so neither can you unless you remain [μένητε] in me. I am the vine, you are the branches. Whoever remains [ὁ μένων] in me and I in him will bear much fruit, because without me you can do nothing. Anyone who does not remain [μένῃ] in me will be thrown out like a branch and wither; people will gather them and throw them into a fire and they will be burned. If you remain [μείνητε] in me and my words remain [μείνῃ] in you, ask for whatever you want and it will be done for you. (John 15:4–7)

This exhortation to remain (John 15) even precedes the words of institution that enables eucharistic remaining (John 6). Then in the era of eucharistic fellowship, "God remains in us [ὁ θεὸς ἐν ἡμῖν μένει]" through communal love, through the gifts of the Spirit, and through the ongoing authority of Jesus (1 John 4:12–16). Although the Greek term is lacking, one might see a trace of manence in Mary's abiding with Jesus in her heart (Luke 2:51), abiding at the foot of the cross (John 19:25), and abiding in the home of the beloved disciple (John 19:27), or even in the *dwelling* of the incarnation itself (John 1:14).

Given its prevalence in the New Testament, manence is indubitably theological, even essentially eucharistic, as Falque's usage underscores. Yet beyond its Christian valence, manence has an indisputable philosophical ancestry of its own. Manence denotes the ground of immanence (*in-manere*),

---

2. See Falque, "De la préposition"; "À demeure"; cf. *Wedding Feast*, 255n15. Following Falque's English translators, I use the French word (*manence*) as a technical term in English.

3. Falque, *Wedding Feast*, 60; cf. e.g., Marion, *In Excess*, 30–53; *Being Given*, 159–73. See further Romano, *Event and World*.

the remaining-in-finitude that marks off the methodological domain of most philosophical traditions. In Plato and Plotinus, μένειν names an action, quality, or trace of the One; as μονή it unifies the Proclian circuit of procession (*e-manatio*) and return. Thanks to this double heritage, manence enacts the *crossing* of philosophy and theology within itself.[4] Manence is not simply another instance of crossing; it is a kind of transcendental "crossing" that makes possible all the others, as the double condition of immanence, on the one hand, and Christic abiding, on the other. We should keep in view the full complexity of this crossing, even if we must postpone for now a further complication: that one of Martin Heidegger's final names for the temporal horizon of Being is precisely abiding, remaining, or dwelling (*wohnen, bleiben, sich aufhalten*, or *währen*).[5]

To clarify the stakes of manence, I first compare Stanislas Breton's retrieval of the concept with Emmanuel Falque's appropriation. Then I outline the differential emergence of manence—and its contrary—in late antique pagan and Christian Neoplatonism. Finally, I nominate an unexpected medieval author whose account of manence most closely resembles Falque's own.

Manence from Breton to Falque

Stanislas Breton first defines manence when analyzing the post-Heideggerian ontological possibilities of *being-in* and *being-toward* in Thomas Aquinas and Meister Eckhart.[6] In the course of explaining Eckhart's henological sources, Breton points readers to the pivotal Theorem 35 of Proclus's *Elements of Theology*, which sets forth the emanationist triad of μονή, πρόοδος, and ἐπιστροφή.[7] Eckhart's commentary on Exod 3:14 (*ego sum qui sum*) uses the term *mansio*, which Breton translates *demeurer* and compares to μένειν in John 15.[8] In Breton's reading of Aquinas, God's being is not simply *esse* as substance but a dynamic, relational being—as *esse in* or *remaining-in* (*demeurer dans*). The divine persons of the Trinity do not simply subsist but *abide in* each other (the immanent Trinity, relating among themselves) and only as such abide in the world (the economic Trinity, active in Creation).

4. See Falque, *Crossing the Rubicon* §§16–18, 122–36.

5. See, e.g., Heidegger, "Bauen Wohnen Denken"; "Dichterisch wohnet der Mensch"; cf. Falque, *Wedding Feast*, 51.

6. Breton, *Philosophie et mystique*, 44–45. On μένειν as *demeurer* see Breton, *Vivant miroir*, 42. *Philosophie et mystique* develops Breton's 1947 doctoral thesis, which would be published as *L'esse in et l'esse ad dans la métaphysique de la relation*. See Falque, "De la préposition," 17–18.

7. On Proclus, see Breton, *Philosophie et mathématiques*.

8. On Eckhart, see Breton, *Deux mystiques*.

Being-in is not an inert substance but an action, an active conservation that is a continuous creation, as Breton describes.⁹ The Eucharist is the supreme site of *esse in*, where in one singular locus the divine persons remain in each other (Trinity), God remains in humanity (incarnation), God remains in the host (transubstantiation), and humanity remains in God (communion).¹⁰

Falque praises Breton as the *pioneer* of his own paradigm for performing philosophy and theology together, a *practique commune* in which, until Falque, Breton was nearly *unique* (*un hapax*). "No one more than Breton, in contemporary philosophy at least, has been able to remain [*demeurer*] a philosopher while also pursuing theology," he writes admiringly.¹¹ Like Breton, Falque emphasizes the eucharistic sense, citing John 6 and 15. But then he links eucharistic remaining to three theological triads: "Abode [*demeure*], birth, childhood; manence [*manence*], origin, growth; Eucharist, resurrection, kingdom."¹² If Heidegger glossed *Wohnen* as *Denken*, and Jean-Yves Lacoste glossed thinking (*penser*) as prayer (*prier*), Falque insists that the originary identity of *Wohnen* must be a "mode of 'remaining' [*demeurer*], one that is proper to phenomenology, certainly, but even more to Christianity."¹³ Along these lines, Breton's initially ontological retrieval of μένειν opens the way for Falque's theological specification. "It's not enough to 'remain' [*rester*] or even to 'make an effort to remain' [*faire effort pour demeurer*]," he explains. "The 'remaining' [*la 'demeure'*] as such must be *consecrated* as a place to inhabit."¹⁴ For Falque, remaining, precisely as a philosophical concept, is already indelibly eucharistic.¹⁵

In the *Philosophical Triduum*, Falque associates the past with the unknown of birth (*Metamorphosis of Finitude*) and the future with the unknown of death (*Guide to Gethsemane*). In between our past and future, the time of manence names the duration of human embodiment associated with the animality of eating and sexuality (*Wedding Feast of the Lamb*). In that present time of abiding in the flesh, however, the body cannot be

---

9. Falque, "De la préposition," 25–26; "À demeure," 273.

10. Falque, "De la préposition," 27.

11. Falque, "À demeure," 268.

12. Falque, "À demeure," 271. On childhood and the kingdom of God, see Falque, *Metamorphosis of Finitude*, 152.

13. Falque, "À demeure," 272. See Lacoste, *Experience and the Absolute*, 34–37.

14. Falque, "À demeure," 270 (italics mine).

15. Put differently—after a Johannine fashion—what is "consecrated" is not only the bread of Passover, as in the Synoptic gospels, but the immanent bodies of the disciples themselves, remaining at table in their ordinary finitude, when, before the sacramental words are spoken, Jesus first petitions the Father to "consecrate *them* in the truth" (John 17:17–19); cf. Falque, *Wedding Feast* §31 ("Consecration"), 209–13.

treated as reified substance; as Breton argued, to remain is not to subsist.[16] Instead, Falque defines three aspects of manence in *Wedding Feast of the Lamb* §11 and §36.[17] The first we have already seen: in the Gospel of John manence denotes abiding in Jesus. After John the Baptist hails Jesus as the Lamb, two unnamed disciples ask him "Where do you dwell?" (ποῦ μένεις). When he invites them to come and see, they *remained* (ἔμειναν) with him all day (John 1:38–39). Remaining with Jesus, Falque comments, means dwelling with him in the chaotic animal body that all humans share with him.[18]

Second, eucharistic remaining has a limiting or negative function. "The viaticum," writes Falque, "keeps us in our humanity in God incorporate."[19] That is, the consecrated host of the Eucharist responds anticipatorily to the human temptation toward departure. It fixes the communicant to the immanence of body and flesh. It is not a means of supernatural escape that removes us from the burdens of finitude or allows us to excuse ourselves from being creatures by flight into another world, but rather keeps the human being *in via*, in the given course of embodied life. In short, it is a gift of a limit that, in the words of Charles de Bovelles, "consolidate[s] him in his humanity or . . . stop[s] him from going beyond the bounds of the human."[20] The finitude of birth and death are not disguised or mitigated by eucharistic remaining, but entered more intensively thanks to its restraints. The Eucharist means that the animality of the body is unsurpassable as a mode of proximity to God.

Finally, the structure of remaining has a hortatory force. I *ought* to remain, even when the exhaustions of finitude tempt me to depart. Manence is not a quality of substance enduring through time, like a stain on clothing or money in a bank. Manence is a task: "we need not simply to abide there, me in him and him in me; we need to strive together to abide."[21] One *strives* to remain. Jesus has achieved a superior remaining in the flesh that we are invited to appropriate as a task: "Remain [μείνατε] in me, as I remain in

16. Falque, *Wedding Feast*, 52. Falque considers critiques of transubstantiation made by Heidegger, Jacques Derrida, and Jean-Luc Nancy.

17. Note Falque's remark in "De la préposition," 27n11: "Nous renvoyons sur ce point [viz. on *eros* and *manence*] à notre ouvrage à venir, et dans lequel le 'demeurer charnel' trouvera probablement une large place: À corps perdu, Essai philosophique sur le corps et l'eucharistie." After *Le passeur de Gethsémani* (1999) and *Métamorphose de la finitude* (2004), it appears that Falque's reading of Breton in 2006 played a role in inspiring the turn to manence in the book that would come to be titled *Les noces de l'agneau: Essai philosophique sur le corps et l'eucharistie* (2011).

18. Falque, *Wedding Feast*, 227

19. Falque, *Wedding Feast*, 52.

20. Falque, *Wedding Feast*, 52.

21. Falque, *Wedding Feast*, 52.

you" (John 15:4). As Falque comments: "Organic calls to organic and takes on itself each day the Chaos of our animality to convert it into humanity."[22] There are not two worlds but only one; and yet, there are two paths open to us within that one world: *to stay and abide*, or to *refuse* the world, withdraw, depart. We must eschew both Platonism and nihilism and, in the words of Breton, make the "effort to dwell in the presence."[23] "We must try, with the aid of grace, to stay or dwell in our created humanity, rather than always wanting to abandon it," Falque adds. "It is in reality more difficult to 'be man' and to 'dwell in man,' and thus to respond to our condition as a creature, than to wish to break those limits and go beyond our nature."[24]

In *Wedding Feast of the Lamb*, Falque hints at a univocal sense of remaining that would encompass both the eucharistic abiding of God and human as well as the erotic abiding of male and female. Yet rather than use the term *manence*, he prefers the somewhat euphemistic phrase *flesh in common*. The *sacrament of sacraments* is also a *sacrament of unity* in which the difference of God and human, or man and woman, are overcome by the same "coincidence of their bodies."[25] God's fidelity to the human body in the incarnation, Eucharist, and resurrection invites a response of fidelity to the flesh in Christian practice, both in the "erotic gift to the one from whom he is differentiated in a face-to-face, and in the eucharistic offering from the depths of his unspoken interior Chaos."[26] This is the closest Falque comes to directly comparing sexual remaining and eucharistic remaining: "The body and blood are offered to us to abide in our daily lives . . . in the creative fidelity of sexual difference, as also in the unique sacrifice of the eucharist gift."[27]

In his most recent book, *La chair de Dieu* (2023), Falque revisits manence.[28] He suggests that contemporary phenomenology has overemphasized intention and meaning over events of non-sense, experiences of the flesh (*la chair*) over those of the body (*le corps*), and passive weakness over active strength regarding the ethics of the Other. Manence, according to Falque, promises to correct each of these imbalances—both in its erotic aspect, as the union of bodies in intercourse, and in its eucharistic aspect, as communion with the body of Christ. Here Falque approaches a more directly univocal denomination of the double sense of manence. Manence

22. Falque, *Wedding Feast*, 57.
23. Falque, *Wedding Feast*, 227–28.
24. Falque, *Wedding Feast*, 59.
25. Falque, *Wedding Feast*, 231–32.
26. Falque, *Wedding Feast*, 234.
27. Falque, *Wedding Feast*, 228.
28. Falque, *Chair de Dieu*, 90–92.

names the unflinching embrace of the chaos of our lived bodies, whose very animal capacities, before language, are able to passively remain with the other precisely through an active gift of self, whether that gift be sexual or eucharistic. "Manence, or the act of 'remaining' [*demeure*], not only possesses a Eucharistic finality, but also serves as the source of erotic finality," he writes. "We remain as a couple as we remain in the Church—'abide in me and I in you'—in a body-to-body relation [*corps-à-corps*] that is as much a matter of desire as of fidelity."[29] Here, as Falque recognizes, he draws quite close to St. John Paul II's theology of the body, in which the conjugal act of spousal union is itself the "primordial sacrament."[30]

Remaining and Event in Neoplatonism

Before its prominence in Johannine texts, μένειν appears widely in pre-Christian Greek Platonism. Yet there it emerges as the contrary of another concept, the *event* of the timeless instant.[31] The concept of event emerges when Plato converts the older temporal particle ἄφνω into a substantive signifying an instant or sudden moment (τὸ ἐξαίφνης), in order to solve a dialectical problem encountered by Socrates in *Parmenides*. If the One is not, Socrates reasons, it stands entirely beyond being, pure transcendence; yet if the One is, it also takes on the manifold features of being, pure immanence. If the One relates to Being in both ways, how can we think the transition from one state to the other, from identity to difference, or One to Many? To answer this riddle, Plato posits *the sudden* (τὸ ἐξαίφνης) as an impossible instant, a place without place (φύσις ἄτοπος) and time without time (ἐν οὐδενὶ χρόνῳ) in which the transition from One to Many occurs: it is a "strange instantaneous nature, something interposed between [μεταξύ] motion and rest, not existing in any time."[32] In other words, the sudden mediates the One and the Many composed from pure impossibility: an evanescent irruption into presence, an event that cannot be anticipated.

In Plato suddenness is by no means divine; it is simply a necessary henological postulate that supports his philosophy of the One. After *Parmenides*, however, other Platonists would characterize the divine One not as a sudden momentary event, but as a sovereign perdurance in time. The

---

29. Falque, *Chair de Dieu*, 91.

30. See Falque, *Chair de Dieu*, 89n1; *Wedding Feast*, 65n5, 138–39n9; cf. John Paul II, *Man and Woman*, 500–529.

31. See the important surveys by Beierwaltes, "'Εξαίφνης oder"; Golitzin, "ἐξαίφνης in Ps.-Dionysius."

32. Plato, *Parmenides* 156DE (Fowler, 298–99).

Neopythagoreanizing Middle Platonist, Theon of Smryna (70–135 CE), wrote a popular handbook for navigating Plato's mathematics. There Theon links remaining or abiding to the unity of the monad: "The monad, insofar as it is number, is indivisible. It is called *monad* because it *remains* [μένειν] unchangeable.... However much it is multiplied, the monad abides [μένει μόνας]."[33] The most characteristic activity of the One is to remain the One.

A century after Theon, Plotinus constructed his own synthesis of Academic Platonism, Middle Platonism, and Neopythagorean impulses, coordinating both ἐξαίφνης and μένειν. His usage of the former largely follows Plato: the vision of the Good arrives as an unforeseen surprise. One is "carried out of [study] by the surge of the wave of Intellect itself and lifted on high by a kind of swell and sees suddenly [ἐξαίφνης], not seeing how. The vision fills his eyes with light and does not make him see something else by it, but the light itself is what he sees."[34] Elsewhere Plotinus underscores the negative aspect of the Good's arrival: "Suddenly appearing [ἐξαίφνης φανέν], alone by itself in independent purity, ... Intellect is at a loss to know whence it has appeared [ἀπορεῖν ὅθεν ἐφάνη], whether it has come from outside or within."[35] The suddenness of illumination defeats the search for its provenance. This is not a theorem of mediation, but the mode of the Good's manifestation beyond anticipation or reckoning, which reduces its beholder, bereft of an object, to silent wonder. Yet Plotinus also develops μένειν in new ways. The One is that which *abides by itself* (ἑατοῦ δὲ μένον) and to which we should in response *remain in contemplation* (μένων ἐν τῇ θέᾳ).[36] What abides (μείνασα μὲν αὐτὴ) throughout the sudden appearance and withdrawal of Intellect is the Good.[37] Through its remaining life and intellect *abide*.[38]

For his part Proclus does not foreground ἐξαίφνης, but rather seizes upon μένειν to describe the reserve of self-inherence that abides in causes even amidst their constant flow into effects. Every cause *remains* (μένει) in itself during its procession out of itself, and only thereby can effects complete their return.[39] That is, remaining is what enables the emanative cycle of Proclian Platonism so important for Ps.-Dionysius, John Scotus Eriugena,

---

33. Theon of Smyrna, *Exposition*, 28; cf. Plotinus, *Enneads* 5.5.4–5 (Armstrong, 165–71). On Neopythagoreanism and its relation to Augustine, see Albertson, *Mathematical Theologies*, 40–89.

34. Plotinus, *Enneads* 6.7.36 (Armstrong, 200–201).

35. Plotinus, *Enneads* 5.5.7 (Armstrong, 178–79).

36. Plotinus, *Enneads* 1.6.7 (Armstrong, 254–55).

37. Plotinus, *Enneads* 6.7.36 (Armstrong, 200–201).

38. Plotinus, *Enneads* 6.6.18 (Armstrong, 72–73).

39. See Proclus, *Elements of Theology* props. 26, 30, 33, 35.

Meister Eckhart, Nicholas of Cusa, and other Christian Neoplatonists.[40] By contrast to his favored master, Proclus, and yet returning to the pattern of Plato and Plotinus, Ps.-Dionysius the Areopagite embraces the *sudden*, in a brief but significant passage. In *Letter 3* to Gaius, Ps.-Dionysius constructs his own fourfold theology of suddenness. The sudden is an unforeseen arrival (τὸ ἐξαγόμενον) that arises contrary to expectations and *against hope* (παρ'ἐλπίδα). As an arrival, it passes from the concealed to the openly manifest. Despite its arrival, the sudden remains fundamentally *hidden* (κρύφιος), throughout the revelation and afterwards. As hidden, it remains *unspeakable* (ἄρρητον) and *unknowable* (ἄγνωστον). Hence, the sudden is not primarily a conceptual function, but the particular event of the incarnation of the Word in Jesus. Ps.-Dionysius makes two fundamental alterations to Plato: he transforms *suddenness* into a dialectical event of revelation, and he identifies it with the incarnation.[41] The sudden is no longer a feature of the One, but of the Word.

In the *Divine Names*, Ps.-Dionysius makes another alteration to both Plotinian and Proclian Neoplatonism: he depicts God's own erotic madness as paradoxically the supreme instance of remaining. For Ps.-Dionysius, the signature of divine desire is its unique subjective displacement through ecstasy. The Creator *comes to be outside of himself* (ἔξω ἑαυτοῦ γίνεται) due to an overwhelming *excess of erotic loving* (δι'ὑπερβολὴν τῆς ἐρωτικῆς ἀγαθότητος). God is *charmed* or *enchanted* (θέλγεται) by the world and *falls in love* (ἀγαπήσει καὶ ἔρωτι).[42] Stirred by violent desire, the divine Lover finds he can no longer remain exalted beyond the world. Given such burning desire for the world, God *could not remain barren within* (ἄγονον ἐν ἑαυτῷ μένειν) but must become fruitful. Hence God "was stirred to accomplish, through that abundance, the engendering of all things [κατὰ τὴν ἁπάντων γενητικὴν ὑπερβολήν]."[43] The overflow of God's desire gives birth to the cosmos. Yet for Ps.-Dionysius, God's madness takes place without any flailing, or loss of identity. In this singular divine instance, ecstatic displacement into the beloved is achieved *without roaming* (ἀνεκφοίτητον) beyond the self. Only God can demonstrate "an ecstatic, transcendent capacity to remain Godself [κατ'ἐκστατικὴν ὑπερούσιον δύναμιν ἀνεκφοίτητον ἑαυτοῦ]."[44] God leaves Godself, becoming all things, but miraculously, throughout this

---

40. See Gersh, *From Iamblichus to Eriugena*; Riccati, *"Processio" et "explicatio."*
41. Ps.-Dionysius, *Epistula 3* (1069B) (*Corpus Dionysiacum*, 2:159).
42. Ps.-Dionysius, *Divine Names* 4.13 (712A–B) (*Corpus Dionysiacum*, 1:158–59).
43. Ps.-Dionysius, *Divine Names* 4.10 (708B) (*Corpus Dionysiacum*, 1:155).
44. Ps.-Dionysius, *Divine Names* 4.13 (712A–B) (*Corpus Dionysiacum*, 1:158–59).

self-emptying into the world, God nevertheless *remains* Godself (μένων ἐφ' ἑαυτοῦ).[45]

We have already seen that μένειν is prevalent in the Gospel of John, but there are sudden events throughout the Hebrew Bible and New Testament. "See, I am sending my messenger to prepare the way before me," writes the prophet Malachi, "and the Lord whom you seek will suddenly [ἐξαίφνης] come to his temple" (Mal 3:1–2). In the Lukan infancy narrative, the angels appear to the shepherds *suddenly* (ἐξαίφνης / *subito*) (Luke 2:13). In Jesus's eschatological sermons in Mark, the Lord returns to the house *suddenly* (ἐξαίφνης / *repente*) in the middle of the night (Mark 13:35–36). On the road to Damascus, Paul *suddenly* (ἐξαίφνης / *subito*) was surrounded by the light of Jesus (Acts 9:3; cf. 22:6).

Augustine of Hippo was a careful student of Plotinus and an expert reader of Scripture. One might expect the Latin father to embrace the Platonic aesthetic of suddenness. However, much like Nicholas of Cusa after him, Augustine shows disinterest in the event, if not impatience with its constraints.[46] In *Confessions*, Augustine views *suddenness* with skepticism. Indeed, his emphasis on the intimate proximity of the Creator complicates the very notion of God's *sudden* arrival. In his very different ascents in book 7 (as failure) and in book 9 (as success), Augustine nevertheless resents the momentary quality of *sudden* experience in both instances. As subjectively experienced, suddenness is a function of the finitude of sense perception; it is not a sign of theophany, but a source of human disappointment.[47] For Augustine, God is already so near to the self that no distance is opened for God to traverse.[48] If God is *interior intimo meo*, from whence (*unde*) does God arrive as an event? As he prays: "Where [*quo*] do I call upon you, since I am already within you [*in te*]? Or from what place [*unde*] do you come into me [*in me*]?" Likewise, Augustine asks where could God suddenly arrive where God does not already dwell: "Which place in me exists where my God could come into me?"[49]

---

45. Ps.-Dionysius, *Divine Names* 9.5 (912D) (*Corpus Dionysiacum*, 1:210).

46. In book 12 of *De genesi ad litteram*, Augustine analyzes mystical visions at length, yet never mentions the temporal discontinuities of a sudden ecstasy or an event of rapture. See Augustine, *De genesi ad litteram* 12.16–18 (Zycha, 402–7). Nicholas of Cusa combines Augustinian and Dionysian impulses in his concept of God as *non aliud*, construed as radical anteriority, self-gift, and remaining, namely, the exact inverse of the sudden event. On Nicholas of Cusa, see Albertson, "Plötzlichkeit und Schweigen."

47. Augustine, *Confessiones* 7.17 (23) (O'Donnell, 84); cf. 9.10 (25) (O'Donnell, 114).

48. See Marion, *In the Self's Place* §38 ("Aporia of the Place"), 237–43.

49. Augustine, *Confessiones* 1.2 (2) (O'Donnell, 3).

Instead, Augustine constructs an alternative to the Platonist *event* that we might even describe as a counter-event. For Augustine, God is closer to the self than the self is to itself. This situation certainly allows for the event of one's own self-arrival into authentic identity, but it renders impossible any such event on the side of God. Rather than arrive in a sudden event, God abides, always already present as a non-event or anti-event, remaining infinitely and inescapably proximate to the self despite the self's own habitual instability, self-alienation, even dissolution. How do we characterize this mode of divine presence, if not by event? In *Confessions*, the verb *maneo* fills this role.[50]

Augustine uses remaining (*maneo*) in two ways that we can hear indicated in his famous phrase *interior intimo meo et superior summo meo*.[51] God remains in *Confessions* in two senses: *superior* above the self, eternally in heaven, and *interior* within the self, waiting for the self's return. When Augustine applies *manere* to God in the superior sense, he uses the term simply to express God abiding in eternity, following the common usage of *manet in aeternum* in the Vulgate.[52] In this first sense, we encounter two distinct emphases in different passages. God remains unchangeably: beings arise into being and pass away into non-being, but God remains above the flux in the immutable first principles of creation (*incommutabilis manes super omnia*).[53] And God remains above (*desuper mihi manes*): the soul passes through its memory to attain the God who abides above it.[54]

But the more original and complex use of *manere* is Augustine's second, interior sense. God remains more within the self than does the self itself, waiting patiently for the self to return. For Augustine, divine Love is primarily the guarantee always to remain and never to abandon the departed self. "I wandered through the wide ways of the world," he writes, "yet you never deserted [*deserebas*] me."[55] After reflecting on the death of his friend in book 4, Augustine pleads with his soul:

> Now you listen: the Word itself shouts for you to return, and there lies a place of indisturbable quiet, where your love will not

---

50. Augustine uses *manere* and its variants (*remanere, permanere, mansio*) some fifty-four times in *Confessiones*. Of these fourteen can safely be counted as trivial. Augustine applies the term to himself (or to himself along with readers) ten times. The remaining thirty uses fall somewhere on the spectrum of "superior" and "interior" uses, with over half appearing in the former category.

51. Augustine, *Confessiones* 3.6 (11) (O'Donnell, 27).

52. Augustine, *Confessiones* 9.6 (8) (O'Donnell, 151).

53. Augustine, *Confessiones* 10.25 (36) (O'Donnell, 134); cf. 1.6 (9) (O'Donnell, 5).

54. Augustine, *Confessiones* 10.17 (26) (O'Donnell, 129).

55. Augustine, *Confessiones* 6.5 (8) (O'Donnell, 62).

> be deserted, if it does not desert [*deserat*]. Look how things pass away, and other things take their place, and at bottom the whole amounts to no more than its parts. "But do I ever pass away?" says the word of God. There fix your dwelling place [*mansionem tuam*]; there, my soul, so tired of these deceits, there commend whatever you might possess within. . . . And as they decline those things will not drag you downwards, but they will stand firm with you and remain present to the ever-steadfast and ever-remaining God [*permanebunt ad semper stantem ac permanentem deum*].[56]

The Word of God remains present to the self, waiting for the self's return, and that very remaining provides the conditions according to which a return can be made. God remains within the self as the very locus of return that God never departs. Indeed, so little does God ever recede from the human heart that, for a lack of any distance, says Augustine, "we scarcely even return" to God (*vix redimus ad te*).[57]

In book 10, we encounter a second characteristic of interior remaining. Augustine interprets God's remaining with the self as a remaining *in memoria*. Augustine had established early in book 1 that God's presence should not be construed spatially, even as a maximal spatial extension. Now Augustine's use of *manere in memoria mea* connects God's non-spatial presence and the memory's non-spatiality.[58] Searching throughout his memory, he has not found God outside it. Yet he underscores that there is no single place where he finds God.[59] How to reconcile these truths? The answer is that "you remain in my memory [*manes in memoria mea*], and there I find you, when I remember you and delight in you."[60] God remains in his memory from the first day Augustine learned of God. But *where* in the memory does God remain? "Where do you remain in my memory, Lord, when you remain there? . . . You have conferred this honor upon my memory, that you remain in it, but now I am considering in which part of it you remain."[61] In the end Augustine ends the search for God without resolution, since

---

56. Augustine, *Confessiones* 4.11 (16) (O'Donnell, 39).

57. Augustine, *Confessiones* 8.3 (8) (O'Donnell, 91).

58. See Augustine, *Confessiones* 10.24–25 (35–36) (O'Donnell, 133–34), where *manere* denotes God six times and *habitare* three more.

59. Augustine, *Confessiones* 10.26 (37) (O'Donnell, 134).

60. Augustine, *Confessiones* 10.24 (35) (O'Donnell, 133).

61. "Sed ubi manes in memoria mea, domine, ubi illic manes? . . . tu dedisti hanc dignationem memoriae meae, ut maneas in ea, sed in qua eius parte maneas, hoc considero" (Augustine, *Confessiones* 10.25 [36] [O'Donnell, 133]).

his search presupposed the spatial locality he had previously denied of the memory and God alike.

Augustine's two senses of remaining coincide at the moment when the self begins to return. At that point, the self sees that God's superior remaining above time has fixed the possibility of the self's return in time, which is God's interior remaining. The truth of God's eternal remaining is that to which the self has recourse when it returns to itself. God's remaining provides a kind of unshakeable wellspring from which souls can draw sustenance and refreshment. "It is good for me to be fixed to God, since if I do not remain in him, neither will I be able to remain in myself; for God, remaining in himself, makes all things new."[62] God's remaining is the means by which individual natures abide in themselves and collapse the alienating distance within them, renewed in their particular identities.

Far from appearing as an event, God's self-revelation for Augustine is too near to ever arrive; much less does God arrive to the self suddenly in an instant. Somewhat anachronistically, but perhaps all the more urgently for that reason, we ought to understand Augustine's understanding of God in *Confessions* as an anti-event—as the God who remains. God is too close to the self to arrive, because God is the condition of the self's own arrival. God remains above the self eternally as the truth which guarantees the self's safe passage back to itself. God's love is known as a patient refusal never to abandon or desert the self, remaining uncomfortably close despite our own temptation to flee. As Falque writes of manence: "We must try . . . to stay or dwell in our created humanity, rather than always wanting to abandon it . . . [and] to respond to our condition as a creature, than to wish to break those limits and go beyond our nature."[63]

Hadewijch of Brabant on Remaining in Finitude

Emmanuel Falque has engaged a chorus of medieval philosophers: most of all Bonaventure, but also Aquinas, Eckhart, and Duns Scotus; twelfth-century masters like Anselm of Canterbury, Hugh and Richard of St. Victor, Aelred of Rievaulx, and Bernard of Clairvaux; and even radical Neoplatonists like John Scotus Eriugena or Nicholas of Cusa. But to my knowledge he has yet to explore the embodied philosophy of medieval women typically classified as *mystics*. Beyond their claims to special visions or illuminations,

---

62. "id enim vere est quod incommutabiliter manet. mihi autem inhaerere deo bonum est, quia, si non manebo in illo, nec in me potero. ille autem in se manens innovat omnia" (Augustine, *Confessiones* 7.11 [17] [O'Donnell, 82]).

63. Falque, *Wedding Feast*, 59.

authors like Hildegard of Bingen, Marguerite Porete, or Julian of Norwich are eminently worthy of philosophical retrieval for the same reasons that Bernard of Clairvaux or Aelred of Rievaulx—only philosophers in an eccentric sense—might be. I have tried to outline new ways to read such medieval women beyond the often-limiting frame of mystical visions.[64] When it comes to the concept of manence, one voice stands out: Hadewijch of Brabant (fl. ca. 1250).

Hadewijch was a lay woman who wrote *Letters*, *Songs*, *Poems*, and *Visions* in Middle Dutch. She is the earliest known author to write Christian mystical texts in the vernacular. Although we cannot be sure, it seems likely she was affiliated with a Beguine community in the Duchy of Brabant near Antwerp.[65] At some point Hadewijch was expelled from her home community; although she experienced a real material exile, she evolved a secondary concept of spiritual exile as she reckoned with its meaning. If her controversial teachings about mystical experience precipitated her exile, the exile in turn must have confirmed her teachings. Among other achievements, Hadewijch's account of remaining-in-exile (*bliuen* in Middle Dutch) rivals Ps.-Dionysius and Augustine in sophistication. But more than them, her version foreshadows two features of manence found in Falque's thought: remaining in finitude as an affirmation of immanence; and the inner connection between erotic remaining and sacramental remaining.

Hadewijch's spiritual exile is an exile into immanence. The locus of her exile—the territory of remaining—is the finitude of embodied human life.[66] For Hadewijch, moreover, exile is a task, a matter of voluntary obedience, a traumatic separation to take on board as a mission to fulfill. As she wanders in exile, she longs for God and reaches out with human love, finding strength as she endures the distance from her Beloved. On principle she refuses any religious consolation or self-compensation beyond sheer fidelity to divine Love. "Neither want nor demand anything from God," she warns her students. "Do not demand the satisfaction which comes from Him in any form of rest or consolation."[67] Or as she writes to another, "From time to time, someone is so wounded by charity that he has to renounce God [*dat hi hem gode ontsegghen moet*], in his enjoyment and bliss."[68] Bereft of

---

64. See Albertson, "Cataphasis."

65. For background, see Fraeters, "Hadewijch of Brabant"; McGinn, *Flowering of Mysticism*, 199–265. On Hadewijch and the Beguine movement, see Simons, *Cities of Ladies*; Faesen, "Was Hadewijch a Beguine."

66. On Hadewijch's philosophy of exile, see Albertson, "Immanence as Exile."

67. Hadewijch, *Letter* 6 (ll. 208–11). This significantly reformatted bilingual translation follows the 1947 edition by Jan van Mierlo (*Brieven*, 72).

68. Hadewijch, *Letter* 2 (ll. 126–29) (*Brieven*, 30).

God and barred from transcendence, Hadewijch has only her immanent humanity left over in its finitude. But precisely in her sorrow, she wields that bare human nature as means to touch Love in silence.

Staying at her station in finitude, Hadewijch finds union with the derelict body of Jesus. She remains with God by remaining without God, in solidarity with God's own humanity. As Hadewijch is keen to point out, Jesus refused what was his by right—to call upon God's power—and "did not regard equality with God something to be grasped" (Phil 2:6). Instead, Jesus deliberately chose humility, weakness, obedience, and death. Hadewijch's insight is to apply this principle to the task of loving God. "One does not find it written that Christ ever in his entire life relied at all on His Father or on His mighty nature to enjoy rest," she insists.[69] Hence she invites Christians to forego divine transcendence and embrace human finitude, lest in appealing to that *mighty nature* they escape into delusions of piety and end up compromising the one task greater than knowing God: loving God in the darkness of immanence.

Remaining or manence takes on several distinct but interrelated senses in the thought of Hadewijch. In a preliminary sense Hadewijch understands remaining (*bliuen*) as dwelling (*wonen*). Her few autobiographical letters express her concerns about the communities where her female students dwell without her following her expulsion. She asks a favorite named Margriet to dwell (*wonenne*) with her again rather than remain dwelling (*wone noch en bliue*) with Hadewijch's opponents.[70] Hadewijch explains that only divine Love has the ultimate power to dwell, intimately possessing her beloveds. "Love in herself is always desiring and touching [*ghereinende*] and digesting [*terende*]," she writes. "Love can indwell [*wonen*] all things. Love can indwell love of neighbor [*wonen in caritaten*], yet love of neighbor cannot indwell Love."[71]

For Hadewijch, remaining is also a state of wandering. To be exiled from Love by Love delivers her into the paradox of staying far from the beloved out of love for the beloved. "I am wandering [*dolen*] alone, and I have to remain [*bliuen*] far from Him . . . for whom I so much long to be perfect love."[72] She expresses her desire for God by refusing rest, certainty, and comfort. In *Vision 6*, some *wander* (*dolen*) away from God, while others have

---

69. Hadewijch, *Letter* 6 (ll. 86–94) (*Brieven*, 64).

70. Hadewijch, *Letter* 25 (ll. 27–31) (*Brieven*, 302); cf. *Letter* 26 (ll. 10–14) (*Brieven*, 306).

71. Hadewijch, *Letter* 20 (ll. 65–80) (*Brieven*, 232).

72. Hadewijch, *Letter* 26 (ll. 28–30) (*Brieven*, 308).

the strength to *remain* (*bleuen*).⁷³ Yet there is another sense of wandering that is opposed to remaining. Hadewijch defines reason as both antagonist and stimulant of desire. When reason performs its role, it recognizes its limitations and total indenture to the love that ultimately exceeds it. But, as Hadewijch explains at length in *Letter* 4, reason *strays* (*dolen*) whenever it forgets its relative vocation; reason can mistakenly come to fear the greatness of God, to observe rules unduly, to pursue devotions for their own sake, to draw distinctions among beings.⁷⁴ When God enlightens reason, then "a new force shall remain [*bliuen*] with it"—a power to remain within its finitude and not stray beyond its limits.⁷⁵

The most common sense of manence in Hadewijch is her resolve to remain in finitude, endure the pain of divine absence, and renounce superficial spiritual consolations. When Hadewijch courageously pursues Love, "she remains [*blijft*] too far out of my reach."⁷⁶ Love *remains unseen* (*blijft onghesien*), but Hadewijch strives to *remain* (*bliven*).⁷⁷ Whether Love sends her victory or loss, Hadewijch prays to *endure* (*doghen*). "I want to remain steadfast [*staen*] in her hold [*bedwanc*]," she says in one poem.⁷⁸ In another, she yearns to *endure* (*ghevoelt*) "the weight of gentle love."⁷⁹ Love's vigor makes Hadewijch weak, and Love's sovereignty takes her freedom: "She does with me according to her pleasure. / Nothing of myself has remained to me [*Mijns selves en es mi bleven niet*]."⁸⁰ Humility is one strategy of endurance. Hadewijch is fond of the Marian imagery of the valley: "Whoever rises up, I remain in the dale [*Wie oprijst ic blive int dal*], / Without the consideration of rich comfort, / And always weighed down with heavy burdens."⁸¹

73. Hadewijch, *Vision* 6 (ll. 49–59). I use the edition of Hofmann, *Buch der Visionen*, and the translation by Columba Hart (*Complete Works*, 88).

74. Hadewijch, *Letter* 4 (ll. 32–110) (*Brieven*, 44–48).

75. Hadewijch, *Letter* 4 (l. 29) (*Brieven*, 42).

76. Hadewijch, *Song* 21 (ll. 60–63). This bilingual translation follows the standard 1942 edition by Jan van Mierlo (*Strophische Gedichten*, 156). Hadewijch is credited with couplet poems (many pseudonymous) and stanzaic poems, but recent research suggests the latter are closer to songs. See Fraeters et al., *Hadewijch*.

77. Hadewijch, *Song* 22 (ll. 34, 71–72) (*Strophische Gedichten*, 160–62).

78. Hadewijch, *Song* 30 (ll. 12, 18) (*Strophische Gedichten*, 210).

79. Hadewijch, *Song* 6 (ll. 28–29) (*Strophische Gedichten*, 68).

80. Hadewijch, *Song* 24 (ll. 47–48) (*Strophische Gedichten*, 174).

81. Hadewijch, *Song* 35 (ll. 6–8) (*Strophische Gedichten*, 236); cf. *Song* 38 (l. 31) (*Strophische Gedichten*, 256). "In the heights of love one finds depth [*sale dal*], / Whoever then perceives elevation in that depth [*dale sal*], / Has deep discernment" (*Song* 23 [ll. 61–63] [*Strophische Gedichten*, 168]; cf. *Song* 29 [ll. 47–50] [*Strophische Gedichten*, 204]).

Hadewijch learns to brace herself for misfortunes, but also comes to respond to Love's neglect with ever greater desire. One must "Remain steadfast [*ghestane*] in stormy ardor, / And stand up [*ghestaen*] to love by persisting, / And become equally strong."[82] Those who submit to Love "receive heavy strokes from her / Of which they remain utterly unhealed [*onghenesen af bliven*] . . . / Before they completely gratify love."[83] Love sends sufferings to Hadewijch until she is *utterly noughted* (*niete werden*). If in response she "stands up to love with ardor [*met niede dan besteet*]," absorbing the attack by reciprocating with even greater desire, then Hadewijch gains *power* (*cracht*) to abide in Love's presence.[84] "If anyone dare take on love with vehement ardor," she writes, "she cannot withstand [*verweren*] that fiery storm, / And therein will he dwell [*wone*] with her: her peer."[85] Only those who refuse *to turn back* (*kere*) can *remain* (*bleven*) in the kingdom of Love, as Love's witting and willing captives.[86] The one who *endures* (*doghen*) exile will find his beloved's kingdom in the end, but only as an anonymous refugee, "remaining unknown [*blijft . . . onbekinde*] to love / In his vagrant's wear."[87]

The maximal practice of manence is to remain with Jesus in his humanity, and ultimately "to remain on the cross [*an den cruce gestaen*]" with him.[88] Jesus "remained not-lifted [*onuerheuen af bleef*]" until he was "lifted up [*verheuen*]" on the cross. God remained fully within the conditions of immanence up to the point of death.[89] The cross that we *carry* (*draghen*) is also *endured* (*draghet*) while patiently awaiting the manifestation of Love.[90] Those who remain renounce the premature *rest* (*rasten*) of transcendence. Hadewijch exhorts her students to embrace Jesus's kenosis into immanence: "With God's Humanity, you shall live here [*hier leuen*] in exertion and misery, but with the mighty, eternal God you shall love and jubilate within in sweet surrender."[91] In the present conditions of embodied life, it is too soon to delight in God; one must remain as Jesus did, without relief from finitude. "We all want indeed to be God with God, but—God knows!—few of us want to live as a human being with His Humanity and want to carry [*draghen*] His cross with Him

---

82. Hadewijch, *Song* 23 (ll. 74–76) (*Strophische Gedichten*, 168).
83. Hadewijch, *Song* 32 (ll. 60–64) (*Strophische Gedichten*, 222).
84. Hadewijch, *Song* 38 (ll. 49–56) (*Strophische Gedichten*, 258).
85. Hadewijch, *Song* 38 (ll. 58–60) (*Strophische Gedichten*, 258).
86. Hadewijch, *Song* 2 (ll. 88–90) (*Strophische Gedichten*, 52).
87. Hadewijch, *Song* 9 (ll. 21–28) (*Strophische Gedichten*, 84).
88. Hadewijch, *Letter* 6 (l. 375) (*Brieven*, 86).
89. Hadewijch, *Letter* 30 (ll. 85–95) (*Brieven*, 370, translation modified).
90. Hadewijch, *Letter* 6 (ll. 350–52) (*Brieven*, 84).
91. Hadewijch, *Letter* 6 (ll. 116–19) (*Brieven*, 66).

and want to hang on the cross with Him," Hadewijch observes.[92] Such resolute refusal to depart the immanence of the human condition requires "standing firm [*volstaen*]" and "going to the end [*volgaen*]."[93]

For Hadewijch, the very proximity to the cross brings with it, if not spiritual consolation, then an opportunity to gaze upon the divine Face. The opponents who censured her departed too quickly from suffering, never having seen God's Face in it. But those subject to Love find strength in gazing upon the "great Face of sovereign Love."[94] In the face of Jesus crucified, Hadewijch finds the strength to remain. "With a full heart," she tells her students, "you should gaze upon your dear God, so that the united eyes of your desire remain fixed upon [*bliue ane hanghende*] the Face of your Beloved by the penetrating nails that touch you with a burning that will not cease."[95] The one who "inseparably clings [*hanghet*] to God" and *reads* the divine Face "remains [*bliuet*] in peace."[96]

To embrace the humanity of Christ is to remain within the limits of immanence. This renunciation of transcendence governs all of Hadewijch's theological predication and every possibility of embodied experience in her *Songs* and *Letters*. The only exception to this rule is that which goes beyond the possible: namely, the impossible experiences recounted in her fourteen *Visions*, which take place in a realm of that which cannot be and yet is. (This principle is only reinforced when reminiscences of the *Visions* appear as recollections within a handful of *Songs* and *Letters*.[97]) In the surreal, oneiric *Visions*—always occurring during an episode of eucharistic communion—Hadewijch encounters impossible things: infinite chasms, crystal thrones, St. Augustine in avian form, shapeshifting infants, angelic proclamations, even her own ethereal *Doppelgänger*. If Hadewijch's task in exile is to remain faithful to Love despite her deprivations, abiding resolutely in the humanity

---

92. Hadewijch, *Letter* 6 (ll. 231–34) (*Brieven*, 74).
93. Hadewijch, *Letter* 6 (ll. 298–308) (*Brieven*, 80).
94. Hadewijch, *Letter* 18 (l. 153) (*Brieven*, 213).
95. Hadewijch, *Letter* 18 (ll. 179–83) (*Brieven*, 214, translation modified).
96. Hadewijch, *Letter* 18 (ll. 109–11) (*Brieven*, 208).
97. In *Song* 14, Hadewijch references the abyss or whirlpool of *Visions* 1 and 12. "In the deepest whirlpools, on the highest levels / Love's being remains one and undivided [*Blijft hare wesen in een*]" (Hadewijch, *Song* 14 [ll. 77–78] [*Strophische Gedichten*, 116]). At the end of *Letter* 28, Hadewijch describes the qualities of abiding in divine union, "with God in God": dwelling in silence, ceasing to make distinctions, and allowing her identity to be subsumed in God. In the final lines she shifts from prose to poetry and from concept to image: "Therein I remained standing [*bleuic staende*], above everything and in the middle of everything. Then I looked out, above everything, in the gloriousness without end" (Hadewijch, *Letter* 28 [ll. 269–70] [*Brieven*, 344]).

of Jesus, then the *Visions* constitute an exceptional time and space, where she enjoys proleptic sensory experiences of dwelling in God without difference.

Hadewijch's visionary accounts often conclude with a reference to "remaining" in God. At the end of *Vision 3*, she returns to herself and is able to comprehend the experience she has just had. Then there is one more thing to do: "And I remained to gaze fixedly [*ende bleef starende*] upon my delightful sweet Love."[98] At the closure of *Vision 9*, Hadewijch wins dominance over Reason and is embraced by Love. Ecstatic and inebriated, she again ends the vision with remaining, this time prostrate, as she "remained lying [*bleef ligghende*] until late in the day."[99] In *Vision 11*, Hadewijch experiences spiritual union with Augustine of Hippo himself, who not coincidentally defined *maneo* as a Christian modification of μένειν. Grateful but reflecting on her achievement, Hadewijch realizes that she prefers union with God alone. Unlike her union with Augustine, union with God is a kind of remaining: "For I wished to remain in his deepest abyss [*woude bliuen in sine diepste afgronde*], alone in fruition.... I likewise wished to remain [*woudics bliuen*] in him alone."[100]

In *Vision 7*, Hadewijch notoriously experiences a physical sexual union with the male body of Jesus. While often interpreted as a sign of gender fluidity in medieval Christian culture, the *Vision* also enacts a perfect fusion of erotic and eucharistic manence.[101] Hadewijch narrates the events of a eucharistic liturgy in a virtual space of augmented reality. An eagle flies from the altar as she falls to her knees; Jesus appears as a three-year-old child offering her the ciborium. Finally, the mature male Jesus appears "in the form of clothing of a man [*mans*]"—she underscores: "both human being and man [*mensche ende man*]."[102] Then Jesus makes an active gift of himself, at once erotic and eucharistic:

> After that he came himself to me, took me entirely in his arms, and pressed me to him; and all my members felt his in full felicity [*alle die lede die ic hadde gheuoelden der siere in alle hare ghenoeghen*], in accordance with the desire of my heart and my humanity. So I was outwardly satisfied and fully transported. Also then, for a short while, I had the strength to bear this [*cracht dat te draghene*]; but soon, after a short time, I lost that

98. Hadewijch, *Vision 3* (ll. 25–28) (*Buch der Visionen*, 70; *Complete Works*, 272).

99. Hadewijch, *Vision 9* (ll. 69–71) (*Buch der Visionen*, 108; *Complete Works*, 286).

100. Hadewijch, *Vision 11* (ll. 84–92) (*Buch der Visionen*, 120; *Complete Works*, 290).

101. See, e.g., Hollywood, *Acute Melancholia*, 149–62; Murk-Jansen, "Mystic Theology"; "Use of Gender."

102. Hadewijch, *Vision 7* (ll. 64–67) (*Buch der Visionen*, 70; *Complete Works*, 281).

manly beauty outwardly in the sight of his form. I saw him completely come to nought and so fade and all at once dissolve that I could no longer recognize or perceive him outside me, and I could no longer distinguish him within me. Then it was to me as if we were one without difference.[103]

In this passage, Hadewijch visually comments on the eucharistic reception of the bread dissolving in her stomach with another image, an image of sexual union with the body of Jesus. The moment of ingestion is simultaneously represented as a moment of intercourse. The passing of one body into another, and even the indistinct auto-affection of each body, is figured simultaneously as eating and as a spousal union. At the height of this interpenetration, Hadewijch finds the "strength to remain [*cracht dat te draghene*]." After it comes to an end, Hadewijch abides in a paradox: "I remained in a passing away [*bleef ic in enen veruaerne*] in my Beloved, so that I wholly melted away in him and nothing any longer remained to me of myself [*mi mijns selues niet en bleef*]."[104] She remains in Jesus because she no longer remains. As Veerle Fraeters has shown, *Vision 7* stands out among Hadewijch's other visions, which most often recount ecstatic experiences of mind or spirit. But according to Fraeters, *Vision 7* is *non-ecstatic* and uniquely corporeal. Hadewijch thus abides in eucharistic communion in two senses: she remains in time without a sudden ecstatic event, and she remains within the body's organic finitude.[105]

In her final *Vision 14*, God gives Hadewijch supernatural strength to remain in her sufferings without fleeing them, so long as she abides in Jesus:

> The new power [*gheweldecheit*] he then gave me, which I did not possess previously, was the strength [*cracht van sijn selues wesene*] of his own Being, to be God with my sufferings according to his example and in union with him, as he was for me when he lived for me as Man. That was the strength to endure

---

103. Hadewijch, *Vision 7* (ll. 74–88) (*Buch der Visionen*, 94–96; *Complete Works*, 281).

104. Hadewijch, *Vision 7* (ll. 94–96) (*Buch der Visionen*, 96; *Complete Works*, 282).

105. "Vision 7 is, therefore, not a spiritual or intellectual vision perceived by the inner sensorium of the soul's mind. Rather, it is a corporeal vision perceived with the bodily senses.... This sensorial and intensely erotic embrace can, in my view, be seen as the corporeal counterpart of the moment of revelation in the ecstatic visions" (Fraeters, "Mystic's Sensorium," 34–35). Rob Faesen has suggested that Hadewijch's experience of bodily union with Christ's humanity is focused on his earthly passion, closer to receiving the stigmata of Francis than an erotic embrace. Her corporeal experience fuses with his until they dissolve into one body, sharing one eucharistic life. See Faesen, "Body of Christ," 36–49.

[*ghedraghen*], as long as the fruition of Love was denied me; really to endure [*ghedraghen*] the arrows Love shot at me.[106]

For Hadewijch—as for Emmanuel Falque—Christian experience is not a means of escaping this world into another world, but rather empowers one to remain fully in this one world of our common embodiment, where God himself dwells in his own body on the cross.

This paradigm of erotic-eucharistic manence in *Visions* 7 and 14, grounded in the body and yielding new strength, appears in other places across Hadewijch's writings. In two letters in particular, she analyzes past episodes of union with God that presumably occurred during eucharistic communion as reported in her visionary texts. In *Letter* 9, Hadewijch defines the interpenetration of lovers as both dwelling and remaining:

> How wondrously sweetly one beloved indwells the other [*dat een lief in dat ander woent*], and so through and through indwells the other [*Ende soe dore dat ander woent*], that neither of them recognizes himself, but they mutually enjoy each other, mouth in mouth, and heart in heart, and body in body [*lichame in lichame*], and soul in soul, and one sweet divine nature flowing through them both, and both of them one through each other and also both remain, yes, so they remain [*Ende al eens beide bliuen, Ja ende bliuende*].[107]

Then in *Letter* 11 Hadewijch recounts an early episode of being so "intensely dominated [*bedwonghen gheweest*] by passionate love" that God had to grant her "special strength [*sonderlinghen cracht*]" to survive the erotic experience. Amidst her pleasure God reveals himself with tokens of love, as do friends who "conceal little . . . and show much," whenever they share *intense feeling* (*gheuoelne*) with each other. To express the quality of this intimate exchange, Hadewijch uses images of ingestion, comparing herself and God to two lovers who are *eating, drinking, savoring* (*smakene*), and "devouring one another."[108] Here eucharistic imagery is the only language able to convey the depth of erotic remaining experienced by Hadewijch and the strength she receives from it. Eucharistic remaining gives her the power to remain in her humanity, counteracting the temptation to flee the world and consolidating her within the limits of immanence, where indeed she finds God.

---

106. Hadewijch, *Vision* 14 (ll. 11–20) (*Buch der Visionen*, 152; *Complete Works*, 302).

107. Hadewijch, *Letter* 9 (ll. 6–14) (*Brieven*, 106); cf. *Song* 34 (ll. 41–44) (*Strophische Gedichten*, 232).

108. Hadewijch, *Letter* 11 (ll. 10–29) (*Brieven*, 120).

"To remain in Christ is the fundamental act of being a Christian."[109] Breton's statement—a gloss on Thomas Aquinas—is commended by Falque on more than one occasion. Yet if manence is indeed so fundamental, it must have appeared in multiple guises and conceptual configurations during the development of ancient and medieval Christian thought. Its renewed pertinence today after Heidegger, Breton, and Falque, precisely at the intersection of theology and philosophy, should encourage us to inquire which figures of remaining might inform contemporary approaches to immanence, dwelling, and the event in the continental philosophy of religion. Which version of manence, beginning from Greek traditions in Plato, Theon, Plotinus, Proclus, and Ps.-Dionysius, anticipates Falque's retrieval the most closely, both theologically and philosophically? Remarkably, even more so than Augustine of Hippo or Nicholas of Cusa, Hadewijch of Brabant remains the best.

Bibliography

Albertson, David. "Cataphasis, Visualization, and Mystical Space." In *The Oxford Handbook of Mystical Theology*, edited by Edward Howells and Mark A. McIntosh, 347–68. Oxford: Oxford University Press, 2020.

———. "Immanence as Exile: Hadewijch as Philosopher of Finitude." In *Radical Thinking in the Middle Ages: Proceedings of the 15th International Congress of the Société Internationale pour l'Étude de la Philosophie Médiévale*, edited by Monica Brinzei et al., 263–74. Turnhout: Brepols, 2024.

———. *Mathematical Theologies: Nicholas of Cusa and the Legacy of Thierry of Chartres*. New York: Oxford University Press, 2014.

———. "Plötzlichkeit und Schweigen: Nikolaus von Kues im Dialog mit christlichen Neuplatonismus." In *Nikolaus von Kues—Denken im Dialog*, edited by Walter Andreas Euler, 9–26. Philosophie: Forschung und Wissenschaft 30. Münster: LIT, 2020.

Augustine. *Confessions*. Edited by James J. O'Donnell. Vol. 1. Oxford: Clarendon, 1992.

———. *De genesi ad litteram*. Edited by Joseph Zycha. Corpus Scriptorum Ecclesiasticorum Latinorum 28. Vienna: Hölder-Pichler-Tempsky, 1894.

Beierwaltes, Werner. "Ἐξαίφνης oder: Die Paradoxie des Augenblicks." *Philosophisches Jahrbuch* 74 (1967) 271–382.

Breton, Stanislas. *Deux mystiques de l'excès: J.-J. Surin et maître Eckhart*. Paris: Cerf, 1985.

———. *L'esse in et l'esse ad dans la métaphysique de la relation*. Rome: Angelicum, 1951.

———. *Philosophie et mathématiques chez Proclus*. Paris: Beauchesne, 1969.

———. *Philosophie et mystique: Existence et surexistence*. Grenoble: Éditions Jérôme Millon, 1996.

---

109. "Demeurer dans le Christ est l'agir fundamental de l'être chrétien" (Breton, *Philosophie et mystique*, 33, cited in Falque, "De la préposition," 26).

———. *Le vivant miroir de l'univers: Logique d'un itinéraire philosophique*. Paris: Cerf, 2006.

Faesen, Rob. "The Body of Christ and the Union 'Without Difference': Hadewijch's Eucharistic *Vision 7–8* Reconsidered." In *The Materiality of Devotion in Late Medieval Northern Europe: Images, Objects, Practices*, edited by Henning Laugerud, et al., 36–49. Dublin: Four Courts, 2016.

———. "Was Hadewijch a Beguine or a Cistercian? An Annotated Hypothesis." *Cîteaux: Commentarii cistercienses* 55 (2004) 47–64.

Falque, Emmanuel. "À demeure: habiter, naître, enfanter; Des existentiaux chez Stanislas Breton." In *Philosophie et mystique chez Stanislas Breton: Colloque de Cerisy-La-Salle (août 2011)*, edited by Jean Greisch et al., 267–83. Paris: Cerf, 2015.

———. *La chair de Dieu*. Paris: Cerf, 2023.

———. *Crossing the Rubicon: The Borderlands of Philosophy and Theology*. Translated by Reuben Shank. New York: Fordham University Press, 2016.

———. "De la préposition à la proposition: Mystique et philosophie chez Stanislas Breton." *Transversalités* 99 (2006) 17–36.

———. *Metamorphosis of Finitude: An Essay on Birth and Resurrection*. Translated by George Hughes. New York: Fordham University Press, 2012.

———. *The Wedding Feast of the Lamb: Eros, the Body, the Eucharist*. Translated by George Hughes. New York: Fordham University Press, 2016.

Fraeters, Veerle. "Hadewijch of Brabant and the Beguine Movement." In *A Companion to Mysticism and Devotion in Northern Germany in the Late Middle Ages*, edited by Veerle Fraeters, 47–71. Leiden: Brill, 2014.

———. "The Mystic's Sensorium: Modes of Perceiving and Knowing God in Hadewijch's *Visions*." In *Mystical Anthropology: Authors from the Low Countries*, edited by John Arblaster and Rob Faesen, 28–40. New York: Routledge, 2017.

Fraeters, Veerle, et al., eds. *Hadewijch: Lieder. Originaltext, Kommentar, Übersetzung und Melodien*. Berlin: De Gruyter, 2016.

Gersh, Stephen. *From Iamblichus to Eriugena*. Leiden: Brill, 1978.

Golitzin, Alexander. "ἐξαίφνης in Ps.-Dionysius." *Studia Patristica* 37 (2001) 482–91.

Hadewijch of Brabant. *Brieven*. Edited by Jan van Mierlo. Antwerp: Standaard-Boekhandel, 1947.

———. *Das Buch der Visionen*. Translated by Gerald Hofmann. Vol. 1. Stuttgart-Bad Canstatt: Frommann–Holzboog, 1998.

———. *The Complete Letters*. Translated by Paul Mommaers and Anikó Daróczi. Leuven: Peeters, 2016.

———. *The Complete Works*. Translated by Columba Hart. Mahwah: Paulist, 1980.

———. *Poetry of Hadewijch*. Translated by Marieke van Baest. Leuven: Peeters, 1998.

———. *Strophische Gedichten*. Edited by Jan van Mierlo. Antwerp: Standaard-Boekhandel, 1942.

Heidegger, Martin. "Bauen Wohnen Denken." In *Vorträge und Aufsätze: Gesamtausgabe*, edited by Friedrich-Wilhelm von Herrmann, 4:145–64. Frankfurt am Main: Vittorio Klostermann, 2000.

———. ". . . dichterisch wohnet der Mensch . . . ." In *Vorträge und Aufsätze. Gesamtausgabe*, edited by Friedrich-Wilhelm von Herrmann, 7:189–208. Frankfurt am Main: Vittorio Klostermann, 2000.

Hollywood, Amy. *Acute Melancholia and Other Essays: Mysticism, History, and the Study of Religion*. New York: Columbia University Press, 2016.

John Paul II. *Man and Woman He Created Them: A Theology of the Body*. Translated by Michael Waldstein. Boston: Pauline, 2006.

Kierkegaard, Søren. *Fear and Trembling*. Translated by Sylvia Walsh. Cambridge: Cambridge University Press, 2006.

Lacoste, Jean-Yves. *Experience and the Absolute: Disputed Questions on the Humanity of Man*. Translated by Mark Raftery-Skehan. New York: Fordham University Press, 2004.

Marion, Jean-Luc. *Being Given: Toward a Phenomenology of Givenness*. Translated by Jeffrey L. Kosky. Stanford: Stanford University Press, 2002.

———. *In Excess: Studies of Saturated Phenomena*. Translated by Robyn Horner. New York: Fordham University Press, 2002.

———. *In the Self's Place: The Approach of St. Augustine*. Translated by Jeffrey L. Kosky. Stanford: Stanford University Press, 2012.

McGinn, Bernard. *The Flowering of Mysticism: Men and Women in the New Mysticism, 1200–1350*. New York: Herder & Herder, 1998.

Murk-Jansen, Saskia. "The Mystic Theology of the Thirteenth-Century Mystic, Hadewijch, and Its Literary Expression." *Medieval Mystical Tradition in England* 5 (1992) 117–28.

———. "The Use of Gender and Gender-Related Imagery in Hadewijch." In *Gender and Text in the Later Middle Ages*, edited by Jane Chance, 52–68. Gainesville: University Press of Florida, 1996.

Plato. *Cratylus; Parmenides; Greater Hippias; Lesser Hippias*. Loeb Classical Library 167. Translated by Harold North Fowler. Cambridge: Harvard University Press, 1926.

Plotinus. *Plotinus*. Translated by A. H. Armstrong. Vols. 1, 5, 7. Loeb Classical Library 440, 444, 468. Cambridge: Harvard University Press, 1966, 1984, 1988.

Proclus. *Elements of Theology*. Edited and translated by E. R. Dodds. Oxford: Clarendon Press, 1963.

Ps.-Dionysius the Areopagite. *Corpus Dionysiacum*. Edited by Beata Regina Suchla et al. 2 vols. Berlin: de Gruyter, 1990–1991.

Riccati, Carlo. *"Processio" et "explicatio": La Doctrine de la création chez Jean Scot et Nicolas de Cues*. Naples: Bibliopolis, 1983.

Romano, Claude. *Event and World*. Translated by Shane Mackinlay. New York: Fordham University Press, 2009.

Simons, Walter. *Cities of Ladies: Beguine Communities in the Medieval Low Countries, 1200–1565*. Philadelphia: University of Pennsylvania Press, 2001.

Theon of Smyrna. *Exposition des connaissances mathématiques utiles pour la lecture de Platon*. Edited and translated by Jean Dupuis. Paris: Hachette, 1892.

Sense and Non-Sense

"Become, Never Cease to Become What You Are"

Chaos, Struggle, and Creation in Nietzsche

Gaël Trottmann-Calame

I am in the first place he who knows not where to go—or rather, he who knows not where he is going and who knows it only once he has gone there.

—Emmanuel Falque

"Become what you are"—surely few thinkers have echoed Pindar's imperative more than Nietzsche.[1] Indeed, the Greek poet's words reappear regularly in the writings of the philosopher from Sils-Maria. From their first discreet appearance as the epigraph to an essay by Nietzsche's student in 1864 to their use as the subtitle of *Ecce Homo* in 1889, Pindar's words run like a leitmotif [*fil rouge*] throughout Nietzsche's work.[2] Nevertheless,

---

1. Pindar, *Pythian* 2.72.
2. Among others, see Nietzsche, *Gai savoir* §27; *Schopenhauer éducateur* §4; *Richard Wagner à Bayreuth* §1; *Humain, trop humain I* §263; *Ainsi parlait Zarathoustra* IV. "L'offrande du miel"; *Fragments posthumes*," 19[40]; 11[297]; "Letter à L. Salomé" in *Correspondance*.

there are good reasons why retrieving the famous Greek syntagm complicates the field of Nietzschean thought. By interpreting *becoming* in a way closer to the eternal flow of Heraclitus rather than to Aristotelian teleology, Nietzsche seems to assert that it is impossible for all *becoming* to debouch [*déboucher*] into any being whatsoever.[3] At the same time, by categorically rejecting the *fixist*, ontological, and idealist interpretive prism of reality in favor of that of interpretation or the will to power, Nietzsche radically disqualifies the notion of being[4]—which is not without posing a problem anew when it comes to *becoming* what we *are*. To preserve a meaning that satisfies the demands of perpetual becoming, should we go so far as to invert Pindar's imperative, as Emmanuel Falque insists (after Maldiney), by asserting "be whom you become [*sois qui tu deviens*]"? Does the reversal by the author of *Hors phénomène*—according to whom "it is not being that makes becoming, but becoming that makes being"[5]—suffice to exhaust the radically new meaning that the lyric poet's formula takes on under Nietzsche's pen?

In addition to the above question, further and more complicated problems arise from Nietzsche's reworking of the famous Greek syntagm. As we know, Nietzsche is the thinker who radically refuted the idea of the *ego* (unity and simplicity) by showing what a fiction it is.[6] Indeed, there can be no doubt that, after Nietzsche, there seems to be nothing left of the "famous old 'I'"[7] which modern philosophy takes for its foundation. What's more, the thinker who philosophizes with a hammer remains the one who shattered the very notion of "Self" [*Selbst*] into a formidable multiplicity (struggle), an unspeakable impersonality (chaos), and an incessant process (becoming). This is so much so that Nietzsche condemns the "I have sought myself" of Heraclitus as a never-ending quest, but above all, the Socratic "know thyself" as a dead end. The question then arises: *how* is it possible, despite everything, to uphold the call to "become what you are," and above all, *why* does this exhortation persist, coupled with a call to *egoism*? Inconsistency? Incoherence? Or is this new *egoism* that denies the reality of the *ego* even possible? Could it be that there is "something new to create: no *ego*, no *you*, no *omnes!*"?[8] Could it be that a new *oeuvre* must be accomplished, a new *oneself* [*soi-même*] to be conquered and created, enabling us to become,

---

3. "Le devenir n'a aucun état final, ne débouche pas sur un 'être'" (Nietzsche, *Fragments posthumes*, 11[72]).

4. "Being is an empty fiction" (Nietzsche, *Crépuscule des idoles* §2).

5. Falque, "Tempête sous un crâne," 270.

6. "Le sujet est une fiction" (Nietzsche, *Fragments posthumes*, 9[91]); "L'erreur du moi" (*Fragments posthumes*, 11[21]).

7. Nietzsche, *Par-delà bien et mal* §17.

8. Nietzsche, *Fragments posthumes*, 11[21].

to *never stop becoming who we are*, even if this is in not knowing, in "not realizing that we are engaged in this task"?[9]

As we can see, it's imperative to understand what Nietzsche means by "becoming what you are." And this cannot be done without clarifying "how one becomes what one is," as *Ecce Homo* sets out to do. Perhaps then we'll see what creative effort, poetic force, artistic intoxication, self-transcendence—or, to put it in Falque's language, what *metamorphoses* or *transformations*—are required to *become oneself*. Even more precisely, when *becoming* proves to be an agonal process devoid of any finality other than the search for resistance and the feeling that power is growing, the self is reduced to an impulsive multiplicity to be educated (*Selbstzucht*) and to chaos to be organized and dominated in a perfect *egoistic* logic (*Selbstsucht*) of independence and novelty.

What *I* am Not

How do we become what we are? The first step in this process is to remember *what* you *are not*, or more precisely, what *I* am not. This is to avoid misinterpretation, erroneous definition, or even loss in an impersonal, generic self—"I am such and such. Above all, don't misunderstand me."[10] It's important, consequently, to shed the burden of false metaphysical and moral interpretations, the burden of what we are not, a veritable molt heralding a "metamorphosis"[11]: the conquest of a singular, autonomous, and processual self.

Yet, to keep what is not *me* away from oneself, Nietzsche paradoxically proposes, at least at first glance, taking up the question of *egoism* (its definition and value). His "I want to rehabilitate egoism"[12] is a surprising phrase from a philosopher who denies the *ego*'s reality with the greatest firmness and consequence. It's important to understand. Here, far from showing any inconsistency, Nietzsche, according to a habit peculiar to his *new language* [*neue Sprache*], takes a classic term, empties it of its usual epistemological content, and rethinks it, even if it means keeping it only as a metaphor. So, in defending the "hardest selfishness [*Selbstigkeit*],"[13] Nietzsche takes up and revalues *egoism* [*Selbstsucht*], freeing it from a strictly moralistic

---

9. Nietzsche, *Ecce Homo* §9.
10. Nietzsche, *Ecce Homo* §1.
11. Cf. Nietzsche, *Ainsi parlait Zarathoustra*, "The Three Metamorphoses."
12. Nietzsche, *Fragments posthumes*, 6 [74].
13. Nietzsche, *Ecce Homo* §9.

understanding by giving it a "good conscience"[14] and liberating it from the usually depreciatory connotation attached to this sickly search or quest for the self [*Selbstsucht*]. So much so that, for our philosopher, the *I*, far from being *hateable* (Pascal), becomes loveable and to be cherished. And from then on, this greedy quest or conquest of the self takes on the allure of virtue, self-satisfaction, joyful self-affirmation or *good mood* [*Heiterkeit*], and even more of *necessity*. And this, Nietzsche reminds us, because all forms of egoism, whether we speak of *defensive egoism* (the right to defend oneself, the need to protect oneself) or *aggressive egoism* (the right to attack, the thirst for power), "are necessities for every living being" and "are not a matter of choice . . . but the very inevitability of life."[15] It was an illusion of morality, this "Circe of humanity," to lead us to believe that egoism was a matter of *free will* and that *non-egoistic* instincts were possible.[16] Properly understood, *egoism*—compelling necessity, an irreconcilable search for *interests*, egoism—is never more than the irrepressible and natural *push* of needs expressed by the internal struggle of the (corporeal) drives of the *individual* striving to *be more*, to "feel itself 'more.'"[17]

Nietzsche may well claim that egoism is indeed "an insulting and dirty term for what is the fact of every living being—*to want to grow and create by surpassing oneself*."[18] The imperative of growth and creation, this avid quest for self, as *Ecce Homo* insists, invites us to make ourselves a veritable *masterpiece* of egoism. So, when Nietzsche appeals after Pindar to become what *I* am, it is primarily an exhortation to detach myself from what *I* am not. And this, by rejecting the Western moral tradition (Platonism and Christianity) insofar as it forces a negation of the *strong* and autonomous *I*, an equalization and belittling of the singular and exceptional *I* by means of the *virtues* of self-denial, self-sacrifice, altruism, disinterest (benefiting the *weak*). Thus, becoming oneself begins with the refusal of morality that, while condemning the *subjective self*, defends an impersonal, universal, common, gregarious self—a self that thinks *we* when it says *I*, a self that

---

14. Nietzsche, *Fragments posthumes*, 16 [15].

15. Nietzsche, *Fragments posthumes*, 14[192].

16. "Des actes non égoïstes sont impossibles; 'instinct non égoïste' sonne à mes oreilles comme 'fer en bois'" (Nietzsche, *Fragments posthumes*, 26[54]); "Un être qui serait uniquement capable d'actions pures de tout égoïsme est encore plus fabuleux que l'oiseau Phénix. . . . Comment *pourrait-il* même faire quelque chose qui n'eût aucun rapport avec lui, c'est-à-dire sans nécessité intérieure? . . . Comment l'*ego* serait-il capable d'agir sans *ego*?" (*Humain, trop humain I* §133).

17. Nietzsche, *Par-delà bien et mal* §220.

18. Nietzsche, *Fragments posthumes*, 18[32] (italics mine).

is a "herd"[19]—what could be more sadly impersonal than to be reduced to an *ego*, to "a substance whose whole essence or nature is *only* to think" (Descartes)? This morality, which cuts off the *ego*'s impulse towards itself, extinguishes its aspiration towards itself, curbs its joyful affirmation and moderates its jubilant exhilaration at *becoming* itself, is, therefore, to be rejected. So, at this stage, I know at the very least that *I* am not what this morality says about *me*.

So it's easy to understand why, in the pen of the man who, with rare patience, rigor, and precision, denied the reality of the *ego*, the *I* should appear so often where it would have been easy to opt for the impersonality and universality customary in philosophical discourse (we, us). This explains why, in Nietzsche, "the little word 'I'"[20] although reduced to a mere fiction, is anything but discreet, but on the contrary displays and asserts itself in full view: *Ecce Homo*—"*ego ipsissimus*, and even, if I may be permitted a prouder expression, *ego ipsissimum*."[21] It is not possible to *become oneself* without a formidable *egoism*.

Nevertheless, the question of how we become who we are is not resolved here. Indeed, the problem seems even more complex since Nietzsche rehabilitates *egoism* while firmly maintaining that "the ego itself is nothing but a 'supreme fraud,' an 'ideal.'"[22] Could it be that "egoism without ego" (Wotling) is possible, that *becoming what you are* does not presupposes the *ego*?

Contest and Abyss

If we follow the thinking of the philosopher from Sils-Maria, it's not only idealistic morality that fails to express *who we have to become* but also idealistic epistemology and metaphysics. As we know, according to Nietzsche, the theories of the subject, the great modern *egologies*—whether they affirm the ego as a metaphysical substance (Descartes), as a synthesizing formal unity (Kant), or even as an intentional subject (Husserl)—only refer to an unfortunate but useful fiction: that of the *subject-atom*. And Nietzsche never ceases to point out and demonstrate that this fiction of the subject—a pure philosophical prejudice relaying the ancient belief in the soul—masks the formidable richness of the human person by not seeing it or by not wanting to see it. A structure of irreducible plurality, a profound body,

---

19. "La moralité est l'instinct du troupeau dans l'individu" (Nietzsche, *Gai savoir* §116).
20. Nietzsche, *Fragments posthumes*, 2[193].
21. Nietzsche, *Humain, trop humain II* §1.
22. Nietzsche, *Ecce Homo* §5.

the human being is, above all, a multiplicity of mutually interrelated (*en rapport*)[23] drives, instincts, forces, and affects. As a result, we can no longer speak of the unity and simplicity of the subject (atomism). But that's not all. This mutual relationship of drives is conflictual, agonal, and a struggle. For Nietzsche, far from being defined as an attempt to annihilate what stands in the way (polemical struggle or war), the mutual relationship of drives must be thought of as the search for resistance (agonal struggle or jousting), as the need to establish an ephemeral hierarchy (command and obedience) between various competing drives, with the sole aim of increasing the feeling of power, of *feeling more* of creating. As the fundamental character of all that is, the character of the will to power,[24] struggle thus characterizes *the mode of the becoming of becoming*. It's important to realize that becoming is not the realization of an essence, of a being, but rather the recognition and expression of an irreducible multiplicity in struggle, driven by various fundamental needs or *self-interests* (egoism), most of which are subconscious.

As a result, and Nietzsche insists relentlessly on this point, if this struggle is not at all teleological but solely *oriented* by the search for the feeling that power is growing if this struggle is indeed the character of the "whole"[25]—the human body and the body of the world—then all that is reveals itself to be devoid of purpose, meaning, order, and harmony. Now, since it is elusive, changeable, unspeakable, multiple, devoid of background and foundation [*grundlos*], far from being a *cosmos*, the whole can only be approached as closely as possible by recourse to the *metaphor* of chaos— "*Chaos sive natura*," "the general character of the world is . . . from all eternity chaos,[26] not in the sense of the absence of necessity, but on the contrary in the sense of the absence of order, articulation, form, beauty, wisdom."[27] And, as Nietzsche reminds us—for this is an important point—to assert that everything is chaos is to claim that man himself, "as a multiplicity of 'wills

---

23. Nietzsche, *Gai savoir* §333.

24. "Chaque expression de la volonté de puissance présuppose donc déjà une pluralité de volontés de puissance. La réalité que le philosophe nietzschéen atteint au final consiste dans la multiplicité des volontés de puissance rapportée à des oppositions mutuelles et constituant dans une telle relation le monde un" (Müller-Lauter, *Problème de l'opposition*, 475); "C'est l'opposition qui fait la volonté de puissance" (478).

25. "Il s'agit en fait de rapports de forces qui s'établissent sans laisser place à quoi que ce soit d'autre, une totale brutalité sans le moindre adoucissement. . . . Ce qui règne, c'est le caractère d'absolue instantanéité de la volonté de puissance"(Nietzsche, *Fragments posthumes*, 40 [55]).

26. Nietzsche, *Fragments posthumes*, 11 [197].

27. Nietzsche, *Gai savoir* §109; cf. Nietzsche, *Fragments posthumes*, 11 [225]: "Le 'chaos du tout' . . . une nécessité déraisonnable au mépris de toute considération formelle, éthique, esthétique."

to power': each with a multiplicity of means of expression and forms"[28] is *chaos*, carries chaos within himself.[29]

But then, to follow the hypothesis of *a* chaos within oneself, to accept to interpret oneself as *chaos* in the Anaxagorean sense of the most absolute mixture and the deepest abyss, implies that we no longer envisage ourselves as a subject with any self-identity, as an agent of knowledge and will, as an *ego*-monad, as "the affirmation of one being in the face of many (instincts, thoughts, etc.)," as *ground* (*Grund*). Discovering that we carry chaos within us rather implies that we interpret ourselves "as an unstable sphere of bubbles and moods,"[30] as impermanence and, beyond that, as a *body*, as "a plurality of personalized forces, sometimes one and sometimes another of which comes to the fore as ego . . . making the dominant element the *whole* ego."[31] This presupposes, as always, that we interpret ourselves as an arena in which impulses or wills to power joust, as an "effect of the self," as an abyss, as becoming a constant metamorphosis.

As we have seen, a major problem arises here: does Pindar's imperative, taken up by Nietzsche, still make any sense in a perspective where *becoming* is an agonizing struggle without end or finality, and where *what you are* is an abyss, chaos, total multiplicity, and indeterminacy?

Master and Founder of Yourself

Many readers of Nietzsche have seen this impasse. Still, few have succeeded in circumventing or overcoming it, as Emmanuel Falque has done, if not completely, then at least in part: "Let's say it following Henri Maldiney, or even Nietzsche. . . . There is something more radical than the incessant repetition of Pindar's formula 'become what you are.' Namely, its inversion: 'be what you become.' For it is by accepting to transform oneself, and to be transformed, that one becomes what one was not before, and not simply by actualizing predetermined potentialities."[32] A remarkable inversion, which, in keeping with Nietzschean logic, gives priority to an infinite becoming, the antithesis of the actualization of an essence, of a being, and recognizes

---

28. Nietzsche, *Fragments posthumes*, 1 [58].

29. Cf. Nietzsche, *Ainsi parlait Zarathoustra* §5; *Fragments posthumes*, 4 [213], 14 [61]; *Par-delà bien et mal* §224.

30. Nietzsche, *Humain, trop humain I* §376.

31. Nietzsche, *Fragments posthumes*, 6 [70].

32. Falque, "Tempête sous un crâne," 270. La question de l'inversion de la formule de Pindare et le dialogue avec Maldiney y relatif sont déjà présents dans *Hors phénomène* §62, "Je suis qui je serai," 363–65.

the *becoming-self* (if not the *self* itself) as a succession of incessant metamorphoses or transformations. There can be no becoming that results in the actualization of potentiality; there can be no well-earned *rest* in being after an exhausting becoming. Condemned never to reach a determined self, never to *become* (Aristotle) a self, the *self* must always *become* (Heraclitus)—"be what you become" or the reminder that, paradoxically, "you are *but for* becoming or *to* become" also formulated by Maldiney: "Become what you are. You are only what you become."[33]

The fact remains, however, that while the inversion hits the nail on the head, showing the sempiternal nature of becoming, of the incessant process of the constantly renewed joust of drives that we *are*, it fails—at least in our view—to convey the tremendous creative effort, self-mastery, self-training, and self-transcendence that *becoming what you are* implies in Nietzschean writing. To *become what you are* is not to let yourself go, tossed about like a plank on the chaotic waves of becoming. *Becoming* is not to let oneself happen randomly or passively as the product of an affecting exteriority. *Becoming* does not mean discovering what we have become or are becoming, like an astonished spectator, and having as our sole task to welcome and assume this ever-new *I*. Rather—and Nietzsche is most precise: "Become, never cease to become who you are—*the master and founder of yourself.*"[34]

As we can see, *becoming oneself* is not simply a *flowing river* into which we can plunge and then let ourselves be carried away from metamorphosis to transformation. Far from it, "becoming, the ceaseless becoming oneself" presupposes the strength to dominate the struggle we *are* (master of ourselves) and to "master the chaos we are: forcing our chaos to become form"[35] (founder of ourselves). And so, returning to *egoism*, to this constant, sickly search for oneself [*Selbszucht*] as *becoming*, Nietzsche, in a happy play on words, adds the necessity of *creation*, of elevating oneself through a veritable "training of the self [*Selbstsucht*]."[36] Formidable creation, "spectacle of the force that a genie employs, *not upon oeuvres, but upon oneself as an oeuvre.*"[37] The *Selbstsucht* expresses the courage and strength of a man who plunges into the abyss or chaos of struggling impulses that he is, and feels capable of imposing a certain direction and form on them. At the same time, *Selbstsucht* signifies the ability to distinguish what in the *I* is the inheritance of the gregarious needs proper to weakness, from what makes

33. Maldiney, *Penser l'homme*, 285.
34. Nietzsche, *Fragments posthumes*, 11 [297] (italics mine).
35. Nietzsche, *Fragments posthumes*, 14 [61].
36. Nietzsche, *Ecce Homo* §9.
37. Nietzsche, *Aurore* §548.

the distinction of a singular, strong type wanting to be what it is. Thus, *Selbstsucht* and *Selbstzucht* announce themselves as the double task of the self-master and self-former, like "the Dionysian artist [who] dominates even the chaos of the will that has not yet become form, and can from there give birth to a new world at every creative moment," and in whom "greatness is measured by the force of tension of his will, by the sureness with which chaos obeys his artistic command and becomes form."[38]

The creative process of ceaselessly becoming what we are presupposes that the individual is aware of the impersonal abyss (chaos) above which it causes to emerge (absence of *ego*) and incorporates this assumption as a means of breeding: he must "carry chaos within himself" and be able to impose a form on it. But at the same time, he needs to be able to do violence to an entire tradition incorporated within him, and, in this domination of struggling impulses, he can then assert what is most personal in himself and tyrannize himself if need be: "to be able to give birth to a dancing star."[39]

Nevertheless, anticipating any misinterpretation of this fundamental *egoism* and training of the *self*, Nietzsche warns, "That one becomes what one is presupposes that one does not suspect in the least what one is," "the most serious danger in tackling this task would be to perceive oneself."[40] To those who still believe that *becoming oneself* means defending one's *ego* and personal interests, Nietzsche reminds us that the *ego* is a fiction and that no interest is *personal* or individual since the human being is nothing but a multiplicity of competing drives whose ephemeral and changing interests, specific to each group of drives, are as diverse as they are contradictory. There is no "defense of form" (Hölderlin) here, only the imposition of form on chaos. Nietzsche is keen to emphasize the subterranean, subconscious, blind nature of part of the process of *becoming oneself* or *doing work*. This becoming, this constant metamorphosis or transformation is much more effective, direct and assured, if the intellect does not exert its influence here. Far too hesitant and prone to illusion and error, the conscience is more likely to hinder and divert this realization of a *masterpiece* of *egoism*. So, as Nietzsche insists, the work of hierarchical drives must, in part, remain unconscious and blind, not knowing precisely what it is aiming at or, at the very least, not always making it visible to the conscious mind. You must indeed be the master of the struggle (dominating an anarchic drive), but you also have to have the courage to let it have a spontaneity of its own;

38. Nietzsche, *Fragments posthumes*, 16 [49].

39. "Je vous le dis: il faut encore porter du chaos en soi pour pouvoir donner naissance à une étoile dansante. Je vous le dis: vous portez encore du chaos en vous" (Nietzsche, *Ainsi parlait Zarathoustra* §5).

40. Nietzsche, *Ecce Homo* §9.

you have to be the founder of a work based on chaos, but you also have to have the strength not to reduce or deny the latter. So, in becoming oneself, one's only role and power will sometimes be to offer this process the necessary conditions (strength) so that it remains an assumption, a blessing of life and not its negation. Only at this price can one be born and constantly become "oneself as a work of art"—or, to put it in the words of Emmanuel Falque, "*I am in the first place he who knows not where to go*—or rather, he who knows not where he is going and who knows it only once he has gone there,"[41] as can be said of the artist who, when contemplating his work, always seems to be discovering it for the first time.

Becoming what you are, mastering the struggle and shaping the chaos that you are, forcing yourself in one direction, imposing a form on yourself, even if it's protean, is a major task worthy of the great human being who sets about it. This surpassing of oneself (*Selbstüberwindung*) presupposes an iron will, a will that is the sign of an energy (intoxication) peculiar to a human type capable of setting itself a goal, a direction (*Selbstzucht*)—far from having them imposed on it (*Selbstsucht*)—and that marks the whole of its work with its creative stamp, its singularity. In this way, he becomes and never ceases to become who he is: "As for the rest of us, we want to become who we are—the new, the unique, the incomparable, those who are their own legislators, those who are their own creators!"[42]

Bibliography

Costa, Joao Paolo. "Un tournant? Interview d'Emmanuel Falque." *Revista Filosófica de Coimbra* 31.62 (2022) 279–90.

Falque, Emmanuel. *Hors phénomène*. Paris: Hermann, 2021.

———. "Une tempête sous un crane." *Revista Filosófica de Coimbra* 31.62 (2022) 265–78.

Maldiney, Henri. *Penser l'homme et la folie*. Grenoble: J. Million, 1991.

Müller-Lauter, Wolfgang. "Le problème de l'opposition dans la philosophie de Nietzsche." *Revue philosophique de la France et de l'étranger* 131.4 (2006) 455–78.

Nietzsche, Friedrich. *Ainsi parlait Zarathoustra*. Translated by Georges-Arthur Goldschmidt. Paris: LGF-Le Livre de Poche, 1972.

———. *Aurore*. Translated by Éric Blondel et al. Paris: GF-Flammarion, 2012.

———. *Correspondance*. Translated by Jean Lacoste. Vol. 4. Paris: Gallimard, 2015.

———. *Crépuscule des idoles*. Translated by Éric Blondel. Paris: GF-Flammarion, 2005.

———. *Digitale Kritische Gesamtausgabe Werke und Briefe* (eKGWB). Edited by Paolo D'Iorio. Berlin: de Gruyter, 1967. http://www.nietzschesource.org/#eKGWB.

———. *Ecce Homo*. Translated by Éric Blondel. Paris: GF-Flammarion, 1992.

41. Costa, "Un tournant?," 289.
42. Nietzsche, *Gai savoir* §335.

———. *Fragments posthumes*. In *Œuvres philosophiques complètes*, edited by Giorgio Colli and Mazzino Monotinari. Paris: Gallimard, 1968–1997.
———. *Le gai savoir*. Translated by Patrick Wotling. Paris: GF-Flammarion, 1997.
———. *Humain, trop humain I*. Translated by Patrick Wotling. Paris: GF-Flammarion, 2019.
———. *Humain, trop humain II*. Translated by Éric Blondel et al. Paris: GF-Flammarion, 2019.
———. *Par-delà bien et mal*. Translated by Patrick Wotling. Paris: GF-Flammarion, 2000.
———. *Richard Wagner à Bayreuth*. Translated by Marie Baumgartner. Schloss Chemnitz: E. Schmeitzner, 1877.
———. *Schopenhauer éducateur*. Translated by Henri Albert. Vol. 5.2 of *Œvres complètes de Frédéric Nietzsche*. 16th ed. Paris: Mercure de France, 1922.
Pindar. *Pythian* 2. Translated by Diane Arnson Svarlien. Perseus Digital Library. https://www.perseus.tufts.edu/hopper/text?doc=urn:cts:greekLit:tlg0033.tlg002.perseus-eng1:2.

Meister Eckhart and the Logic of Non-Duality

Sean J. McGrath

IF THERE IS SUCH a thing as a perennial philosophy, it surely includes the thesis concerning the non-dual nature of absolute reality. One finds this claim in Madhyamika schools of Buddhism, in Chan and Zen, which emerge from it, in the Advaita Vedanta of medieval Hinduism, and paralleling these Eastern traditions, in Roman and Greek Neoplatonism, in the Christian mystical theology which succeeded it, and in modern European idealism. Non-duality (ND) goes by many names—*Henosis*, the *Tao*, *Saccidannda*, *Nirvanna*, *Advaita* ("not two"), *Nirguna Brahaman*—but in each case what is named is functionally the same: not a positive content but the necessity of the negation of distinction in absolute reality.

Paradoxically, the empirical and logical point of departure for the philosophy of ND *is* distinction. Take, for example, what might be regarded as the founding distinction of Western philosophy, the distinction between appearance and reality: this too must disappear in the absolute. Appearance thus *is* reality, ordinary mind *is* Buddha mind, as the Madhyamika school of Buddhism puts it. But such paradoxical statements do not delegitimize distinction as a point of departure for elaborating ND. Here, as in

Wittgenstein's early philosophy, one must kick away the ladder one relied on to reach the higher standpoint, but one must first use it.[1]

On the level of appearance, we perceive differences among things: differences between this and that, things and their properties, between here and there, or more epistemically conceived, between the knower or the subject and the known or the object. Difference or duality (for the purposes of this essay, the same thing) are basic to human experience. Individuation, basic human emotions (fear and hope), and indeed, the passage of time itself are expressive of difference. Without the consciousness that the past no longer is, and is to that degree different from the present, there could be no sense of temporality as such. But duality is also the essence of human ignorance. We cannot know the variety of all the things that are and could be. On a more radical conception of knowing, we cannot truly be said to know anything whatsoever so long as what is to be known remains other than the faculty of cognition. The goal of knowledge is the identity of the subject with the object, and at least in ordinary patterns of cognition, this never entirely occurs.[2] Indeed, insofar as we do not fully know ourselves, insofar as our desires remain obscure to us, and as the apostle Paul put it, the good that we would do, we do not (Rom 7:19), we can be said to be divided in ourselves. Beneath the multiplicity and dividedness of beings, times, and spaces, non-dual philosophies posit an undivided continuum of being. At this level, there are no things and their properties, no subjects and objects, no here and there, no this and that, no here and now, nor any desire, need, or competition among beings, because everything is one. This unity of being is bliss, eternity, and peace without interruption.

If all distinctions disappear in the absolute, so must the distinction between God and the soul disappear for the Christian who has broken through to the divine ground of being. It was on this very point, this refusal to absolutize the divine-human distinction, that Meister Eckhart fell afoul of the Inquisition, narrowly escaping with his life.

---

1. "My propositions are elucidatory in this way: he who understands me finally recognizes them as senseless, when he has climbed out through them, on them, over them. (He must so to speak throw away the ladder, after he has climbed up on it.) He must surmount these propositions; then he sees the world rightly" (Wittgenstein, *Tractatus* 6.54).

2. "For, in the case of those things which have no matter, that which thinks and that which is thought are the same; for contemplative knowledge and that which is known in that way are the same" (Aristotle, *De anima* 3.4, 430a, 3–5).

In agro dominico and Eckhartian Non-Duality

Concerned with the ongoing battle with the heresy of the free spirit, the Avignon Pope John XXII condemned twenty-six Eckhartian theses as heretical in 1329, a year after the Meister's death. In the defense leading up to the condemnation, shortly before his death by natural causes, Eckhart reinterpreted his teachings on ND for the Inquisition in a non-heretical way and renounced any heretical implications they might contain. The consensus of scholars today is that the papal bull *In agro dominico* contains among its anathematized theses so many orthodox claims that are basic to Catholic mystical theology that the condemnation of Eckhart can no longer be maintained.[3] Eckhart is now regarded as rehabilitated.

At the center of the fourteenth-century debate was Eckhart's approach to the non-duality of the infinite. Eckhart was charged with going too far with the otherwise unimpeachably orthodox doctrine of divine simplicity, to the point of denying the distinction between creator and creature, and, most disturbing for the Hierarchy, the necessity of moral and ecclesial law. The allegations outlined in the papal bull *In agro* were deadly serious. The Beguine Margarite Porete was burned at the stake in Paris in 1310 for publishing a mystical treatise *The Mirror of Simple Souls Who Are Annihilated and Remain Only in Will and Desire of Love*, a text which is replete with Eckhartian-style paradoxes based on presupposition of the non-difference of the ground of God and the ground of the soul.

The non-dual identity of infinite being is the root of Eckhart's signature concepts: *Gottheit, Gelassenheit, Abgeschiedenheit, Gottesgeburt*. It is also the source of his most paradoxical claims. For Eckhart identity overtakes every distinction within being and renders creation in *essence* identical to the divine. At the same time creation and Creator are existentially so incommensurable that no language can be deployed to speak of both. Thomas Aquinas did not go this far. God alone is *being itself* (*ipsum esse*) and so exists in a different sense than anything else, Aquinas argues.[4] Still created things *are* in their own way and have a grammar appropriate to them (*their proper modi significandi*). Nor is God's being entirely beyond human language for Aquinas. Some words, such as the divine names (goodness, truth, infinity, unity), bridge the divide between these two orders of being (created/uncreated).[5] For Eckhart, by contrast, God alone is; creatures in themselves are nothing. Whatever is real in them is God, whatever is not

---

3. *In agro dominico* as well as documents related to Eckhart's defense are translated in McGinn's *Complete Works of Meister Eckhart* (1981).

4. *Summa Theologica* 1a, q. 13, a. 11.

5. *Summa Theologica* 1a, q. 13.

God in them is not real. The language with which we speak of creatures is inappropriate for God and vice versa. If we say *God is*, then we must also say *creatures are not*. If, by contrast, we say *creatures are*, we must say *God is not*.

The difference between Aquinas and Eckhart on this point hinges on their alternative approaches to the *analogia entis*, the Scholastic doctrine of the similarity and dissimilarity that obtains between created being and uncreated being. Whereas for Aquinas the analogy of proportionality allows us to maintain a finite sense of being, Eckhart insists on a stark analogy of attribution that prevents him from simultaneously attributing any sense of being to God and to creatures.[6] Analogy for Eckhart is not a connective relationship but a relationship of dependence. It does not explain what something is but where it comes from. While this starkly negative doctrine of analogy prevents Eckhart from making categorical claims of God, symbolic language allows him to gesture towards the divine source of things by speaking of a thing "as it is in the principal," as it is insofar as it is "not other in nature" from its divine source.[7]

If there are no absolute relations in the infinite, then there are also no relations outside the infinite. How, then, to account for the existence of the soul? At the core of the soul, the human being is not different from God. As such it needs not go out of itself to find God. It need not even look for God, for it is never without God. The claim is primarily practical, not speculative. One ought to live out of this truth, which for Eckhart means detaching

---

6. See McGinn, *Mystical Thought*, 4–5: "When Eckhart says, 'It does not now seem to me that God understands because he exists, but rather that he exists because he understands,' he has stood Thomas on his head in the service of a different form of metaphysics. Eckhart's criticism of 'ontotheology,' that is, a metaphysics centering on being, or *esse*, marks an important stage in his intellectual development. His teaching is rooted, in part at least, in a distinctive doctrine of analogy, which appears here for the first time. 'In the things that are said according to analogy, what is in one of the analogates is not formally in the other. . . . Therefore, since all created things are formally beings, God will not be a being in the formal sense. Since *esse* here is being treated as the first of creative things, it cannot as such be in God. What is there is the *puritas essendi* which Eckhart identifies with *intelligere*." See Eckhart's *Commentary on John* cited in McGinn, *Mystical Thought*, 11: "In analogical relations what is produced derives from the source . . . [and] is of another nature and thus not the principle itself; still, as it is in the principal, it is not other in nature or supposit."

7. Another way of putting Eckhart's difference from Aquinas on analogy is in terms of Eckhart's emphasis on God's formal causality of creation, which got him into trouble at the Cologne and Avignon trials (McGinn, *Mystical Thought*, 180). "Analogates have nothing of the form according to which they are analogically ordered rooted in positive fashion in themselves, but every creative being is analogically ordered to God in being, truth, and goodness. Therefore, every creative being radically and positively possesses existence, life, and wisdom from and in God and not in itself" (Eckhart, *Sermons and Lectures on Ecclesiasticus*, cited in McGinn, *Mystical Thought*, 91).

oneself from all particularity, from one's own sense of separate self as much as from the objects of our desires. As the *Gottheit* itself is untarnished by attachment or relation, so should the soul practice detachment (*Abgeschiedenheit*) from all things.

There is nothing radical in Eckhart's approach to negative theology and asceticism; similar teachings can be found in most of the church fathers. Eckhart, however, pushes detachment further than most theologians. We ought to become so detached and poor as to no longer have a God above us. The one who is attached to religious practices and devotions entrenches an objectifying relation to the divine being and remains as fettered to multiplicity and particularity as the most dissolute hedonist. To be one with the One is to have no God. Not having a God in this Eckhartian sense is a hyperbolic intensification of finitude, to the point where the infinite no longer horizons the finite as its other. The finite becomes indiscernible from the infinite without ceasing to be finite. There is nothing spiritual here to enjoy, no object to contemplate, nor any image of the divinized self to lord over others. The poor man forgets God as he forgets his own name and lives, without why. "A poor man is one who wants nothing, knows nothing, and has nothing."[8] In this infamous sermon, which is a principal target of *In agro*, Eckhart prays for deliverance from conventional religiosity: "Let us pray to God that we may be free of 'God.'"[9]

Eckhart's German sermons contain his most radical claims concerning ND. It should be remembered that they were not speculative treatises defended amongst Scholastics; they were delivered in rough vernacular medieval German in cloisters to groups of men and women monastics whose entire daily existence was preoccupied with acts of religion. In their zeal for God, Eckhart said, they were in danger of mistaking the means for the end and fetishizing the rule, under the delusion that through works and effort they could *achieve* mystical union or what Eckhart calls the *breakthrough* (*Durchbruch*) into the *ground*. The breakthrough is not an achievement or a work. It is rather the effect of ceasing to work. We need only stop doing what we habitually do and the *breakthrough* to *Gottheit* will occur. *Breakthrough* is here in italics because it is not an event at all; nothing happens in the breakthrough; rather what usually happens stops happening.[10] The only

8. Eckhart, *Sermon 87*, in *Complete Mystical Works*, 420.
9. Eckhart, *Sermon 87*, in *Complete Mystical Works*, 422.
10. See Eckhart, *Sermon 56*, in *Complete Mystical Works*, 294: "Everything that is in the Godhead is one, and of that there is nothing to be said. God works, the Godhead does not work: there is nothing for it to do, there is no activity in it. It never peeped at any work. God and Godhead are distinguished by working and not-working. When I return to God, if I do not remain there, my breakthrough will be far nobler than

thing to be done is to stop doing, to stop dividing that which is one, to let be, to become so surrendered or *gelassen* as to no longer even will the good.

Such a *gelassene* man or woman does not become otherworldly, disengaged from ordinary concerns, or indifferent to life. In a truly paradoxical *coincidentia oppositorum*, perfect Eckhartian *Gelassenheit* leads to a life of active engagement in the world. It is not often noted that Eckhart preferred the *vita activa* over the *vita contemplativa*, since the contemplative remains attached to the distinction between sacred and profane, the divine and the worldly.[11] The perfectly *gelassene* Christian no longer lives out of this distinction and so can find as much of God in the stable and the kitchens as he can in the cloister and at prayer.[12] She does not remove herself from the world, quite the contrary. Like the incarnating logos himself, the *gelassene* Christian becomes yet more immanent and gives birth to God, just as Mary gave birth to Jesus in Bethlehem: the soul is the mother of the Christ, who is reborn and reincarnated in every devout life.

Eckhart bases his notion of breakthrough on a strictly logical metaphysics of *imago Dei*. If we are, as Genesis says, the image of God, then our essence does not have any being in itself; its being is in another. "An image is not of itself or for itself; it is solely that thing's whose image it is, and all that it is belongs to that. Whatever is alien to that which it represents, it is not and does not belong to. An image takes its being solely from that of which it is the image and has one essence with it and is the same essence."[13] What makes an image and its original two is the order of dependency. The image depends on the original and not vice versa. The image only is insofar as the original is, but the original is what it is regardless of its image. Imaging is a doubling of an original. An image is by definition derivative and secondary. If the image were to make its difference from the original into its substantial identity, it would become identified with nothingness, i.e., with that negation which makes it other than the original.

The emphasis on the nothingness of the created is only one side of the Eckhartian teaching: the other side is the affirmation of creaturely cognition as in itself divine. God needs the creature in order to know Godself as God,

---

my outflowing. I alone bring all creatures out of their reason into my reason, so that they are one with me. When I enter the ground, the bottom, the river and fount of the Godhead, none will ask me whence I came or where I have been. No one missed me, for there God unbecomes."

11. See Emmanuel Falque's analysis of Eckhart's inverted reading of the relation of Martha to Mary (Luke 10:38–42) in Falque, *God, the Flesh, and the Other*, 82–86.

12 Eckhart, *Sermon 13B*, in *Complete Mystical Works*, 110.

13. Eckhart, *Sermon 14B*, in *Complete Mystical Works*, 116.

Eckhart taught, in a claim that greatly impressed Hegel.[14] "If I were not, God would not be either."[15] The creature's knowing God is God's knowing the creature, for there is no sense in which they could be ultimately different. It is not hard to understand why Eckhart would be summoned before the Inquisition in Avignon to explain such claims. Although he died before the defense, it is my contention that Eckhart's paradoxes can indeed be defended, and on purely logical grounds.

Non-Duality is a Rational Position

While in religion, ND is usually presented as an *experience* of an ecstatic or transformed consciousness, an experience of enlightened mind, or in Eckhart's language, *ein Durchbruch*, ND can also be advanced as a conclusion of argumentation. The logical approach to ND has a certain advantage over the mystical: where mysticism speaks of gift, of grace, of the elevation of a single individual to the divine, and so is by its nature aristocratic, if not exclusive, certainly incommunicable, the logic of ND democratizes the mystical. Logic includes and distributes; it de-privileges certain kinds of persons (sages, monastics, etc.) who are otherwise elevated into a mystical priesthood above the rest of us. Logic renders ND a universal basis of *all* consciousness. Precisely because it relativizes distinction, ND renders all beings equally distant from and, at the same time, equally near to the center. "God is equally near all creatures," Eckhart says, in a word, anticipating the flattened ontology of Protestant modernity and threatening the hierarchy of being upon which medieval society was founded.[16] But because ordinary consciousness is constitutively dualistic—intentional of objects or always *consciousness of*—non-dual identity with God can only be equally distributed if we posit an irreducible and to some degree unrecoverable unconscious experience at the basis of ordinary divided consciousness. On the logical reading, mystical experiences of ND are momentary breakthroughs

---

14. The connection between Eckhart and Hegel (and between German medieval mysticism and German idealism more generally) is mapped by Benz, *Sources Mystiques*. Hegel's reception of Eckhart is captured in the comment he made to Franz von Baader in 1824, after reading with him some passages of Eckhart's sermons: "Da haben wir es ja, was wir wollen" (cited in Benz, *Sources Mystiques*, 12). On the Hegel/Baader/Eckhart nexus see the analysis in Magee, *Hegel*, 224–27. H. S. Harris makes the claim that Hegel encounters the medieval mystics much earlier than 1824, already in 1795, while working on his essay on the positivity of Christianity. See Harris, *Hegel's Development*, 230–31.

15. Eckhart, *Sermon 87*, in *Complete Mystical Works*, 424.

16. Eckhart, *Sermon 69*, in *Complete Mystical Works*, 353.

to true being. Such experiences are anything but exclusive; rather, they are as common as cognition itself.

Three families of arguments for ND are found in the Western tradition. One is the epistemic argument, which is common to modern idealists and focuses on the subject/object duality in ordinary cognition. A second is a grammatical argument. It is more classical, departing from the subject/predicate duality in discursive knowledge claims. A third is ontological, an argument based on the logic of infinity. On all of these arguments, duality is shown to be founded; duality cannot be basic but indicates a defection or departure from an underlying identity. All three arguments are primarily negative, showing why dualism is logically untenable without saying anything positive about the non-dual, but this does not render them ineffective. On the contrary, the relativization of ordinary consciousness is exactly the point of the arguments. Divided everyday consciousness cannot be taken to be ultimate or final.

The three families of arguments—epistemic, grammatical, and ontological—lead to three basic negative claims:

(1) Since consciousness presupposes subject/object, ND cannot be conscious or an object of consciousness.

(2) Since to speak of anything is to predicate things of other things, ND cannot be spoken of categorically but only indirectly.

(3) Since finitude presupposes duality (to be finite is to stand opposed to that which one is not), ND cannot be finite.

A word on each of these arguments is necessary to show that Eckhart's paradoxes are not mystical in some supernatural, esoteric sense but rational and exoteric.

The Epistemic Argument

As the actualization of a human potential, knowledge presumes a distinction between a subject who is sometimes knowing and an object that is in part known, in part unknown. Knowledge on this account is a provisional and partial victory over the duality of the knower and the known. To know anything is in some way to become identical with it, as Aristotle argued against Plato.[17] And yet insofar as knowledge remains a discrete act, the act of one who is sometimes knowing and at other times not, and insofar as discrete achievements of knowledge are expressed in determinate concepts

---

17. Aristotle, *De anima* 3.4, 430a, 3–5.

and language *by means of negation (determinatio est negatio)*, the quest for knowledge, which is nothing less than the effort to overcome the duality of thought and being, inevitably falls short of its goal and only further entrenches the difference between subject and object. If what is to be known is being, and if being is only partially and occasionally known, then absolute knowledge as such is impossible. I either know being, in which case I am one with being, or I do not. I cannot know being partially and still claim to be knowing without qualification. If, on the other hand, I can be said to partially know being, this partial knowledge is at best a recovery of an underlying identity with being rather than a precarious and partial conquest of an unknown continent. The identity recovered in acts of knowledge is not alien or outside of reason, for if it were it would not be identity but difference. Partially recovered identity is nothing other than the identity of thought and being itself, which is always already grounding the acts of the subject as it does the discrete objects the subject partially knows. Insofar as it asserts itself to be true without qualification, partial knowledge is distortive. Otherwise put, knowledge of being cannot be built up piece by piece. Knowledge is only possible if the subject and its object are originally one. To the degree that discrete achievements of knowledge maintain the presupposition of subject/object duality, they are not adequate to being, which must be non-dualistically conceived.[18]

The Grammatical Argument

Every act of saying something about something, that is, every discursive knowledge claim, fuses two parts of speech that are other than each other and cannot be fully identified: subject and predicate in attributive propositions ("Socrates is good"), individual and universal in identity propositions ("This is a university"). If knowledge is the total sum of truth claims expressible in propositions, it is an infinite and impossible task of trying to create unity out of things that are essentially heterogeneous and only further fractures reality with every effort.

The form of the proposition itself betrays the duality upon which it is founded. Let the form of the proposition be *A is B*, where A is singular and individual and B is a universal predicate. In what sense can A be said to be

18. For a modern representation of this argument, which is found in pre-Socratic philosophy (e.g., Parmenides) as well as in Advaita Vedanta in ancient Hinduism and in the Madhyamika school of ancient Buddhism, see Schelling's identity philosophy, which Schelling developed in lectures at the Universities of Jena and Würzburg between the years 1801 and 1806. For a translated selection, see Schelling, *Idealism*, 139-94.

B? Are they not opposed in every way, occupying mutually exclusive spaces: that which is individual, incommunicable, and substantial on the one side, and that which is universal, transferable, and predicable (requiring another in which it can subsist) on the other? If they could be identified without remainder such that the subject becomes the predicate and vice versa, we would lose the proposition. And inasmuch as the proposition is the site of the knowledge claimed, its loss would be the loss of knowledge itself. Or, in another register, if we are to say that A is a *that* and B is a *what* (as we do when we deploy the *is* of identity, i.e., *this is a university*), the opposition is just as insurmountable as it is between subject and predicate. A is a singular existent, as Aristotle puts it, that which is never said of anything, and B is the *whatness* or universal, that which is never in itself but always said of something. The two can never be one. "This" can never be identical to "university."

As Schelling writes in his *Freedom Essay*, every proposition first divides what it proposes to identify.[19] If "A is B" is a knowledge claim and not a tautology, it presupposes that A is *not* B and can never be reduced to B. The truth of the proposition depends upon a concealed identity, which the terms of the proposition fail to recapture, indeed, which they can be said to have rendered impossible in some sense. The copula identifies that which it in the same act dis-identifies. It is a relation that stands for something concealed, something absent, which cannot be present in the terms of the proposition. Some X which is in one respect A is in another respect B. But X is neither A nor B and cannot be identified with either A or B. Every proposition breaks up what is originally one for the sake of putting it back together inadequately. To assert a claim is to break being in two for the sake of reassembling it with a crack down the middle. Assertion fractures and deals only with composites. It follows that every asserted unity can be taken apart again. As an expression of knowledge, *A is B* does not attain what it intends; it is at best a partial recovery of a lost identity, which conceals that which it seeks to express. It produces a sign, and not the thing itself, a sign which must ultimately be discarded when that which it signifies is recovered.[20]

---

19. Schelling, *Philosophical Investigations*, 340.

20. This argument is as old as German idealism itself and can be found in various forms in Fichte, Schelling, and Hegel. But its first articulation was Hölderlin's, in the 1795 fragment, *Urteil und Sein*. The German word for judgment, *Urteil*, literally means primordial division.

The Ontological Argument

The ontological argument for ND proceeds from the nature of the infinite, or God, to a denial of all oppositional relations in it or outside of it. The infinite that is posited as the other of the finite is not genuinely infinite. This dialectic of the finite and the infinite is the centerpiece of Hegel's philosophy of religion, if not of the system itself. Hegel holds the interprenetration of finitude and infinity to be the core of Trinitarian theology, but let us leave that aside for the moment. Let us stick with the negative point: "If infinity is thus set up against finitude, each is as finite as the other."[21] Monotheistic one-sided transcendence, according to Hegel, is logically untenable. The only alternative is to understand the finite as the self-mediation of infinity, that is, as belonging to infinity and inseparable from it. "In the Idea, however, finite and infinite are one, and hence finitude as such, i.e., as something that was supposed to have truth and reality in and for itself, has vanished. Yet what was negated was only the negative in finitude; and thus the true affirmation was posited."[22] The finite that insists on remaining transcended by infinity, by a wholly other, has disavowed its finitude and absolutized itself and the negation which is constitutive of it.

In the Dominican Scholastic tradition to which Eckhart belongs, God is held to be being itself, that which is most real in everything that is, and which pervades all things in the infinite act of being, the *actus essendi*. God is what is innermost to everything that exists, Aquinas argues, because he is the act of being upon which every finite thing depends both for its essence and its existence. God is the efficient, formal, and final cause of everything that exists or else he is not God. And he must *be* in a primary sense if he is the source of the derivative being of everything that exists. There can be nothing

---

21. Hegel, *Faith and Knowledge*, 66.
22. Hegel, *Faith and Knowledge*, 63. Similar claims are strewn throughout the Hegelian corpus from the *Phenomenology of Spirit* to the *Encyclopedia*. It is a major point of contact between Hegel and Eckhart, as was said in note 7 above. See Dubilet, "Speculation and Infinite Life," 57: "For Hegel, to critique the subject in order to exalt some form of transcendence surreptitiously reinforces the very perspective of finitude that it means to subvert. What is at stake is not the opening up of finitude to transcendence, however conceived, but the diagnosis of the correlation between finitude and transcendence, and in turn the subversion of that entire correlation. To annihilate finitude for Hegel is to remove the very negative constraint of transcendence that structures its entire theoretical and affective matrix, and in this way to hallow life, to release it from the determination as essentially finite. In other words, one must resist merely choosing between the affirmation of a self-possessed subject and its self-negation as a way of valorizing transcendence; instead, the task of the speculative enterprise becomes the collapse of the entire conceptual field governed by finitude, in order to articulate finitude itself as a moment of infinite generation of immanence."

positive in things which does not have its source in him, for he is the source of everything. What makes things different from God is not anything positive; rather, it is that which is negative in things which differentiate them. That which makes a thing other than another thing makes it limited, contingent, dependent, or finite. The differentia are nothing positive, not qualities of being, but negations of being and privations of its infinite fullness. Paradoxically, that which is purely existent, because it excludes the negations which make being determinate and actual in any sense in which we can understand it, is equivalent to nothing (not the *ouk on* but the *me on* of Plato's *Philebus* 23c). The negations that make one thing different than another thing and other than God are negated in the divine. God is the *negatio negationis* (*das Verneinen des Verneinens*).[23] It is these illusory differentiae, these unsustainable one-sided negations to which we are attached, which are burnt away in hell, which for Eckhart is nothing other the divinization process.

> You must be free of nothing. The question is asked, what burns in hell. The masters generally say it is self-will. But I declare in truth: nothing burns in hell. Here is a simile. Take a burning coal and put it on my hand. If I said the coal burnt my hand, I would do it injustice. Were I to say truly what burns me, it is negation, for the coal contains something that my hand has not. It is this not that burns me. But if my hand contained all that the coal has or can affect, it would be all of the nature of fire. Then, if anyone were to take all the fire that ever burnt, and poured it out on to my hand, that could not hurt me. In the same way, I say, just because God and all those who stand before His face have on account of their true blessedness something which they who are separated from God have not, this very not torments the souls in hell more than self-will or any fire. I say truly, insofar as not adheres to you, to that extent you are imperfect. Therefore, if you want to be perfect, you must be rid of not.[24]

It is clear even to Aquinas that God could have no ontological or substantial distinction within his being.[25] He cannot be composite, for to be composed is to stand in potency to that which is other, either as overarching genus or as cause of the composition. God is pure act (*actus purus*), which means he is without potency. He has no capacity or potency to be anything that he actually is not, for as pure actuality he lacks nothing. Hence God is

23. Eckhart, *Sermon 97*, in *Complete Mystical Works*, 467. The expression *negatio negationis* is in Aquinas, *Quodlibet* 10, q. 1, a. 1 ad 3. It also occurs in several places in Eckhart's Latin works.

24. Eckhart, *Sermon 13B*, in *Complete Mystical Works*, 109.

25. Aquinas, *Summa Theologica* 1a, q. 3.

simple. For the same reason, God or infinity cannot stand in relation to beings that are other than it, for such beings, as other than God, would stand as limitations to the being that God is, rendering him less than infinite. The experience of difference is one-sided, as indeed are all distinctions, and only pertains to creaturely consciousness. On God's *side*, there are no differences. God does not look upon us as something other than Godself; rather, God sees in us only God. And as Eckhart argues, it follows from the principle of divine simplicity that we do not so much see God as participate in God's seeing of us. "The eye with which I see God is the same eye with which God sees me: my eye and God's eye are one eye, one seeing, one knowing and one love."[26]

The Logic of ND

The indeterminacy of the purely existent can be represented to a certain degree through the Boolean connector, logical NOR.

All the Boolean connectors are operations on two logical values, typically the values of two propositions. NOR only produces a value of true if both of its operands are false. Conversely, it produces a value of false if at least one of its operands is true. NOR is the symbolic formula for the *negatio negationis*. It is the denial of determinacy and the logical symbol of ND.

To understand Eckhart's *Durchbruch*, we need only substitute the distinction which most concerned him (and his inquisitors), that of God and soul, for A/B. Only where there is neither God nor soul, does the connector obtain (=*Durchbruch*). If soul (B) and no God (A), then no breakthrough. If God (A) and no soul, no breakthrough. If God (A) *and* (soul) no breakthrough. One sees from the above truth table that the result of NOR is purely negative. That is, a sentence of the form (p NOR q) is true only when neither p nor q is true—i.e., when both possible values (p and q) are *false*. NOR negates all the other Boolean operators (AND, OR, NOT), each of which is a form of negation, including the one-sided *not* that would negate one of two without negating the other (thereby asserting the other). The background in the Venn diagram for NOR, which in the other operators is negative (white), becomes here positive (black): the negative space becomes positive space in the *negatio negationis*. This is the figure for the *me on*, the nothingness which is not mere absence of being, but the sheer possibility of

---

26. Eckhart, *Sermon 57*, in *Complete Mystical Works*, 298. According to Magee, this is the only passage of Eckhart that Hegel cites in his *Lectures on the Philosophy of Religion*. See Hegel, *Lectures*, 1: 347–48; Magee, *Hegel*, 225.

determination: indeterminacy, not merely the absence of determination but the presence of infinite (unlimited) determinability.

The NOR operator is also known as Peirce's arrow, after C. S. Peirce introduced the symbol ↓ for it. Soul↓God means neither a soul nor God is given. It does not mean that at some other level, or at a later moment, soul and God could not exist in interdependence, which is just what Eckhart says when he says that God needs the soul in order to be God. Thus S↓G does not deny a contingent internal relatedness of the soul and God. But it does deny AND or S∧G, the necessary relation between the two values such that the one cannot be thought without the other. Insofar as the soul/God relation is thought of as necessary, logical, and essential, as though wherever the soul is thought, so too must God be thought, we do not have Eckhartian ND. And S↓G also denies OR, S∨G, insofar as it refuses the idea that the soul can exist without God. However, it does not refuse the contingent possibility that God might not have created anything.

To be sure God would not have been God without the soul, but nothing is thereby decided about a preexistence of the infinite, an infinite which is not (yet) God.[27] And here we strike a problematic ambiguity in all words for the divine. We need a word for the divine in itself and another for the divine in its role as creator. This is precisely Eckhart's point: the divine in itself he calls *Gottheit*; the divine creator he is happy to call God, the Father, the Creator, etc.

Through this logical detour, we see the thrust of Eckhart's so-called *mysticism*. His aim is not to achieve an extraordinary state of consciousness but to return us to a level of being prior to the untenable distinction between soul and God, prior to all distinctions, to return to the uncreated, or the *Grund*. "As surely as the Father in His simple nature bears the Son naturally, just as surely He bears him in the inmost recesses of the spirit, and this is the inner world. Here God's ground is my ground and my ground is God's ground. Here I live from my own as God lives from His own."[28] Because there can be no relations where there are no distinctions, and there can be no distinctions in the ground (for to distinguish is to negate and there is no negation or exclusion in the ground), there are no *absolute* relations. Relations are always relative, or as F. H. Bradley would say, they always pertain only to appearance, never to reality.[29] But that does not mean that we are not bound to relations in our creaturely existing, thinking, and speaking.

27. Here is the point of connection between Eckhartian ND and Boehmian/late Schellingian theogony, the distinction between *ungrund* and God, which is not a topic I can deal with here.

28. Eckhart, *Sermon 13B*, in *Complete Mystical Works*, 109.

29. Bradley, *Appearance and Reality*, 11–34.

The poor man is so poor that not only does he have no way out of relational, relative being but he does not even desire a way out.

How then to account for the soul as a distinct but related substance, that is, as finite or created? For Eckhart, the creature-creator distinction can only be appearance; in the ground, the soul is not different from God. God's ground and the ground of the soul are not two. As such the soul need not go out of itself to find God. It should not even look for God, for it is never without God.

> When I flowed forth from God, all creatures declared, "There is a God"; but this cannot make me blessed, for with this I acknowledge myself as a creature. But in my breaking through, where I stand free of my own will, of God's will, of all His works, and of God himself, then I am above all creatures and am neither God nor creature, but I am that which I was and shall remain for evermore.[30]

But why strive to return to the uncreated? Is this nihilistic, a refusal of creation and a reversal of God's will in willing something rather than nothing? For Eckhart, at least, the return to the uncreated ground is not nihilism. It is rather a claim, again deeply Schellingian, that ground remains ground, even or perhaps especially when something else has emerged out of it and is supported by it. We souls, existing in internal relatedness to one another and to the God who created us, legitimately experience otherness, and hence are capable of love and hate and other inter-subjective relations. And these are not illusions, but neither do they exhaust reality.

On the contrary, Eckhart claims: the non-dual ground of the soul abides and remains a place of refuge for it, when the dividedness becomes intolerable, or evil, or produces false ideas. If by mysticism we mean a special or supernatural experience of God, given in a moment of privileged and altered consciousness, there is nothing mystical about it. It is a logical point, or better an onto-logical point.

A Last, Logical Defense of Eckhart

As we have seen, for Eckhart, the identity of God and creatures in the ground overtakes every distinction within being and renders creation *essentially* but *not* existentially identical with the divine. God alone is, creatures in themselves are nothing. "All creatures are mere nothing, neither angels nor

---

30. Eckhart, *Sermon 87*, in *Complete Mystical Works*, 424.

creatures are anything."³¹ God *negates* everything that we know *is*; but this negation of *all* that is opens up a new order of being in which our distinction between what is and what is not no longer obtains. "God as *negation negationis* is simultaneously total emptiness and supreme fullness."³² Eckhart expresses such claims indirectly, that is, symbolically, through careful use of indexicals, symbols, analogies, and metaphors, primarily in the context of his German preaching. The point of such indexical statements is not to categorically define a theological issue in some alarmingly heterodox way. Nor does Eckhart aim to give his hearers an idea or a new theology to consider. Rather, Eckhart's intention is to direct the attention of those who hear him to an abiding but pre-predicative experience of ND, which is always betrayed in categorical claims. All propositional knowledge (categorical claims) presuppose duality: the epistemic duality of subject and object, the grammatical duality of subject and predicate, and the ontological duality of infinity and finitude. Therefore, a propositional or categorical claim of ND is inherently self-contradictory since it denies the very distinctions which it presupposes in making the claim. ND, whether in preaching or teaching, can never be categorically articulated without contradiction; it is not and cannot be a discursive claim.

In order for Eckhart's ND claims to be heretical, they would have to be categorically formulated. But as we have just said, they are not and cannot be categorically formulated. Pope John XXII and his inquisitors misread Eckhart's ND claims as categorical claims. Eckhart's more dramatic German expressions are not so much heretical as self-deconstructing claims. As symbols, however, they *point* to the limits of the categorical, which is a Christian gesture as old as Paul. "For now we see through a glass, darkly; but then face to face: now I know in part; but then shall I know even as also I am known" (1 Cor 13:12). Eckhart the preacher was not trying to change dogma but to elicit a change in his hearer, and not so much on an intellectual as an existential level. A preacher does not define matters of dogma but exhorts a change of heart in his hearers. As exhortations, Eckhartian paradoxes are underdetermined, paradoxical, and ambiguously intended. They are formulated precisely so as to refuse categorical interpretation.³³

To sum up the Eckhartian exhortation: we ought to become so detached and poor so as to no longer have a God above us. The one who

---

31. Eckhart, *Sermon 13A*, in *Complete Mystical Works*, 105.

32. McGinn, *Mystical Thought*, 94.

33. It is worth remembering that in his early Freiburg lectures, Heidegger drew on Eckhart to design a method of expression (the formal indication) that would leave the phenomena intact, not cut it to fit a preconceived, categorical frame. See Heidegger, *Phenomenology of Religious Life*; McGrath, "Logic of Indirection."

remains attached to religious practices and devotions is entrenched in an objectifying relation to the divine being and every bit as fettered to multiplicity and particularity as the most dissolute hedonist. To be one with God in the ground is to have no God. But this not having a God is not a disavowal of finite consciousness; rather, it is a hyperbolic intensification of finitude to the point where the infinite no longer horizons it as its other, and therefore, to be finite, paradoxically, without discernible and definable limits. But before we start proclaiming our intrinsic divinity, we ought to remember that for Eckhart there is nothing spiritual here to enjoy, no object to contemplate, nor any image of the divinized self to lord over others. The poor man forgets God as he forgets himself. "Out of this inmost ground, all your works should be wrought without why."[34]

This language comes directly out of the Christian Neoplatonic tradition.[35] And yet it has become the root of a popular misreading of Eckhart traceable back to Reiner Schürmann but also found among some proponents of the Kyoto school.[36] Eckhart destroys the onto-theological basis of medieval Catholicism, we are told, and liberates the non-theistic experience of truth, best expressed in Zen, from Scholastic ideology. Eckhart is a *realized being* trapped in the mythological age of medieval Catholicism. He is in fact (so the story) an atheist who is not permitted because of his time to confess his lack of faith. But in order for Eckhart to be an atheist, that is, one

---

34. Eckhart, *Sermon* 13B, in *Complete Mystical Works*, 110. See Falque *God, the Flesh, and the Other*, 89:"Eckhart certainly abolishes differences, which gives rise to perhaps an appropriate suspicion that he has not fully respected the necessary difference between Creator and creature. But it is not the case that in this ontological suppression there hides a mystical position more than a philosophical thesis. In order to give his entire place to God man no longer has a place: not as if he wanted to leave his place (deification), or even to fill all place (pride), but rather that the action of having a place is for him some sort of 'de-place' (detachment)—whereas it is for God alone to take the place that he will have determined in constituting our egoity (attachment): 'man ought to be so poor that he has no place where God would be able to operate [as I have already indicated, following Eckhart].There where man guards a place, he guards a difference'" (Falque cites *Sermon* 87/32, in *Complete Mystical Works*, 308.5).

35. See Milbank, *Monstrosity of Christ*, 189: "Eckhart read paradoxically does not become Žižek's Hegel, who interprets incarnation as signifying that 'the ordinary and disappointing is after all the All . . . there is no creation but only nature (or worse) and no man as a creature in the image of God, but only rather a weird, crippled, but dangerously complex animal.' For Eckhart, God does not disappear as a vanishing mediator into man (Hegel's reading of him) but rather finitude and infinite co-exist as non-competing totalities."

36. Schürmann, *Meister Eckhart*; Ueda, *Gottesgeburt in der Seele*. Illuminative is the debate between Thomas Merton and D. T. Suzuki on the degree to which Eckhart is or is not representative of Christian mystical theology. It is clear that Suzuki is out of his depth here. See Merton, *Zen and the Birds*, 99–138.

who maintains the proposition *there is no God*, the symbols of his preaching would also need to be read as categorical claims. His prayer to be rid of God would have to be then read literally, about a desire for the freedom to be atheist. Eckhart the preacher can no more be an atheist than he can be a heretic for the simple reason that, at least in his preaching, he refuses us the language with which to express these positions.

There is another, more ambiguous result to this investigation. If I am right and ND is a rational position,[37] then ND is not the privileged insight of seers and mystics. To be sure, Eckhart never said it was. No mystic in the Catholic canon is less taciturn or enthusiastic about mystical experiences. The *Durchbruch* sounds like a supernatural event, but one needs to read Eckhart's breakthrough passages alongside his deflationary arguments to see that it is not. The experience of God is quotidian (God is to be found in the kitchen and by the fireside as much as in the church), ubiquitous (everyone is equally near and equally far to the divine ground), and non-phenomenal (defying all objective manifestation). The poor man who is so poor that he no longer has a God is miles distant from a Teresa of Ávila, whose visions and mystical experiences clutter her autobiography and include what could only be described as intercourse with an angel (the seraph with the arrow) and a heavenly wedding in which she is betrothed to Jesus. This is not to discredit Teresa or to deny the possibility of supernatural experiences of divinity (on what grounds, other than those of a dogmatic and narrow rationalism, could they be denied?). It is rather to contextualize ND. It is not properly a mystical experience, it is a rational experience, or better, an experience of the essence of reason itself. Such an argument goes some distance to explaining why ND is found in all of the major religious traditions of the world.

Bibliography

Aquinas, Thomas. *Summa Theologica*. Translated by Fathers of the English Dominican Province. New York: Benzinger, 1948.
Aristotle. *The Complete Works*. Edited by Jonathan Barnes. Princeton: Princeton University Press, 1984.
Bradley, F. H. *Appearance and Reality: A Metaphysical Essay*. London: G. Allen, 1916.
Benz, Ernst. *Les sources mystiques de la philosophie romantique allemande*. Paris: J. Vrin, 1981.
Dubilet, Alex. "Speculation and Infinite Life: Hegel and Meister Eckhart on the Critique of Finitude." *Russian Journal of Philosophy & Humanities* 1.2 (2017) 50–70.

---

37. The late Schelling called ND "negative philosophy" or "the purely rational philosophy." See McGrath, *Philosophical Foundations*.

Eckhart, Meister. *The Complete Mystical Works of Meister Eckhart*. Edited and translated Maurice O'C. Walshe. New York: Crossroad, 2009.

———. *Meister Eckhart, the Essential Sermons, Commentaries, Treatises, and Defense*. Translated and edited by Bernard McGinn. New York: Paulist Press, 1981.

Falque, Emmanuel. *God, the Flesh, and the Other: From Irenaeus to Duns Scotus*. Translated by William Christian Hackett. Evanston, IL: Northwestern University Press, 2014.

Harris, H. S. *Hegel's Development: Towards the Sunlight, 1770–1801*. Oxford: Oxford University Press, 1971.

Hegel, G. W. F. *Faith and Knowledge*. Translated by Walter Cerf and H. S. Harris. Albany: State University of New York Press, 1977.

———. *Lectures on the Philosophy of Religion*. Edited and translated by Peter C. Hodgson et al. 3 vols. Berkeley: University of California Press, 1984.

Heidegger, Martin. *The Phenomenology of Religious Life*. Translated by Mathias Fritsch and Jennifer Anna Gosetti-Forencei. Bloomington: Indiana University Press, 2004.

Hölderlin, Friedrich. *Urteil und Sein: Sämmtliche Werke*. Vol. 4. Stuttgart: Cotta Kohlhammer, 1959.

Magee, Glenn Alexander. *Hegel and the Hermetic Tradition*. Ithaca: Cornell University Press, 2008.

McGinn, Bernard. *The Mystical Thought of Meister Eckhart: The Man from Whom God Hid Nothing*. New York: Crossroad, 2001.

McGrath, Sean J. "The Logic of Indirection in Aquinas and Heidegger." *Heythrop Journal* 54 (2013) 268–80.

———. *The Philosophical Foundations of the Late Schelling: The Turn to the Positive*. Edinburgh: Edinburgh University Press, 2021.

Merton, Thomas. *Zen and the Birds of Appetite*. New York: New Directions, 1968.

Milbank, John, with Slavoj Žižek. *The Monstrosity of Christ: Paradox or Dialectic?* Edited by Creston Davis. Cambridge: MIT Press, 2011.

Plato. *Complete Works*. Edited by John M. Cooper and D. S. Hutchinson. Cambridge: Hackett, 1997.

Schelling, F. W. J. *Idealism and the Endgame of Theory*. Edited and translated by Thomas Pfau. Albany: State University of New York Press, 1994.

———. *Philosophical Investigations into the Essence of Human Freedom*. Translated by Jeff Love and Johannis Schmidt. Albany: State University of New York Press, 2006.

Schürmann, Reiner. *Meister Eckhart, Mystic and Philosopher. Translations with Commentary*. Bloomington: Indiana University Press, 1978.

Ueda, Shizuteru. *Die Gottesgeburt in der Seele und der Durchbruch zur Gottheit: Die mystische Anthropologie Meister Eckharts und ihre Konfrontation mit der Mystik des Zen-Buddhismus*. Baden-Baden: Karl Alber, 1965.

Wittgenstein, Ludwig. *Tractatus Logico-Philosophicus*. Translated by C. K. Ogden. London: Kegan Paul, Trench, Trubner, 1922.

Emmanuel Falque, Reader of Sigmund Freud

From the Id to the Extra-Phenomenal

Matthew Nini

Introduction: The Philosopher on the Couch

STRANGE, ONE MIGHT REMARK, that Emmanuel Falque—philosopher, theologian, specialist in phenomenology and medieval thought—would write a book on Sigmund Freud. Yet far from being a curiosity, «*Ça*» *n'a rien à voir* (2018) is an integral part of Falque's work. In its author's words, the book is an exploration of the *backlash* or *counterblow* (*choque-en-retour*) or influence of psychoanalysis on phenomenology. At stake is the question of how philosophy, confined as it is to discourse, can say anything about what is by definition beyond discourse without objectifying it and thereby invalidating it. This question is one that must be asked in regards to both Freud's theory of the Unconscious and Falque's *extra-phenomenal*, expounded in the work *Hors phénomène* (2021)—that is, the idea that certain human experiences not only surpass the realm of phenomena, but extinguish our very capacity for the phenomenal. It is ultimately by means of his engagement with Freud that Falque is able to conceive of what escapes the phenomenal.

Herein, I will argue that the methods Freud uses to deploy the Unconscious from within the discursive realm of consciousness exert a strong influence on Falque's manner of treating the extra-phenomenal from within the world of phenomena. Given these structural similarities, the main criticisms of the Freudian unconscious also apply, *mutatis mutandis*, to the extra-phenomenal. I take Jean-Paul Sartre's criticism of Freud's Unconscious to be paradigmatic in this regard. Sartre essentially accuses Freud of *bad faith*: if the unconscious is not a *second self*, a redundant double of consciousness, then either it is known to me and isn't unconscious at all, or the lack of knowledge of unconscious material constitutes a deliberate lie that I tell myself.

Aside from defending against an objection that, if true, would invalidate both the Unconscious and the extra-phenomenal, addressing Sartre's objections also serves to clarify the nature of discourse in Freud, whose example Falque will follow. I will argue that Freud's own writings preclude Sartre's arguments, establishing a form of indirect discourse that shows what the Unconscious is without transforming it into an object for consciousness. This Freudian theory of discourse is to be found in Freud's *The Joke and Its Relationship to the Unconscious* (1905). Freud's analysis of jokes exemplifies a theory of self-referentiality that distinguishes between a *what* and a *how*, content and performance: the joke performs what the ego cannot say. Sartre's critique ignores this distinction, arguing about the relation of two kinds of discourse, two *whats*: those of consciousness and the unconscious. In his reading of Freud, Falque will deploy this same strategy, *performing* a philosophy of the unconscious, making *jokes* of his own. In reading the wordplays and puns that constitute his *Freudbuch*, we must therefore be just as attentive to what they perform as what they say, much in the same way that in a clinical context, Freud is listening for an act of repetition and not just content. From Freud, then, Falque learns how to approach what resists appearing. This will allow for an oblique approach to the extra-phenomenal, to those traumatic experiences that stand outside the bounds of phenomenality.

Sartre's Seriousness

In Freud's *Interpretation of Dreams* (1900), the human psyche is divided into conscious and unconscious aspects because certain elements of experience are unacceptable to consciousness, and have therefore been repressed. This barrier is enforced by *censorship* (*Zensor*). But in sleep, the defenses of the conscious mind are weakened.[1] Dreams, then, are susceptible to containing

---

1. "Falling asleep at once involves the loss of one of our mental activities, namely our power of giving intentional guidance to the sequence of our ideas" (Freud,

unconscious material that could not be expressed by the waking mind. The dream is therefore a form of wish fulfillment: the desires that I dare not admit to myself in waking life find their way into my dreams.[2] But if the dream material is to be made intelligible to waking consciousness, it must be disguised in order to slip past the censor that is fully operative when the dreamer has awakened. Freud refers to this process as dream distortion, and likens it to a war-time journalist trying to slip information past censors: the censor will have to be tricked, otherwise the material will once again be repressed.[3] Dreams are therefore constituted by symbolic images and require subsequent interpretation in language because they are crafted by two opposed psychical forces within us: one which seeks to express a wish, and a second that seeks to thwart that expression.[4] Freud will argue that the complex process of repression, wish fulfillment, censorship, and dream distortion is only substantiated in practice. It is the interpretation of a dream that transforms latent content into manifest content, and helps the dreamer-patient better understand themselves, ultimately moving towards the alleviation of symptoms.[5] The theory is valid, in other words, because it works.

In *Being and Nothingness*, Sartre attempts to subvert Freud's concept of the Unconscious by criticizing the related notions of the *censor* (*Zensor*) and repression. Sartre finds the censor in particular to be philosophically problematic. How can I talk about unconscious material if, by definition, what is unconscious escapes consciousness, and consciousness is the place where knowing is expressed? Sartre puts the argument thus:

> The very essence of the reflexive idea of hiding something from oneself implies the unity of one and the same psychic mechanism and consequently a double activity in the heart of unity, tending on the one hand to maintain and locate the thing to be concealed and on the other to repress and disguise it. Each of the

---

Interpretation of Dreams, SE 4:54). All references to Freud are taken from the *Standard Edition* (SE) followed by the volume and page number.

2. SE 4:122-33. At 134, Freud emphatically states that the meaning of every dream is the fulfillment of a wish.

3. SE 4:142. Freud first used the censorship metaphor in *Studies on Hysteria* (SE 2:1-252).

4. SE 4:143. It is not altogether clear from Freud's text whether the dream as symbol is crafted by the first agent in an attempt to slip by the censor; by the second agent, the censor, as a means of distorting a wish that it could not fully suppress; or a cooperation of both, reaching a sort of tacit compromise with the unacceptable wish being disguised, but not destroyed.

5. See SE 4:163-64.

two aspects of this activity is complementary to the other; that is, it implies the other in its being. By separating consciousness from the unconscious by means of the censor, psychoanalysis has not succeeded in dissociating the two phases of the act, since the libido is a blind *conatus* toward conscious expression and since the conscious phenomenon is a passive, faked result. Psychoanalysis has merely localized this double activity of repulsion and attraction on the level of the censor.[6]

Sartre is claiming: (1) In order to censor what is unacceptable to consciousness, the censor must have knowledge of what that unconscious content is. There is therefore an agency that has knowledge of both my consciousness and what is acceptable to it, and my unconscious content. (2) All of these processes and content are *mine*, they belong to one individual. (3) I *cannot* view my psychic processes as if from without: my point of view is that of consciousness. (4) The censor therefore leads to a contradiction: the censor *must* belong to me, since all my psychic life is *mine*; the censor also must be another person, since I cannot see the totality of my psychic life as if from without. One could rehearse the same argument using the concept of repression. Put philosophically, it is a logical error to assert, as Freud does, that conscious *per se* is somehow broader than self-consciousness. To Freud's imperious claim that the model is true because it works, Sartre can reply that there is a divorce between what its truth claims are, and what it does: the truth claims are about a hypostatized *Second Mind* that is the censor; the therapeutic activity that supposedly works is about a *First Mind* that is consciousness.[7]

Sartre's argument hinges on the accusation of self-contradiction: Freud is asserting that there is something that *cannot* be said (i.e., unconscious content), but whose saying is constitutive of the speaking subject (i.e., consciousness). The argument is a transcendental one, ultimately asking *how* we know *what* we know, and seeing whether the two contradict each other.[8] In Sartre's case, however, focusing on the *content* of the unconscious and consequently erecting the censor as a *Second Mind* flattens the very distinction between a *How* (*Wie*) and a *What* (*Was*). Ultimately, Sartre has confused two kinds of speech in Freud, conflating what is simply discursive

---

6. Sartre, *Being and Nothingness*, 53–54, quoted in Gardner, *Irrationality*, 47.

7. My expression of this argument, particularly regarding the theory of a "Second Mind," is a partial reconstruction of Gardner, *Irrationality*, 41–52. Gardner offers his own convincing solution to the problem. Mine is an alternative one.

8. My conception of transcendental argumentation (and the argument from performative self-contradiction found therein) is taken from Thomas-Fogiel, *Death of Philosophy*, 142.

with what is performative, erecting each as a discursive subject. Freud is aware that one cannot, in the normal mode discourse, talk about the unconscious, since that would objectify it, transforming it into consciousness. The unconscious is *absent*, and speech cannot make it present. One can, however, make its absence felt in speech, a performative kind of language that, when employed in the clinical context, allows it to occupy its foundational place precisely *as* absent—as Freud famously says, "*wo Es war, soll Ich warden* (where the Id was, the I shall be)."[9] In other words, it is precisely the absence of unconscious material that is the condition of the presence of consciousness.

Freud's Humor

The whole therapeutic technique that Freud initiated is predicated precisely on this question of enactment. He describes this practical insight as one that was hard won. At the beginning of his experiments with the so-called *talking cure*, Freud adopted an intellectualist approach. If, as therapist, some aspect of the patient's behavior became clear him, but was still unclear to the patient, he was quick to share it with them. Inevitably, the patient resisted, and the content, the *what* that Freud had shared, found no place in the patient's own understanding. Conscious understanding was incapable of surmounting the patient's resistance. Instead of this *intellectualist* approach, the therapist must reserve any insight gained until the patient has talked it through—that is, until the patient has *performed* the symptom, has circumnavigated the hole that it leaves in the fabric of the ego's discourse, and then appropriates it for themselves.[10] This is the essence of the Freudian concept of *repetition*, one of the most fundamental *therapeutic performances*. Writes

9. Freud, *Neue Folge der Vorlesungen*, in *Gesammelte Werke*, 15:86.

10. Compare the intellectualism of *Studies in Hysteria* (1895), SE 2:274, to Freud's admonitions to therapists in *On The Beginning of Treatment* (1913): "It is true that in the earliest days of analytic technique we took an intellectualist view of the situation. We set a high value on the patient's knowledge of what he had forgotten, and in this we made hardly any distinction between our knowledge of it and his. We thought it a special piece of good luck if we were able to obtain information about the forgotten childhood trauma from other sources—for instance, from parents or nurses or the seducer himself—as in some cases it was possible to do; and we hastened to convey the information and the proofs of its correctness to the patient, in the certain expectation of thus bringing the neurosis and the treatment to a rapid end. It was a severe disappointment when the expected success was not forthcoming. How could it be that the patient, who now knew about his traumatic experience, nevertheless still behaved as if he knew no more about it than before? Indeed, telling and describing his repressed trauma to him did not even result in any recollection of it coming into his mind" (SE 12:141).

Freud, "The patient does not remember anything of what he has forgotten and repressed, but acts it out. He reproduces it not as a memory but as an action; he repeats it, without, of course, knowing that he is repeating it."[11] The *content* of what the patient says might be a "confused mass of dreams and associations," shame about undergoing psychotherapy, or hostility directed towards the analyst,[12] but what this *performance* says is, "See what happens if I really give way to such things? Was I not right to consign them to repression?"[13] There is no second-self-as-censor speaking here, because this declaration is precisely what goes *unsaid*—it is not that there is nobody to say it; rather, there is nothing to say. In line with this, the analyst should not correct irrational behavior stemming from repetition-performance, but merely incubate it, trying to prevent the patient from committing acts of self-harm until the performance has, so to speak, played itself out. The analyst therefore *believes* the patient, never doubting or contradicting the latter's claims. But believing the patient does not mean believing *what the patient says*, but rather, as direct object, believing *the patient themselves*. The truth-value of what the patient says is less important than what the speech-performance shows.

I would like to suggest that Freud became aware of this particular function of the patient's discourse in *The Joke and its Relation to the Unconscious* (1905). The joke internalizes all the mechanisms of repetition and performs it within the confines of self-referentiality. In speaking, one relies on possibility-conditions that cannot become the object of speech; whenever one speaks, one hides as much as one reveals, since it is the speech-act that suggests what its conditions are, and simultaneously hides them in order bring particular content into view. Consequently, speaking about oneself implies hiding things about oneself.

With a joke, such implications become clear when we ask *why* we enjoy it. A joke is funny because of what Freud calls "condensation accompanied by the formation of a substitute."[14] That is, one condenses opposing concepts into a composite, and then proposes this new composite as a substitute for a familiar state of affairs. While this is best exemplified by wordplay, Freud states that it belongs to the nature of all jokes. For it is our *enjoyment* of the joke that indicates what is being repressed in serious discourse. This is not a simple matter of linguistic content being hidden or revealed,

---

11. Freud, *Remembering, Repeating, and Working Through*, SE 12:150.
12. SE 12:150.
13. SE 12:152–53.
14. *Joke and Its Relationship*, SE 8:19.

but of some repressed material being alluded to rather than objectified.[15] The joke and its enjoyment are a single act that constitute a *performance*, a *mise-en-scène* of what is repressed. For example, in a *comedy of manners* (Molière's *Tartuffe*; Shakespeare's *Much Ado About Nothing*) politeness and social conventions are often mocked by an exaggerated, obsequious politeness. Such mockery of the norms of politeness expresses the very impolite animal desires of the unconscious precisely through the politeness it would like to contravene. The joke *performs* what the ego cannot say.[16]

Part of what is performed but not said is precisely that which escapes language—the deep past of language, the pre-linguistic origins of the ego. Consciousness has a past, going all the way back to the mineral world. Our language is not rooted in a dis-incarnate symbol, as Lacan would have it, but in our *bodies*. Metaphorically, we evoke *the body speaking* or *the language of the body* to talk about the symptom. But this *speech* is not speech at all. And older than the symptom is the original homeostasis of the mineral, elemental self. Ego-discourse has a pre-discursive past, and it must remain so if our discourse is to make any sense. To speak of it too seriously is already to objectify it.

Id Goes Without Saying: Falque and the Joke

My central claim, therefore, is that in his book on Freud, *Nothing to It* («*Ça» n'a rien à voir*, 2018), Emmanuel Falque deploys the method implied by the theory of self-referentiality contained in the Freudian joke. The book's title, as well as the titles of all its chapters, are puns on the word Ça (*Id*, the French translation of the Freudian *Es*). Each of these is an example of the Freudian joke, of "condensation accompanied by the formation of a substitute." Given this, one's understanding of Falque's analysis of Freud is incomplete if one remains on the level of content: each pun *performs* an element of Freudian psychoanalysis. This non-objectifying performance is meant to exist in

---

15. "It is most instructive to observe how the standards of joking sink as spirits rise. For high spirits replace jokes, just as jokes must try to replace high spirits, in which possibilities of enjoyment which are otherwise inhibited—among them the pleasure in non-sense—can come into their own: 'Mit wenig Witz und viel Behagen' [*Faust, Part I*, V, in Auerbach's cellar]. Under the influence of alcohol the grown man once more becomes a child, who finds pleasure in having the course of his thoughts freely at his disposal without paying regard to the compulsion of logic" (SE 8:127).

16. I base my analysis on Michael Billig's excellent paper, "Dialogic Unconsciousness." Billig sees "dialogical consciousness" as a constitutive factor of subjectivity. This is not due to a separation in the self, but rather the nature of language, which always speaks according to structures of alterity, even when making a self-referential point. The joke is a way of highlighting this state of affairs.

harmony with what is performed, namely, the idea that the Freudian Id is key to understanding what Falque calls the *Hors phénomène*: events which not only are beyond our field of experience, but obliterate the possibility-conditions of subjective experience. The extra-phenomenal, like the Freudian unconscious, is precisely that which cannot be talked about, since it escapes experience. In a later work, *Hors phénomène: Essai aux confins de la phénoménalité* (2021) Falque will adopt Freud's strategy in approaching the unsayable. From Freud, then, Falque learns how one deals with the extra-phenomenal, and his apprenticeship with Freud consists in learning how to tell jokes. For the English speaker, this crucial element of Falque's appropriation of the Freudian method is lost in translation. What follows, then, is an analysis of Falque's Freudian puns—not an attempt at explaining away his jokes, but rather, in Freudian terms, asking what is indicated by the enjoyment thereof.

"Ça" n'a rien à voir. The first and most obvious of the wordplays is Falque's title. The expression is a common French locution roughly equivalent to the English "nothing to do with [something]." A crucial difference with the English, however, is that the French expression constitutively includes the demonstrative pronoun *ça*. Meaning *de cela* or *of that*, this little word is more than a literal translation of the English *it*, but, much like the German *Es* can function variously as an indicator or placeholder: it is, somewhat akin to the Latin *res*, a *pragma* or what one talks about when one talks.[17] In this manner, one can use *ça* to express surprise (*ça alors!*), enthusiasm or distress (*ça oui! ça non!*), ironic approbation (*c'est ça*) or salutation (*ça va?*). The *ça* stands in for the absent object of discourse. *Ça* is also the French translation of Freud's *Es*, rendered in English as the neologism Id.[18] Falque's

17. For more on the "res" as mode of discourse (e.g., res publicum, res nullia), see Legendre, *Inéstimable objet*, 25.

18. The Id makes its first appearance in *Beyond the Pleasure Principle* [1920], and is more fully developed in *The Ego and the Id* [1923]. It belongs to a revision of Freud's topography of psyche, initially composed of the Unconscious, Pre-conscious, and Consciousness. Due to some of the problems we have encountered above, Freud developed the idea of an "ideal of ego-consciousness," the Superego. Additionally, he was obliged to address problems in distinguishing between unconsciously repressed material and drives that are deeply related to the unconscious (in that they cannot fully come to consciousness)—that is, between "static" and "active" parts of the Unconscious. The relationship between the two systems (Unconsciousness, Pre-Consciousness, Consciousness; Es, Super-ego, Ego) is difficult to define. On the one hand, Freud never saw them as being at odds with one another, and indeed, the latter terms can easily be superimposed over the earlier ones. But they also constitute a new way of conceiving of psyche, one that is subjective and active rather than "topographical." Falque, as we shall see, considers the introduction of the second system to constitute a break with the first. Writes Freud, "Now I think we shall gain a great deal by following the suggestion of a writer who, from

initial use of this expression is therefore a wordplay on a common locution, but one that evokes the Freudian Id, the *ça* that lurks in the background of conscious speech. The broadest application of this wordplay, outlined in the Preface, *Ouverture*, and Introduction, is what Falque calls the *backlash* (*choque-en-retour*) of psychoanalysis on philosophy, and phenomenology in particular. The question is whether or not the Unconscious, the *Id*, can have anything to do with a science whose goal is a return to objects. Falque, however, would like to go further, following Merleau-Ponty in asserting that both phenomenology and psychoanalysis have a *part d'ombre*, a shadowy nether region, and that psychoanalysis, for its part, has descended into this nether region, its *sous-sol* (basement).[19] In sum, this shadow, this basement of consciousness, is Freud's Id, linked as it is to primordial human drives. In shifting from a topography of psyche that speaks merely of an Unconscious to a subjective-dynamic system that speaks instead of an *Id*, Freud is responding to a series of traumatic events, especially the First World War, that demonstrate that the possibilities of psyche are broader than human agency—the ego, in other words, can be overwhelmed by *unspeakable* (both in the literal and figurative sense) primordial drives. In such situations, the psychoanalyst is confronted with the limits of experience—in the war, for example, the interplay of egos is eventually overwhelmed by the barbarity of violence, and people are reduced to flesh, to mere cannon fodder. Phenomenology, on the other hand, remains beholden to intentionality, which keeps it firmly within the limits of phenomenal experience. Falque claims that this is inadequate. From Freud's Id, we can learn that there are experiences so terrible that they annihilate the very possibility of the phenomenon—and yet, when they have passed by, the ego is still present, still alive. Addressing such experiences phenomenologically would imply accounting for something that is not an *excess* of phenomenality, but that rather *resists* phenomenality altogether. This is the lesson of the Id: it is not a remainder,

---

personal motives, vainly asserts that he has nothing to do with the rigors of pure science. I am speaking of Georg Groddeck, who is never tired of insisting that what we call our ego behaves essentially passively in life, and that, as he expresses it, we are 'lived' by unknown and uncontrollable forces. We have all had impressions of the same kind, even though they may not have overwhelmed us to the exclusion of all others, and we need feel no hesitation in finding a place for Groddeck's discovery in the structure of science. I propose to take it into account by calling the entity which starts out from the system [Perception-Consciousness]. and begins by being [Pre-conscious] the 'ego,' and by following Groddeck in calling the other part of the mind, into which this entity extends and which behaves as though it were [Unconscious], the 'Id'" (Freud, *Ego and the Id*, SE 14:23; cf. Groddeck, *Buch vom Es*). Both Groddeck and Freud were aware of Nietzsche's use of the term "Es" to describe impersonal forces at work in individuals.

19. Falque, «*Ça*» *n'a rien*, 30.

but a resistance. It is, says Falque, "something that is not nothing [*n'est pas rien*], something that looks at me and concerns me [*me regarde*], buries me in the hiding-place of a fault-line [*faille*] that one must inhabit rather than try to escape or pull oneself out of."[20]

Circulez, y a rien à voir. The title of the first chapter does not contain the word ça. Its Freudian *substitution* involves the *rien*, the *nothing*. Ultimately, the Id will reveal itself to be this *nothing*. The expression itself refers to what a police officer might say to bystanders who, seized by morbid curiosity, observe the scene of a crime or accident. What the police officer, the symbol of a censor or Super-ego, judges to be nothing, is in fact the something that the ego-consciousness wants to see. Psychoanalytically, there might in fact be precisely *nothing* for the ego to see, since the unpleasant scene will have been repressed. What remains is the suffering it has caused, in the form of a symptom. In the transition that takes place in Freud's work around the time of the First World War, the emergence of the concept of the Id is precisely meant to account for this *nothing*, ultimately caused by trauma. In the earlier *topography of psyche*, the goal of psychoanalysis was to bring to consciousness what was unconscious, which would inevitably cure the patient. Falque sees in this earlier Freudian thesis all the hallmarks of Enlightenment thought: Freud the *Aufklärer* thinks that by making the Unconscious conscious, the rational resources of consciousness will be able to fix all of its own problems—and this, not only on an individual level, but on a societal one.[21] But, claims Falque, the experience of the First World War taught Freud that some experiences are so traumatic that they simply cannot be brought to consciousness—their severity simply eradicates the very foundations of conscious experience. Freud's acknowledgement of this comes in the form of the Id, which is not simply an assemblage of material that can be repressed or uncovered, but the wellspring of desires that the ego can sometimes tame and control, but by which it is at other times

---

20. "Quelque chose qui n'est pas rien, me regarde et me concerne, m'enfouit dans le cache selon une faille qu'il convient d'habiter plutôt que de vouloir en être tiré ou de chercher toujours à en remonter" (Falque, «Ça» n'a rien, 36 [translation mine]).

21. Falque cites in support of this Freud's keynote address at the second international meeting of psychoanalysts in Nuremberg, *Future Prospects of Psychoanalytic Therapy* [1910]: "I will let you go, therefore, with the assurance that you do your duty in more than once sense by treating your patients psycho-analytically. You are not merely working in the service of science, by using the only and irreplaceable opportunity for discovering the secrets of the neuroses; you are not only giving your patients the most efficacious remedy for these sufferings available at the present time; but you are contributing your share to that enlightenment of the many from which we expect to gain the authority of the community in general and thus to achieve the most far-reaching prophylaxis against neurotic disorders" (SE 11:152).

overwhelmed. If philosophy has not learned this lesson, it is because it is beholden to a vision-intuition model of knowing, which Falque calls Idealism. Seeing was theorized into intuiting, and this became the model for knowledge. Vision is the *modus operandi* of metaphysics. How, then, does one describe what escapes one's paradigm? Falque evokes Merleau-Ponty's chiasm as the right kind of movement, but does not subsequently propose a phenomenology of touch. Rather, as if he were in a therapeutic context, he continues to *talk around* the idea of trauma without addressing it as object. If the joke performs what the ego cannot say, Falque's wordplay on the "*nothing*" evokes the Id that is unseeable. This wordplay is an effort to sneak past the censor-police: if what is said is "nothing to see here," what is meant is, "beware this nothing, which is the Id."

Prends garde à ça. This title is based on the French expression *prends garde*, often *prends garde à toi*, or *keep your wits about you*. While the term can also be applied to other objects (e.g. *prends garde à la porte*, watch out for the door), the real Freudian substitution is between *toi/ça*, you/Id. To beware of *Id* is to beware of oneself, since the self is host to desires that it cannot always control. Moreover, successfully navigating the world as ego-consciousness implies that one cooperates with these desires, that one respects the Id and lets it occupy its proper place—for if it is ignored, it will invisibly take over. In the traumatic experience that was the First World War, the most primitive of desires, the death drive (still inchoate in Freud's writings until 1920) rises to the fore: in the trenches, one's enemies cease to be other humans and become mere flesh, cannon fodder, as the ego is overwhelmed by something bestial.[22] The violence of evil therefore becomes something ineffable. Writes Falque, "When violence reaches the summit of its blindness, radical evil or the 'pitiless' no longer allows us to 'see' or even 'suffer' insofar as the 'I' is suddenly and radically reduced to an 'it,' or said otherwise, to identity with anonymity above all otherness."[23] The lesson here is that there are desires in the psyche that are older, more fundamental, and more primitive than the products of ego's rational conduct. Before there is an *Ich*, an ego, there was the *Es*, the Id. To beware of the Id, or *prendre garde à ça* does not only mean being vigilant about these primitive desires rising

---

22. This is the lesson that Falque sees in Freud's *Thoughts for the Times on War and Death* [1915], SE 14:275–300. The text—along with Freud's 1914 correspondence on the same subjects with Lou-Andreas Salomé—provides the main theme of the second chapter.

23. "Quand la violence atteint le point extreme dans son aveuglement, le mal absolu ou 'l'Impitoyable' ne laisse plus 'voir,' ni même 'souffrir,' en cela à tout le moins que le 'Je' devient soudainement et radicalement réduit au 'ça,' ou autrement dit l'identité à l'anonymat en-deçà de toute altérité" (Falque, «*Ça» n'a rien*, 77 [translation mine]).

up, it means acknowledging that they are in me; specifically, in my body, the confluence of the somatic expressions of the self.

Ça n'est pas rien. In English, one would express this positively: *that's [really] something*. In French, however, one says *it's not nothing*. The importance of the subject matter in question is affirmed through a negation. Given what was previously established, the wordplay here consists in affirming that the *nothing*, the Id, is indeed something, but since it is older and broader than ego discourse, it cannot be circumscribed by the ego's understanding. Its locus is not the thought of ego, but rather the body. It is precisely this root in the body—and neither in ego, nor an idealized conception of "flesh" derived from ego-perceptions—that defines the Id, and links it to the ego. The body, in other words, is the past, the foundation of consciousness. When consciousness first comes on the scene, its inquiry into its limits, origins, and capabilities requires such a *past*, a point of origin which it must presuppose, but to which it cannot return *qua* consciousness. Put otherwise: the dynamic human subject is host to multifaceted desires, to drives, that traverse the whole spectrum of psyche from Id to ego. When the ego, the standpoint of discursive thought, seeks to understand these drives, part of them resist understanding—they are older than discursive thought, because they are grounded in the body.

C'est quoi ça? The simply interrogation, *what is it?* is here so close to what is actually meant that it is less a joke than another form of Freudian expression, the *uncanny* (*das Unheimliche*). Even those unfamiliar with Freud know the feeling—one sees something, a wax figure for example, that is so close to being human that one is perturbed by the remaining element of inhumanity within it. In Freudian terms, the image, a *repetition* of something insofar as it is a likeness, evokes for the one who sees it his own Id.[24] Here, the *ça* of *what is it* is so close to the products of my own ego-consciousness (overlapping, as it does, with *my body*, from which this consciousness arises) that I can sense, but not describe, the ineffable difference between ego and Id. There is, therefore, a remainder in my experience of myself, grounded in the body, that, when untethered from the world of consciousness, language, and sublimation, can express itself brutally in violence and evil. It is not that

---

24. See Freud, *Uncanny* [1919], SE 17:218–52. Freud's argument is difficult to follow, but in support of my summary, one reads, for example: "We are able to postulate the principle of a repetition-compulsion in the unconscious mind, based upon instinctual activity and probably inherent in the very nature of the instincts—a principle powerful enough to overrule the pleasure-principle, lending to certain aspects of the mind their daemonic character, and still very clearly expressed in the tendencies of small children; a principle, too, which is responsible for a part of the course taken by the analyses of neurotic patients. Taken in all, the foregoing prepares us for the discovery that whatever reminds us of this inner repetition-compulsion is perceived as uncanny" (SE 17:238).

there is anything evil in my bodily nature. But when the animal ground of drive is unleashed from the rest, it behaves in a way that the I of consciousness, ego, perceives as evil—or more properly said, the ego is traumatized by the experience, and dissociates from it. In asking, *c'est quoi ça*? one senses *that* some remainder exists, but it cannot be placed within the totality of one's perspective. The Id is always just beyond my grasp. And this is because consciousness has a somatic history, one stretching all the way back to the anorganic,[25] to the mineral foundations of what will eventually become consciousness. This *before* is with me immemorially, and if I cannot *know* it, I am connected to it by desire: the drives at work in me have not only led me from it, but manifest a return to it. Indeed, if the later Freud's theoretical work identifies the pleasure-principle and the desire for transcendence as being united in *eros*, the human psyche also contains *Thanatos*, a death drive that seeks to restore the homeostasis of anorganic life.[26] The uncanny remainder of experience derives from the ineffable *before* and *after* of drive, the anorganic that is both my origin and destiny.

Ça me regarde. This locution means "this concerns me," but can be literally translated as *it looks at me*. If *prendre garde à ça* is an injunction to beware of the brutality within me, and asking *c'est quoi ça* leads to the anorganic that is both my origin and my destiny, ça me regarde is a statement of appropriation: the somatic source of these drives is mine, and the Id, while sometimes behaving as an *it*, is ultimately *me*, just as much as the ego. Moreover, the border between ego and Id is fluid, meaning that the two interact and together constitute the dynamic subject that I am. Central to this chapter is Falque's adoption of Freud's equestrian metaphor. The ego is like a rider, and the Id, its horse. The ego constantly seeks to bring his mount under control, but does not always succeed—sometimes, the horse will rebel, and the rider can only follow it, waiting for the moment when he can regain control. Ultimately, the two must work in tandem in order to reach their destination.[27] The ego, then, can draw on the Id's power in order

---

25. This word, borrowed from the French, is closely related to "inorganic." Both highlight the lack of organs or constitutive parts. Falque's use of *anorganique* refers to the building blocks of life, the most basic chemical elements whose subsequent relation and interaction produce life-forms.

26. See *Beyond the Pleasure Principle* [1920], SE 18:57.

27. "The functional importance of the ego is manifested in the fact that normally control over the approaches to motility devolves upon it. Thus in its relation to the Id it is like a man on horseback, who has to hold in check the superior strength of the horse; with this difference, that the rider tries to do so with his own strength while the ego uses borrowed forces. The analogy may be carried a little further. Often a rider, if he is not to be parted from his horse, is obliged to guide it where it wants to go; so in the same way the ego is in the habit of transforming the Id's will into action as if it were its own" (Freud, *Ego and the Id* [1923], SE 19:25).

achieve its goals. Prerequisite, of course, is that it *beware* or *prend garde* of the Id, since it can easily be overpowered by it.

Ça me touche. A similar expression to ça me regarde, ça me touche means, *it affects me*, but in the literal sense means, it touches me. In the same way that the two expressions overlap, so does the content of the two chapters: not only does the Id concern me (i.e., *I* the ego must coexist with this other in me), it affects me—that is, informs my self-understanding. There is, to use Merleau-Ponty's language, a *chiasm* of Ego and Id, a constant interrelationality and crossing-over, but one that implies a hidden aspect. When one hand touches another hand, an unknown element is evoked: There is an obscure fourth moment involved in touching-touched when intersubjectivity is introduced: I feel, I feel that I feel, I feel that the other feels, but I cannot feel *what* the other feels. Psychoanalytically, this is the *resistance* of the Id, which can be neither represented as a phenomenon, nor conceived of as an excess of phenomenality.[28]

The Irony of Id all: The Extra-Phenomenal

Falque's book on Freud *does* more than it *says*. This is because, as I have tried to demonstrate, it is a protracted Freudian joke, an act of condensation and substitution that seeks to perform what discourse cannot say. This strategy is a way of tricking the Id into playing the ego's game, or phenomenologically speaking, integrating that which resists phenomenality into a science of phenomena. The key move here is the transition from *Nothing*, which is how the Super-ego censor, agent of repression, presents unconscious material, the Id, namely something that only partly coincides with the phenomenal world, and has a dark nether region that can be performed, but not talked about. Philosophically, Falque has established a methodology according to which the extra-phenomenal, that which resists appearing, can be included in discourse on the phenomenon without being objectified. The expansion and protracted use of this methodology strictly within the limits of phenomenology has yielded a book-length study, *Hors phénomène* (2021)—one that would have been impossible without the work previously done on Freud.

28. "Loin de toute philosophie ou théologie negatives, nous l'avons dit, le ça est resistance à une puissance (l'ego et sa volonté de diriger) plutôt que reste d'une dependence (Dieu ou l'au-delà du discours). Non seulement inassimilé, il demeure inassimilable, et donc imprenable. *Ni* logique, *ni* négation, *ni* jugement de valeur, *ni* représentation du temps, le ça n'appartient pas à la privation ou à l'au-delà du discours ... mais il est à proprement parler hors phénomène ou expropriation: non pas irreprésentable mais échappant, voire détruisant, l'idée même de représentation" (Falque, «Ça» n'a rien, 131–32).

Appropriately, the preface (*Ouverture*) of *Hors phénomène* is entitled, "Ça me tombe dessus." This expression—the first of many wordplays—refers to something that arrives out of the blue and requires my attention. Following the wordplay, the *thing* that comes seemingly out of nowhere is the Id, highlighting its extra-phenomenal character. "I do not only suffer from what happens to me inexplicably [*ce qui me tombe dessus*]," writes Falque, "but my very capacity to suffer is thereby sometimes annihilated."[29] To the Id belong those traumatic experiences that simply leave a hole in our experience, the *troumatisme* (another wordplay that combines *hole* [*trou*] and trauma). Their very occurrence destroys the possibility-condition of subjective experience. Falque offers five examples of such experiences: death, the separation of a couple, the death of a child, natural disasters, and pandemics. Others are possible; any time an *Es*, some unknown force, rises up and causes destruction, subjectivity is at risk of being annihilated, and the extra-phenomenal comes into play. In such experiences, one cannot speak of resilience, or the subject's ability to *bounce back* after the trauma, but rather the miraculous discovery, after the fact, that *I am still there*.[30] Without any point of reference, one finds oneself in the chaos of formlessness, in the abyss of the *hors phénomène*. But this chaos, says Falque, is not the absence of thought. Indeed, accepting that one is simply *still there* in the face of trauma invites the conception of the subject as *hors-je(u)* (out of bounds/out of self), which lets the unthinkable, the unassimilated, enter into the human experience: beyond the idealist's reduction of what exists to the thinkable, the human subject in its fullness is confronted with chaos, that which allows for the arrival of something new.

The problem of the extra-phenomenal we find here is the same one that Freud faced at the beginning of the Great War: the challenge of conceiving the inconceivable.[31] The enormity of trauma introduces chaos into the very fabric of the self; my "I," the ego, no longer feels any control—an invisible Id (ça n'a rien à voir) wells up from some unknown corner of my own psyche and takes over (ça me tombe dessus).[32] On the level of ego-consciousness, this involves a degree of self-estrangement; indeed, even if I cannot *see* or understand the phenomenality of what is occurring, the foundational possibility-condition of all human experience, the body, is still present, as inalienably mine. But *this* ego becomes estranged from *this* body,

---

29. "Je ne souffre pas seulement de ce qui me tombe dessus, mais mes capacités d'en souffrir elles-mêmes sont parfois néantisées" (Falque, *Hors phénomène*, 11 [translation mine]).

30. See Falque, *Hors phénomène*, 28.

31. Falque, *Hors phénomène*, 152.

32. Falque, *Hors phénomène*, 262.

and my own experience becomes uncanny.³³ If this Freudian uncanniness has Nietzschean origins—there is an *Es* (Id) that is older than the *Ich* (I), and it speaks when it wants to, and not when I force it to³⁴—it is perhaps better expressed by Rimbaud's phrase *Je est un autre*.³⁵ The extra-phenomenal has an event character, and belongs to that primordial world that is broader than ego-consciousness, and speaks to me *as if* it came from another. In a rare moment of accord with Lacan, Falque cites one of the former's notorious *bon mots*: "je pense là où je ne suis plus (I think when I am no more)."³⁶ More than an epistemological reading of *Wo Es war, soll Ich werden*, this wordplay ultimately seeks to account for self-alienation (which for Falque, contrary to Lacan, is incarnate, and felt in the body) performatively, as a Freudian joke. If symptoms express themselves in the body as a response to the ineffability of trauma, trying to say them verbally is not a cure by means of objectification, but a way of bringing the body's activity into discourse by means of performance. Writes Falque, "*Aux maux de la psyche répondent les mots du langage, nécessaires aussi pour penser*."³⁷ The *words* (*mots*) of language answer the *ills* (*maux* [homonym of *mots*]) of psyche.

Linked to the concept of the extra-phenomenal is the task of providing an ontology of solitude. Subsumed under the tyranny of the phenomenal is the tyranny of otherness.³⁸ We always talk about solitude as if it were already a form of alterity. To speak of solitude, then, will imply using the Freudian methodology of *substitute formation*. To talk about solitude authentically implies *talking in one place and being in another*, in such a manner that this solitude, the hidden object that never comes to discourse, is obliquely present. In this way, discourse accounts for itself without leaving itself. The culmination of the discursive possibilities first explored in «*Ça*» *n'a rien à voir* is therefore achieved with this "lieu propre en soi inaccessible de soi à soi."³⁹

To make his point, Falque refers to Marcel Proust's *In Search of Lost Time*. There, the death of the narrator's lover Albertine leads to a pithy declaration of solitude: "*Jamais [Albertine] ne reviendra. . . . Nous existons seuls*."⁴⁰ This is not a lament for Albertine. Rather, it is the beginning of the narrator's desire to purge his memory of her, to confine her to the past. The

---

33. Falque, *Hors phénomène*, 34, 266–67.
34. Falque, *Hors phénomène*, 267; cf. Nietzsche, *Beyond Good and Evil* §17.
35. Falque, *Hors phénomène*, 269.
36. Falque, *Hors phénomène*, 267; cf. Lacan, *Écrits*, 517.
37. Falque, *Hors phénomène*, 454.
38. Falque, *Hors phénomène*, 410–11.
39. Falque, *Hors phénomène*, 411.
40. Proust, *À la Recherche du temp perdu*, 1943.

solitude at stake here is not an originary ontological aloneness, but something that escapes the otherness-structure of discourse. Discursively, the primordiality of solitude requires an initial negation: before my beginning *alone*, there is an immemorial otherness hidden in the past. If the constitution of subjectivity in Proust ultimately lies in a collusion between the past and the present, then the death of Albertine helps constitute a foundational forgetting, much like birth for Otto Rank,[41] which allows solitude to be there precisely at the beginning. The birth of the individual, separate from the originary relatedness of the womb, moves towards the constitution of a "*noyau de solitude*." Following Winnicot, Falque sees the ability to be alone not as something innate, but a sign of maturity, the fruit of human development and flourishing.

Otherness is older than solitude, chaos older than order, the Id older than ego. These ancestral concepts remain in a past that is ontological rather than merely temporal. They must remain in the past in order for the present to be possible. Falque's point in exploring the *Hors phénomène* is therefore not one of closing off possibilities in the human experience, but rather one of opening them up: from the *Krisis* of the past emerges something new. Indeed, once one examines the ontological results of the phenomenological game that is the Freudian joke, one understands that it is precisely what *cannot* come into the phenomenal realm that is the catalyst for phenomenality in the first place. If one could *say* what the extra-phenomenal is, then either it would be a projection and objectification of the transcendental subject (as Sartre contended above) or it would simply not exist at all. Ontologically, this would ultimately imply the impossibility of the emergence of anything *new*. The world would merely be the constant rearrangement of its ontic elements. Newness comes from crisis and chaos.

---

41. Falque evokes Otto Rank's idea of the trauma of birth several times in *Hors phénomène*. Most importantly: "Il faut reconnaître que 'naître,' c'est fracturer . . . et qu'aux yeux du 'naissant' à tout le moins le 'pêle-mêle' prime sur 'l'ouvert,' le plein sur le vide, le Chaos sur le Cosmos, ou le confus sur l'ordre et la beauté. Otto Rank . . . l'a montré. Il est un '*Traumatisme de la naissance*' (das Trauma der Geburt) qui n'est pas d'abord uniquement celui de l'accouchement, mais aussi pour l'enfant de la 'perte' du premier objet, à savoir sa mère. D'où la quête de tous les 'objets transitionnels' (doudous, tétines, peluches, poupées . . .) qui seront sinon inventées, au moins trouvés, pour y remédier. Le traumatisme est *originel*, comme il y a la 'rupture' et non pas 'l'ouverture,' que l'on 'construit autour du trou'" (Falque, *Hors phénomène*, 353). In other words, the original trauma of rupture, an extra-phenomenal event, is constitutive of our subsequent capacity for alterity, for entering into relation. No phenomena without an extra-phenomenal in the past.

Bibliography

Billig, Michael. "The Dialogic Unconsciousness: Psychoanalysis, Discursive Psychology, and the Nature of Repression." *British Journal of Social Psychology* 36 (1997) 139-59.

Falque, Emmanuel. *«Ça» n'a rien à voir: Lire Freud en philosophie*. Paris: Cerf, 2018.

———. *Hors phénomène: Essai aux confins de la phénoménalité*. Paris: Hermann, 2021.

Freud, Sigmund. *Gesammelte Werke*. 18 vols. Frankfurt: Fischer, 2010-2011.

———. *The Standard Edition of the Complete Works of Sigmund Freud*. Translated by James Strachey et al. 24 vols. London: Hogarth, 1953-1974.

Gardner, Sebastian. *Irrationality and the Philosophy of Psychoanalysis*. Cambridge: Cambridge University Press, 1993.

Groddeck, Georg. *Das Buch vom Es: Psychoanalytische Briefe an eine Freundin*. Leipzig/Wien/Zürich: Internationaler Psychoanalytischer, 1923.

Lacan, Jacques. *Écrits*. Paris: Seuil, 1966.

Legendre, Pierre. *L'inéstimable objet de la transmission: Étude sur le principe généalogique en Occident*. Paris: Fayard, 1985.

Nietzsche, Friedrich. *Beyond Good and Evil*. Translated by Walter Kaufmann. New York: Vintage, 1966.

Proust, Marcel. *À la Recherche du temp perdu*. Paris: Quarto Gallimard, 1999.

Sartre, Jean-Paul. *Being and Nothingness: An Essay on Phenomenological Ontology*. Translated by Hazel Barnes. London: Methuen, 1958.

Thomas-Fogiel, Isabelle. *The Death of Philosophy: Reference and Self-Reference in Contemporary Thought*. Translated by Richard A. Lynch. New York: Columbia University Press, 2011.

When Meaning Breaks

Thinking Sense and Suffering with Emmanuel Falque

SARAH HORTON

IN *HORS PHÉNOMÈNE* (THE Extra-Phenomenal), Emmanuel Falque endeavors to "think the unthinkable" and to write of that which shatters our interpretive categories.[1] Such a task might seem paradoxical: how indeed can thought grapple with that which breaks the very conditions of thought, even as if those conditions never were? Yet it is also essential, for the crisis in which no meaning can be found spares no one: it is a matter of a *crack* that runs through us all. Here I seek to follow Falque in his effort to think

---

1. Falque, *Hors phénomène*, 151. All translations from *Hors phénomène* are my own. Falque's phrase *le Hors phénomène* is usually translated as "the extra-phenomenal," which also translates *l'extra-phénoménal*. Literally, *le Hors phénomène* translates as "the Outside phenomenon," an unacceptable rendering because it suggests a phenomenon characterized by outsideness, while the *Hors phénomène* is not experienced phenomenally and should not be conceived in spatial terms. I translate *le Hors phénomène* as "the Outside-the-phenomenon," thereby maintaining something of the distinction between the preposition *hors* and the prefix *extra*. Granted, "the Outside-the-phenomenon" sounds odd in English (the hyphenation is to make it read more naturally), while *le Hors phénomène* sounds natural in French; thus, as the *Hors phénomène* is extra-phenomenal, the translation "the extra-phenomenal" is unsurprising. Still, the relative bluntness of *outside* or *hors*, as full words in comparison to the prefix *extra*, is worth maintaining because it accentuates the stark reality of non-phenomenal chaos. While standard English capitalization might suggest writing "the Outside-the-Phenomenon," I capitalize only the *O* to emphasize *Outside*.

this chaos or non-sense that destroys thought and to examine the sense of survival in the midst of suffering. Ultimately, I argue that it is impossible to separate sense and non-sense, or the phenomenon from the outside.

Outside All Sense

The extra-phenomenal, or the Outside-the-phenomenon, is neither the supra-phenomenal, which exceeds the categories of thought, nor the infra-phenomenal, which is preparatory to phenomena.[2] On the contrary, it breaks the categories, destroying the very possibility of phenomenality. As Falque puts it, the unthinkable is "that which stands 'outside' of the limits of thought, not by a defect or by excess, but by the annihilation, or even the destruction, of the very capacities of the thinkable, or at the very least of the imaginable (the *extra*-phenomenal)."[3] Having reproached phenomenology for overemphasizing the saturated phenomenon at the expense of the limited phenomenon, Falque now reaches a limit of thought and phenomenology outside which there is no phenomenon, saturated, limited, or otherwise. Before the saturated phenomenon, thought falls short; beneath the weight of the Outside-the-phenomenon, thought shatters into nothing. This nothing is not the absence that still presents itself as a meaningful phenomenon, as when, in Sartre's example, I arrive at a café to find that my friend Pierre, whom I expected, is not there;[4] when it comes to the Outside-the-phenomenon, the very notion of expectation is senseless, and this nothing does not *mean* at all. The French *sens* may mean sense, meaning, or direction, and the extra-phenomenal destroys sense (*sens*) in every sense of the word, for by breaking meaning, it also breaks one's relation to the sensible world and the possibility of orienting oneself within the world.

Thinking the extra-phenomenal, the Outside-the-phenomenon, is therefore thinking the unthinkable—and this is the task that Falque sets himself and his readers. *Hors phénomène* highlights five traumas—illness, separation, death of a child, natural disaster, and pandemic—that break the very possibilities of thought and of phenomenality.[5] A crisis—note that while these five traumas are all crises, Falque's list does not exhaust all possible crises[6]—"break[s] all capacity to phenomenalize,"[7] shattering any

2. Falque, *Hors phénomène*, 91–103.
3. Falque, *Hors phénomène*, 153.
4. Sartre, *Être et le néant*, 43–46; *Being and Nothingness*, 41–44.
5. "Separation" refers to the breakdown of a relationship with a spouse or partner.
6. Falque, *Hors phénomène*, 31.
7. Falque, *Hors phénomène*, 61. "That which should not happen (to me) and which

possibility of the coherence that is necessary for me to say that *I* am experiencing *something*. A crisis has no sense: it is not that *I* cannot make sense of it but that *it* renders sense-making impossible. Because it is non-sensical and breaks down the very possibility of phenomenal experience, a crisis is extra-phenomenal; in other words, it does not appear or become present as a phenomenon. Crucially, crises can befall us only because *the crisis* has always already befallen us: there is a crack in thought itself that is more fundamental than any instance of suffering. Indeed, how could thought break under the weight of particular crises if, within thought, there were not a fracture that rendered thought susceptible to crises? When Falque writes that "the unthinkable is a rupture, even a 'crack [*fêlure*],' by which everything collapses, unto the very capacity to construct or reconstruct,"[8] he is referring not to a problem that some might avoid by luck or effort but to a fundamental fact of our common humanity, and this irreparable, originary crack or fracture is the crisis. The Outside-the-phenomenon—that which does not belong to the domain of phenomenality, which indeed destroys the possibility of phenomenal experience—does not, therefore, come to me from without, as though imposed on me by some external force, but rather confronts me from within: it is constitutive of my very humanity, and as such, it always already conditions phenomenal experience and the categories of thought. "It *befalls me*,"[9] and there is no way to dodge it by remaining safely inside. Because there is no inside without an outside, nothing in our existence can properly be thought without also thinking the extra-phenomenal.

The seemingly impossible task of thinking the unthinkable thus requires reckoning with the fact that through each one of us runs a crack that is the sheer chaos—that is, the utter non-sense that is in fact prior to sense itself[10]—by which we may be submerged. So irreparable is the crack

---

has happened (to me) or which befell (me) . . . has made what should have been a mere 'exception' in my life my *whole* life, such that I have 'become' that which I dreaded and still 'become' it" (Falque, *Hors phénomène*, 303). In a crisis, I am wholly absorbed in the senseless of what befalls me.

8. Falque, *Hors phénomène*,155.

9. Falque, *Hors phénomène*, 7.

10. See Falque, *Hors phénomène*, 195–98, in particular, Falque's remark that "it is not *Chaos* that is drawn from *Cosmos*, or the Elements that make the Mixture, but on the contrary Cosmos that comes from *Chaos*, or the Elements from the Mixture. *Chaos* is first or it is not" (*Hors phénomène*, 197), as well as *Hors phénomène*, 215, where Falque describes *Chaos* as "this 'mass of phenomena'—in its density, its confusion and its mixture for us who receive it to the point of the annihilation of our very capacity for receiving." Submerged by chaos, we can make sense of nothing, yet chaos is prior to sense, such that the crack in us is constitutive of our being.

that the very notion of repair is itself nonsensical: it is no thing that could even hypothetically be closed or removed. To be human is not to have a crack within an otherwise solid self but to be cracked. Against a culture that tends to recognize only solvable problems on the one hand and identities to be affirmed on the other, Falque emphasizes that being thus cracked is not a pathology. The crises that shatter thought "are certainly never to be wanted or desired, and are even always to be repulsed,"[11] and he recognizes medicine and psychiatry as potentially necessary responses to them.[12] But specific crises differ from the common human condition only "by degree," for "'being-in-crisis' is in reality constitutive of the human subject, such that he never will and never should stop 'changing.'"[13] Neither an abnormal but treatable pathology nor a stable identity, *the* crisis—that is, the fundamental crack that runs through each person and that is the condition of possibility for every particular crisis that may befall one—reveals that being human is never a matter of safety or changeless, self-identical stability. Rather than seeking an impossible closure of the crack, we must never "renounce 'being ceaselessly modified' and therefore living as a 'metamorphosed subject.'"[14] While *The Metamorphosis of Finitude* envisions a transformation of our finitude brought about through Christ's resurrection, *Hors phénomène*—"taking here, therefore, the baton from *The Metamorphosis of Finitude*,"[15] as Falque himself puts it—points out that finitude is already a matter of constant metamorphosis, even aside from any reference to God. The metamorphosis that the resurrection of Christ brings about in the believer's manner of living in the world[16] is thus a metamorphosis of his or her manner of undergoing metamorphoses.[17]

The Impossibility of Impossibility

Falque's work is marked by the insistence that our condition as humans *tout court* is first to be thought positively, rather than in the negative terms

11. Falque, *Hors phénomène*, 312.
12. Falque, *Hors phénomène*, 310.
13. Falque, *Hors phénomène*, 312.
14. Falque, *Hors phénomène*, 312.
15. Falque, *Hors phénomène*, 283.
16. See Falque, *Métamorphose de la finitude*, 303–15; *Metamorphosis of Finitude*, 102–12.
17. Cf. Falque's observation that "binding up our wounds, [Christ] does not come to remove them, but in a way to heal them. . . . There is nothing to prevent us from thinking that the stigmata of our trials, or rather of our traumas without cause or sin, remain in us by way of 'traces' that are never truly erased" (*Chair de Dieu*, 155; "God Extra-Phenomenal," 213).

of lack or privation,[18] and this point still holds with regard to the extra-phenomenal. Thinking the human condition positively means considering first what it is (e.g., finite and temporal), while thinking it negatively means seeking first to describe it by reference to its lack of qualities typically attributed to God (e.g., humans are non-infinite and non-eternal), as though the experience of being human were originarily an experience of lacking or being deprived of the divine perfections. In reality, though, our experience of being human begins not with what we are not and can never be but with what we are: hence the importance, for Falque, of thinking the human condition first in terms of what it is and therefore in terms of our primordial experience of it. Certainly, it is better not to be undergoing any specific crisis: someone who is seriously ill or whose child dies would be better off if the crisis were not befalling her. Even the breakdown of phenomenal experience that occurs in a crisis is not, however, best understood in terms of privation, for the crisis is not the experience of loss—not even the experience of losing experience—but is non-experience or an-experience. As Falque explains,

> The "de-thought" [*le dé-penser*]—or the "negation of thought"—does not designate, or no longer designates, something that one should have and that one suddenly no longer has (privation). It designates, rather, what one does not have as if one had never had it, while no longer being sure that one day one will have it again, if it is even the case that once at least one did have it (negation).[19]

Although the terms *de-thought*, *unthinkable*, *an-experiential*, and *extra-phenomenal* incorporate a reference to what they are not, Falque is contrasting the unthinkable with experiences that belong to the human condition, not experiences that are alien to humanity. Rather than suggesting that our condition is one of regrettably failing to be divine, he shows that human existence is constituted by the unthinkable and the an-experiential at least as much as by the thinkable and the experiential. And the terms *unthinkable* and *an-experiential* do not refer to a lack of something that we ought always to have.

A crisis that shatters sense, as if sense never was or will be, is not experienced as a privation because it is the undoing of experience and hence is not experienced at all. Moreover, in a crisis, there is no possibility of experience because there is no one to experience it: a crisis forces the self outside itself such that there is no longer a self to speak or to speak of. The encounter

18. See, for instance, Falque, *Métamorphose de la finitude*, 191–99; *Metamorphosis of Finitude*, 15–20.

19. Falque, *Hors phénomène*, 156.

with the extra-phenomenal is a non-experience precisely because thought's categories shatter such that the thinker herself breaks down: "If there are still 'some' thoughts, it then becomes uncertain, at least in view of trauma ... whether I can still continue to constitute them as 'mine.'"[20] Again, such a crisis is bad. That we should not insist on looking on the bright side by rushing to find meaning in suffering is central to Falque's argument. Crises, however, "arise *positively* there as if 'without contrary,'"[21] since one is trapped in them and broken down as if no alternative were possible.

Recall, moreover, that we cannot and should not be cured of *the* crisis, even as we do and should seek to resist crises. It is precisely because one cannot escape the crisis that the crisis is transformative: as Falque argues,

> Confronted with the Outside-the-phenomenon, the subject is, conversely, "pushed to the limit [*à bout*]," or as if cornered into itself [*acculé à soi*], held in a "corner" of its existence from which it cannot withdraw itself. It thus becomes, as if without realizing it, "hyper-subjectified," for it is from "oneself" that one suffers here, even though in the anonymity of existing. Therefore one will not, and one will never, suppress subjectivity, though it should become totally unrecognizable and transformed. "Metamorphosed," the subject will thus never remain "the same" but will always become "other"—not from an alterity of "oneself as another" that always permits recovering oneself but from a "transformed subject" that is ceaselessly renewed.[22]

During a crisis, one might say that one will never be the same again; in fact, since one is always already in crisis, one was never the same in the first place. Not being the same does not, however, mean ceasing to be. Being in crisis is being trapped outside phenomena, outside sense, outside oneself, as though there had never been an *inside*. Yet because the Outside-the-phenomenon is "the impossibility of possibility,"[23] it is also the impossibility of the possibility of a complete nullification of the self by which one could escape the breakdown. There would be no crisis if a crisis or the crisis meant the cessation of existence. "It's not the end of the world," we say, sometimes in response to minor problems, other times in response to crises that do shatter the world of the afflicted one—yet even when one's world breaks, it is not simply the end, for *it* does go on. If *it* did not, there would be no

20. Falque, *Hors phénomène*, 221.
21. Falque, *Hors phénomène*, 335.
22. Falque, *Hors phénomène*, 297.
23. See Falque, *Hors phénomène*, 355. The phrase "the impossibility of possibility" recurs throughout.

suffering. Beset by the Outside-the-phenomenon, one seems to be nothing but suffering, with no hope of becoming or having been anything else. Yet one is suffering because one cannot discard the crack by which one may be thus laid bare for suffering—which means, since this crack is constitutive of one's existence, that one is suffering from not being able to discard oneself.[24] Thus one is truly *hyper-subjectified*, unable to rid oneself of a cracked subjectivity that is, in truth, the only possible subjectivity. Under such pressure, one cannot remain the same but can only be transformed.

Even one who is not undergoing any specific crisis remains cracked, however much one might like to pretend otherwise. It is not that we are all constantly suffering and in denial—though it bears noting that no one goes through life without suffering. Rather, we are never safe within some realm of guaranteed sense and identity but are always already laid open to chaos. As Falque puts it, "The 'source' of the Outside-the-phenomenon first finds its point of emergence *in each of us*, although such layers are usually approached, it is true, only on the occasion of an *extra*-phenomenality."[25] Thus each of us is always in the midst of being transformed by the very impossibility of ridding oneself of a cracked subjectivity. To go on living is to be unceasingly changed by virtue of the sheer impossibility of sheltering oneself from the crack. The very categories of thought are not fixed but might at any moment collapse such that I can no longer ignore or pretend to ignore the Outside. Since the ego, the world, and thought itself cannot protect me, going on requires a constant creation of the new—and this creation and creativity cannot be attributed to the powers of a fixed ego. Because the resources to continue are not inscribed in any stable thing that will survive the breakdown in its supposed prior state, continuing demands ever-new resources, and the creativity that brings them forth cannot deny the breakdown.

That such creation may arise even from the impossibility of possibility is astonishing. As Falque observes, "For such is the paradox. We *continue* (usually) *to live*, or at the very least *to survive*, in the crisis."[26] If the Outside-the-phenomenon is unthinkable, that life should continue seems scarcely

24. Cf. Falque on illness: "The lived experience of suffering is practically no longer mine because the self [*le moi*] destroys itself [*se détruit*] through suffering. I who believed that here or there I had a hurt (pain), now I become *only this* hurt (suffering)" ("Éthique du corps épandu," 39; "Toward an Ethics," 97, translation modified). But the point that it is "practically no longer mine," not simply "no longer mine," remains crucial. I become suffering, such that I cannot think it or be intentionally directed toward it, but I cannot be rid of the crack by which I have become this suffering, and since that crack is fundamental to my existence, I cannot be rid of myself.

25. Falque, *Hors phénomène*, 305.

26. Falque, *Hors phénomène*, 375.

less so. But continue it does, and even though the catastrophes that shatter the world are most assuredly to be resisted, it is because of the Outside-the-phenomenon that the transformations by which life continues may arise. I propose, therefore, that the impossibility of possibility is also the impossibility of impossibility. The impossibility of impossibility is not a return to mere possibility, as Falque makes clear in his discussion of "creative action"[27] (though without using the phrase "impossibility of impossibility"). But mere impossibility is not the last word either, since the impossibility of possibility throws the self back on itself, rendering impossible even the escape of a total annihilation of subjectivity. The impossibility of impossibility is precisely this impossibility of a complete destruction that would put an end to everything, such that there would be no more inside or Outside. Mere nothing has its sense; negation is, after all, an operation in formal logic. The impossibility of possibility and of impossibility is a crucial condition for a creativity that is beyond the dichotomy of the possible and the impossible.

Surviving the Breakdown

It is necessary, however, to reckon with the fact that one does not always continue to live. Falque's analysis may call to mind Sartre's remark that "I carry the weight of the world that is mine on my own, without it being possible for anything or any person to alleviate it.... Suicide is one way among others of being-in-the-world."[28] Thus Sartre argues that suicide remains an action that one takes and is therefore not a way of divesting oneself of the weight of one's freedom within the world. Here one may think of Falque's contention that the Outside-the-phenomenon is not the absolute suppression of subjectivity, but Sartre does not envision the breakdown of any mode of being-in-the-world. Indeed, for Falque, it is the very fact of surviving the breakdown of the world that necessitates continual transformation. Falque's analysis of the Outside-the-phenomenon suggests, therefore, that survival itself may be a resource from which one gains the strength to remain alive. This argument is not the Sartrean insistence that there is no way to exist or to have existed as anything other than a free being within the world: the point is that one may survive the very breakdown of freedom and of the world. When one is "*a subject outside of being*"[29] and "*a living dead one* (living as if I were dead),"[30] one finds that one is not in fact utterly anni-

27. Falque, *Hors phénomène*, 387.
28. Sartre, *Être et le néant*, 600; *Being and Nothingness*, 721.
29. Falque, *Hors phénomène*, 281.
30. Falque, *Hors phénomène*, 117.

hilated. And when one discovers, through the other, that the world is not utterly annihilated either, one finds also that nothing can be done except "creating new possibilities": "the crisis is born of not being able to yield to it, of surprising oneself by not renouncing (living), and of working at the necessity of creating new possibilities."[31] It is undeniably true that not everyone survives—but that one finds oneself surviving, and not only in spite of the Outside-the-phenomenon but even by virtue of it, may itself lead one to go on living.

Judged in light of Camus's remark that "there is but one truly serious philosophical problem, and that is suicide,"[32] *Hors phénomène* is, therefore, assuredly a serious philosophical book, even without explicitly analyzing the question of suicide. Camus adds that "judging whether life is or is not worth living amounts to answering the fundamental question of philosophy. All the rest—whether or not the world has three dimensions, whether the mind has nine or twelve categories—comes afterwards."[33] *Hors phénomène* implicitly takes up this challenge by considering survival when the categories are shattered and one is so disoriented that the dimensions of the world are utterly irrelevant. Strictly speaking, that life continues is not a reason to live, since life continues amid the breakdown of reason. Perhaps it is in part because the question "Is life worth living?" implies reasoned evaluation and judgment that Falque here does not thematize it as such. More fundamental than reason and judgment is survival itself. Or, to paraphrase Pascal, survival has its reasons of which reason knows nothing.

Falque argues that survival and creativity are not to be understood in terms of a resilience that bounces back from the crisis, as if the crisis could be over and done with. The notion of resilience, he warns, risks implying that one is in control of one's life and that an inability to leave the crisis behind merits condemnation.[34] Indeed, one could compare the notion of resilience to theodicy (though Falque does not make this point directly): both seek to eliminate the crisis by subjecting it to a master narrative in which it ceases to have a place, whether because it is supposedly over and done with or because it is allegedly justified. The narratives of resilience and theodicy fail to recognize the impossibility of putting an end to the crisis by assigning it a place as part of a narrative, concerning one's life in particular or even the universe as a whole, that has become fully coherent, fully submitted

---

31. Falque, *Hors phénomène*, 377.
32. Camus, *Mythe de Sisyphe*, 17; *Myth of Sisyphus*, 3.
33. Camus, *Mythe de Sisyphe*, 17; *Myth of Sisyphus*, 3.
34. Falque, *Hors phénomène*, 336–38.

to sense.[35] And he cautions us against "too quickly go[ing] from 'collapse' (*breakdown*) to 'creative thoughts' (*breakthrough*)."[36] Transformation and creativity cannot move past the crisis that belongs to our finitude. Neither do they deny mortality—which, as Falque has argued, also belongs to our finitude. Referencing Augustine, Falque writes in *By Way of Obstacles* that "Adam 'was able to die' (*posse mori*) by virtue of his natural condition or of his animal body 'and' 'was able not to die' (*posse non mori*) according to divine goodwill."[37] Mortality, then, is not alien to us, yet while the actuality of death in general can be explained theologically with reference to sin, it remains that we cannot, and should not attempt to, adequately explain why a particular person dies or falls mortally ill at a particular time. Survival up to a certain point does not prove that one will live on; if anything, it proves that one has come closer to death. When reason breaks, neither the sufficiency nor the insufficiency of survival for the continuation of life are matters of reason. But one of the key insights of *Hors phénomène* is that the breakdown of sense is not itself a reason or an argument in favor of death: one may survive sense itself, even as though sense had never been, and from this survival one may draw the strength to still keep going.

Creativity and the Other

Falque argues for a fundamental solitude of the self, but this solitude is not a solipsism or an absolute isolation that would render speech or writing impossible. Although one cannot leave the crisis behind, one is not forever cut off from sense or from others. Thus Falque writes,

> I do not *exit from* the Outside-the-phenomenon, but perhaps I am *no longer alone* there. . . . It is by seeing "from" the other rather than by seeing the other (who sees me) or, better, by seeing that the other, like me, remains riveted or not to her own "core of solitude" that she makes me see that my sole real in which I am cornered is not the sole horizon of all existentiality.[38]

In other words, the other, precisely because of her difference from me, enables me to see that the world is not reducible to my suffering. There is no question of the other saving me from the crisis or giving a meaning to

---

35. My thanks to Martin Koci for suggesting that I make explicit this challenge to theodicy.

36. Falque, *Hors phénomène*, 306. *Breakdown* and *breakthrough* are in English in the original.

37. Falque, *Parcours d'embûches*, 74; *By Way of Obstacles*, 28.

38. Falque, *Hors phénomène*, 377.

the crisis, which would deny the reality of suffering. For that matter, the other is necessarily also in crisis. But even the other's crisis shows that one can inhabit the world otherwise than I do, and I thereby discover that my reality, in which my suffering has foreclosed all possibilities, does not have the final word.

One is necessarily transformed by the extra-phenomenal, but it is by recognizing that the other inhabits the world otherwise that I realize that I may myself come to inhabit the world otherwise—differently than the other does and differently than I have done hitherto. Thus it is no longer only that transformation befalls a subjectivity that somehow survives but that I may in fact act transformatively—that is, create. The realization that the world is not mine alone is crucial for transformation to become creativity. Certainly, I am transformed in ways that do not depend on or derive from my actions, but I am also capable of creating. What I have called the impossibility of impossibility is yet more profound than the earlier discussion indicated: not only am I not utterly suppressed, I find that the world is not destroyed either, since someone else dwells within it. By virtue of the crisis, I am in solitude: in each of us there is a "core . . . of *extra*-phenomenality that founds and is the crux of our ownmost being."[39] The "core of solitude"[40] is, in Falque's view, an argument against the claim that the self is constituted from the start by intersubjectivity. Yet "this *common inaccessibility* also makes us connected. . . . I am not 'without' the other in my solitude, since the other 'watches over' my own solitude—without, however, penetrating or violating it."[41] I am therefore alone in the crisis but also alongside the other in a world that no longer reduces to the cracked thought in which I am cornered.

Precisely because the other is other, I cannot take on her manner of living within the world. The other does not open definite possibilities for me, nor do I discover definite possibilities that lead to some clear and distinct future. Rather, drawing on Bergson, Falque points out that one knows only after the fact what will have turned out to be possible: thus I do not receive or discover possibilities but create them. As Falque puts it,

> It is, on the contrary, by trusting in, and entrusting oneself to, the act of the writing of oneself, and by drawing on the Self, that one sees, as if *after the fact*, that what is now "real" (the work that one holds there in one's hands) was then "possible" (the book that one had initially projected but without truly knowing what it *would be*).[42]

39. Falque, *Hors phénomène*, 419.
40. Falque, *Hors phénomène*, 420.
41. Falque, *Hors phénomène*, 448.
42. Falque, *Hors phénomène*, 388.

What is true of writing is true of living. One does not escape the crisis, but one often survives it. Surviving, one is continually transformed by it, and one thus continues to live. And seeing the other living within the world shows one that the world also survives. It would be too simple to say that one thereby discovers the possibility of creativity. The dichotomy between possibility and impossibility breaks down because one will know that creativity was possible only after creating. Falque writes that "one will recognize only—but this is already a great deal—that *there is some possible that is not me and that stands there 'around' me and even 'with' me*."[43] One does not discover what is possible for oneself except by acting and realizing afterwards what happened. But that other also inhabits the world shows that the world is not summed up in impossibility: there is space for the possible. My survival and the other's survival reveal the impossibility of impossibility: my survival shows that I am not yet destroyed, and the other's survival shows that the world is not only my own being-in-crisis. To be sure, I do not leave the crisis: my own creativity arises from the continual transformations of myself that the crisis brings about. Without the crisis, I would be static, frozen into myself, and therefore unable to create. Creativity cannot be separated from crisis.

The Intertwining of Sense and Non-Sense

In the spirit of the *loving struggle*, I here mark a difference from Falque: I propose that sense and non-sense are intertwined, such that if there is no experience that is free of the crisis, neither is an-experience ever free from the plea for interpretation. Consider Derrida's assertion that "there is no outside-the-text."[44] But is the Outside-the-phenomenon (*Hors phénomène*) also an outside-the-text (*hors-texte*)? The Outside-the-phenomenon, as a non-sensical chaos, seems obviously non-textual. Derrida's challenge to our powers of interpretation is not Falque's: for Derrida, there is no way out of interpretation, while for Falque, the crisis forces us out of interpretation by shattering it, leaving nothing to interpret—a nothing that is not even blank space. A *hors-texte* is, however, also an illustration included in a book on a non-numbered page, which might be taken as a guide to interpreting the text, as the immediate meaning that the text represents. And in this sense the *Hors phénomène* is assuredly not a *hors-texte*: because it breaks down our powers of interpretation, it cannot stand outside the world to tell us how

---

43. Falque, *Hors phénomène*, 377.

44. Derrida, *De la grammatologie*, 220; *Of Grammatology*, 158 (translation modified).

to interpret the world. This point might seem trivial: granted that outside the phenomenon there is no *hors-texte*, but there is no text either, so are we not again faced with the impossibility of interpretation? For that matter, the extra-phenomenal breaks down even our ability to tell whether there is anything to interpret. One does not calmly look at chaos and interpret it as non-interpretable, for one's powers of interpretation are simply broken. Falque argues that the Outside-the-phenomenon can leave us unable to call or to respond: "It will become impossible, within the framework of *extra*-phenomenality... to 'appeal [*faire appel*]' (juridical sense) in order for the call [*appel*] (phenomenological sense) to resound anew."[45] I maintain, though, that the Outside-the-phenomenon still gives rise to a call, for there is a protest against enclosure within suffering.

Falque highlights a phrase that Deleuze attributed to Kierkegaard: "The possible, the possible, or I will suffocate!"[46] Although I need to discover "that *there is some possible* that is not me,"[47] it does not follow that the afflicted one is actually capable of calling for the possible or even of recognizing his or her need for it. Already suffocating, one who is broken down by the crisis has no breath to cry out. Consider also, however, Falque's remark in "Toward an Ethics of the Spread Body" that "silence is called for when the body is exposed. By talking too much or too technically one runs the risk of suffocating the pain that nevertheless tries to express itself."[48] The anguish of suffocation is itself a mute cry, even if no subject thinks to send it, even if it is not intended for anyone. Not a juridical appeal that expects a judgment or resolution, it arises simply because the body does not so easily surrender its strength: the very notion of suffocation implies a struggle to keep breathing. Even the act of suicide testifies by its violence to a struggle that preceded it. And this struggle to go on, whether it succeeds or not, is not without its own sense. I do not suggest that the struggle justifies or gives a sense to suffering but rather that suffering is protested against and that this protest has sense. As *Hors phénomène* reminds us, we must avoid overwriting non-sense with sense or glorifying suffering by claiming it is intrinsically meaningful. Insisting on sense would be a way of "suffocating the pain that nevertheless tries to express itself,"[49] to borrow Falque's words. But proposing that what has no sense remains entangled with sense and

45. Falque, *Hors phénomène*, 457.
46. Falque, *Hors phénomène*, 367; see also 377–78.
47. Falque, *Hors phénomène*, 377.
48. Falque, "Éthique du corps épandu," 24–25; "Toward an Ethics," 91–92 (translation modified).
49. Falque, "Éthique du corps épandu," 24–25; "Toward an Ethics," 92 (translation modified).

recognizing the sense of the cry, "This suffering does not make sense," is not necessarily a privileging of sense over non-sense: it may, on the contrary, be an act of care by which one acknowledges, alongside the afflicted one, the senselessness of the affliction. Importantly, it is not necessarily the sufferer-as-subject who cries out; the struggle itself cries out that suffering is senseless, even if the subject is too submerged by the suffering to protest or even try to protest. One might object that one who is struck down by the Outside-the-phenomenon cannot even struggle, but I reply that survival itself indicates that there is a struggle. The subject may no longer be capable of willing to struggle or of recognizing the struggle, yet the body presses on, and not senselessly. The struggle of survival remains a protest against suffering even when it ceases to register as such because one's relation to the body has broken down. For survival has its reasons of which reason knows nothing: hence surviving the breaking of sense is already a creation of a sense outside of sense.

Moreover, this protest against suffering ought to be heard. The afflicted one may not hear it; others, also afflicted, may not hear it either. Falque emphasizes the possibility of such a breakdown of communication, but the breakdown does not annul the *ought*. The protest solicits me even if I am unable to hear it, for in our different solitudes we remain alongside each other in the world. Thus solitude itself is surrounded by protests against the crisis, and it is only by hearing these protests that I realize that the world too survives, with enough oxygen for creativity.[50] In other words, the encounter with the phenomenal requires both the an-experience of the Outside-the-phenomenon and the encounter with others alongside oneself in the world. Through being alongside others, one becomes able to "think the unthinkable" and also to "think the thinkable," not on its own but always in relation to the unthinkable that cannot be separated from it.

Rather than opposing sense and non-sense and elevating the former over the latter, I propose to think them as inescapably intertwined. Solitude and alterity are also intertwined, since the protest against suffering calls out to others whether or not there is a subject capable of intending or hearing the call. To be constituted by intersubjectivity is not, from this perspective, to be wholly known or to seek to be wholly known; far from it. It means,

---

50. Cf. Marcelo, responding to *Hors phénomène*: "It remains to wonder if a subject postulated as being ontologically alone can still build its world and what the real conditions of possibility are for re-subjectification to be able to take place" ("Métamorphoses du sujet," 340, translation mine). I argue that the subject is not only alone: one is alone in that one cannot be wholly known or wholly know another, but one is always surrounded by protests against suffering, even if one cannot hear them, and it is through being able to hear them that one may become a creative subject.

rather, that the cry of the struggle for survival ought to be heard, that there are such cries alongside me whether I am capable of hearing or not, and that it is only through hearing them that I will be able to act creatively within the world. There is no inside without an outside, but neither, I contend, is there an outside that is wholly separated from an inside, even if that inside is only the mute cry of continued survival in the teeth of suffering. Outside the phenomenon, outside any subject's will, survival in the midst of suffering is a struggle that begs for interpretation, begs to be recognized as having sense and for its suffering to be recognized as senseless. The Outside-the-phenomenon does not call us to interpret, but survival begs for interpretation and recognition. Even when death comes, the survival that preceded it still pleads thus; even if the afflicted one can recognize no sense to survival, survival still cries out for the recognition of its sense beyond sense. There is, then, no absolute an-experience, for although the Outside-the-phenomenon defies interpretation, it cannot be separated from the plea, even the mute plea, for interpretation, for the recognition of survival. Such interpretation may at times be best and most caringly expressed through silence, though the effort to think and write the unthinkable may also be a way of interpreting and recognizing the plea.

Outside texts, though not a *hors-texte*, suffering is inseparable from the cry that begs to be a text, to be interpreted as meaningful. Moreover, since creativity cannot be separated from crisis, all writing arises from the crisis. Elsewhere Falque asks, "*Would you but die of not writing*? . . . Writing is first an 'existential challenge' before it is a matter of intellectual stakes or a public profession."[51] Indeed. Writing is an existential challenge because existence threatens to be lost in the extra-phenomenal that is neither text nor *hors-texte*, that suffocates meaning and mediation. Truly, one would die of not writing, for all the acts of creation by which one lives are also a manner of writing. And I conclude by thanking Emmanuel Falque for an œuvre that, by giving rise to thought, offers occasions for further writing.

Bibliography

Camus, Albert. *Le mythe de Sisyphe*. Paris: Gallimard, 2012.
———. *The Myth of Sisyphus and Other Essays*. Translated by Justin O'Brien. New York: Vintage International, 2018.]
Derrida, Jacques. *De la grammatologie*. Paris: Éditions de Minuit, 1967.
———. *Of Grammatology*. Translated by Gayatri Chakravorty Spivak. Baltimore: Johns Hopkins University Press, 1997.

51. Falque, "Conclusion," 203.

Falque, Emmanuel. *By Way of Obstacles: A Pathway through a Work.* Translated by Sarah Horton. Eugene, OR: Cascade, 2022.
———. *La Chair de Dieu.* Paris: Cerf, 2023.
———. "Conclusion: To Die of Not Writing." Translated by Megan Megaher. In *Transforming the Theological Turn: Phenomenology with Emmanuel Falque*, edited by Martin Koci and Jason W. Alvis, 203–6. Lanham, MD: Rowman and Littlefield, 2020.
———. "Éthique du corps épandu." In *Éthique du corps épandu suivi de Une chair épandue sur le divan*, by Emmanuel Falque and Sabine Fos Falque, 11–85. Paris: Cerf, 2018.
———. "God Extra-Phenomenal: For a Phenomenology of Holy Saturday." Translated by Jan Juhani Steinmann. *Journal for Continental Philosophy of Religion* 4.2 (2022) 190–217.
———. *Hors phénomène: Essai aux confins de la phénoménalité.* Paris: Hermann, 2022.
———. *Métamorphose de la finitude.* In *Triduum philosophique*, 165–363. Paris: Cerf, 2015.
———. *The Metamorphosis of Finitude.* Translated by George Hughes. New York: Fordham University Press, 2012.
———. *Parcours d'embûches: S'expliquer.* Paris: Éditions Franciscaines, 2016.
———. "Toward an Ethics of the Spread Body." Translated by Christina Gschwandtner. In *Somatic Desire: Recovering Corporeality in Contemporary Thought*, edited by Sarah Horton et al., 91–116. Lanham, MD: Lexington, 2019.
Marcelo, Gonçalo. "Les métamorphoses du sujet à l'aune du trauma." *Revista Filosófica de Coimbra* 31.62 (2022) 331–42.
Sartre, Jean-Paul. *Being and Nothingness.* Translated by Sarah Richmond. New York: Washington Square, 2018.
———. *L'être et le néant.* Paris: Gallimard, 1976.

God and Finitude

God and Human Being

An Ellipse in Emmanuel Falque's Work

CARLA CANULLO

Wrestling with the Angel

EMMANUEL FALQUE'S WORK COULD be defined by the biblical episode of Jacob wrestling with the angel on the banks of the Jabbok. Falque himself confirms this interpretation when, in *Le combat amoureux*, he comments on Eugène Delacroix's painting *Jacob's Struggle with the Angel*[1] and declares that his work is nothing other than this *hand-to-hand combat*. This struggle between man and God is the meaning of the ellipse theme that I have chosen for this homage to the work of Falque, to whom I have dedicated other texts.[2] Falque's work, in other words, sketches an ellipse in which two irreducibles, i.e., God and human beings, can *recognize* each other in mutual union, without one being assimilated into the other, and indeed still remaining in a *loving struggle* (*combat amoureux*).

These two irreducibles, that are held together as the two foci of the ellipse are, also appear in a Cartesian expression that Falque likes to quote

---

1. This struggle gives its title to a book of studies on philosophy, theology, and religion written by Ciancio, *In lotta con l'angelo*.

2. Allow me to refer to the following texts for other explorations of Emmanuel Falque's work: Canullo, "À visage découvert"; "Esperienza del credere"; "*Oportet transire*"; "Il Passaggio possibile," in Canullo and Gilbert, *Emmanuel Falque*, 5–11.

and which closes *Crossing the Rubicon: The Borderlands of Philosophy and Theology*,[3] the well-known *Larvatus prodeo*, which he transforms into *Larvatus pro Deo*. If *larvatus* in Latin means covering one's face with a mask, Falque instead removes this mask by doing philosophy bare-faced or with the face uncovered, an expression that opens his book *Le combat amoureux*. "With the face uncovered," *A viso scoperto*, is the Italian translation of Clive Staples Lewis's book *Till we have faces*, translated into French as *Un visage pour l'éternité*,[4] whose plot is inspired by the myth of Cupid and Psyche, that is, a struggle for love. The protagonist of Lewis's novel is the princess Orual, who is obsessed with her sister Psyche. When the gods deprive her of her beloved sister, she sets out to search for her in the farthest reaches of her kingdom. This search leads her to the mountain, where she is *face to face* with the gods and fights her own *struggle with the angel*. Orual's struggle is the opportunity to make her own accusation against those gods who, out of sheer selfishness and indifference to all human love, have robbed her of her sister's love. The assembly of gods listens in silence to this address until the presiding god asks her if justice has been done to her. Orual replies that yes, this justice has been done, for the very possibility of making her accusation and hearing her voice is the possibility of receiving an answer. The greatest justice, in fact, is to be able to speak, to hear and hear oneself, to understand and understand oneself, and thus to interpret, interpret oneself and understand oneself. This is what Falque has done with his work.

"Till We Have Faces"

The myth of Orual, who stands *bare-faced* before the gods, shows, in my opinion, Falque's philosophical attitude. The theme of the flesh and the body, which the author interprets in an original way continuing the analyses of Husserlian phenomenology and its French reception, confirms this philosophical attitude of Falque. His analysis of the body was at the heart of the third volume of what Falque himself described as a *triduum philosophique*, namely *Les noces de l'agneau: Essai philosophique sur le corps et l'eucharistie*,[5] and *Dieu, la chair et l'autre: D'Irénée à Duns Scot*. If this second book is about the history of medieval philosophy, in the first (*Les noces de l'agneau*), Falque *barefacedly* deals with the phenomenological question that, with

---

3. Falque, *Crossing the Rubicon* §24.

4. The English title of the novel, *Till We Have Faces*, is well rendered both in the Italian translation, *A viso scoperto*, and in the French edition, *Un visage pour l'éternité*.

5. The other books of this *triduum* are *Passeur de Gethsémani* and *Métamorphose de la finitude*.

Husserl, distinguishes body and flesh, showing the extent to which this second element has been emphasized. Falque calls this emphasis an *embardée* of the flesh, which is attested by French phenomenology, especially by Maurice Merleau-Ponty and, in a different way, by Michel Henry.[6] In contrast to the two phenomenologists mentioned above, who insist on the flesh, Falque privileges the body (*corps*), speaking specifically of the extended body (*corps épandu*), in order to limit this *embardée*.[7] We could say, however, that not only this book but Falque's entire work is an attempt to understand the body and the embodied voice, and in order to do so, the author places himself *barefaced* before philosophy, but also before theology. In doing so, he privileges the body and not the invisible flesh (as Merleau-Ponty and Henry did) and, as Jacques Derrida affirmed, he states that also the voice is a phenomenon that hermeneutics interprets and understands, just as Orual interpreted and understood her own voice before the gods—barefaced.[8]

One will argue that what has just been said is surpassed by *Hors phénomène: Essai aux confins de la phénoménalité*, an original and difficult book that begins with the suggestive phrase "ça me tombe dessus."[9] With this expression, Falque reminds us that man allows himself to be caught "on the edge, à la limite," as traumatic experiences testify. It is only as "ça tombe dessus" that we really feel the blow of "illness, separation, the death of a child, a natural disaster, a pandemic," all traumas that destroy existence by suddenly happening to those who exist. Thus, *hors phénomène* is the appropriate expression for these situations because it does not deal with the *infra-phénomène* that precedes phenomenality or the *supra-phénomène* of excess. Quite simply, *hors phénomène* signals that one exists insofar as the *outside* takes priority over any possible phenomenal manifestation.

To announce the effects of such a *hors phénomène* on the subject, Falque writes in the *Ouverture* to the book: "Ni extase ni instase, ni 'ouverture' ni 'auto-affection,' le sujet subsiste comme 'Hors de soi' dans le trauma, et ne voit ni ne croit en un quelconque 'possible' capable de résoudre le 'réel' de son exister."[10] In this quotation, we discover the aim of Falque's philosophical attempt, that is to arrive at the limits of the possibility of a *pure phénoménalité*. The leitmotif of the Falque's attempt to go up to and beyond *the limits of phenomenality* is the *adagio* "il faut savoir descender

---

6. By "embardée de la chair" Falque means the fact that in French phenomenology the flesh has been treated forgetting the concreteness of the body. The author explained his opinion not only in *Noces de l'agneau* but also in "Y a-t-il une chair."

7. See Falque, *Noces de l'agneau*, 41.

8. See Falque, *Passer le Rubicon*, 75.

9. Falque, *Hors phénomène*.

10. Falque, *Hors phénomène*, 9.

pour remonter, sinon on ne touche rien de profonde."[11] Therefore, after the description of *Le champ du hors phénomène*,[12] the pages of the book show how the *hors phénomène* that transcends the limits of phenomenality is not just an announcement, but it is actually possible. However, this possibility raises at least two remarks.

By analyzing what he calls the five paradigms that accompany the journey into the non-phenomenal (illness, separation, death of a child, natural disaster, pandemic), Falque cuts across experiences that *fall upon us* and destroy both the phenomenalizing subject and any other horizons of phenomenalization. Far from being an annihilating destruction, these non-phenomenal experiences "degage cette space du 'moi,' y comprise en philosophie où nul n'a accès . . . selon une 'résistance' qui fait le plus fort de mon existentialité."[13] Furthermore, Falque writes,

> Rien ne demeure en effet dans le Hors phénomène, sinon le poids d'un "Soi" à la fois "ignorant le moi" et "faisant le moi." D'où l'inéluctable constat de devoir porter le "Soi," voire parfois de le supporter, jusqu'à accepter la "mue" qui fait que je suis sans cesse transformé. Rien de ma substance donc, ni de mon identité, ne saurait demeurer, sinon ce perpétuel changement selon lequel je suis transformé.[14]

However, we could ask our author if the explanation of the *hors phénomène* doesn't lead to a kind of metaphorization that merely transforms and changes our experience without giving anything more to live for. I call it *metaphorization* because metaphor, before it became a rhetorical figure, was and is a *transport*, a displacement. And what is the *root* of the transformation and the change Falque announces, if not this *displacement* within oneself? If this the case, this change remains a *phenomenon* that we cannot grasp but that can be grasped by someone else. For my self there is maybe this *hors phénomène* but not for the others attesting my trauma, my mourn, my molt. Thus, the *subjectivity* of the other continues to attest the phenomenality of the *hors phénomène* and, then, it remains as last horizon. Perhaps philosophy as phenomenology has more to gain from the suspension that *epochè* and reductions have taught it from its beginning, pushing phenomenology to return again and again to the *roots* of phenomenality. This return, however, has never obliged phenomenology to restrict phenomenality to the limits philosophy has known since its origins, namely, subjectivity and

---

11. Falque, *Hors phénomène*, 21.
12. Falque, *Hors phénomène*, 89–108.
13. Falque, *Hors phénomène*, 453.
14. Falque, *Hors phénomène*, 457.

objectivity. Perhaps the unceasing *work* of reduction can be a caveat to carefully characterize the extra-limits of the *hors phénomène*, attesting that what was *hors phénomène* for me is a manifest phenomenon for someone else. This then restores the *subject* as last horizon.

However, this is only my first remark. The second remark is more of a question: Does *hors phénomène* overcome and contradict Falque's previous books or does it grasp their truth and reveal their true meaning? And above all, how does this book, which forms a kind of *triptyque phénoménologique* with *Le combat amoureux*[15] and *La chair de Dieu*,[16] dialogue both with the philosophical *triduum* already announced[17] and with what has been said about the *barefaced* aptitude with which one stands before the gods (or God)?

In my opinion, it is only by considering the limits of phenomenality and the *hors phénomène* that one can fully understand Falque's earlier work, and in particular the first book of the *triduum*, *Le Passeur de Gethsémani: Angoisse, souffrance et mort; Lecture existentielle et phénoménologique*.[18] To put it more clearly: *hors phénomène* and the limits of phenomenality questioned by Falque allow us to better understand the meaning of the author's first work and, above all, grasp the leitmotif of his philosophical production. This leitmotif is *the passage*, which Falque not coincidentally places at the centre of this beautiful work *Passer le Rubicon*,[19] in which an Italian river also appears, the Rubicon[20]—a river that Falque, as Julius Caesar did, proposes to cross. And it is precisely *Le passeur de Gethsémani*, that is, the first volume

15. See Falque, *Combat amoureux*.

16. Falque announced this book in Falque, *Hors phénomène*, 9, with the title *En chair et en os*. Now the book is published with the title *Chair de Dieu*.

17. See note 6 above.

18. In Italian and Latin, this leitmotif is easy to grasp, since "le Passeur" is the one who "passes through." In English, "passeur" is translated as "guide" and the meaning of the French word (i.e., passage) is lost. Christ, on the other hand, does not limit himself to leading, but by passing through and crossing Gethsemane, makes happen the "hors phénomène" par excellence, that is, himself as man and as God. The English translator explains this difficulty in the translation of *passeur* as follows: "Falque's usage is in the singular, *le passeur*, and refers specifically to Christ in Gethsemane, who undergoes his ordeal there for us. It has seemed most appropriate to translate *passeur* in this book as 'guide,' but, taking into account its connotations, it is worth emphasizing how in French the term strongly suggests not just guiding *but passer (to pass), in the sense of a passing over or across with people or things, and 'passage.'* For Falque *passeur* suggests the passage through Gethsemane to Golgotha and beyond, and in this context it is echoed in the word *pâtir*, to suffer from, take on board suffering, or suffer passively" (Hughes, "Translator's Note," in Falque, *Guide to Gethsemane*, xiii–xiv).

19. I earlier quoted the English translation of this book. The original French edition is *Passer le Rubicon: Philosophie et théologie; essai sur les frontières* (2013).

20. To this subject I have also devoted "*Oportet transire.*"

of what Falque defined as his own *Triduum philosophique*, that can be seen as a kind of threshold for accessing Falque's thought thanks to the leitmotif of his work, the passage. And this happens for two different reasons. First, because of the phenomenological method to which it explicitly refers and, second, because it reveals the aptitude of Falque's thought, i.e., the aptitude for passage and passing, and not for *evasion* or escape. In fact, we can say that passing through issues and problems, and not recoiling from them, is the aptitude that Falque maintains throughout his work. In other words, Falque's aptitude is to cross, to pass through, and to proceed *by way of obstacle*, in order not to avoid or evade any of the components of an unescapable human finitude. And perhaps it is no coincidence that the *Triduum* begins precisely with an *existential reading* of the One who crosses and passes through Gethsemane without fleeing from (and his) existential condition.

The Heideggerian echoes predominate in this volume, although one should not ignore the Kierkegaardian echo that Falque recalls at several points in the book, emphasizing both his own debt and his distance from the Danish philosopher.[21] Only when the patient crossing of existence is possible can the questions that cross it take on the weight that makes them inescapably human. Not inescapable, however, because they weigh so heavily on existence that one wishes for their end. These questions are inescapable because they characterize human existence as such, to the point of being moments in which the human form, i.e., the image that man is, recurs and is fulfilled; or, as Falque writes, "The image of God in us can be read today in the profundity of our nature."[22] It is for this reason that "Christ teaches us first of all to be human beings—that is, precisely, not to flee from our own finitude. He teaches us how we can also, with him, 'abandon' ourselves in death."[23] That is why, in a very dense chapter, Falque insists on the moment of *suffering the world* in order to *cross over to the Father*.[24] Christ, that is, who crosses over from this world to the Father, *s'en fait le gué*, crosses over the ford, and at the same time hands over his pain to the Father—a pain which, as our author points out, is not the result of an experience of sin, but a natural experience.[25] Therefore, "in suffering this world the Son conveys

---

21. For the echoes see, for instance, "The Temptation of Despair or Anxiety over Sin" (chapter 3) in Falque, *Guide to Gethsemane*.
22. Falque, *Guide to Gethsemane* loc. 599.
23. Falque, *Guide to Gethsemane* loc. 608–16.
24. See "From Self-Relinquishment to the Entry into the Flesh" (chapter 9).
25. Falque, *Guide to Gethsemane* loc. 1913.

to the Father (a passage) the weight of finitude experienced in his death," to the point of begging him to cease the pain.[26]

In this passage, no substitution or Promethean act of Christ is seen or proposed; he does not take on the suffering of all, but stands before his own suffering. But it is precisely in this passage that the impossible becomes possible, that is, it becomes possible for man not to submit passively to suffering or to flee from pain or from death, but to go through it, to go through it in and with his humanity. One to might ask how this is possible, a question to which Falque responds by following a path that is not always easy and by explaining that it is the Son who makes it possible. The path, as we have said, is not easy because, first of all, it is not clear what the suffering that Christ experienced in his flesh can say to any man, since each man experiences his own suffering. In other words, even though Christ, by suffering in his human flesh, allows the passage of suffering into God, it is obviously his suffering. What can each person gain from such a passage?

Falque discusses this issue by quoting Jürgen Moltmann, who wrote that "the cross of Christ is not the same as the cross of his disciples."[27] However, Moltmann goes on to complete this statement by writing: "But those who follow him suffer and die in fellowship *with him*."[28] This is the meaning of the possible passage. The fact that Christ's suffering passes on to the Father does not mean a substitution (because everyone is suffering alone), but rather an opening up, the very opening up of a possibility: the possibility of not living in isolation from the experience of pain and suffering, which isolates and closes off par excellence, but the possibility of living with it. Therefore, "to suffer and die 'with' the Son does not mean that one does not any longer suffer and die," because nothing is taken away from the human condition, "nor does it take away the 'mineness' of suffering and death."[29] Falque writes again,

> Christ does not suffer and die in my place. . . . He suffers and dies for me and with me. . . . Like a guide or ferryman [*Passeur*] taking in charge the one who passes or whom he guides [*le passant*], Christ transforms, starting from today, the meaning of my suffering, so that I am able to make it (along with him) the modality of my own life.[30]

26. Falque, *Guide to Gethsemane* loc. 1920.
27. Falque, *Guide to Gethsemane* loc. 2474.
28. Falque, *Guide to Gethsemane* loc. 2474.
29. Falque, *Guide to Gethsemane* loc. 2474.
30. Falque, *Guide to Gethsemane* loc. 2474, 2483.

In this passage, then, the image of the *other* which human beings carries within himself and which Christ allows to be discovered and revealed, develops itself. This the way in which this perception of this image grows up. This passage is a passage to oneself and to the otherness that inhabits the *self*, to one's own finitude, which is not escaped or rejected, nor understood in a more Heideggerian way: on the contrary, it is the possibility of discovering a radical otherness, or rather, an otherness that is the root of the man. Falque calls this dynamic of discovery and revelation "the non-Substitutable Substitution," showing that Christ does not come to take away suffering, but to bring it with man (and in this he is the *Passeur*).[31] The loss of this irreplaceable substitution exposes human being to the risk of "enclosure" "in the pure unbreakable solipsism of suffering and dying flesh."[32] The possible passage thus reveals, in finitude, and especially in suffering finitude, the intimate openness of existence, where "suffering remains . . . that which tears me apart while it reveals me to myself in my own," revealing the radical otherness that inhabits me; "other" before which the alternative of existence opens up, since everyone can always welcome or reject "the presence in everyday reality of this other in myself."[33]

Falque's work is the unfolding of this possible passage towards human beings and their *true image*, where the *other* comes to become *true*, an image that is the expression of the ellipse for which God and human being are always different and always manifest together—as the Syrian bishop Theophilus of Antioch said: "Show me your man, and I will show you my God!"[34]

Passage—*hors phénomène*

Is there a connection between *le Passeur de Getshémani*, whose phenomenology is at the heart of the first work, and *hors phénomène*? Yes, in my opinion, because passing is not a phenomenon, but it is what, *hors phénomène* that makes a phenomenon concrete. A passage as transformation, for example, is not grasped while it is transforming, but through the effects it produces. The passage always remains *outside*[35] the actual transformation and never precedes or follows it. It does not precede the transformation because what precedes it is a state, not a passage; it does not follow it because when a transformation has taken place the previous state no longer *is*. The passage,

---

31. Falque, *Guide to Gethsemane* loc. 2467.
32. Falque, *Guide to Gethsemane* loc. 2499.
33. Falque, *Guide to Gethsemane* loc. 2537.
34. See Theophilus of Antioch, *Ad Autolycum* 1.2.
35. As the "Hors phénomène" is according to Falque.

we might say, is *hors phénomène* because it neither precedes nor follows the phenomenon that manifests itself, but is in a sense the *in-between* of the phenomenon itself. In other words, it is the *in-between/intra* of transformation,[36] that is, the *in-between* of the incessant shaping of the image, which never ceases to take the form that *other* assigns to it. Neither infra-phenomenal nor extra-phenomenal, the passage corresponds perfectly to Falque's principle *autant d'exception, autant de modification*, because the passage is always an act in itself, and therefore an exception, but it is also always a modification, and therefore a transformation. This, I think, is the meaning of the conclusion of *Hors phénomène*, where Falque proclaims the *faille* that characterizes man and makes his transformation possible. In fact, if humanity's *être phénomènale* consists in his "être phénoménale ... comme toujours se transformant," such a transformation is possible because of the *faille* that characterizes man himself, and "être ou se tenir dans cette 'faille' d'un moi sans cesse transformé, est l'unique raison de continuer, fût-ce en s'élevant non pas pour s'évader mais pour toujours davantage peser."[37] And above all, because of this *faille*, one is always open to *other* and therefore always *with it*—which brings us back to the proximity of the ellipse and its meaning.

In fact, "vivre avec quelque chose ou quelqu'un—avec l'homme (*cum homine*) ou avec Dieu (*cum Deo*),"[38] where both human beings and God are inaccessible to each other, it remains *hors phénomène*, i.e., outside the phenomenon and at the limits of phenomenality, even if a transforming *passage* takes (or has taken) place. The passage is therefore *hors phénomène* because "l'être-là pour vivre avec" is "l'Em-manuel d'un présent 'résistant' à la fuite du temps—ancré dans l'impensable (*extra*-phénoménal) plutôt que préparant le manifeste (*infra*-phénoménal) ou ouvrant sur l'inimaginable (*supra*-phénoménal)."[39] Moreover, the passage is *hors phénomène* because it brings about a transformation by leading everyone to the most primordial unthinkable *other*, thanks to which *nous sommes là*, but to which we can never have access as if it were a phenomenon—or how we gain access to

---

36. Trans-formation, that is the act of changing in form or shape or appearance, is a word of Latin derivation, *transformare*, composed of the prefix "trans," meaning to go beyond, and form, form. The prefix "trans" in Greek is "meta-" and trans-formation is metamorphosis. "Meta-," however, does not only mean "beyond" but also "in-between/intra." Thus, transformation can be understood both as changing one's form into something else, and as that minimal interstitial "in-between" that each person has within him or herself and that allows him or her to incessantly assume that form that "other" gives him or her.

37. Falque, *Hors phénomène*, 458.

38. Falque, *Hors phénomène*, 458.

39. Falque, *Hors phénomène*, 458. Both the philosophical passage and the reference to the author's own name, Emmanuel, are interesting in this passage.

phenomena. This unthinkable allows us to understand the meaning of the One who passes through Gethsemane.

Le Passeur de Gethsémani, while he is passing, in fact passes *hors phénomène*. He passes, pushing himself and human beings to the limits of phenomenality, towards that God who is also at the limits of phenomenality, *inaccessible* but connected to man "dans notre commune inaccessibilité."[40] In *The Guide to Gethsemane*, this *inaccessibility* characterizes the silent flesh (*la chair silencieuse*), which theology, in particular in the twentieth century, has set aside in order to privilege linguistic acts for the proclamation of the *kerygma*. Instead, in the passages referring to Peter's discourse at Pentecost, Falque points to the centrality of the inaccessible flesh of Christ. This inaccessible flesh, however, according to him, does not characterize only the flesh of Christ. Following the apostle's speech, Falque stresses that the flesh of Christ would have known corruption if it had been left in the tomb. Then the flesh of Christ is no exception to the agony experienced by all suffering human flesh. This remark is undoubtedly *only* philosophical. However, it comes from a comparison with theology and may perhaps bounce back on theology. And it is to theology that Falque addresses the invitation to understand the proclamation of the *kerygma* not only as an act of language but also as starting from "the silent flesh, or, to use Husserl's phrase, the 'pre-predicative evidence,'" which can speak "better and differently than any discourse."[41]

Finally, what is emerging from these statements, if not a passage to the limit at the crucial point of the proclamation of the *kerygma* of the Risen One announced to any living beings? With this, and then with this passage to the limit and *à la limite*, Falque has taken up and retraced that ancient question, which asks at the same time about God and about human being, who never ceases to question themselves on the two foci of an ellipse. This figure is not a closed one. Rather, it is the tracing of a link that characterizes infinite relationships, always destined to begin by transforming those in the relationship. From beginning to beginning, according to beginnings that will never know an end.

Bibliography

Canullo, Carla. "À visage découvert—un nouveau passage." In *Une analytique du passage: Rencontres et confrontations avec Emmanuel Falque*, edited by Claude Brunier-Coulin, 399–412. Paris: Éditions franciscaines, 2016.

40. Falque, *Hors phénomène*, 458.
41. Falque, *Guide to Gethsemane* loc. 1865.

———. "L'esperienza del credere." In *Passare il Rubicone: Alle frontiere della filosofia e della teologia*, by Emmanuel Falque, 1–15 Translated by Lorenza Bottaccini. Brescia: Morcelliana, 2017.

———. "*Oportet transire*: How 'Crossing' Becomes *quaestio de homine*." In *Transforming the Theological Turn: Phenomenology with Emmanuel Falque*, edited by Martin Koci and Jason Alvis, 135–48. Lanham, MD: Rowman and Littlefield, 2020.

Canullo, Carla, and Paul Gilbert, eds. *Emmanuel Falque: Tra fenomenologia della finitezza e teologia dell'incarnazione*. Firenze: Le Lettere 2014.

Ciancio, Claudio, et al. *In lotta con l'angelo: La filosofia degli ultimi due secoli di fronte al cristianesimo*. Torino: Sei, 1989.

Falque, Emmanuel. *La chair de Dieu*. Paris: Cerf, 2023.

———. *Le combat amoureux: Disputes phénoménologiques et théologiques*. Paris: Hermann, 2014.

———. *Crossing the Rubicon: The Borderlands of Philosophy and Theology*. Translated by Reuben Shank. New York: Fordham University Press, 2016.

———. *Dieu, la chair et l'autre: D'Irénée à Duns Scot*. Paris: PUF, 2008.

———. *The Guide to Gethsemane. Anxiety, Suffering, Death*. Translated by G. Hughes. New York: Fordham University Press, 2019.

———. *Hors phénomène: Essai aux confins de la phénoménalité*. Paris: Hermann, 2020.

———. *Métamorphose de la finitude: Essai philosophique sur la naissance et la résurrection*. Paris: Cerf, 2004.

———. *Les noces de l'agneau: Essai philosophique sur le corps et l'eucharistie*. Paris: Cerf, 2011.

———. *Passer le Rubicon: Philosophie et théologie; Essai sur les frontières*. Paris: Lessius, 2013.

———. *Le passeur de Gethsémani: Angoisse, souffrance et mort; Lecture existentielle et phénoménologique*. Paris: Cerf, 1999.

———. "Y a-t-il une chair sans corps?" In *Phénoménologie et christianisme chez Michel Henry*, edited by Philippe Capelle, 95–135. Paris: Cerf, 2004.

Lewis, Clive S. *Till We Have Faces*. London: Geoffrey Bles, 1956.

———. *Un visage pour l'éternité*. Translated by M. and D. Le Péchoux. French. Paris: Le Livre de Poche, 2007.

———. *A viso scoperto*. Translated by Maria Elena Ruggerini. Italian. Milan: Jaca, 2016.

Theophilus of Antioch. *Ad Autolycum*. Christian Classics Ethereal Library. http://www.ccel.org/ccel/schaff/anf02.html.

SUBSTANTIA

Note on the Use of substantia *by St. Augustine and on Its Belonging to the History of Metaphysics*

Jean-Luc Marion

I

ST. AUGUSTINE'S USE OF *substantia* has given rise to a pluriform debate. There is no discussion about the decisive role he played in introducing this term, which was at the time in competition with *essentia* to translate *ousia*.[1] It is rather a question of assessing whether "the frequent use of this term throughout Saint Augustine's career"[2] establishes his theology as a turning point in the history of metaphysics or if, because of him, Christian theology accomplishes a decisive turn towards metaphysics, that is to say, in the course of Western philosophy. For a century, it has been a common tendency to interpret the appeal of *De Trinitate* (and of other texts) to the *substantive* either as a sign of inclusion of his theology in the (Greek) framework of metaphysics, as a loss of the achievements of the theology of the (also Greek) fathers, or both at the same time (without fear, one will notice, of a great imprecision on what is to be understood as "Greek").

---

1. See esp. the works of Arpe, "Substantia"; Gellinck, "Entrée d'*essentia*," 77–112; Gilson, *Être et l'essence*, 336; Courtine, *Catégories de l'Être*, 12.

2. Giraud, Review of *Au lieu de soi* (Marion), 94.

Starting from an undoubtedly faulty reading of T. de Régnon's work, many theologians (from V. Lossky to K. Rahner, not to mention all their many epigones)[3] have reproached St. Augustine for having abandoned or compromised the reading of the Trinity according to the *economy* (from the origin, the Father, passing to the Son, and to the Spirit, in the deployment of both the auto-manifestation of God and soteriology) in favor of an abstract hypothesis of divine unity, articulated only afterwards in three poles, which no theological logic really justifies but risks a sort of modalism. This reproach, at first restricted to the Trinitarian doctrine, has widened more recently: St. Augustine compromised Christian theology with metaphysics, in the sense that its *constitution* manifests itself today in its necessary *destruction*. Without any textual support, J. O'Leary was thus able to write "the notion of divine substance serves to function as an idol, that is to say that it serves to hypostasize a cessation of the transcendent aim of faith."[4] Following him, E. Falque tried to show that the uses of *substantia* give way, in the end, to yield all of *De Trinitate*, and with it, Latin theology, "under the weight of metaphysics."[5]

We have tried elsewhere to read St. Augustine, on the contrary, as a thinker who was sufficiently pre-metaphysical to play the role of a post-metaphysical thinker today.[6] In this context, one of the most decisive tests is found in the uses of *substantia*: do they not attest to a metaphysical turn in Christian theology, or at the very least an obvious compromise? However, it could be that these occurrences, however indisputable and significant they may be, are not sufficient to decide whether their use to translate *ousia* (in competition with *essentia*) is in any way metaphysical. It could be, on the contrary, that the instability of their *two* uses (for there are indeed two very different ones) prove that the term does not *yet* have in St. Augustine the metaphysical status and stability that it will undoubtedly acquire only after

---

3. On this and many other questions, the point of departure is chapters 9–10 in Kany, *Augustinian Trinitätsdenken*.

4. O'Leary, "Dieu-esprit." He deploys, for this radical critique of St. Augustine, our work "Heidegeger et la double idolâtrie." This text is then taken up in *Dieu sans l'être*.

5. Falque, *Dieu, la chair et l'autre*, 78, takes the argument on the "weight of substance" to include St. Augustine in the history of metaphysics following Heidegger's sense (61–62). This analysis, which contrasts a resistance to *substantia* in book 5, and a submission to it in book 7, has been criticized by Gioia, *Theological Epistemology*, 160n53.

6. One of our adjacent arguments had to do with the non-ontological sense of the term *idipsum*, invented by St. Augustine to hold the role of (deictic) name of God, a non-ontological sense which makes impossible a neo-Thomistic rereading, however widespread, starting from *ipsum esse* (see Marion, *Au lieu de soi*, particularly, "*Idipsum* ou le nom de Dieu" [chapter 7]).

Boethius.[7] Without claiming to undertake a systematic study of all these uses, which alone would allow us to answer the question seriously, our only aim in this note is to *complicate* any solution that is too simple and swift.

II

We must first consider the formulations which appear to fix a definition of *substantia*. In fact, they seem to support two Augustinian theses which could imply a metaphysical doctrine.

First of all, to be, for a thing, means to be substance, since conversely this which has no substance simply is not: "nam quod nulla substantia est, nihil omnino est."[8] Hence it follows that one cannot know a thing except by its substance: "nullo modo autem recte dicitur sciri aliqua res dum eius ignoratur substantia."[9] Nevertheless, this thesis does not properly define *substantia*, but assumes its title in order to determine what is a *res* or an *id quod*. Therefore, *substantia* remains completely indeterminate. Consequently, *substantia* cannot serve as the starting point.

Then, substantiality defines the totality of beings, that is, the totality of the created but also the creator: "omnis igitur substantia aut Deus aut ex Deo, quia omne bonum aut Deus aut ex Deo."[10] Or: "omnis enim substantia quae Deus non est creatura est, et quae creatura non est Deus est."[11] So, precisely because to know a thing implies to know it as a substance, substance offers the univocal horizon of all beingness [*étantité*], a univocity however formal, since *substantia* does not have a precise definition. This thesis allows us to at least distinguish two questions, and not only one. First, if and how substance predicates [*se dire de*] God. Then, if and how substance predicates [*se dire de*] creatures. Most studies omit or neglect the second question.

III

Can *substantia* predicate God?

7. Courtine seems to suggest this when speaking of a "capital reversal" in the Augustinian understanding of *essentia* and *substantia* (Courtine, "Traductions latines," 49).

8. Augustine, *Enarrationes in psalmos* 68.1.5.

9. Augustine, *De Trinitate* 10.16.

10. Augustine, *De libero arbitrio* 3.13.36, 128. "Si omni bono privabuntur [sc. res], omnino nulla erunt: ergo quandiu sunt, bona sunt. Ergo quaecumque sunt, bona sunt, malumque illud, quod quaerebam unde esset, non est substantia, quia, si substantiam esset, bonum esset" (Augustine, *Confessiones* 7.12.18).

11. Augustine, *De Trinitate* 1.6.9.

Undoubtedly, God has the rank of substance and, radically, by comparison with what is not at all, evil: "sic non est substantia peccatum, sed substantia est Deus, summaque substantia, et solus verus rationalis creaturae cibus,"[12] in refuting the Manichean opinion of a *mali substantia quondam*.[13] But the equivalence, elsewhere frequent, of *substantia* with, for example, *natura* does not make it possible to fix its exact meaning: "nescio quam substantiam et naturam summe mali."[14] No more than the equivalence between *substantia* and *essentia*.[15] This indeterminacy goes so far as to admit even the body as one of the possible equivalents of *substantia*: "non est opus certari de nomine: si corpus est omnis substantia vel essentia, vel si quid aptius nuncupatur id aliquo modo est in seipso, corpus est anima."[16] Such imprecisions of the term indicates some impropriety in applying it to God.

Also, St. Augustine does not maintain *substantia* as an adequate concept to designate God, but prefers, despite its novelty, the quasi-neologism of *essentia*:

> Inseparabiliter sint unius eiusdemque substantiae uel, si hoc *melius* dicitur, essentiae. Nam nonnulli nostri et maxime Graeci Trinitatem quae Deus est, *magis* essentiam quam unam substantiam esse dixerunt aliqud inter haec duo nomina esse arbitrantes uel intelligentes.[17]

Or: "Est tamen sine dubitatione substantia uel *si melius* hoc appellatur essentia."[18] Finally, *essentia* indeed replaces *substantia* when it is a question concerning God as Trinity:

> Itaque ut nos *jam* novo nomine ab eo quod est esse, vocamus essentiam, quam plerumque substantiam etiam nominamus: ita veteres qui haec nomina non habebant, pro essentia et substantia naturam vocabunt.[19]

---

12. Augustine, *De natura et gratia* 20.22.

13. Augustine, *Confessiones* 5.10.20.

14. Augustine, *Confessiones* 4.15.24. See also: "omnium naturarum atque substantiarum esse auctorem Deum" (*De moribus Manichaeorum* 2.2); "nulla natura est . . . et omnino nulla substantia" (*Epistula* 11.3).

15. Augustine, *De moribus Manichaeorum* 2.2.

16. Augustine, *Epistula* 166.4. To the point that the heresy, when it uses the term even for the evil, manifests the maximum of its imprecision: "malum . . . quod mihi nescienti non solum aliquam substantiam, sed etiam corporea videbatur" (*Confessiones* 5.10.20).

17. Augustine, *Epistula* 120.17.

18. Augustine, *De Trinitate* 5.2.3.

19. Augustine, *De moribus Manichaeorum* 2.2.

And most importantly:

> Cum enim Deus summa essentia sit, hoc est summe sit et ideo immutabilis sit: rebus, quas ex nihilo creauit, esse dedit, sed non summe esse, sicut ipse est; et aliis dedit esse amplius, aliis minus, atque ita naturas essentiarum gradibus ordinauit (... ab eo, quod est esse, vocatur essentia: *nouo quidem nomine*, quo usi ueteres non sunt Latinii sermonis auctores, sed iam nostris temporibus usitato, ne deesset etiam linguae nostrae quod Graeci appellant οὐσίαν; hoc enim uerbum e uerbo expressum est, ut diceretur essentia).[20]

For what compelling reason does the *De Trinitate*, which opened with the declaration of an *incommutabilis substantia quae est Deus*,[21] end up, and so quickly, by rejecting the use of *substantia* in favour of *essentia* to set forth the Trinitarian logic?

Assuredly, for a very strong reason: in virtue of divine immutability, God does not bear accidents: "Nihil itaque accidens in Deo quia nihil mutabile aut amissibile."[22] Now, the possibility of an accident is due to the function of the substratum of a substance, just like the possibility of an attribute is due to the function of the subject of prediction. So, if there must be in God neither accidents of a substratum, nor attributes predicated of a subject, we must abandon applying the term *substantia* to God. If "manifestum est igitur Deum *abusiue* substantiam uocari; ... ita ut fortasse solum Deum dici oporteat essentiam,"[23] resulting from the inapplicability of accident and attribution to God:

> Est [sc. Deus] tamen sine dubitatione substantia uel si *melius* hoc appellatur essentia, quem Graeci οὐσίαν vocant. Sicut enim ab eo quod est sapere dicta est sapientia et ab eo quod est scire dicta est scientia, ita ab eo quod est esse dicta est essentia. ... Sed aliae quae dicuntur essentiae siue substantiae capiunt accidentias, quibus in eis fiat uel magna vel quantacumque mutatio; Deo autem aliquid eiusmodi accidere non potest. Et ideo sola est incommutabilis substantia uel essentia quae Deus est cui profecto ipsum esse, unde essentia nominata est maxime ac uerissime competit.[24]

---

20. Augustine, *De civitate Dei* 12.2.
21. Augustine, *De Trinitate* 1.1.1.
22. Augustine, *De Trinitate* 5.4.5.
23. Augustine, *De Trinitate* 7.5.5.
24. Augustine, *De Trinitate* 5.2.3.

In other words, in God as unity of the three, it would be better to say that nothing is accidental, nor attributed to a subject, but by contrast, therefore, everything in God is substance; that is to say, with God it is *never* a matter of a *substantia* in the logical sense (attribute), nor in the ontic sense (accident): "In Dei substantia, non esse aliquid tale, quasi aliud ibi sit substantia, aliud quod accidat substantiae et non sit substantia; sed quidquid ibi intelligi potest, substantia est."[25] The best example comes here from charity:

> Sed aptius [i.e., communio consubstantialis aeterna] dicitur caritas; et haec quoque substantia quia Deus substantia et *Deus caritas, sicut scriptum est*. Et ideo non amplius quam tria sunt: unus diligens eum qui de illo est, et unus diligens eum de quo est, et ipsa dilectio. Quae si nihil est, quomodo *Deus dilectio est?* Si non est substantia, quomodo *Deus substantia est?*[26]

Clearly, *God is charity* is not substance in the sense of a subject attribution, nor of a substratum of accident, precisely because charity predicates [*se dire de*] God neither as the one, nor as the other. Therefore, God as such does not receive [charity] as subject, nor as substratum. Thus, not as a substance in the metaphysical sense either, in the sense of "Aristotelica quaedam quae appellant decem categorias."[27]

It is also precisely because the Trinity escapes substantiality in the metaphysical sense that St. Augustine can invent a mode of naming God, which is *neither substantial nor accidental*, but relational:

> Quamobrem nihil in eo secundum accidens dicitur quia nihil ei accidit; nec tamen omne quod dicitur secundum substantiam dicitur.... In Deo autem nihil quidem secundum accidens dicitur, quia nihil in eo mutabile est; nec tamen omne quod dicitur secundum substantiam dicitur. Dicitur enim ad aliquid sicut Pater ad Filium.[28]

---

25. Augustine, *De fide et symbolo* 9.20.

26. Augustine, *De Trinitate* 4.5.7. Same argument in *De Trinitate* 7.5.10: "Deus autem si subsistit ut substantia *proprie* dici possit, inest in eo aliquid tanquam *in subiecto*, et non est simplex, cui hoc sit esse quod illi est quidquid aliud de illo ad illum dicitur sicut magnus, omnipotens, bonus, et si quid huiusmodi de Deo non incongrue dicitur. *Nefas* est autem dicere ut subsistat et *subsit Deus bonitati* suae atque illa bonitas non substantia sit uel potius essentia, neque ipse Deus sit bonitas sua sed in illo sit tamquam *in subiecto*. Vnde manifestum est Deum *abusiue* substantiam uocari ut nomine usitatiore intelligatur essentia, quod uere ac proprie dicitur." God is not subject, and in order not to be subject, God must not even be said to be substance, a term which is strictly valid only for what admits of accidents.

27. Augustine, *Confessiones* 4.16.28.

28. Augustine, *De Trinitate* 5.4.6.

Predication [*se dire*, in French] according to relation (or more exactly according to the relative) becomes possible for God only because he does not fall under the substance/accident dichotomy (contrary to what the Arians think); therefore, because God escapes the metaphysical understanding of *ousia* as *substantia*. If God said himself according to the substance, he could not say himself trinitarianly: "Nam *si* hoc est Deo esse quod subsistere, *ita non* erant dicendae tres *substantiae* ut non dicuntur tres essentiae."[29] One cannot say it more clearly.[30] This exclusion of *substantia* intervenes, we note, exactly in book 7, precisely where it was imprudently seen as "yielding under the weight of metaphysics."

Concluding on the first question: *substantia* does not predicate God, in relation to God *per se*, at least not in the strict sense of a substratum and a subject for the predication of accidents or attributes. Trinitarian theology, particularly, must use the term with the greatest caution and should even dispense with it (for example in favor of *essentia*). In short, *substantia* appears for St. Augustine as problematic as *persona*.[31] This reluctance, which is in fact twofold, marks a step outside the metaphysical use of the two terms, which will be established (if it is established in the *metaphysical* sense) but only after St. Augustine.

---

29. Augustine, *De Trinitate* 7.4.9.

30. Because of course, in good Aristotelian logic, the *ousia* has nothing relative: "Absurdum est autem ut substantia relative dicatur; omnis enim res ad se ipsam subsistit. Quanto magis Deus?" (Augustine, *De Trinitate* 7.4.9) So, for God to say *ad relativum*, while keeping the rank of *res* qui est, he has to go beyond the opposition between the οὐσία and the πρός τι, and thus get rid of the *substantia* in the strict sense. See Gioia, *Theological Epistemology*, "inadequacy of the vocabulary of substance," 152 and 157; and Gilson, *Introduction à l'étude*, 287. Kany rightly notices that the Anomaeans [or Arians] criticized the Nicene Creed precisely because *substantia* always implied accident *for them*, without also seeing the possibility of *ad relativum* (Kany, *Augustinians Trinitätsdenken*, 498). This what Durrant's argument for the so-called "necessary absurdity" of St. Augustine comes down to (Durrant, *Theology and Intelligibility*, 125).

31. We must insist on an obvious paradox: St. Augustine expresses a doubt about (disqualifies, in fact, frankly) the *two* main concepts of the, in principle, normative formula (*una substantia, tres personae*). In fact, the challenge to substantia echoes, more discreetly, the well-known question of *persona* ("Dictum est tamen tres personae, non ut illud diceretur, sed ne taceretur," Augustine, *De Trinitate* 5.9; see 7.4.7; 7.6.11–12). See Gioia, *Theological Epistemology*, 154–55; Boigelot, "Mot 'persona'"; and especially Cross, "Quid tres?"; namely, that *persona* remains a substantial noun, which covers beyond God even man, and thus does not fit the Trinity as such: "Nam persona generale nomen est in tantum ut etiam homo possit hoc dici, cum tantum intersit inter hominum et Deum" (Augustine, *De Trinitate* 7.4.7).

IV

Can *substantia* predicate the creature?

The second question remains, which commentators usually pass over in silence, focusing solely on the Trinitarian vocabulary. Wrongly, as we shall see.

Apparently, the formal univocity of *substantia* is confirmed to the point that even mutable things deserve the title of *substantia*: "Res ergo mutabiles neque simplices proprie dicuntur substantiae."[32] There is even a major text in favor, it seems, of a metaphysical reading of the created being as *substantia* in St. Augustine. This text begins with a determination of God.

> Aeternitas, ipsa Dei substantia est; quae nihil habet mutabile; ibi nihil est praeteritum, quasi iam non sit; nihil est futurum, quasi nondum sit. Non est ibi nisi: Est; non est ibi: Fuit et Erit, quia et quod fuit, iam non est; et quod erit, nondum est; sed quidquid ibi est, nonnisi est.[33]

In fact, this is a very particular meaning of *substantia*: it does not indicate that God *is* a *substantia* (therefore of an ultimately supreme being), but that God only knows eternity, ignores mutability, and therefore maintains and remains (*subsistit*) according to eternity alone: *substantia* here means eternity, the non-mutability of God. This is confirmed, among other things, by this other text:

> Vtrum autem aliqua natura, hoc est substantia prorsus ad nihilum redigatur, disputatio subtilissima est. Sed fides ueracissima Deo cantat "Mutabis eas et mutabuntur; tu autem idem ipse es" (Ps 101:27–28). Nec regit mutabilia bona nisi immutabile bonum, quod est Deus. Porro bona mutabilia propterea bona sunt, quoniam a summo bono facta sunt; propterea mutabilia, quia non de ipso, sed de nihilo facta sunt.[34]

Or:

> Nulla natura est, Nebridi, et omnino nulla substantia, quae non in se habeat haec tria et prae se gerat: primo ut sit [i.e., causa

---

32. Augustine, *De Trinitate* 7.5.10. Let us notice, however, that here such a possibility (mutable beings as *substantiae*) works *against* the use of this concept about God: as *persona* it remains too imprecise and too broad for what it is about.

33. Augustine, *Enarrationes in Psalmos* 101.2.10, invoked by Giraud (in his review already mentioned), against the reading I give in *Au lieu de soi*, 411–12.

34. Augustine, *Contra adversarium legis et prophetarum* 1.6.8.

naturae], deinde ut hoc uel illud sit [i.e., species], tertio ut *in eo quod est manet* quantum potest.³⁵

Here again, *substantia* is worthy of God, only because God alone proves to be *immutabilis (immutabile bonum)*. The caesura always passes between the immutable (only and unique *substantia* because it is the only *substans*) and the created and thus unsubstantial mutables in the sense of the permanent stance. In the same way, "Quod profecto posset [it is a question of the Holy Spirit, who can *permanere incommutabilis*], nisi Dei naturae esset ac ipsius *substantiae*, cui soli *incommutabilitas* atque, ut ita dicam, inconvertibilitas semper est."³⁶

Clearly, *substantia* indicates first and probably only that which has the property of the *incommutabilitas*.³⁷ So that one of the most famous texts on *incommutabilitas* makes it a divine name without passing by *substantia* anymore: "Esse est nomen incommutabilitatis,"³⁸ which has, precisely, only the sense of immutability.³⁹

In fact, *substantia* defines less God than stigmatizes the created, where it is conspicuous by its absence, because [the created] remains essentially marked by mutability: the *substantia* does not so much designate the mode of being of God positively, as firstly, and negatively, what the created is not, immutable. Thus, continues the *Enarrationes in Psalmos* 101.2.10,

35. Augustine, *Epistula* 11.3, which defines "manentia quaedam, ut ita dicam, in qua sunt omnia." On this permanence, see Augustine in *De moribus Manichaeorum* 2.6.8: "Quod summe et maxime esse dicitur, *permanendo* in se dicitur"; and the triad *exire/redire/manere* in Augustine, *Soliloquia* 1.1.3. Is this an anticipation of the *conatus in suo esse perseverndi*? Undoubtedly not, since precisely the created being does *not* dispose of its beingness, and therefore, cannot preserve it persevere in it as in itself, but only as in another than itself: "Nouerimus tamen perire ista, Deum manere. Et si manent quaedam cum Deo, quae facta sunt a Deo, non manent in se, sed in Deo, non recendendo a Deo" (Augustine, *Enarrationes in psalmos* 101.2.13). Good remarks of Kany, *Augustins Trinitätsdenken*, 416.

36. Augustine, *De moribus Manichaeorum* 1.13.23.

37. Many other texts confirm that *substantia* indicates first of all immutability: "Cum enim Deus summa essentia sit, hoc est summe sit, et ideo inmutabilis sit: rebus, quas ex nihilo creauit, esse dedit, sed non summe esse, sicut est ipse; et aliis dedit esse amplius, aliis minus, atque ita naturas essentiarum gradibus ordinauit" (Augustine, *De civitate Dei* 12.2). Or: "In Deo autem nihil quidem secundum accidens dicitur, quia nihil in eo mutabile est; nec tamen omne quod dicitur, secundum substantiam dicitur" (Augustine, *De Trinitate* 5.5).

38. Augustine, *Sermo* 7.7.

39. Same omission of *substantia*, made useless by immutability: "Non est ergo malum nisi priuatio boni. Ac per hoc nusquam est nisi in re aliqua bon. Etsi non summe bona, quoniam summe bona *incorruptibilis et immutabilis* perseuerat, ut Deus est, non tamen nisi in bona, quoniam non nocet, nisi minuendo quod bonum est" (Augustine, *Contra adversarium legis et prophetarum* 1.5.7).

Ego sum. Quis? *Qui sum.* Hoc est nomen tuum? hoc est totum quod vocaris? Esset tibi nomen ipsum esse, nisi quidquid est aliud, tibi comparatum, inueniretur non esse uere? Hoc est nomen tuum. . . . *Qui est misit me ad vos. Ergo sum qui sum: qui estm misit me ad uos.* Magnum ecce *Est*, magnum *Est*! Ad hoc homo quid est? Ad illum tam magnum *Est* homo quid est, quidquid est? Quis apprehendat illud esse? quis eius particeps fiat? quis anhelet? quis adspiret? quis ibi se esse posse praesumat?[40]

In comparison with divine immutability, therefore to its *Est* [Is], human beings are not, so to speak, precisely because they are according to mutability. Hence, the text concludes: "Quis se esse posse praesumat?" In other words, what is not *substantia*, is not either.

We can therefore conclude on the second point: in relation to God, man is (no more than any other creature) *substantia*, for want of being able to claim for himself the least subsistence in presence. Thus, it is only by contrast with the non-subsistence of the created that one can, at most, attribute (as a negation of the non-subsistence of the created) the *substantia* to God. In this negative sense only, or rather, in the *denative sense*. Thus, if we want to say *substantia tua*,[41] we must understand it in opposition to the *non-substantia* of evil: "quaesiui, quid esset iniquitas, et non inueni substantiam, se a summa substantia, te Deo, detortae in infima uoluntatis peruersitatem."[42]

Where does this non-ontological, so to say, use of *substantia* come from? It has, first, a biblical origin, as witnessed by the *Enarrationes in Psalmos* 68.4–5. That is, the commentary on Ps 68:3, according to the Vetus Latina (and the Vulgate): "Infixus sum in limo profundi et non est substantia," translating ὑπόστασις in the Septuagint. The commentary perfectly articulates the problematic.

First (68.4), the *substantia* is reduced strictly to the fact of standing still: "Quid est hoc: *non est substantia*? Numquidnam ipse limus non est substantia? An, ego inhaerendo factus sum non esse substantia?"[43] I am not *substantia*, because I take my footing and support on that which offers no stability, the silt. Neither he nor I are substances since we do not stand firmly. Not only is *substantia* strictly reduced to stability, to dwelling-in-itself [*demeurance en soi*],[44] but above all, it is only recognized by its defect and is conspicuous only by its absence: "Vnde ergo *non est substantia*? An limus

---

40. Augustine, *Enarrationes in Psalmos* 101.2.10.
41. Augustine, *Confessiones* 7.2.3; 4.6.
42. Augustine, *Confessiones* 7.16.22.
43. Augustine, *Enarrationes in Psalmos* 68.1.4.
44. The Hebrew uses the root word for station.

ille non est substantia? Intelligamus ergo, si potuerimus, quid sit: *et non est substantia?*"[45] To understand *substantia* as the very absence of subsistence implies finding a more empirical meaning for it than that of an ontology. And to immediately find the pre-philosophical meaning of the term: *substantia* in the sense of wealth, property, possession. "Substantia quippe dicitur et divitiarum, secundum quam dicimus 'habet substantiam' et 'perdidit substantiam.'"[46] Afterwards, "secundum . . . uerbi intellectum accepi sensus iste . . . ad paupertatem."[47] In other words, *substantia* signifies for us, the created, the non-subsistence in the sense of poverty: "An forte quia ille ipse limus paupertas erat, et divitiae non erunt, nisi quando aeternitatis participes effecti fuerimus? Tunc sunt enim uerae diuitiae, quando nobis nihil deerit."[48] Poverty which St. Augustine will, moreover, immediately understand theologically on the model of Phil 3:6–8 and 2 Cor 8:9. Therefore, *substantia* applies to us only and still negatively, in the sense of the poverty of the stance, of the lack of stability.

But can we also preserve the philosophical meaning of *substantia*? Because there is still an unusual meaning (*res inusitata, verbum inusitatum*), which the rest of the text examines (68.5). Let us admit the ontological sense of *substantia*: "Intelligitur alio modo substantia, illud quod sumus quidquid sumus," from which we will conclude that

> dicitur homo, dicitur pecus, dicitur terra, dicitur caelum, dicitur sol, luna, lapis, mare, aer: omnia ista substantiae sunt, eo ipso quod sunt. Naturae ipsae, substantiae dicuntur. Deus est quaedam substantia; nam quod nulla substantia est, nihil omnino est.[49]

To be is equivalent, therefore, to being substance, but what is adequate to deserve this title? Obviously, God, if only because the three of the Trinity *unius esse substantiae*, each one being of the (*same*) substance (contrary to men who precisely *are* different men, and not the unique and same substance *man*), even if they are respectively Father, Son, and Spirit according to the relation (*secundum id quod ad aliud*). But does man deserve the title of substance? In a sense, man was created a substance and remained so, as long as he was able to avoid falling from his initial condition; but since the fall, he no longer has the rank of substance:

45. Augustine, *Enarrationes in Psalmos* 68.1.4.

46. Augustine, *Enarrationes in Psalmos* 68.1.4. See the commentary on Exodus 12:37–40. This same use is found in Luke 15:12.

47. Augustine, *Enarrationes in Psalmos* 68.1.4.

48. Augustine, *Enarrationes in Psalmos* 68.1.4.

49. Augustine, *Enarrationes in Psalmos* 68.1.4.

Deus fecit hominem; substantiam fecit; atque utinam maneret in eo quod Deus fecit! Si maneret homo in eo quod Deus fecit, non in illo infixus esset quem Deus genuit. Porro autem quia per iniquitatem homo lapsus est a substantia in qua factus est (iniquitas quippe ipsa non est substantia; non enim iniquitas est natura quam formauit Deus, sed iniquitas est peruersitas quam fecit homo): uenit Filius Dei ad limum profundi, et infixus est; et non erat substantia in qua infixus est, quia in iniquitate illorum infixus est. Naturae omnes per illum factae sunt; iniquitas per ipsum facta non est, quia iniquitas facta non est. Substantiae illae per eum factae sunt, quae laudant eum.[50]

Thus man, who was created substance, lost his stature by his iniquity. Therefore, Christ came to be fixed in the non-substance, in the poverty of stance, where the mutable man passes and dies, to restore substances there, which can praise God. Here man loses his substance only through iniquity and finds it again only to praise. How better to say that substance does not belong to ontology?[51]

Thus, *substantia* has only a negative use for the created and a de-negative use for the triune God, never finding the positive and dogmatic use of a categorical determination of the being of created being, even less of the being of uncreated being (supposing that there is one in the case of God in St. Augustine's vision and aim). These uses of *substantia* cannot therefore serve as an argument for including St. Augustine in the horizon of metaphysics.

Bibliography

Arpe, Curt. "Substantia." *Philologus: Zeitschrift für das klassischen Alterturm* 94 (1940) 65–78.

Augustine. *Confessiones*. Edited by L. Verheijen. Corpus Christianorum Series Latina [CCSL] 27. Turnhout: Brepols, 1981.

———. *Contra adversarium legis et prophetarum*. Edited by K. Daur. CCSL 49. Turnhout: Brepols, 1985.

———. *De civitate dei*. Edited by B. Dombart and A. Kalb. CCSL 48. Turnhout: Brepols, 1955.

---

50. Augustine, *Enarrationes in Psalmos* 68.1.4.

51. Another biblical origin of *substantia*: commenting on Vetus Latina Exod 12:38, St. Augustine notes that this Latin term has nothing philosophical here, since it translates a Greek term which is itself perfectly banal: "Ibi enim graecus . . . habet, ubi *substantiam* latinus interpretatus" (*Quaestiones in Heptateuchum*, quaest. Exodi 42.1; the Vulgate has *armenta et animantia*). As it is also the case, he notes, in Gen 43:8 (Judah to his father Jacob: "non moriamur et nos et tu et substantia tua," Vetus Latina; the Vulgate has *ne oriramur nos et parvuli nostril*).

———. *De fide et symbolo*. Edited by J. Zycha. Corpus Scriptorum Ecclesiasticorum Latinorum 41. Gerhard: Verlag der Österreichischen Akademie der Wissenschaften, 1900.

———. *De libero arbitrio*. Edited by W. Green and K. Daur. CCSL 29. Turnhout: Brepols, 1970.

———. *De moribus Manichaeorum*. PL 32.

———. *De natura et gratia*. PL 44.

———. *De Trinitate*. Edited by W. J. Moutain and Fr. Glorie. CCSL 50. Turnhout: Brepols, 1968.

———. *Enarrationes in psalmos*. Edited by D. E. Dekkers and I. Fraipoint. CCSL 39. Turnhout: Brepols, 1961.

———. *Epistula* 11. Edited by R. Daur. CCSL 31. Turnhout: Brepols, 2004.

———. *Epistula* 166. PL 33.

———. *Soliloquia*. PL 32.

———. *Sermones de Vetere Testamento (1–50)*. Edited by C. Lambot. CCSL 41. Turnhout: Brepols, 1961.

———. *Quaestiones in Heptateuchum*. PL 34.

Boigelot, René. "Le mot 'persona' dans les écrits trinitaires de saint St. Augustine." *Nouvelle Revue Théologique* 57 (1930) 5–16.

Courtine, Jean-François. "Les traductions latines d'*Ousia* et la compréhension romano-stoïcienne de l'être." In *Les catégories de l'Être: Etudes de la philosophie ancienne et médiévale*, 11–77. Paris: Presse universitaire de France, 2003.

Cross, Richard. "Quid tres? On What Precisely Augustine Professes Not to Understand in De Trinitate 5 and 7." *Harvard Theological Review* 100 (2007) 215–32.

Durrant, Michael. *Theology and Intelligibility*. London: Routledge, 1973.

Falque, Emmanuel. *Dieu, la chair et l'autre: D'Irénée à Duns Scot*. Paris: Presse universitaire de France, 2008.

Gellinck, Joseph de. "L'entrée d'*essentia, substantia* et autres mots apparentés dans le latin médiéval." *Bulletin du Cange: Achivum latinitatis medii aevi* 16 (1942) 77–112.

Gilson, Etienne. *Introduction à l'étude de saint Augustin*. Paris: J. Vrin, 1942.

———. "Notes sur le vocabulaire de l'être." In *L'Être et l'essence*, 335–49. Paris: J. Vrin, 1962.

Gioia, Luigi. *The Theological Epistemology of Augustine's "De Trinitate."* Oxford: Oxford University Press, 2003.

Giraud, Vincent. Review of *Au lieu de soi: L'approche de saint Augustin* by Jean-Luc Marion. *Philosophie* 104 (2009) 91–95.

Kany, Ronald. *Augustinian Trinitätsdenken*. Tübingen: Mohr Siebeck, 2007.

Marion, Jean-Luc. *Au lieu de soi: L'approche de saint Augustin*. Paris: Presse universitaire de France, 2008.

———. *Dieu sans l'être*. Paris: Fayard, 1982.

———. "Heidegeger et la double idolâtrie." In *Heidegger et la question de Dieu*, edited by Richard Kearney and Joseph O'Leary, 46–74. Paris: Presse universitaire de France, 1980.

Migne, J.-P., ed. *Patrologia Latina* [PL]. 217 vols. Paris: N.p., 1844–1864.

O'Leary, Joseph. "Dieu-esprit et Dieu-substance chez saint Augustin." *Recherches de science religieuse* 69.3 (1981) 357–91.

Conclusion

Fraternity in Finitude

Emmanuel Falque and the Future of Christian Philosophy

DAVID ALBERTSON

H E LEAPT TO THE podium with youthful energy and gripped the lectern with both hands. Pausing for a moment to collect his thoughts, he pushed the hair out of his face and smiled broadly at the audience that had assembled for the opening lecture of a conference at Notre Dame. "It is a privilege to be with all of you at this university," I recall him saying. "And if I may say so, it is my privilege to be Catholic, here with you."

The philosopher and theologian Emmanuel Falque is one of the leading Christian thinkers in the world today, but he is not as well known to American readers as he should be. Jean-Luc Marion, his famous teacher and occasional sparring partner, has attained international renown after being inducted into the Académie Française and awarded the Ratzinger Prize in theology by Pope Francis. Marion's books on love and politics are often reviewed. But Falque's star is rising. Over the past decade his works have been translated into English and he has held visiting posts at American universities. Falque is dean of the Faculty of Philosophy at the Institut Catholique de Paris, the country's Catholic university. In 2015 he founded the International Network for Philosophy of Religion (INPR). Following Marion's retirement from the Sorbonne and the University of Chicago, Falque's network has become the hub for young intellectuals inspired by the so-called "theological turn" in French philosophy, from Michel Henry and Jean-Yves Lacoste to Jean-Louis Chrétien and Marion himself. Falque was formed by this tradition, and over the past two decades his writings have refreshed and reframed it. Now he is working to shape its future.

Falque deserves to be better known for several reasons: the verve of his writing, the quality of his insights, and the range of his erudition. In *God, Flesh, and the Other* (2008) he demonstrates command of the full library of patristic and medieval theologians. Yet he has also written extensively on the twists and turns of the French phenomenological tradition over the past century in *The Loving Struggle* (2014). More valuable still is the timeliness and freshness of his approach, a winning humility and openness that speaks beyond the usual choir of philosophers (and Christians). If Marion was the Catholic philosopher of the Benedict XVI papacy, it would be fair to see Falque as the one most akin to Pope Francis, and not only because of the book he cowrote with Laure Solignac, *François Philosophe* (2017).

The boundary between philosophy and theology in Jean-Luc Marion's works is strictly policed and remains controversial. Falque relishes crossing back and forth from one domain to the other, a shuttle diplomacy that enriches both sides of the boundary by calling each of them into question. "The more we theologize, the better we philosophize," he writes in *Crossing the Rubicon* (2016). Marion established that the methods of modern phenomenology can accommodate the extraordinary events of Christian revelation. By contrast, Falque seeks to begin not from above but from below—from the ordinary skeins of embodied life not yet saturated by divine glory. Not from impossibly far away, but from impossibly near. Falque's 1998 Sorbonne thesis opted for the Seraphic Doctor over Aquinas, a book later published as *Saint Bonaventure and the Entrance of God into Theology*, and his oeuvre has retained that Franciscan signature ever since.

At the same time, Falque resists a merely confessional theology, since the culture within which we operate today is not already Christian. In *Crossing the Rubicon*, Falque warns that "confessing belief" first requires an "ordinary belief" in the world and in others, or what Maurice Merleau-Ponty calls "animal faith." "No one believes in God if he does not first believe in the world," Falque observes. He is a "before all else a philosopher," even if he remains open to theological experience, for the philosopher is the one "who respects and begins with the human per se."

In *By Way of Obstacles* (2016), Falque explains the genesis of his project twenty years earlier. In 1996 he and others convened an interdisciplinary working group for young Catholic intellectuals. Although theological questions had come to the fore in phenomenological circles, Catholic theology itself was impaired by too many divisions and too little dialogue. Falque was convinced that Catholic traditions had something fresh to say if the relationship between philosophy and theology—between culture and faith—could be reconceived.

Falque's subsequent works have carried out this project. His books reach out sympathetically to the religiously indifferent "nones" whom all of us count among friends and families. In the 1940s, Henri de Lubac analyzed the "drama of atheistic humanism" in Marx, Comte, and Nietzsche. Falque is more interested in the *non*-dramatic atheism that reigns in our time—less defiant nonbelief than the weary agnostic shrug that Nietzsche called nihilism. Some are *for* or *against* God, but most simply live *without* God, which is something different. Falque likes to quote Michel Foucault: "Modern man is possible only as a figuration of finitude."

Falque asks what Christians might now say that could actually matter to their post-Christian contemporaries in the academy or the arts who find this strange religion useless or *passé*. But his strategy is precisely the opposite of the histrionic lament one hears from many educated Catholics today; there is not a wisp of nostalgia in his approach. As Falque puts it, the true theological challenge is not to destroy Nietzschean atheism, but to learn from it. We must seek a "grammar in common"—a phrase he borrows from John Paul II. "The Christian, more receptive to difference, will be precisely transformed in his true capacity to differ."

Falque begins from the standpoint of our common bodily experience, the weak flesh that we share with our unbelieving sisters and brothers, all our illnesses, noisy leaks, and despair, *nudus cum nudo Christo*. As much as Falque has learned from Protestants like Karl Barth and Paul Ricoeur, he insists that a *Catholic hermeneutic* cannot remain at the level of texts and ideas. A Catholic method must be embodied, almost materialist—not a hermeneutic of text but a "hermeneutic of body and voice." Christ, he reminds us, saves us first with his body, not his words.

In the sweltering summer of 2022, I attended the annual meeting of Falque's network in Paris. Marion and Falque squared off for an hour, but most of the panels were packed with twentysomethings. When it came time for Falque to read his paper, he put down his notes to emphasize a point, raising a professorial finger in the air. "The non-Christian is other than me as Christian, but I am not better than him," he said. "Other, not better." Like Pope Francis, Falque seems most comfortable on the margins, and in academic circles, this means accepting the growing marginalization of Christianity itself. But Falque meets the unbelieving on their own territory. He is after "the exposition of a credible Christianity" that is not simply a "Christianity for believers." In philosophical terms, this means listening patiently to Friedrich Nietzsche, Martin Heidegger, Michel Foucault, or Gilles Deleuze, who all condemn Christianity for forgetting the body and domesticating death. As Augustine worked with Platonism and Aquinas with Aristotelianism, "today, it is the horizon of finitude for Heidegger, which still waits to be investigated and transformed."

Falque urges Christians to renew their solidarity with unbelieving contemporaries through our shared bodily plight. He mines the depths of human anxiety in the face of death, starting with the groans at Gethsemane. He asks what it means to be born into the world, a first time or a second time; one's birth, he notes, is even less knowable than one's death. Falque's best-known books are his trilogy on Good Friday, Easter Sunday, and Holy Thursday, his *Triduum philosophique*. There he writes, "Only by posing questions about the impossible overcoming of our nature can we open up and force ourselves to live anew our irreducible finitude." The fraternity that we find in finitude passes from birth to death, and then from death to birth again.

Falque wrote the trilogy's first volume, *The Guide to Gethsemane* (1999), after two close friends died in one terrible year. He starts from a single verse, Mark 14:33. In Gethsemane, Jesus was absolutely gripped by fear of death in the garden. More than mere regret at leaving his students behind, Jesus was overwhelmed with a very personal "alarm" or "terror" (*thambos* in Greek). This is the shock of panic one feels in the face of raw vulnerability when retreat is impossible and violence is imminent. In the words of Charles Péguy: "The Christ once feared to die." Jesus recoils at his end and despairs when help never comes. He has no choice but to navigate the ordeal, Falque says, "without resignation or certitude or heroism."

At Gethsemane Jesus enters the full meaninglessness, the Nothing, that intense pain brings. He arrives at the non-sense of human life oriented to death. Language ends, and the body cries out on its own, for only flesh can express anxiety in its full radicality, trembling and sweating mutely. Here Falque quotes the great Jewish philosopher Emmanuel Levinas: "Sobbing . . . announces death. To die is to return to this state of irresponsibility, to be the infantile shaking of sobbing." Like a woman giving birth, Jesus does not rise above his death but abandons himself to its inevitable unfolding. He comes to "envisage his death successively as a way of living his life and no longer as the end of life." He accepts his death as absolutely his own, and he gives his consent to the Father to let him die. He never seeks to overcome his death through tranquility or virility, but allows the Father to overcome it for him. In a perfect "nonmastery of the self," Jesus gives up managing his death in favor of a "childlike and positive irresponsibility." In this weakness we see that is he is a Son of the Father.

The resurrection should liberate us from anxiety about our sin, but it does not spare us from anxiety about death. Jesus himself passed through that alarm and in doing so transformed it into abandonment in God. According to Falque, Jesus dies for me and with me, but not in my place. I still must work through my own particular death. But Jesus's passage through death transforms my death into a way of proceeding through the life I have left. My death becomes a "place of reception of an *elsewhere* or *other* my life"—the Other of the Father, the otherness of God's love. Our love is measured through the welcome we give to suffering, not because this purifies us from sin, but because it allows the *imprint of the other* upon us. I should not flee my suffering or strive to overcome it heroically. When I undergo my pain, even as I recoil from it, resist it, and enter into its absurdity, I can in perfect passivity allow my flesh to end and be given away. I can receive myself anew as one being given away, and this, says Falque, is a kind of birth.

Everything rests on this distinction: sin is not finitude itself—our aging bodies, maladies, ignorance—but is the refusal to accept that condition of finitude and the limits it gives to us. Panic before death and depression at the meaninglessness of suffering are not in themselves sinful, for Jesus felt them viscerally and without reprieve. "Not only nonbelievers fall into despair," Falque observes. Rather, sin is about treating finitude as a prison that needs to be escaped. The desire to deny our finitude, even by pious means, is the sin of sins, the resentful lust for perfection that the serpent exploited in Eden: *You will be like God*. In the incarnation, Jesus teaches us to remain in finitude without illusions. Falque writes: "The agony of Christ . . . confirms a weakness chosen by God that will be forever and forever manifest, and that we bear—we also—even in our own flesh. . . . The full extremity of his power consists precisely in complying with an originary powerlessness . . . that remains always woven into human finitude . . . to which God himself, right to the end and without ever disposing of it, consents."

In anxiety and tears Jesus embodies the humanity that we all experience. His suffering takes places on a plane of immanence shared as much by philosophers as by theologians. Hence Falque's maxim: "Nothing speaks or is spoken without passing through humankind, in that God was made man." When Jesus falls to the ground in the garden, he completes his commitment to dwell on earth. Falque wonders if Christians today can live up to this achievement, or whether Christianity has become an instrument to separate our anxious lives from those of our neighbors, who share the same flesh. The hard lesson of Gethsemane is that I must relinquish myself to *this* world, accept my finitude, without seeking a subtle escape belonging only to Christians. Rather, I find transcendence only in the face of the other who shares finitude with me. Paradoxically, by abandoning oneself to the loss of selfhood in death, one can "break open the circle of one's own isolation."

Falque's strategy to start again from Gethsemane is a brilliant one. For the experience of divine abandonment in the garden matches the contemporary philosophical experience of facing life without God. In the face of the Father's silence, Jesus kneels here with the unbelieving. By the same token, Falque stresses, sharing in Christ's anxiety never turns into a Christian *privilege* that releases one from the anguish of finitude. Rather than trying to hustle philosophers back into the fold, Falque asks Christians to remain in the garden for a while longer, accompanying Jesus and their unbelieving neighbors. For Jesus teaches us "what it is to be one of humankind, when the human being, in human flesh, suffers from no longer understanding God."

If the terrors of finitude that Jesus experienced in Gethsemane were not sinful, then Christianity does not need to rush to convert birth into rebirth, eros into agape, earth into heaven, time into eternity. Our mortal bodies already bear a relation to God, even before we search beyond the world. The basic facts of natural humanity—our ever-past birth, ever-present sexuality, and ever-future death—are the coordinates we share with our unbelieving contemporaries. Yet they are also the beating heart of the cross, resurrection, and Eucharist. This is the productive struggle between Nietzscheanism and Christianity. Philosophy teaches theology to remain in finitude in an *impassable immanence*. But as it does so, philosophy discovers within that immanence new dimensions that it could never find on its own.

Nietzsche announced the death of God and prophesied the advent of a posthuman animal, the Übermensch who embraces the eternal return of the same. Falque recognizes this for what it is: a parody of the resurrection, indeed a self-resurrection. Is Nietzsche right that Christians view the body only as something to be overcome, something never to be affirmed? Or does the Christian idea of resurrection dignify our embodied existence?

The second volume in Falque's trilogy is *The Metamorphosis of Finitude: An Essay on Birth and Resurrection* (2004). What can the resurrection of Jesus mean for us today? Like Nicodemus, we find it hard to imagine what rebirth would look like. Modern Christians are reluctant to say too much, but Falque finds our reticence unwarranted. We need to ask not *what* really happened, but *how* it happens. For if the resurrection is real, it would *change everything*. In truth, it has *already* changed everything. The resurrection "modifies us from the start" by placing within us the longing for the infinite.

The resurrection signals the "cracking and opening up of immanence and temporality," the *transfiguration* of our being in time. The resurrection is not "*another* world nor an event *in* the world" but a "transformation *of* the world." In this way, the finitude that Falque maps in *Guide to Gethsemane* remains the field in which we encounter the resurrection. "We have no other experience of God but human experience," so we must find the "courage to loiter" with our contemporaries within the "blocked horizon" of immanence. In fact, it is the resurrection that allows us to understand this common experience, since the finite creation we know has already been transformed. We have only to pass from the static finitude of death to the dynamic finitude of rebirth, but these are a *single finitude*. By the same token, Falque adds, "there is no finitude of unbelievers and atheists on the one hand and of believers and the elect on the other."

The opening up of finitude comes from God, not humankind. It happens first within the Trinity. In the death of the Son, Falque argues, the Father is transformed. Through the flesh of the Son, the Father undergoes the rough grain of human finitude, as he sees and touches through Jesus's eyes and hands. Falque quotes Hans Jonas on Auschwitz: "God receives an experience from the world." But as the Father endures the Son's death, the Spirit transforms death into a possibility of life. That metamorphosis works its way into every cavity of the body and every instant of time. Everything in our world, from the joy of birth to the pain of suffering, is now *implanted* in God. "Nothing happens to mankind that did not first happen to God, except sin," for sin is precisely the misguided effort to escape from the world. True Christianity promises the "common construction of a bodily world for human beings with God."

Falque offers two ways to think about the resurrection of the body. The first begins with Husserl's distinction between the "organic body" (*Körper*) and the "body of lived experience" or "flesh" (*Leib*). My flesh is my body in time, or the way I appropriate my physical body. According to Falque, the resurrection names both the vanishing of Jesus's body and the manifestation of Jesus's flesh, his way of being. In the incarnation, God becomes a material body; in the resurrection he becomes the "expressivity of his flesh." The strangeness of his appearances to his disciples makes this clear. In the tomb there is only clothing, no body. In the garden Mary cannot touch him, and when Thomas does, Jesus still has wounds. Yet Jesus still feeds his disciples, still gives himself to their gaze, still calls them by name, still teaches and consoles them, as he always had. "When the body withdraws and the flesh becomes manifest, it is then that he shows himself," Falque writes.

The second way to think about the resurrection of the body has to do with time. The resurrection of Jesus is not just another episode in which one man is given life again. The resurrection "makes time," as Falque puts it, by opening a new mode of temporality. The "joy of the eternal" can be discovered in every moment of time. Falque's extended account of Christian joy seems to echo Francis's *Evangelii gaudium*. The joy of God is neither ecstasy nor entertainment, both of which promise a way beyond finitude. No, the joy of God is absolute reception of each moment as something delivered from God to me, in pure receptivity within time. This childlike dependence is the experience of being given into the stream of time—in other words, the experience of being born or born again. The birth of joy is the joy of birth.

I have only scratched the surface of Falque's theology. I have not even touched on the third volume of the philosophical Triduum, *The Wedding Feast of the Lamb* (2011), which unfolds a new theory of the Eucharist: "the Eucharist assumes our animality and saves us from bestiality." In fact, Falque has orchestrated three different cycles of works, and promises a fourth. In the first trilogy, already discussed, phenomenology improves theology and theology improves phenomenology. A second trilogy on method theorizes this connection: *Passer le Rubicon*; *Le combat amoureux*; and *Parcours d'embûches*. A third trilogy comprises Falque's explorations of patristic and medieval sources: *Saint Bonaventure et l'entrée de Dieu en théologie*; *Dieu, la chair, et l'autre*; and most recently *Le Livre de l'expérience* (2017) on twelfth-century monastic theology, from Bernard of Clairvaux to Richard of St. Victor. The fourth cycle will mirror the first in a passage through three days: on Holy Saturday (provisionally titled *L'inquiétude du créé: Essai sur la lutte, le mal et le péché*); on the First Day of creation; and on the Last Day of the end of time. Falque has also written a short book on Freud, *Nothing to It* (2018), and another with his spouse, Sabine Fos Falque, an accomplished psychoanalyst and author in her own right.

It is exciting to consider where Falque's thinking might go next. He has already confronted two of those thinkers Paul Ricoeur called "masters of suspicion," Nietzsche and Freud. Will Falque also take up Marx? Will he explore the female medieval mystics alongside the male monastic authors? Julian, Angela, Hildegard, and Mechthild all wrote on embodiment with at least as much sophistication as Tertullian and Bernard. The French phenomenological tradition has strangely neglected these visionaries to its detriment. Will Falque's interests in eros and birth lead him further into Mariology or a theology of the womb? One might have expected that organ to be more conspicuous in a phenomenology of birth. Will Falque return to Thomas Aquinas to define the method of finitude? Will his remarkable essays on Nicholas of Cusa grow into a volume on philosophy in the Renaissance?

It is a curious fact that the history of philosophy is ordered by duets of thinkers. Time and time again, their proximate contradictions bear witness to an epochal line that has been crossed: Aquinas/Bonaventure, Luther/Calvin, Descartes/Spinoza, Cusanus/Bruno, Kant/Hegel, Husserl/Heidegger, even Balthasar/Rahner. Falque's nearness to Marion, even as he positions himself as an alternative, is another example of the same dynamic. Just in the moment that he contradicts, expands, or exceeds it, Falque underscores Marion's achievement.

Together they offer an auspicious prospect that isn't legible within Marion's works alone: a re-thinking of the Christian legacy, beginning from *ressourcement* in the first half of the last century and passing through the postmodern turn of the second half. This project continues in our own day the theological renegotiation of modernity undertaken by Balthasar, Ratzinger, and Wojtyla, but now in a parlance that engages secular contemporaries who are more at home with Foucault and Derrida. "One can't emphasize sufficiently how much our understanding of the Christian mystery can turn out to be better or differently deployed by those who do not share it—surprising though it may seem," writes Falque in *Metamorphosis of Finitude*. "Probably this is one aspect of its vocation of catholicity."

Like Marion, Falque likes to think with paintings. When my wife and I visited Paris, he insisted we see *Jacob Wrestling with an Angel* in the Church of Saint-Sulpice down the street from his university. The image had inspired his favorite metaphor for the productive tension between belief and unbelief: *le combat amoureux*. Like Jacob and the angel, belief and unbelief should not let go until they bless each other. The virtue required for such intimate fraternity is not strength, but patience.

Index

alienation, 161, 222
Ambrose, 112, 121, 132, 135, 137, 138
Anselm of Canterbury, 2, 4, 21, 23, 163, 182
Aquinas, xii, 49, 50, 153, 163, 172, 190, 191, 198, 199, 205–6, 270, 272, 276
Aristotle, 112, 113, 125, 127, 129, 184, 189, 195, 197, 205
Augustine, xii, viii, xvii, 57, 107, 108, 110–69, 172, 174, 234, 254–66, 272

Balthasar, Hans Urs von, xxii, 109, 276, 277
Barth, Karl, 271
beauty, 26, 108, 109, 111, 123, 133, 139, 144, 170, 182
being-in-the-world, xv, 73, 232
Bergson, Henri, 94–95, 97, 235
Blondel, Maurice, 94, 97, 99, 101, 102, 186, 187
Bonaventure, xii, xiv, xvii, xviii, 163, 270, 276

Calvin, John, 100, 102, 103
conscience: 180, 185
creation: 10, 52, 56, 60–61, 99, 109, 118, 122, 140, 147, 149, 153–54, 161, 180, 184, 191, 202, 205, 231, 238–39, 275–76

Deleuze, Gilles, 35, 45, 47, 237, 271
Derrida, Jacques, xiv, xv, 42, 47, 88, 155, 236, 239, 245, 277
Descartes, René, xvi, 52, 53, 95, 110, 127, 181, 276

Eckhart, xix, 10, 11, 75, 153, 159, 163, 172, 188–206
epistemology, 181, 255, 260, 266
ethics
    Nichomachean, 129
    of spread body, 6, 95, 237
eucharist, xi–xiii, xxii, 3, 5, 10, 59, 100, 108–9, 126, 130, 135–36, 152, 154–57, 169–73, 244, 253, 274, 276
existence, 1, 8, 10, 28, 32, 69–74, 87, 172, 191–92, 198, 227–31, 239, 245, 248, 250, 274

faith, 6, 13, 57
    existential, 126-28, 145-47, 153-54, 167-68, 198
    phenomenological, 133, 139, 141, 147, 148, 204
    theological 126, 141, 147, 255, 270
freedom, 25, 28, 61, 166, 197, 205, 206, 232
Freud, Sigmund, xiv, xv, xix, 4, 6, 11, 26, 31, 92-94, 96, 207-24, 276
Foucault, Michel, 271, 277

grace, 20, 60, 61, 62, 108, 138, 146, 156, 194
Gregory of Nyssa, xxii
Gilson, Étien, 50, 102, 254, 260, 266

Hegel, xiv, xv, 53, 113, 194, 197, 198, 200, 204, 205, 206, 276
Heidegger, Martin, xii, xiv, xix, xvii-iii, xx, 35-36, 53, 73, 75, 77, 88, 90, 101-2, 107, 114, 126, 153-55, 172-73, 203, 206, 248, 250, 255, 266, 271-72, 276
Henry, Michel, xv-xix, 8, 35, 42, 44, 69-88, 110, 245, 270
hermeneutics, 12, 245, 271
hope, xxii, 13, 24, 46, 86, 87, 110, 120, 159, 189, 231
Husserl, Edmund, xii, xv-vi, xvii-iii, xx, 8, 35, 36, 44, 70, 71-77, 80, 88, 90, 92, 95, 98, 102, 126, 181, 244-45, 252, 275-76

Ignatius of Loyola, xii, 4, 50, 57-61, 64
incarnation: xvii, xx,
    christological, 7, 43-56, 70-88, 86, 103, 122, 125, 126, 139, 145, 152, 154, 156, 159
    phenomenological, 43-54, 69-74, 76-78, 82-88, 152-54, 198, 273-75
    mystical, 95, 103, 139, 145

justice, 86, 95, 146, 244

Kant, Immanuel, xvii, 53, 54, 181, 276

kenosis, 55, 57, 167
Kierkegaard, Søren, 151, 174, 237, 248

Lacoste, Jean-Yves, xxii, 154, 270
Levinas, Emmanuel, xx, xix, xviii, 35, 51, 88, 272
liturgy, 132, 134, 136-37, 140, 145
    of eucharist, 169
    of life, 16
logos, 122, 123, 139, 145

Marion, Jean-Luc, ix, xii, xix, xvii-iii, xx, 1, 4, 5, 12-13, 35, 76, 88, 110, 116, 127, 143, 149, 152, 160, 174, 254-55, 266, 269, 270-71, 276-77
Maldiney, Henri, 178, 183-84
morality, 180-81
mysticism, 194, 201-2

Nancy, Jean-Luc, xiv, 47, 149, 155
Nietzsche, Friedrich, viii, xvii, xviii, 6, 10, 93-96, 177-87, 215, 222, 224, 271, 274, 276
nothingness, 72, 79, 82, 88, 193, 200, 209, 210, 224, 226, 232, 240

objectivity, 91, 247

Pascal, Blaise, 31, 44, 180, 233
Plato, xiv, xiii, xvii, xviii, 110, 112-19, 126-27, 134, 137, 144, 146, 149, 153, 156-59, 161, 172, 174, 180, 195, 199, 206, 272

Rahner, Karl, 255, 276
redemption, 70, 129, 137, 144, 146, 147, 148
resurrection,
    as transformation, 3, 5, 47, 56, 70, 86, 87, 88, 103, 116, 122, 125, 126, 154, 156, 173, 228, 272
    as salvation, 70, 86-88, 103, 122, 125-26, 154, 156, 159, 228
Ricoeur, Paul, xiii, xv, 93, 103, 146, 271, 276

Spinoza, Baruch, 90, 103, 276
subjectivity, 61–78

Tertullian, xiv, xvii, 4, 101, 131, 276
theosis, 56–68

trauma, 6, 11, 28–30, 35, 37, 39, 44, 127, 164, 208, 211, 215–30, 245,46

Wittgenstein, Ludwig 189, 206

www.ingramcontent.com/pod-product-compliance
Lightning Source LLC
Chambersburg PA
CBHW021651230426
43668CB00008B/589

"*To Die of Not Writing* brings together major scholars and new voices to engage the work of Emmanuel Falque, one of the most interesting and important philosophers writing today. The chapters range across the impressively diverse landscape of Falque's thought, engaged in a loving struggle, not for victory, but rather for greater insight and for transformation of our understanding. An exceptional collection that makes a major contribution to philosophy of religion."

—**Brian Treanor**, professor of philosophy,
Loyola Marymount University

"*To Die of Not Writing* is a genuinely excellent tribute to one of the world's leading philosophers and theologians on the occasion of his sixtieth birthday. It is also an accomplishment of its own; born out of gratitude for his person as well as his oeuvre, it contains both sympathetic re-enactment and combat amoreux; it engages each of the four principal thematic foci of Falque's exemplary contributions, from patristic and medieval philosophy, and philosophy and theology, to philosophy of religion, and phenomenology; it even reiterates the energy, élan, erudition, and expertise of E. Falque's own thinking. The wide range of Falque's influence, impact, and readership—the vital and dynamic character of the communities that he constellates—is reflected in the variety of contributors. This includes leading international philosophers and theologians (C. Canullo, J.L. Marion, C. O'Regan), exemplary senior scholars and figures (D. Albertson, S. Fos-Falque, S. McGrath), as well as junior (S. DeLay, S. Horton, P. Irizar, M. Knotts, M. Nini) and emerging (G. Trottmann-Calame, W. Connelly, A. Sackin-Poll) scholars. The authors have in common a long-standing and deep engagement of Falque's work; we the readers of this volume are the beneficiaries of their intimacy and insight. Though it will not be the last such Festschrift, or loving struggle, it sets a high bar for all that will follow."

—**Garth W. Green**, John W. McConnell Professor
of Philosophy of Religion, McGill University

"Although Falque speaks of the spread body (corps épandu), it is his mind that spreads itself out (esprit épandu), prodigiously so. In this fitting tribute to the singular Falque, his family, friends, and students engage in the breadth of his thought and extend it even further, demonstrating its fecundity and catholicity. This rich collection is an expression of gratitude to Falque's liberality."

—**Jonathan Martin Ciraulo**, associate professor of systematic theology, The Catholic University of America

"This extraordinary book, a dynamic collection of voices, is a profound and inspiring tribute to the visionary thought of Emmanuel Falque. A towering figure in contemporary philosophy and theology, Falque challenges intellectual boundaries and boldly engages with the depths of human experience in his tireless quest for our 'common humanity.' His ideas are transformative and exhilarating—like a powerful vortex, they captivate and compel, leaving an indelible mark on all who encounter them."

—**João Paulo Costa**, Center for Classical and Humanistic Studies, Faculty of Arts, University of Coimbra

"This volume's contributors traverse Falque's corpus in a shared effort to cross the Rubicon separating philosophy from theology and struggle (in loving fashion) toward a transfiguration of the meaning of catholicity in the twenty-first century. The complementarity of the chapters ensures that, like the angel and Jacob wrestling on the shores of the Jabbok, they succeed by blessing each other in turn."

—**Sean Hannan**, associate professor, MacEwan University